CHRISTIAN'S WORLD

Christian Title

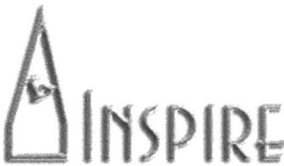

(An Adducent nonfiction imprint)

Adducent, Inc.

www.Adducent.Co

Titles Distributed In
North America
United Kingdom
Western Europe
South America
Australia

Christian's World

Christian Title

ISBN: 9781937592554

Published by Inspire (A nonfiction imprint from Adducent)

Jacksonville, Florida

www.AdducentInc.com

Published in the United States of America

INTRODUCTION

When my brother and I were very young, my father would tuck us in bed and tell us bedtime stories. He had a great imagination and would tell us these fantastic tales and embellish them with descriptions of the characters and places. My brother and I would get excited with all the fun things he would describe. I remember as I got older that I would lie there and make up different endings to his stories that I thought were better.

At the time I had no idea that this creative and stimulating atmosphere would be the foundation for my fantasies. As a young boy my mother nicknamed me the, "Dreamer", as I often escaped into the world of my own fantasies. My mother said I would never amount to anything if I spent all of my time pondering the magical. I have learned that all people and all things are only what is conceived in the mind. I was guided into the art world, and art and music became my sole interests.

Sometime later I discovered girls, then my fantasies became sexual about the women that I knew. It was in a way the means to making interesting evaluations, which in many cases were accurate. I started to illustrate the ideas I had about people and sex and their aberrations. My serious interest in art then paved the road to art schools, good professors and attaining the skill for traditional work. But, in the back of my mind was lingering the mystical and magic of my fantasies. I started to use shorthand symbols that were my own alphabet of meaning, and the scope grew and has never stopped.

I am very much aware that most of my imagery is very foreign to the viewer, but with time and emotional response, I think people will get into my world. I am so entertained while executing the drawing, I can't help but think the viewer can reach this same level. It is my world and I would like to share it with you.

- Christian Title

THE DRAWINGS

I was visiting Christian in his studio in Gulf Harbour, New Zealand. He showed me a portfolio of early drawings that he had done when he was between ten and fifteen years old. They were without question remarkable for a boy of that age. I had never seen any of his work from this early period, but I had previously seen a large selection of pencil works that he had done in Paris. His technical skill had always impressed me and I had made comparisons to other fine works done by many masters.

Now I was confronted by a vast number of pen drawings that he wanted me to see. It had been many years since I had been exposed to his work, and his modern work over the last thirty-five years was only experienced from the hard cover catalogue that I received when he had his seventy-five year retrospective. It was a transition that surprised me, I was aware of his imagination in other realms but the scope of these machinations were staggering. Unlike any other artist that I have seen, they are not only totally individual but possess a dimension and humor that reflects his thoughts on the human condition. I asked myself what kind of a mind thinks in this perspective, and how many artists could record these flights of imagination.

The more I studied the works the more I realized they were not just comments and humor but very serious evaluations of personalities and psychological manifestations of his subjects. They deserve serious consideration and thought, one must contemplate the implications that are there, but you must be willing to invest the mental energy and react emotionally to their message. (translated from French)

- Jean Hilton, 2010

(Jean Hilton passed away in 2012 he was a fine critic and a good friend)

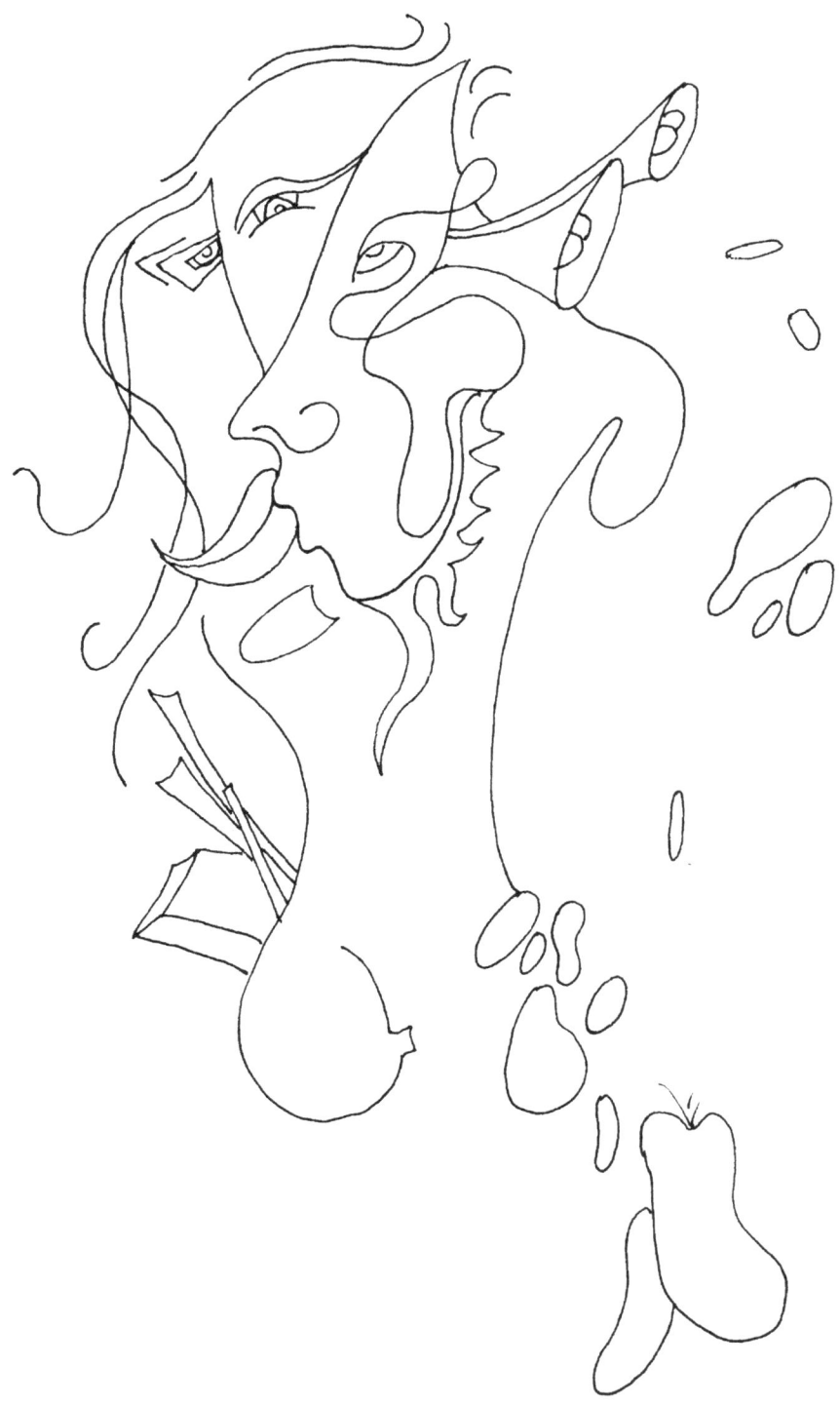

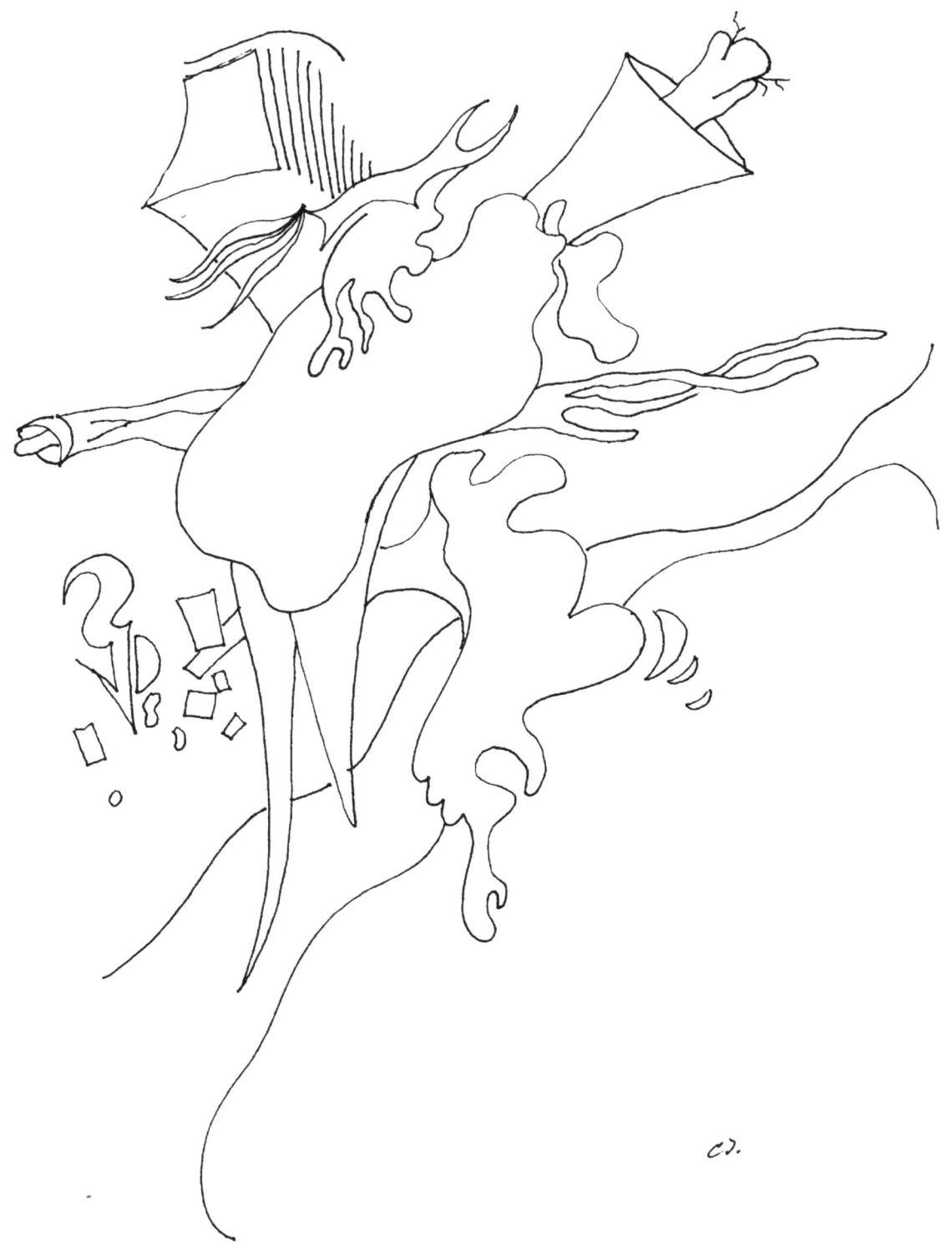

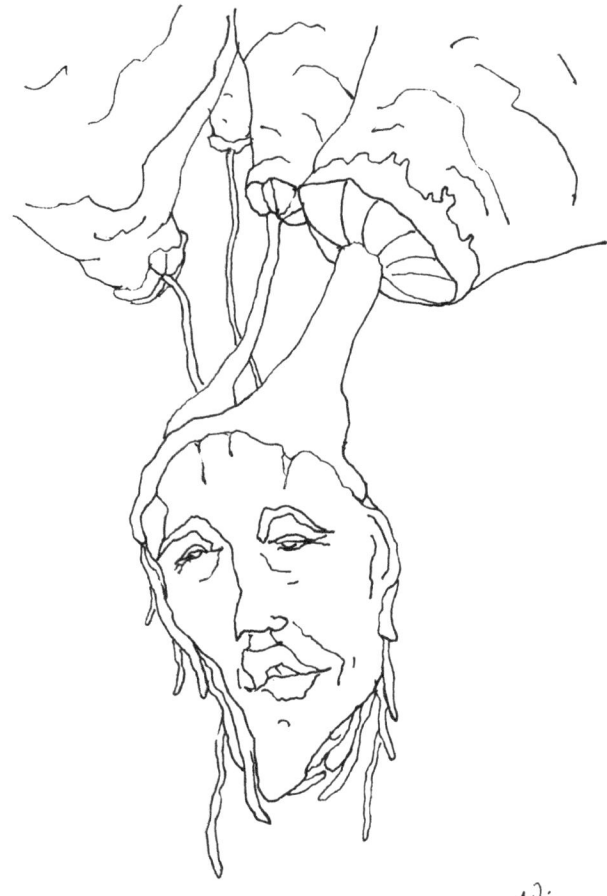

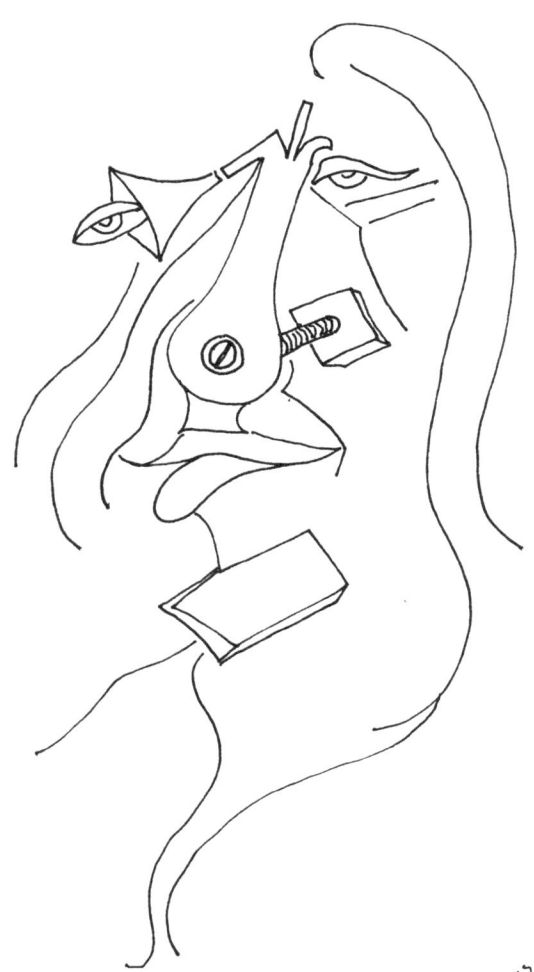

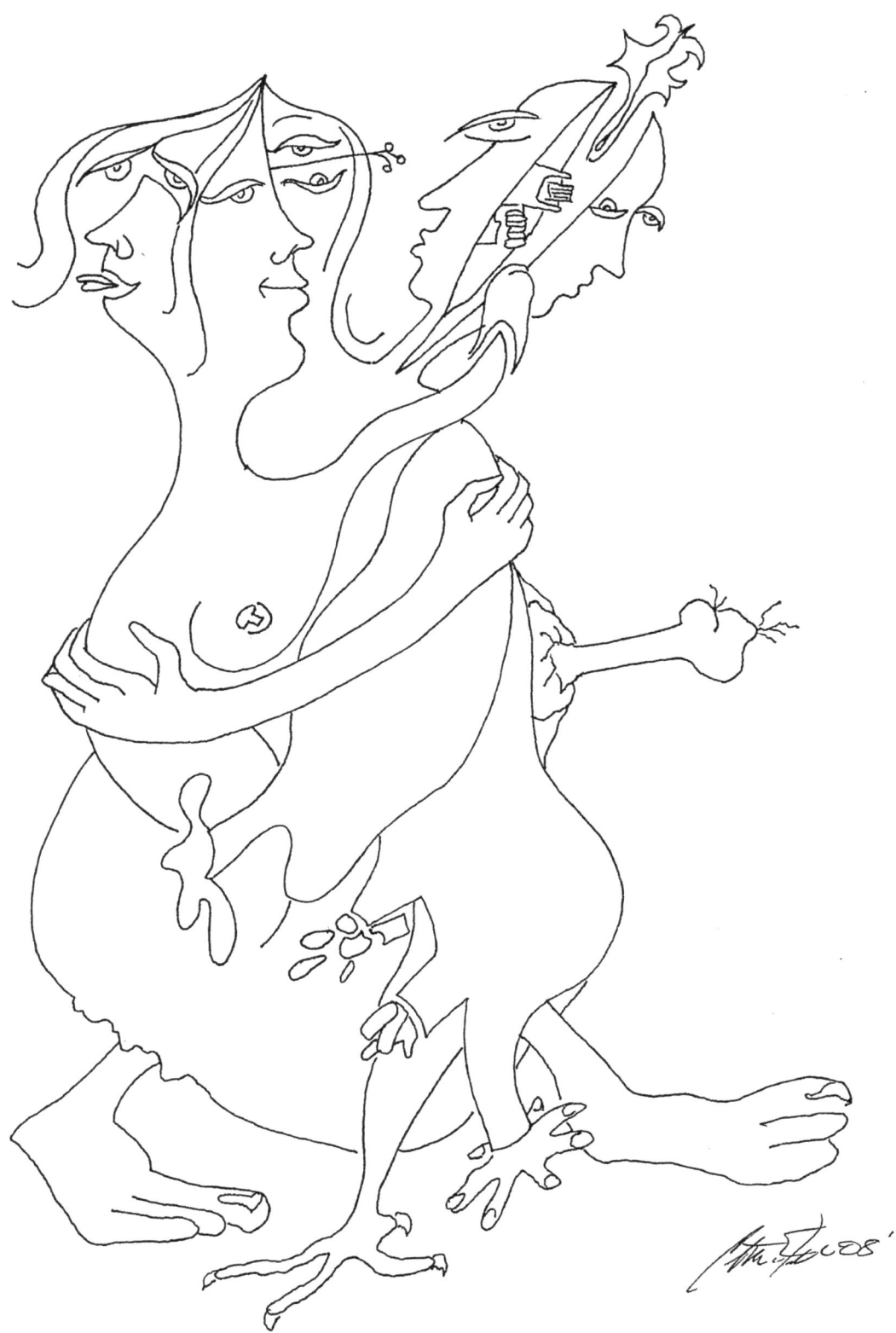

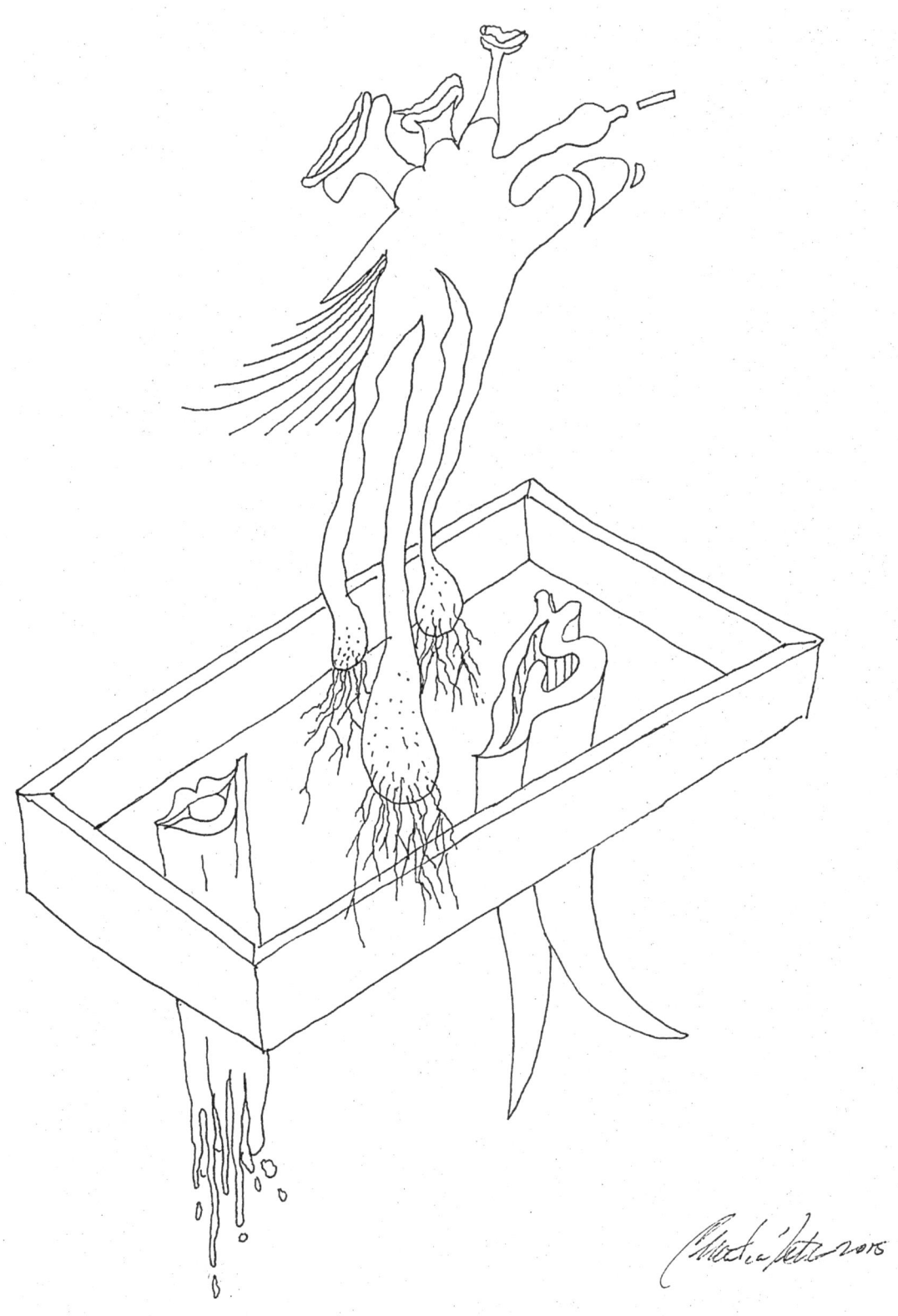

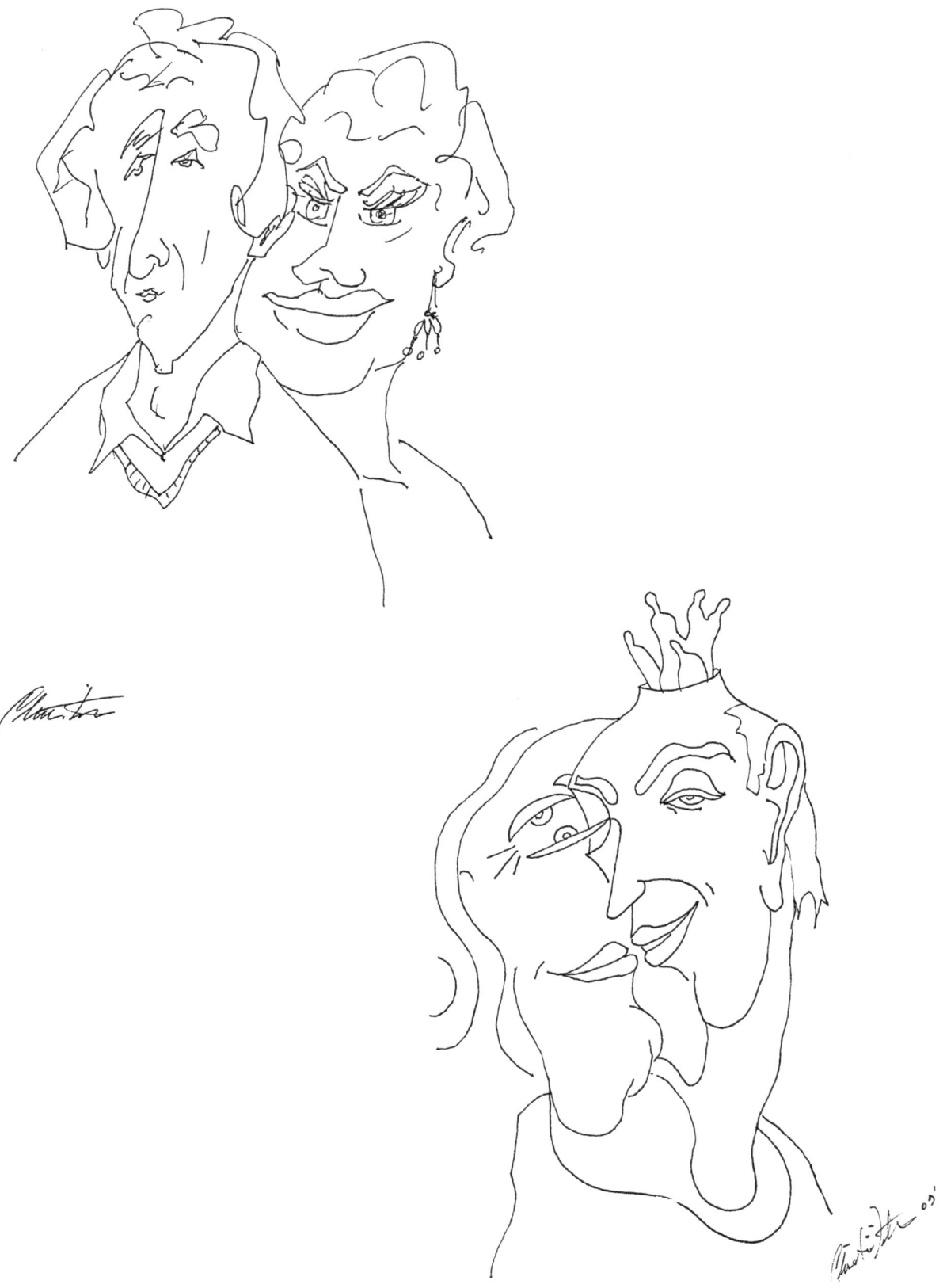

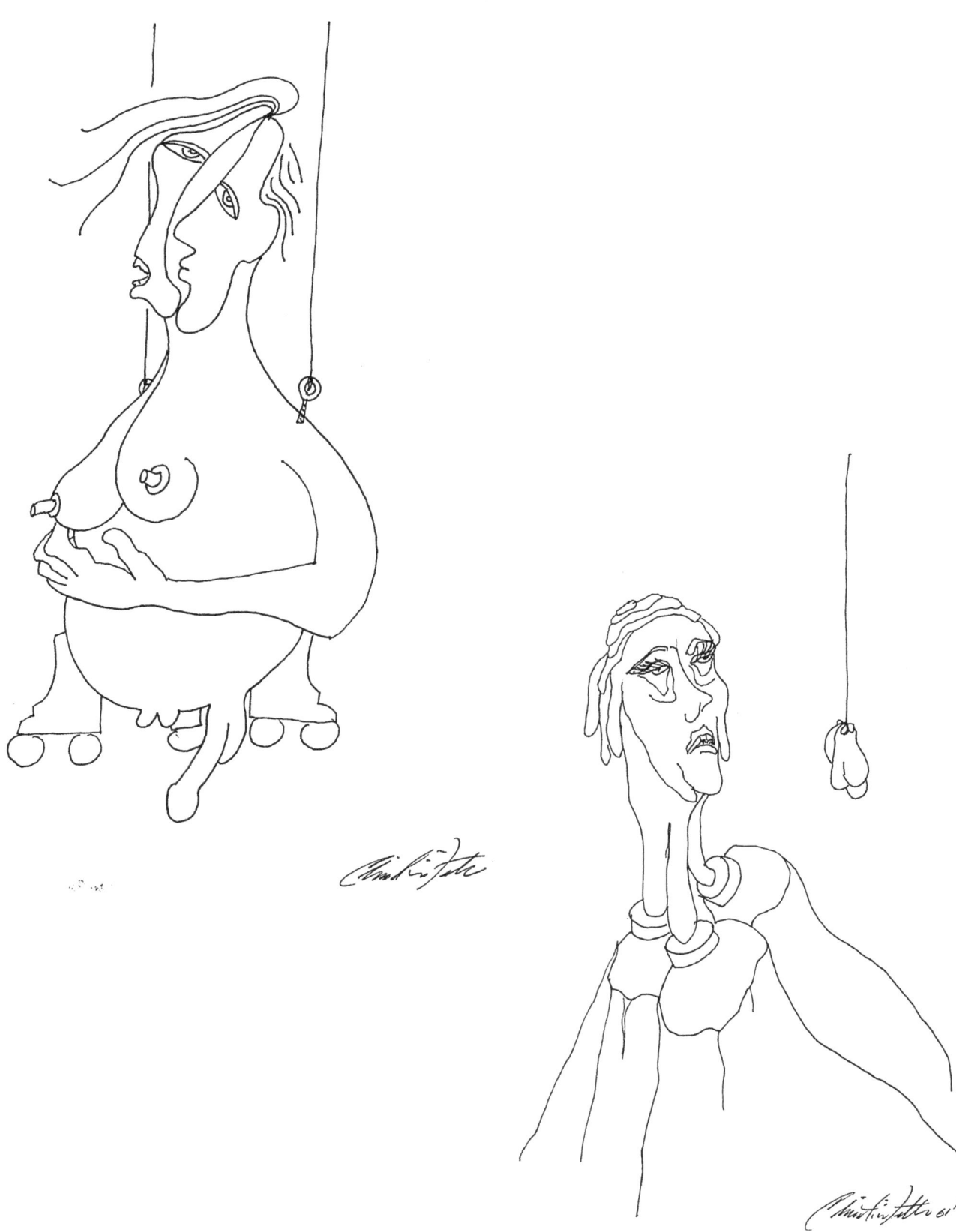

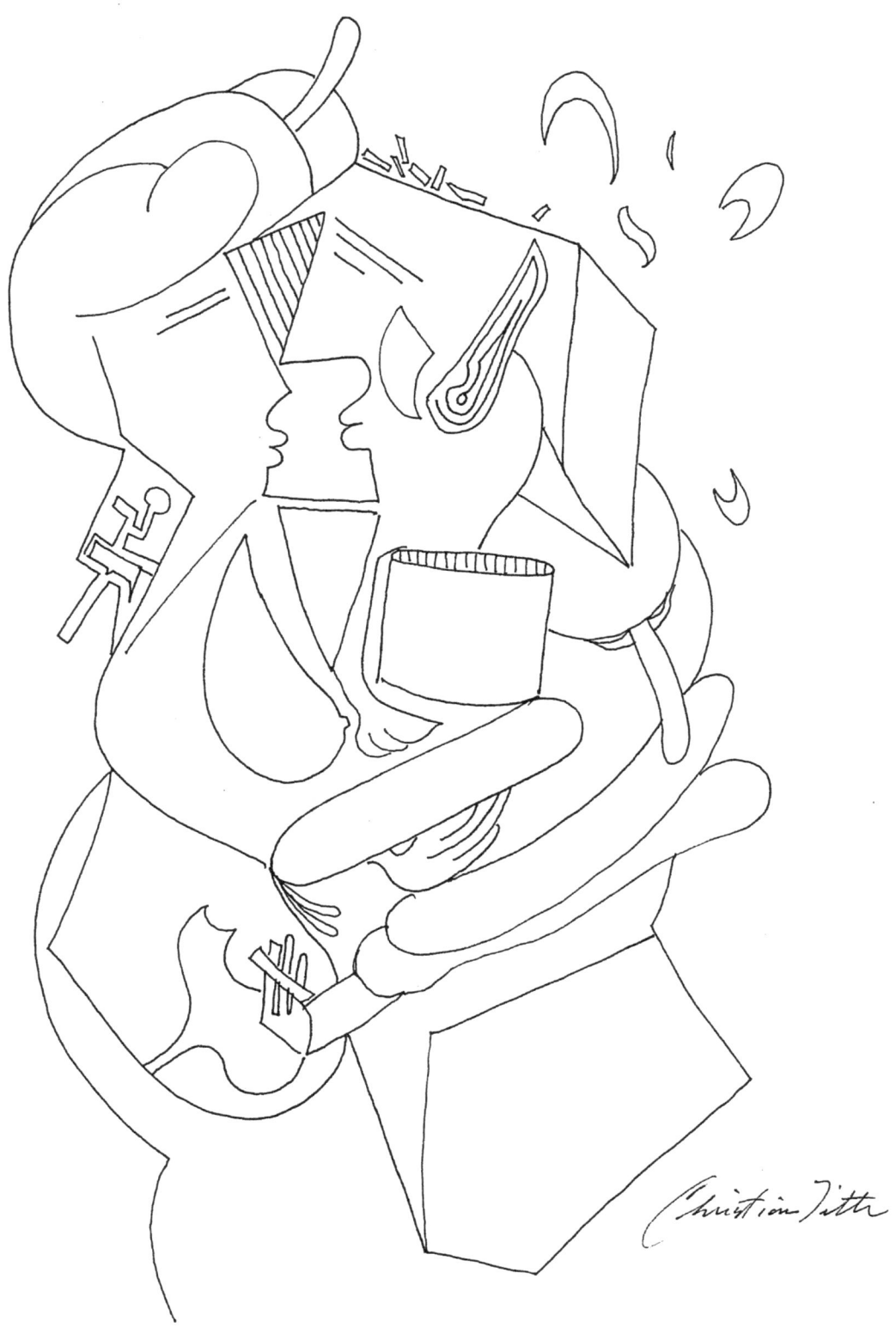

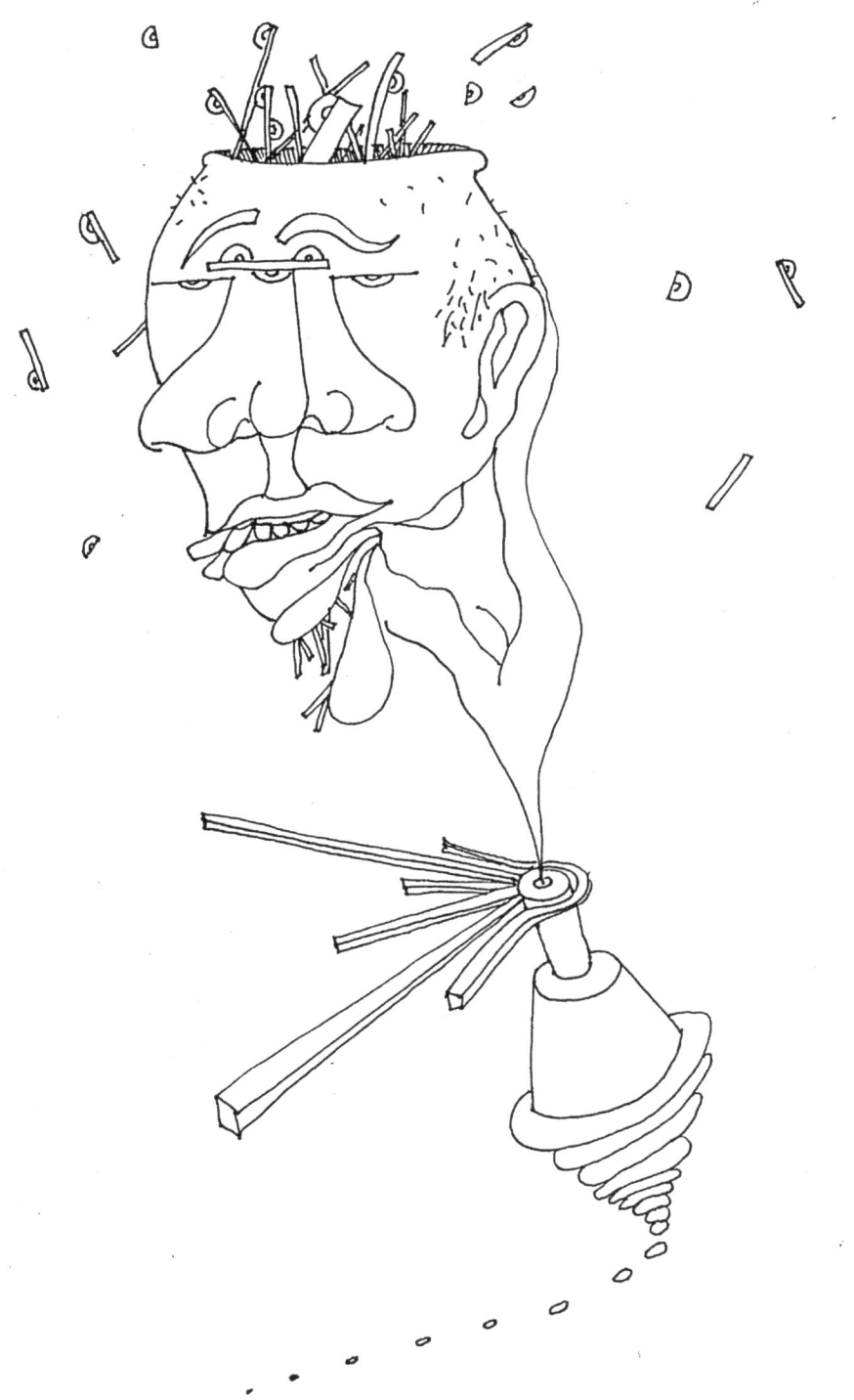

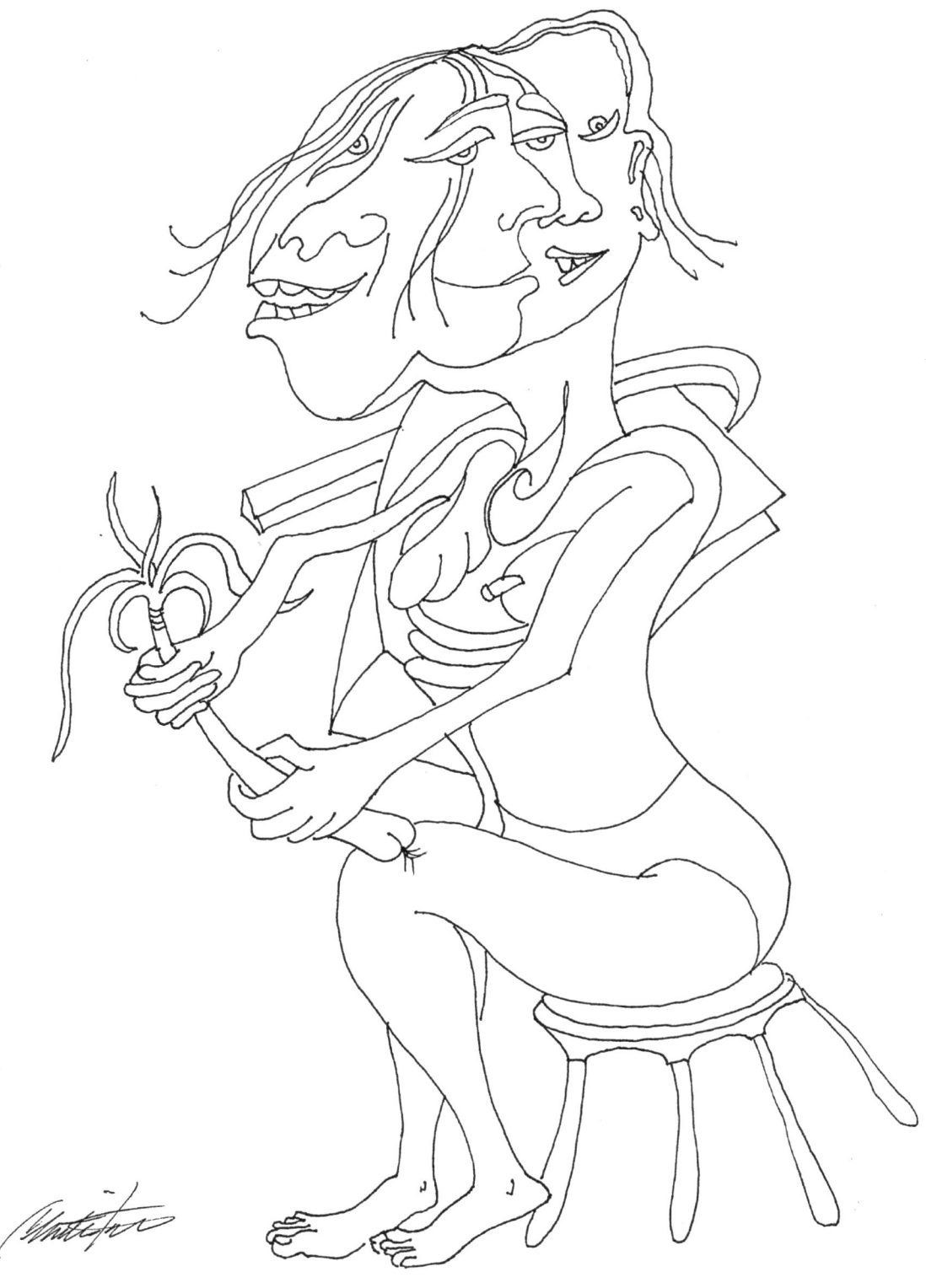

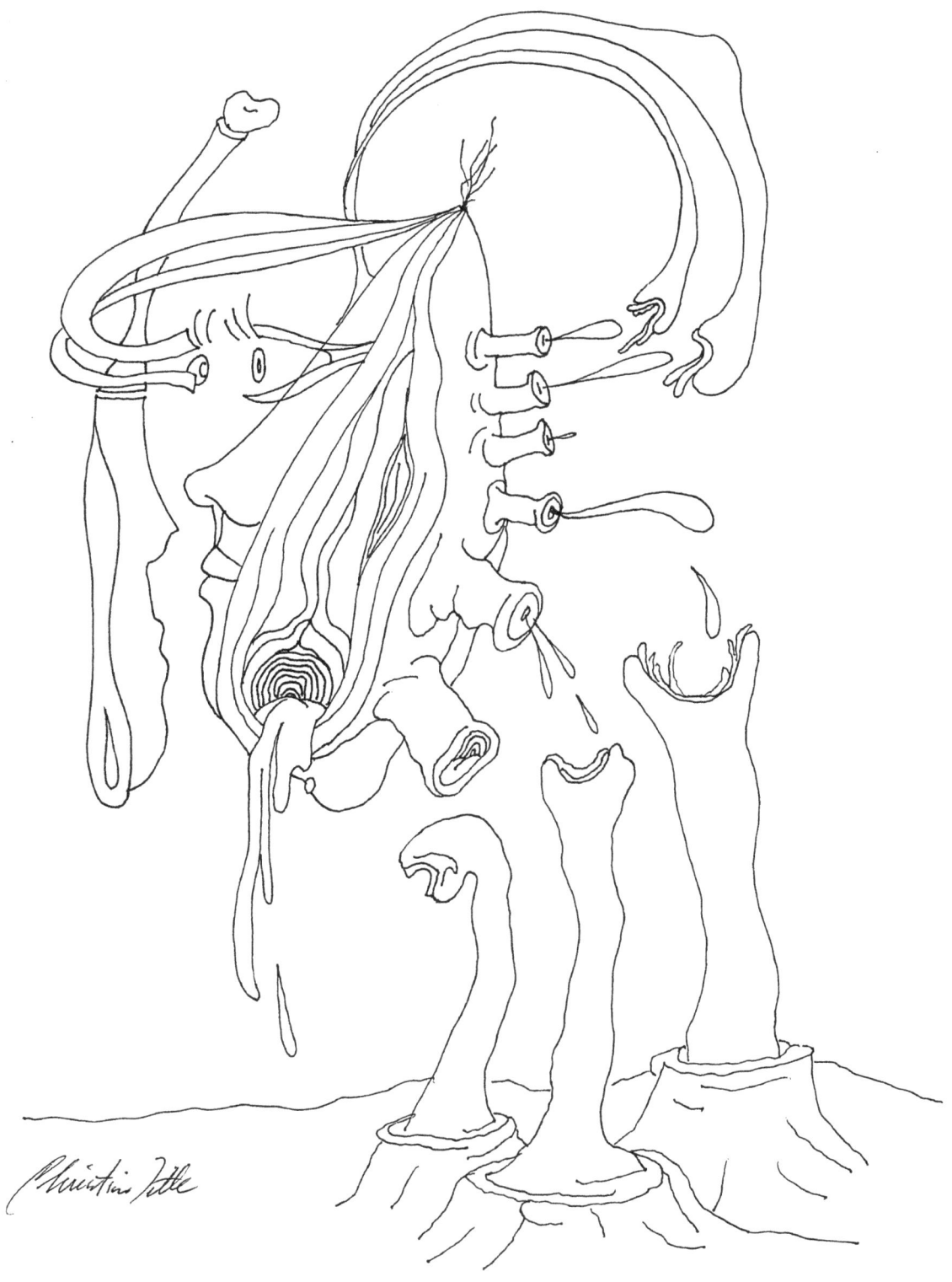

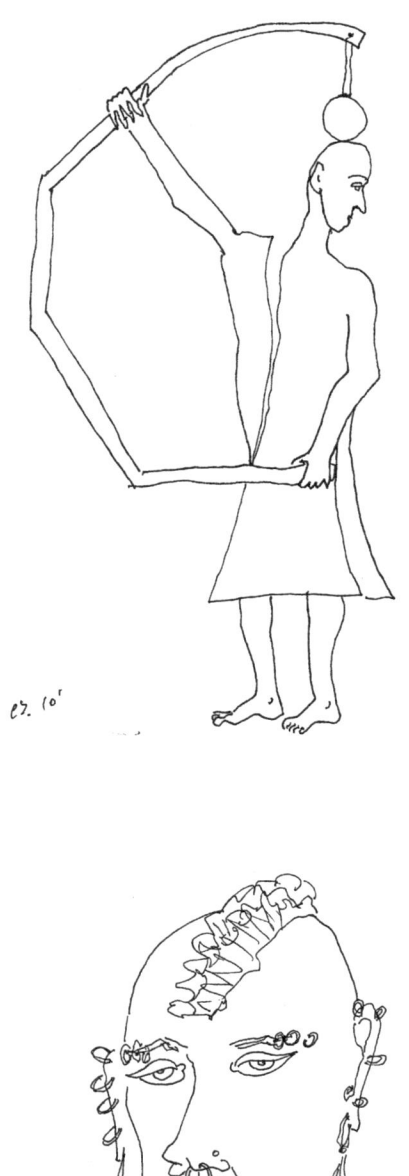

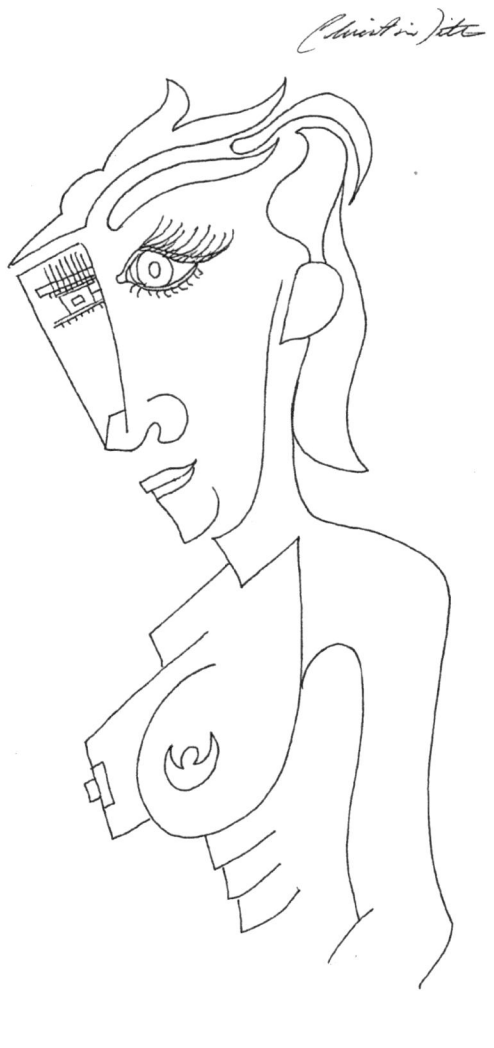

C.T. 2001

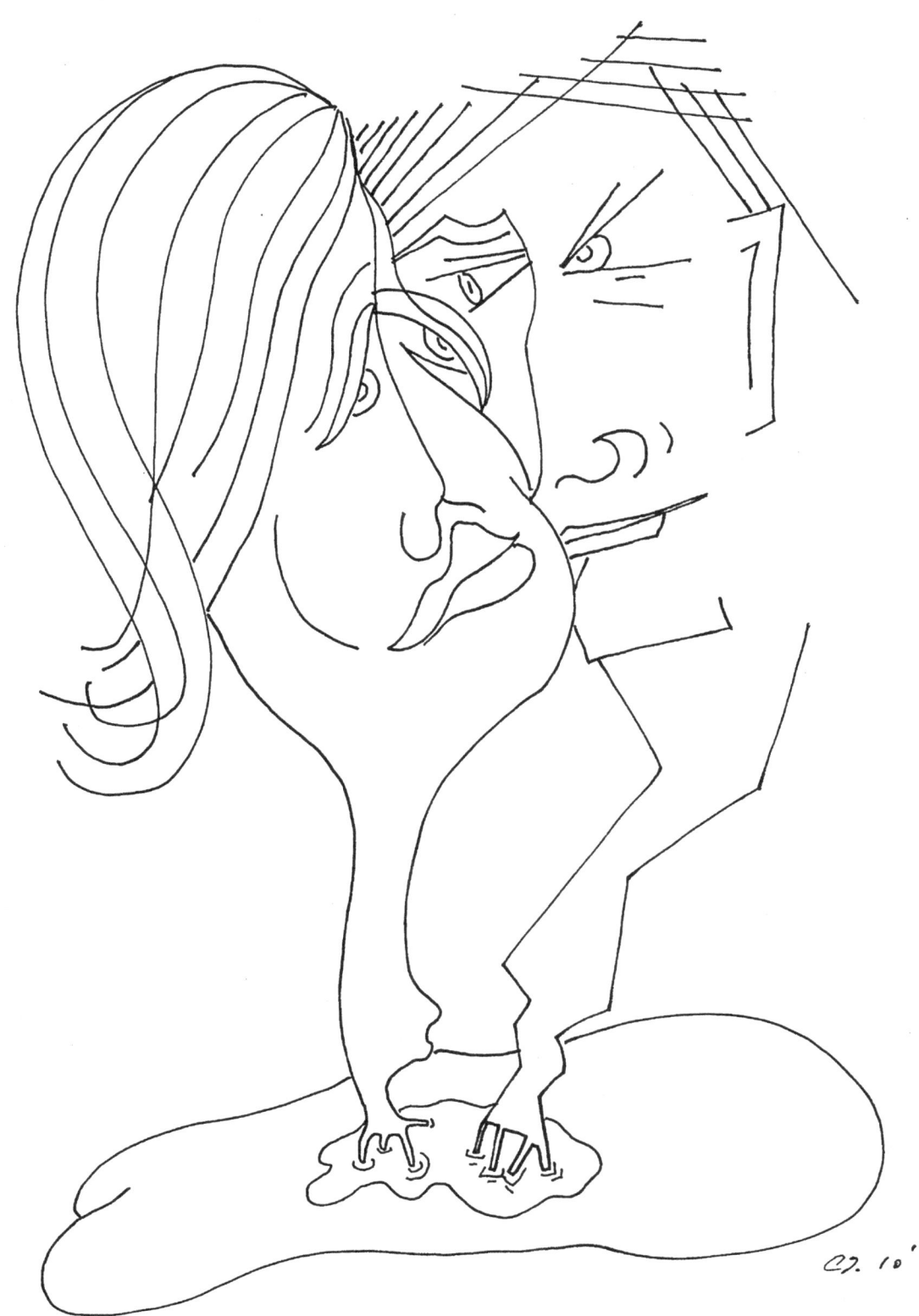

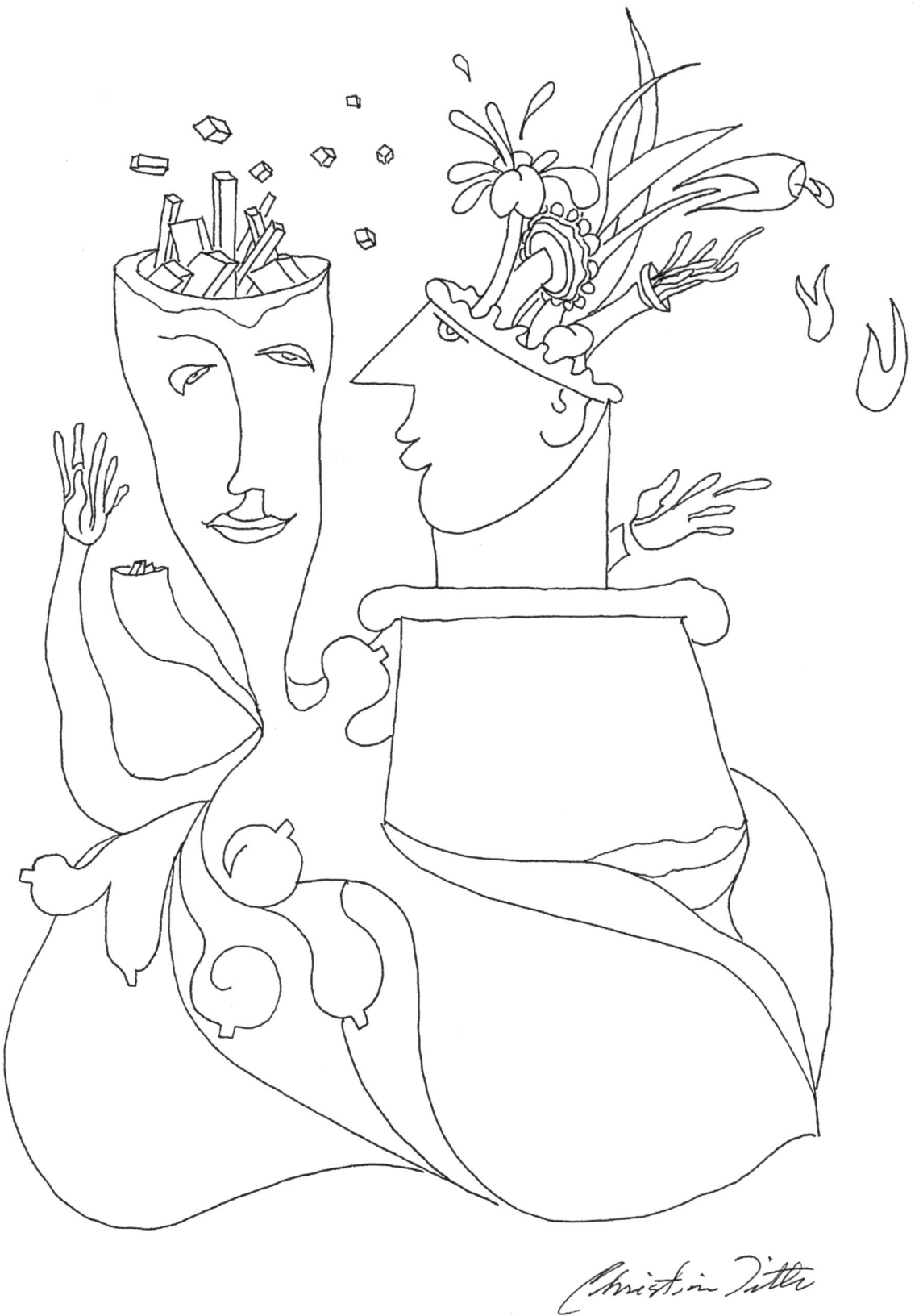

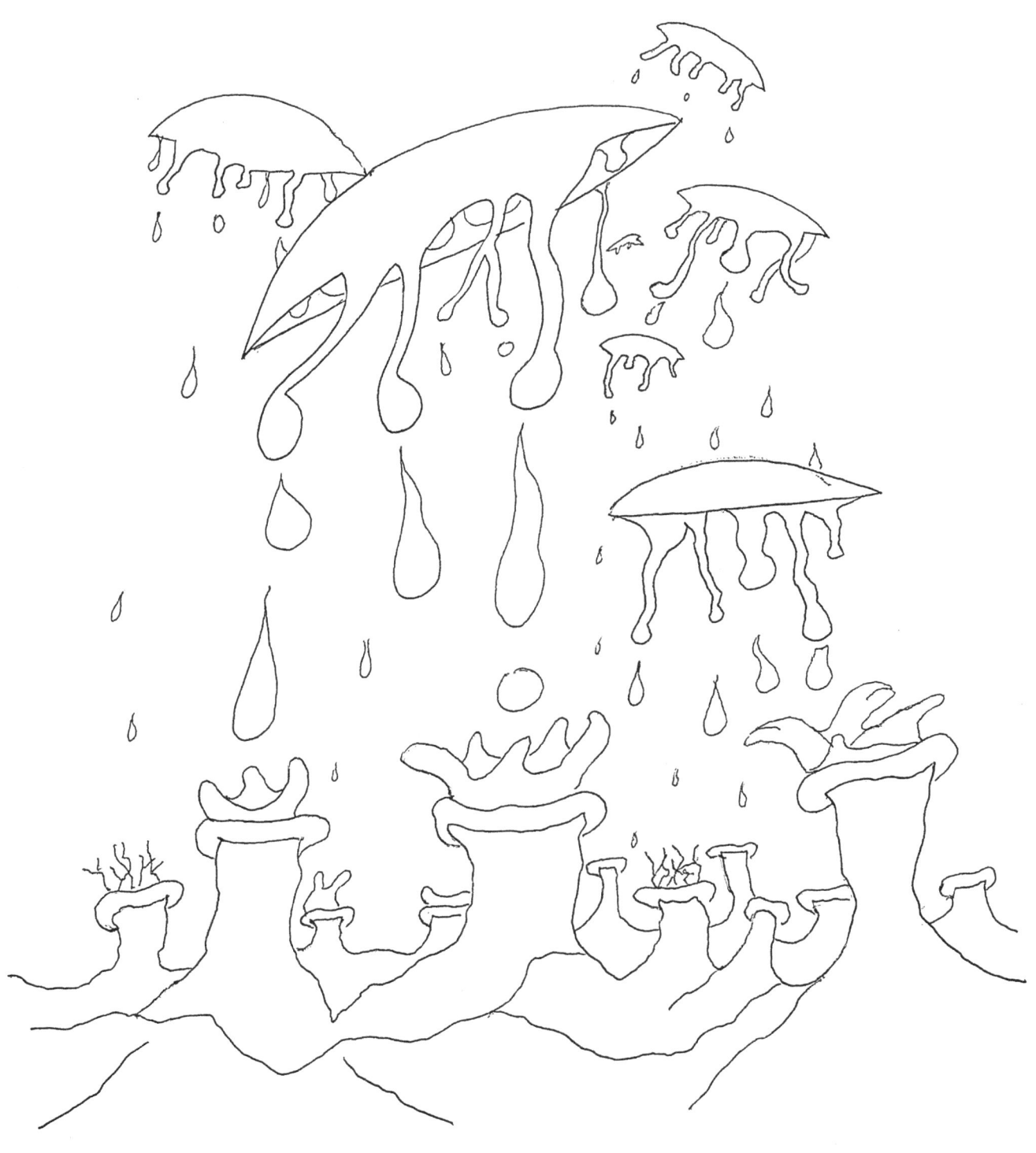

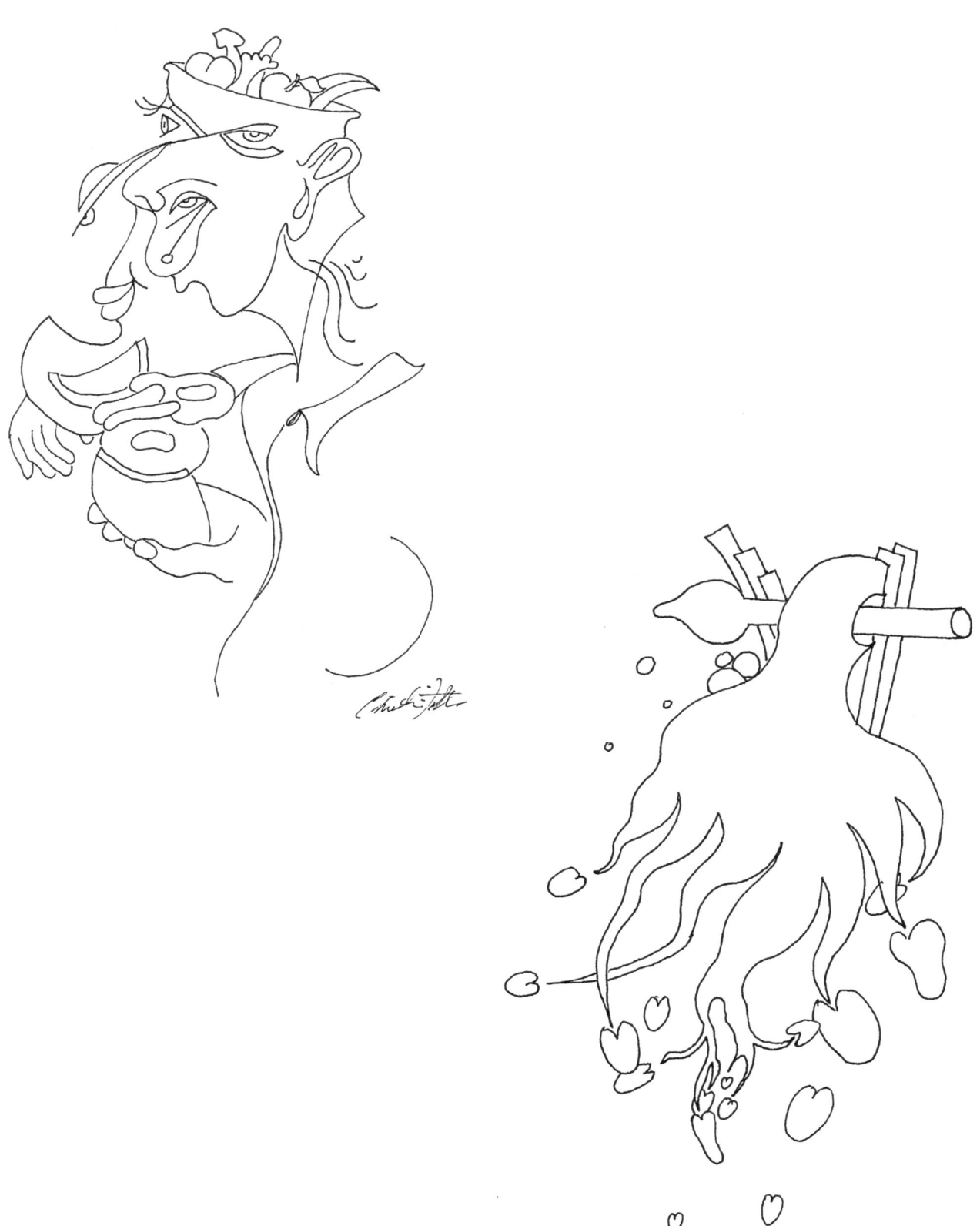

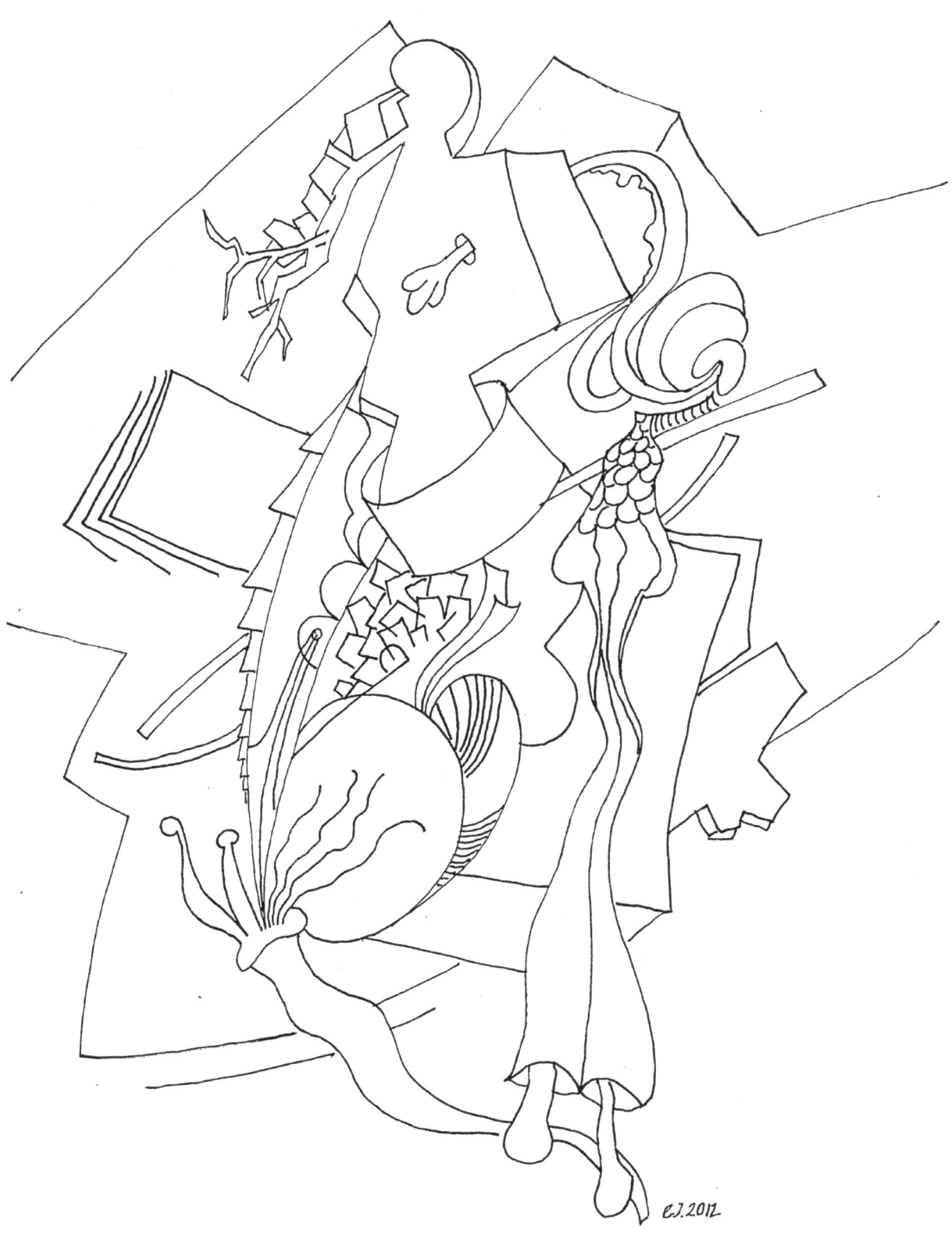

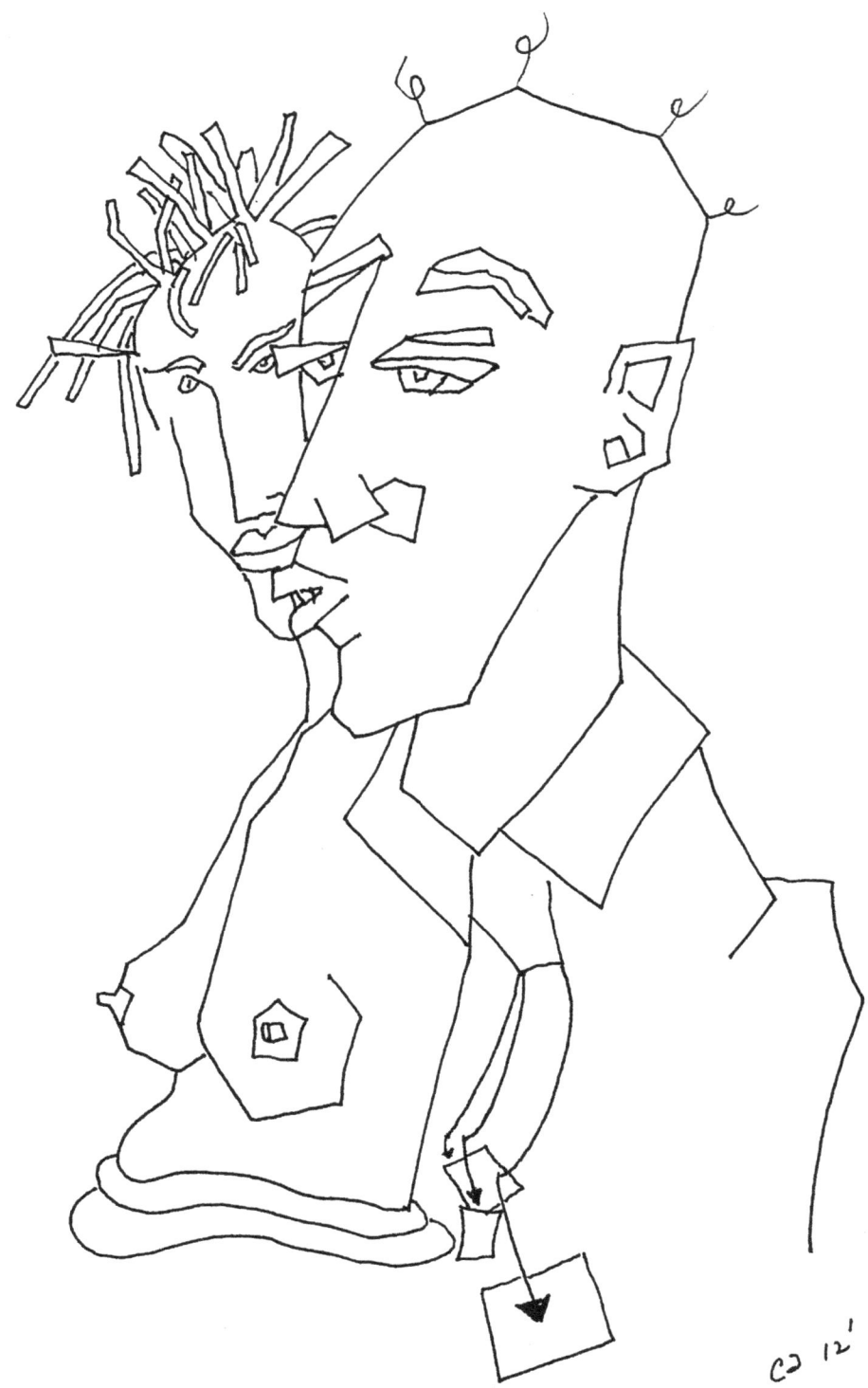

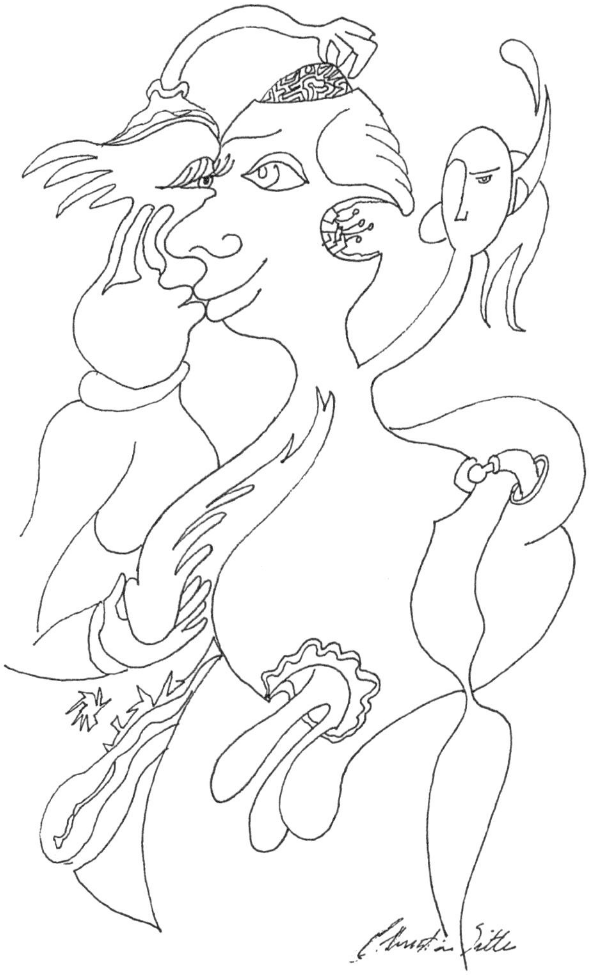

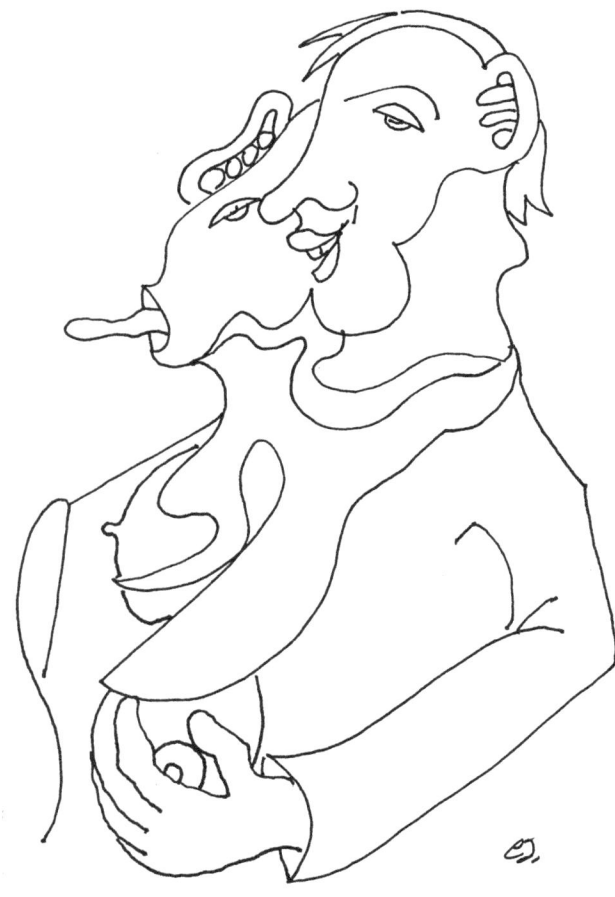

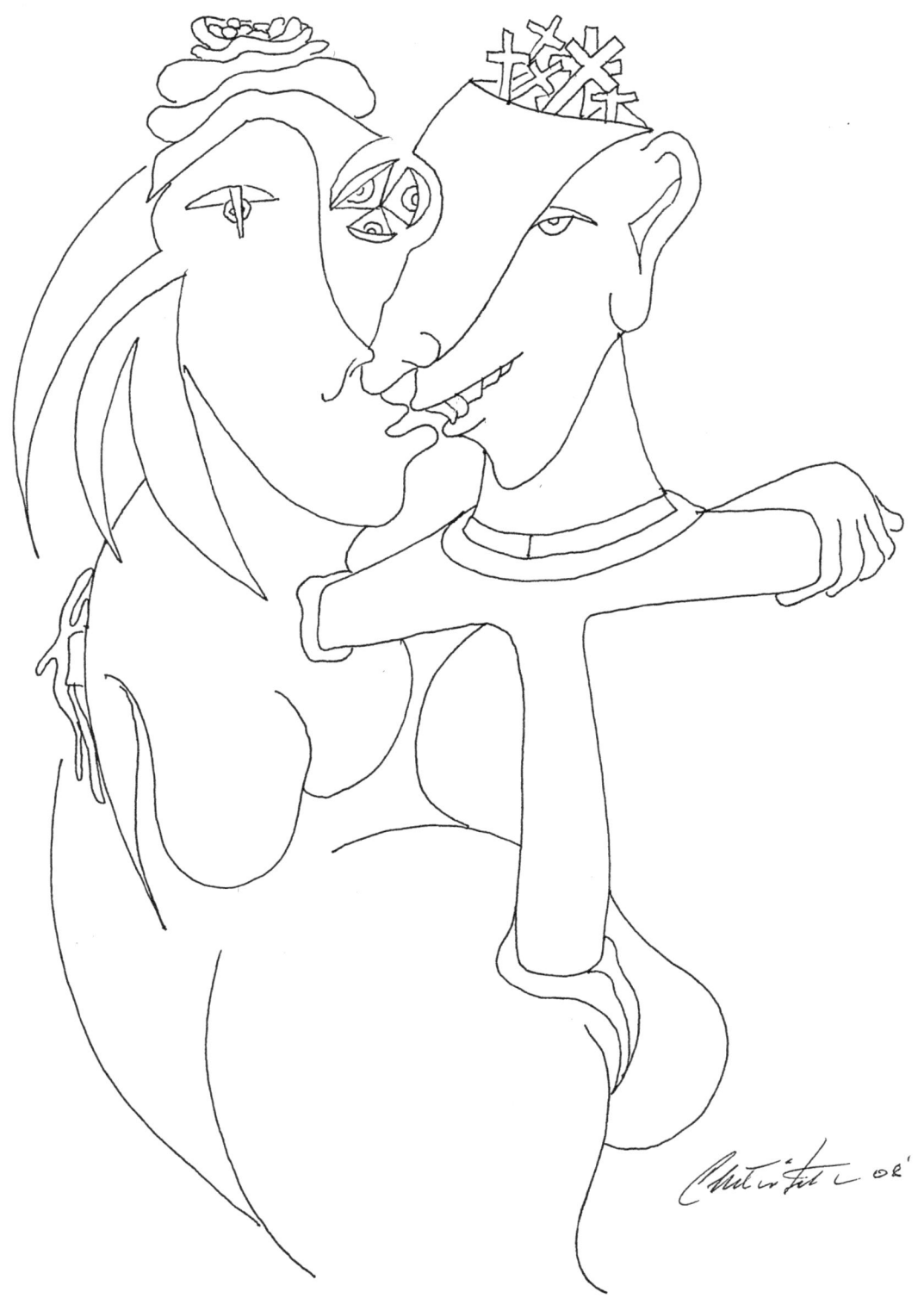

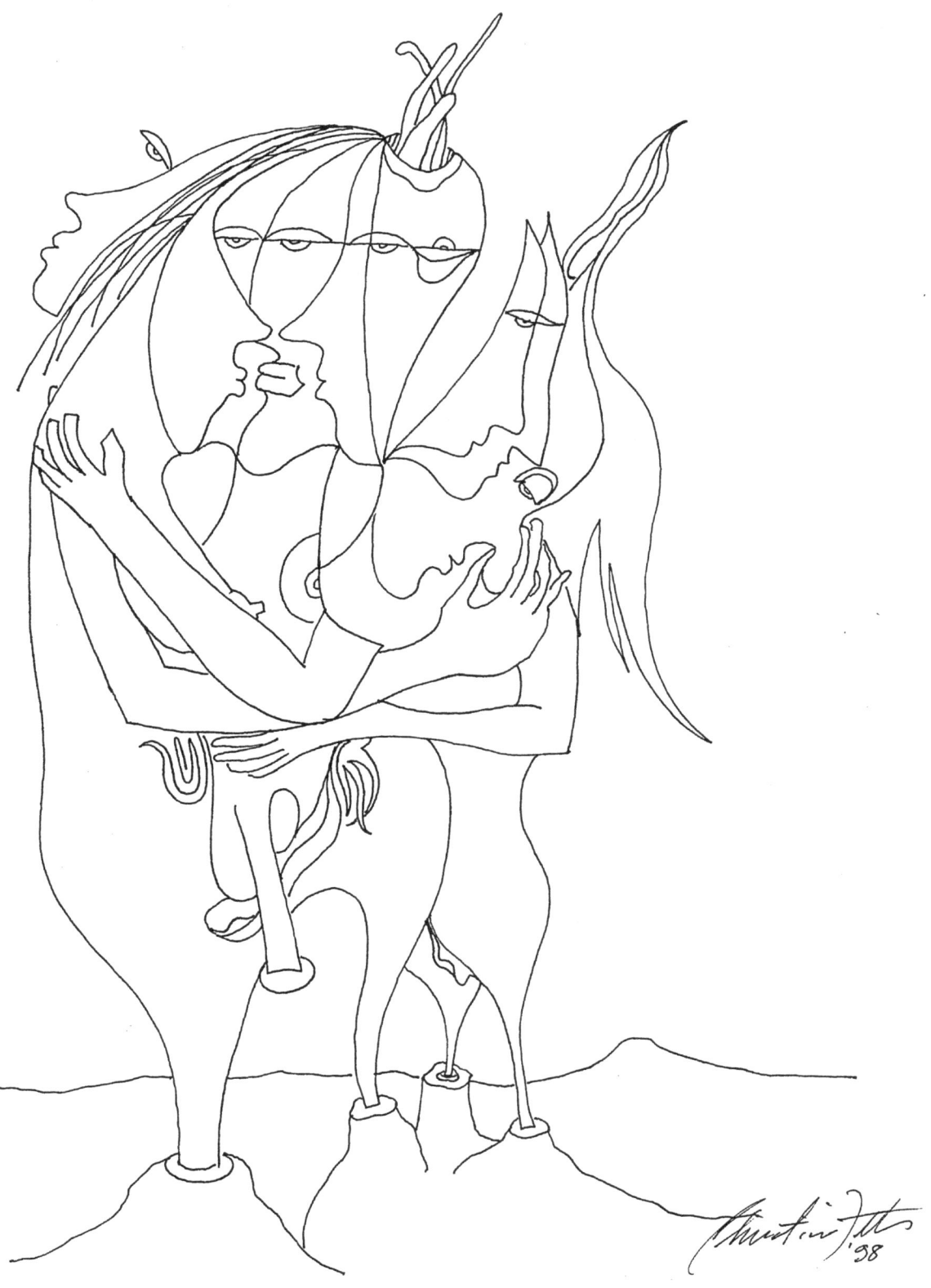

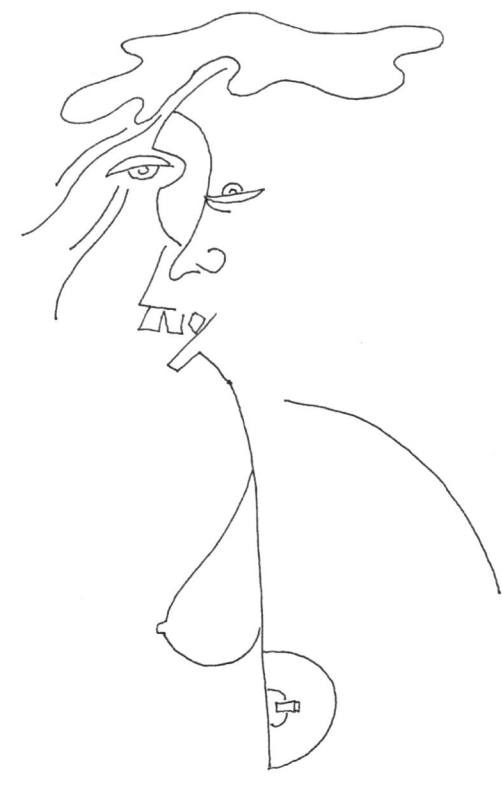

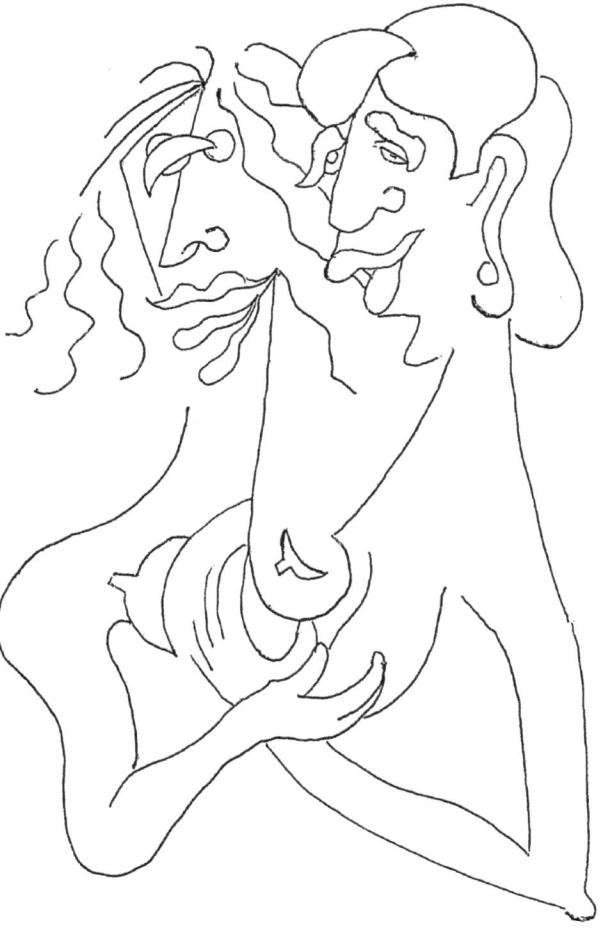

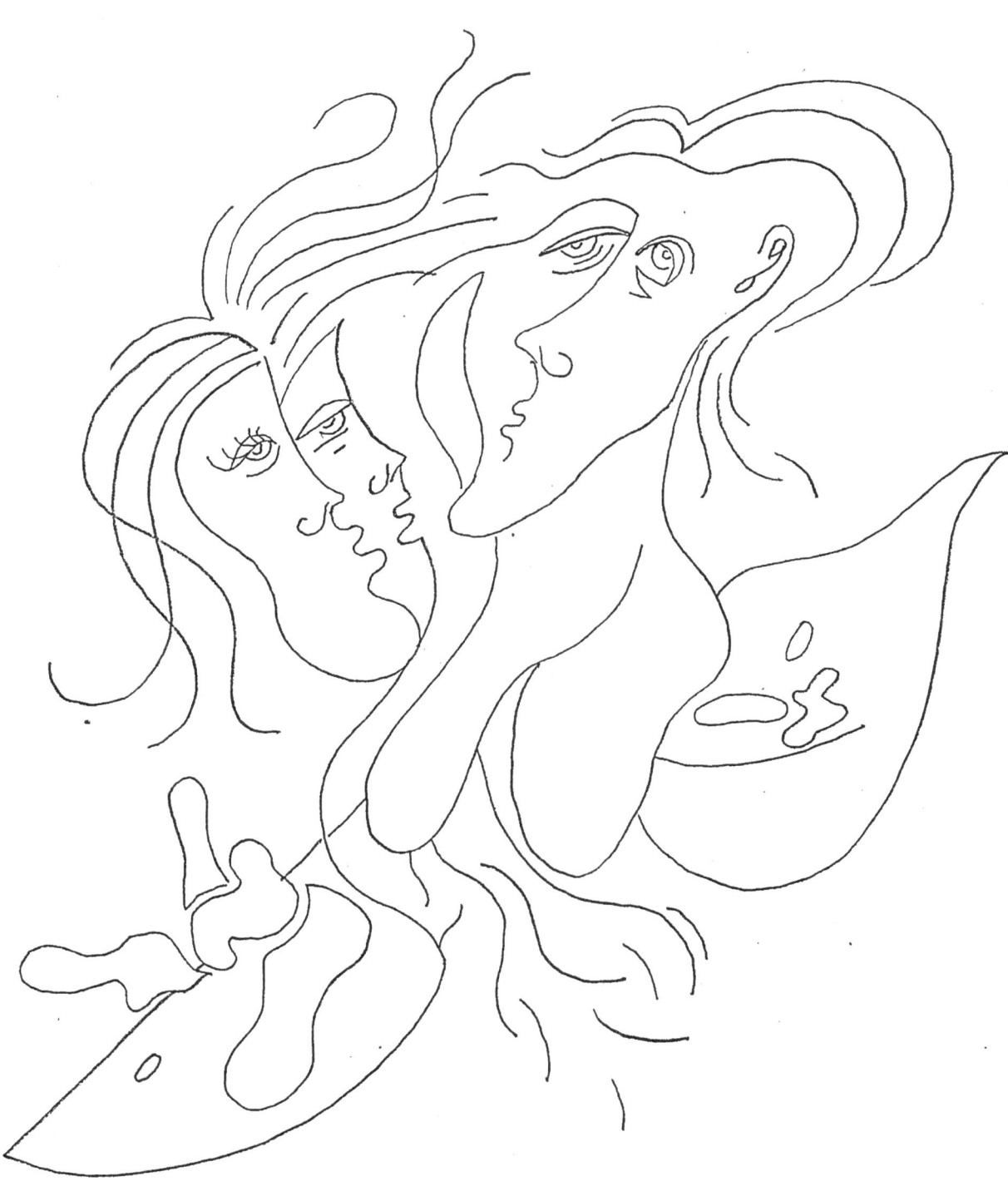

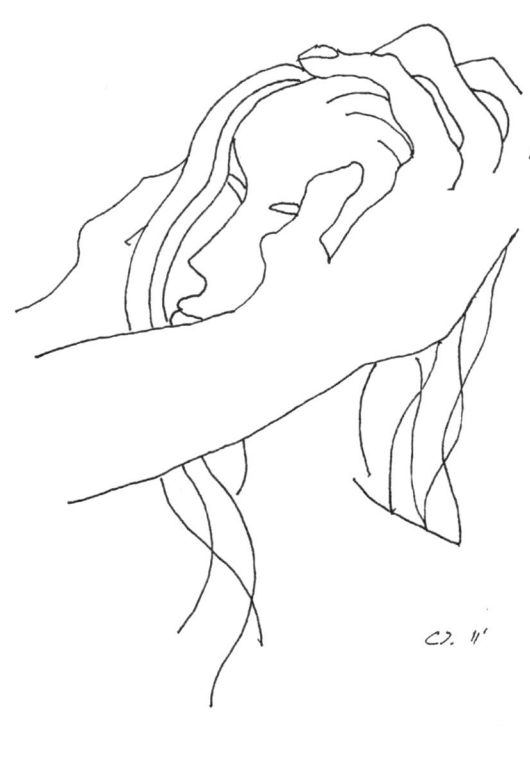

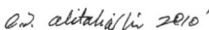

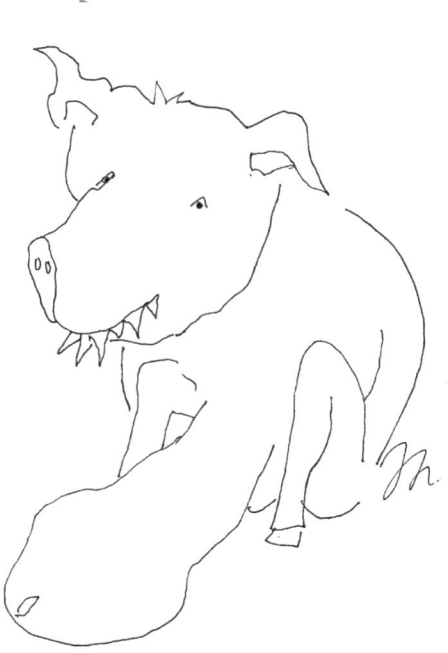

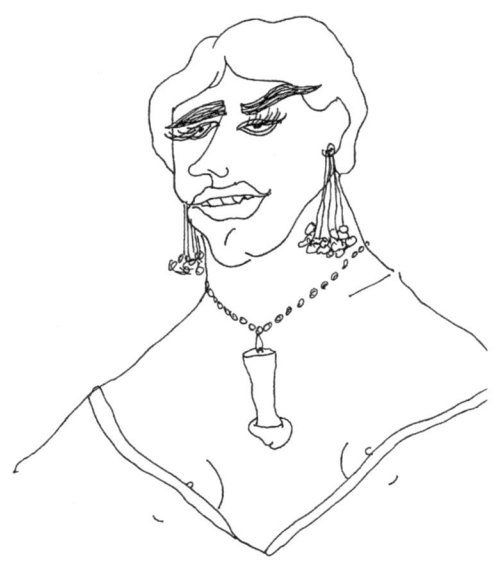

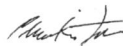

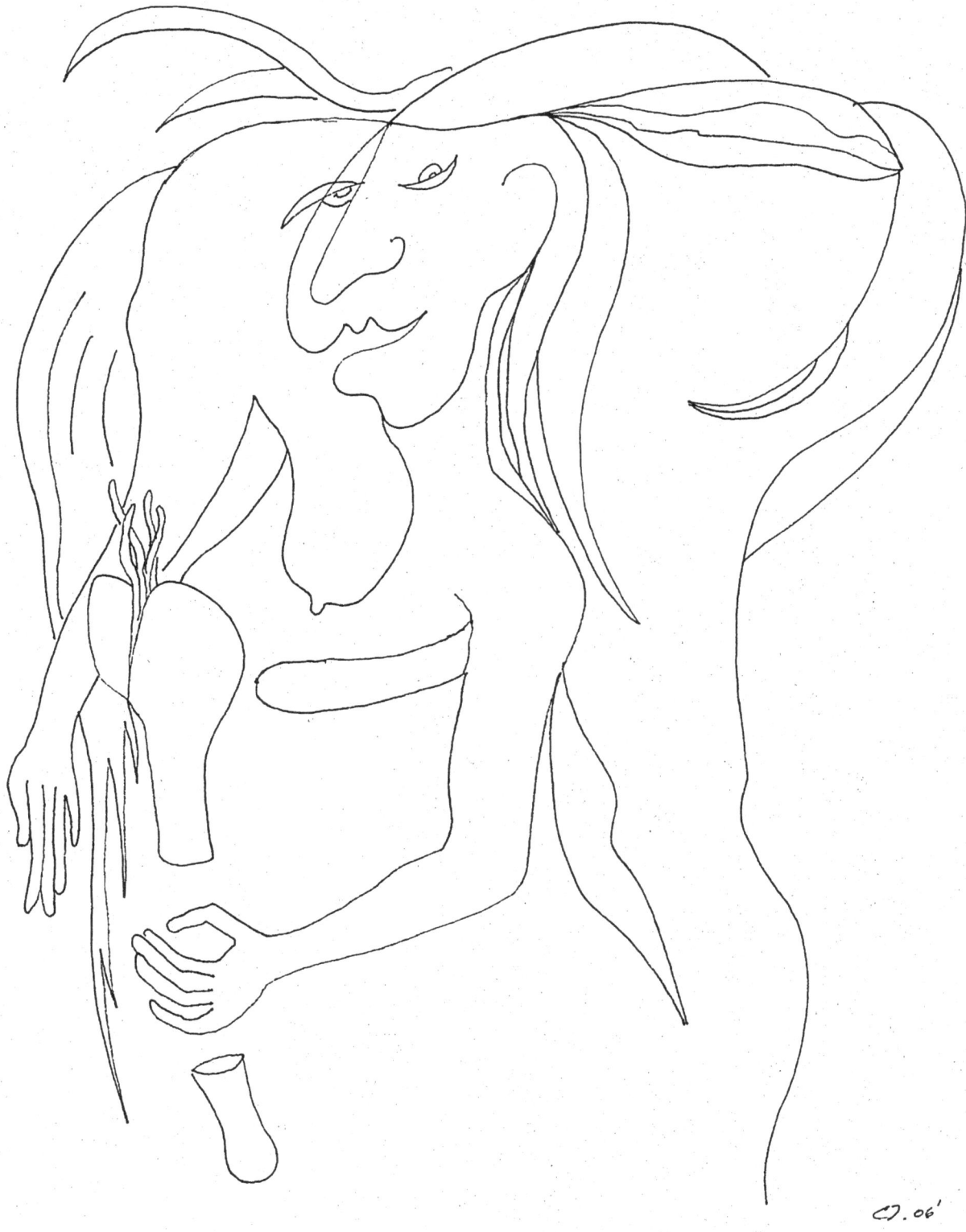

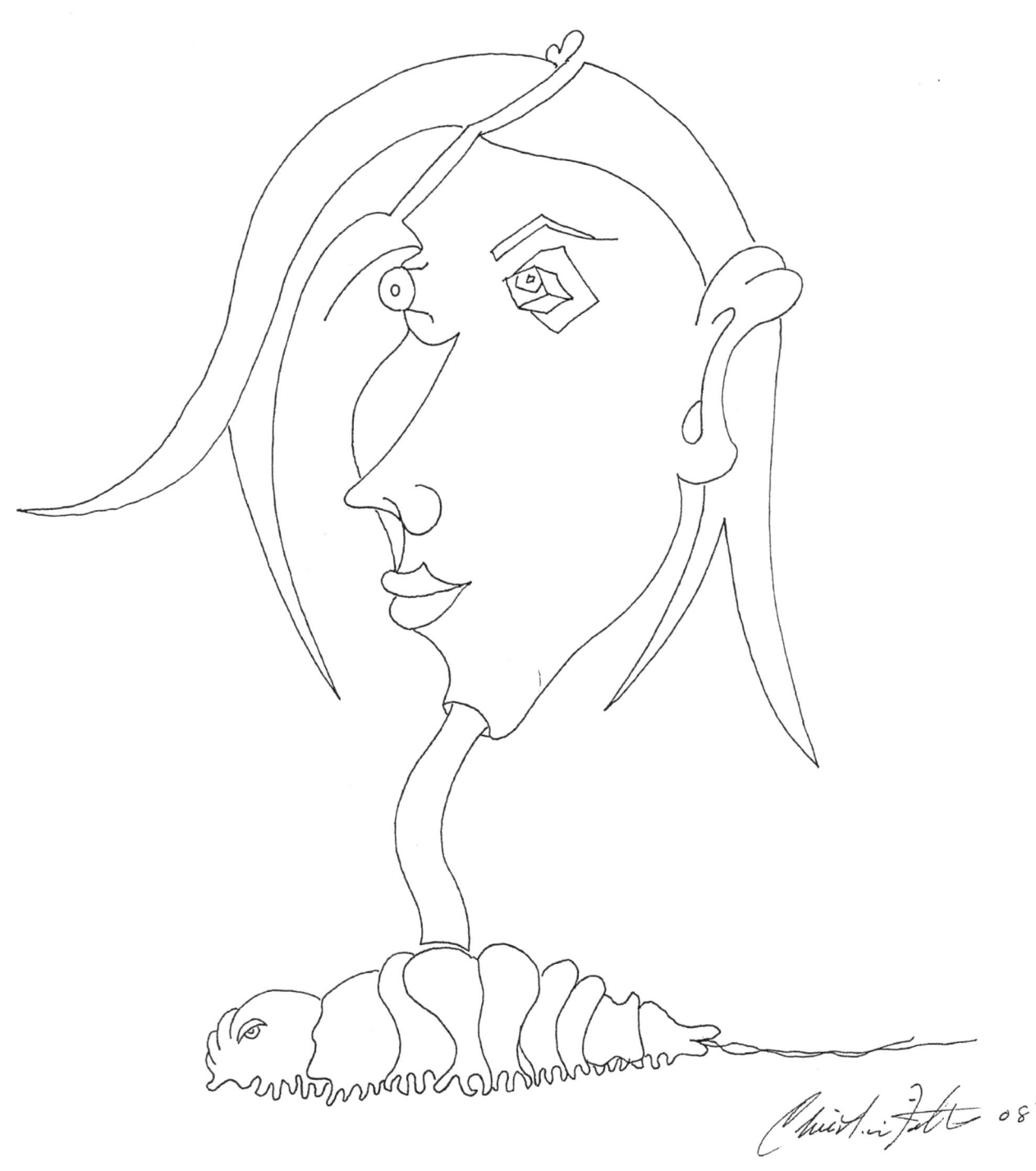

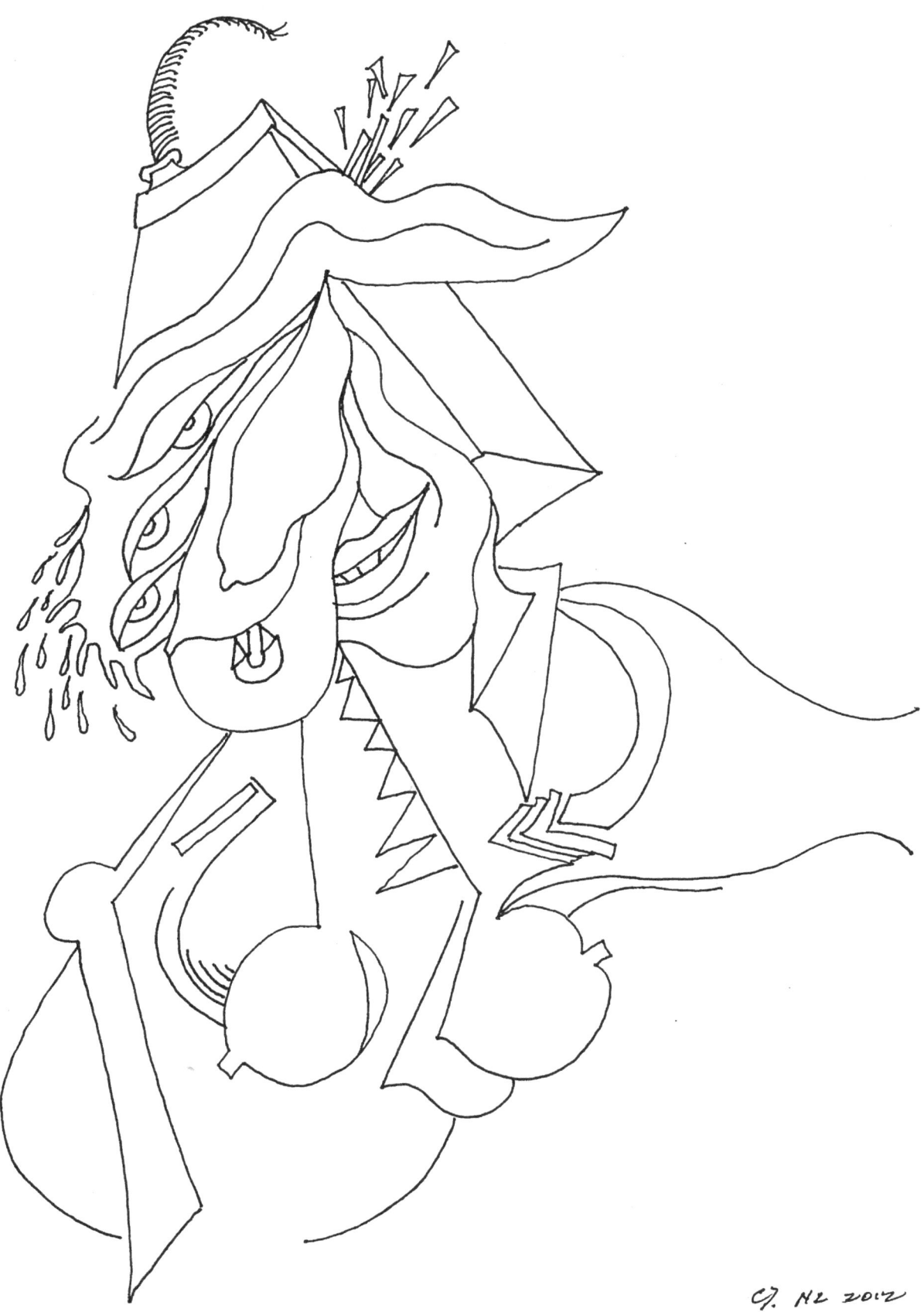

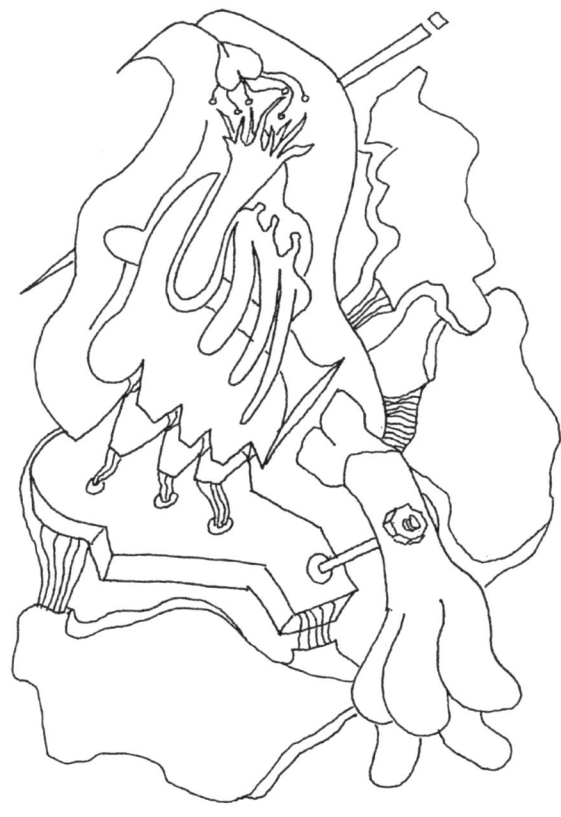

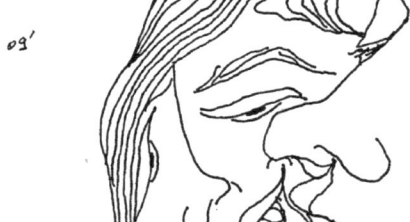

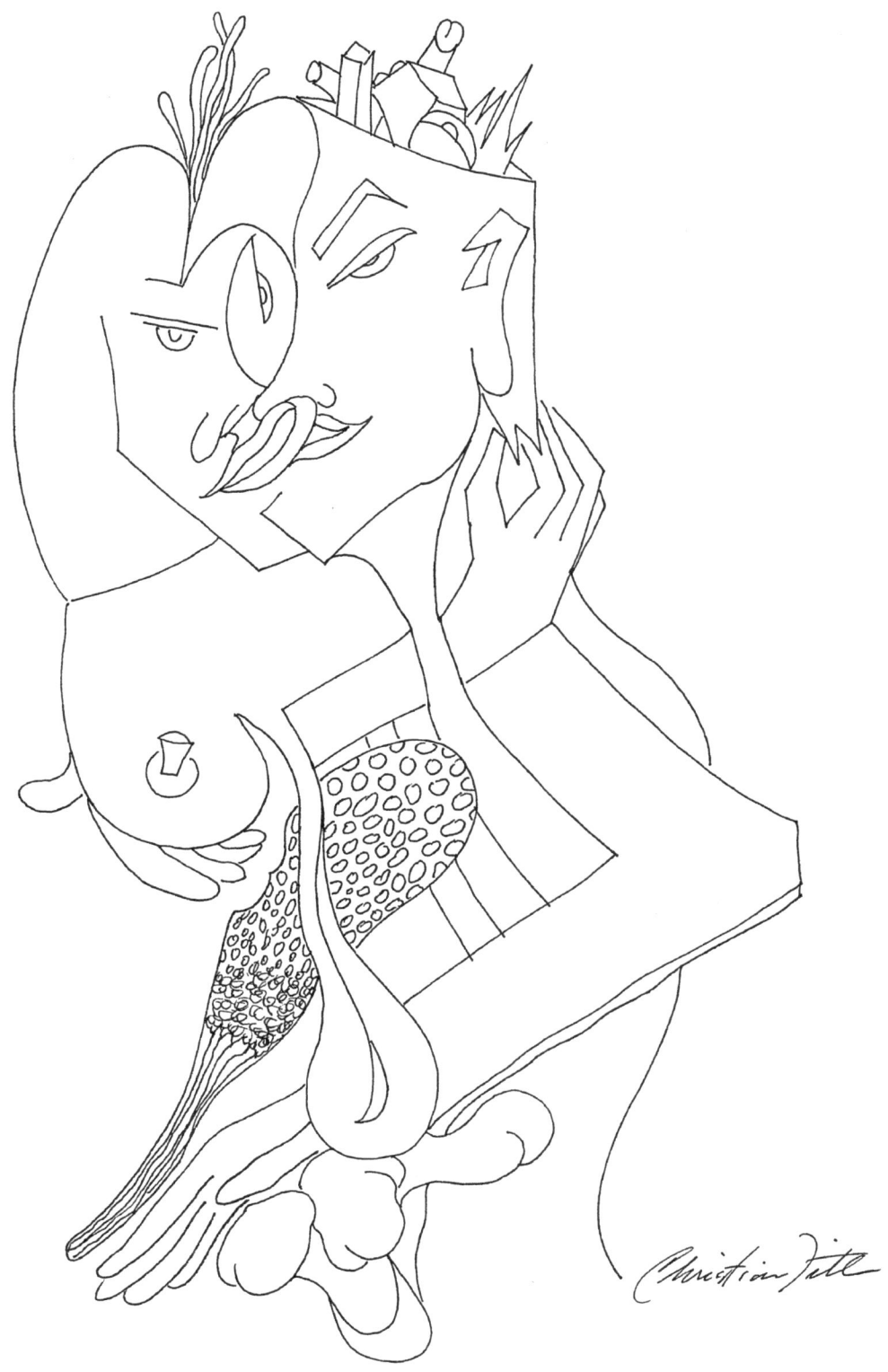

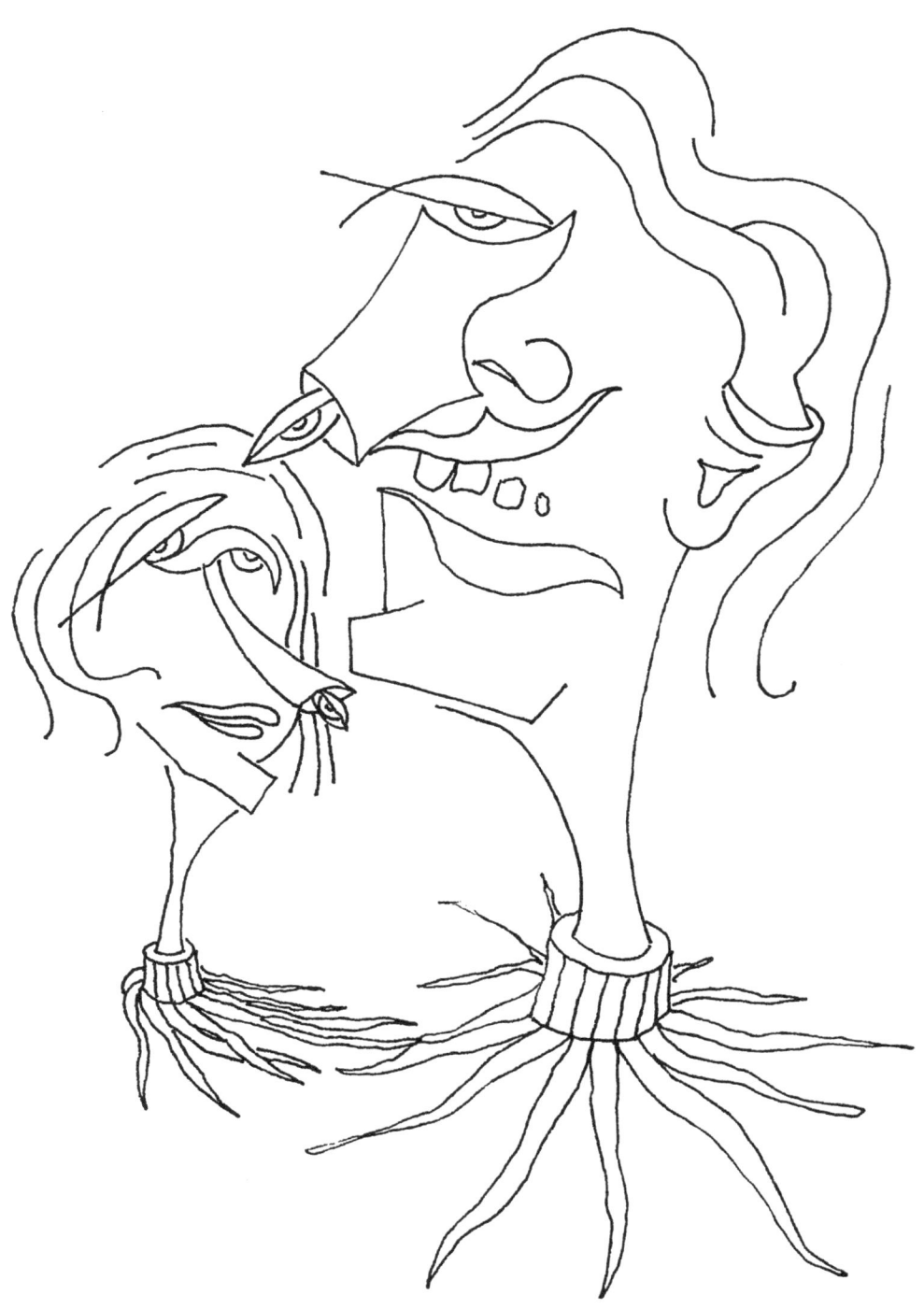

CJ 2014

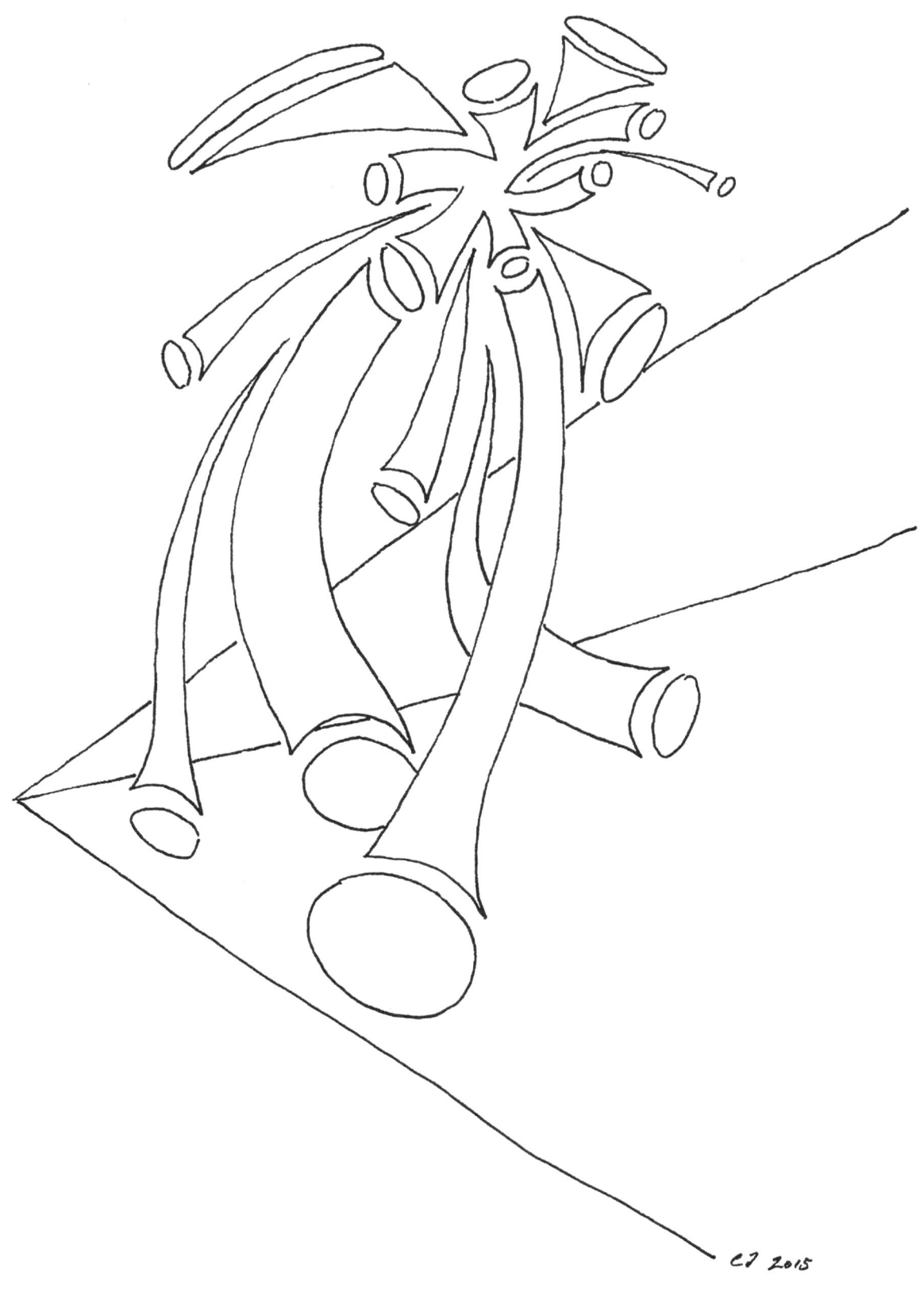

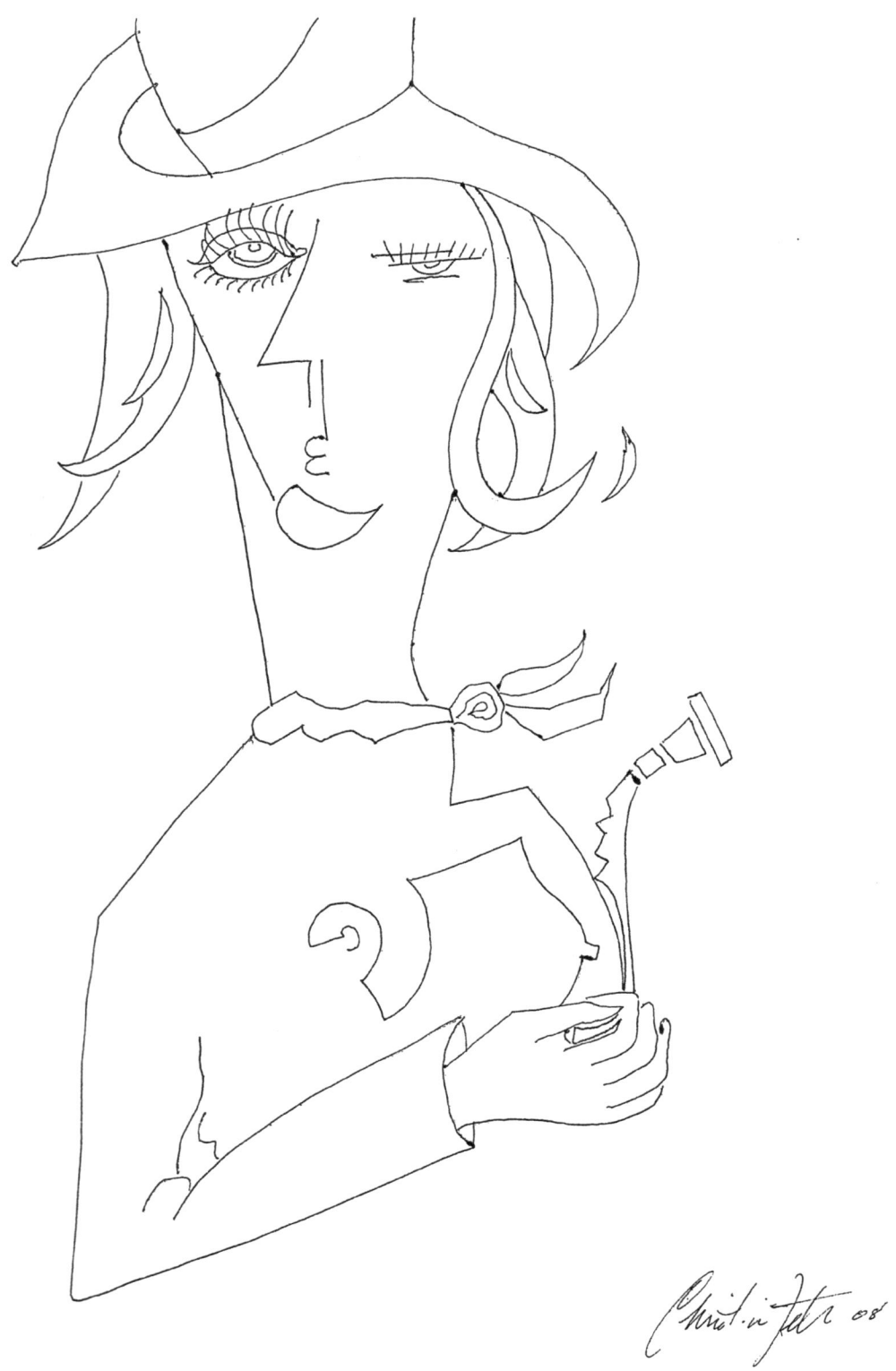

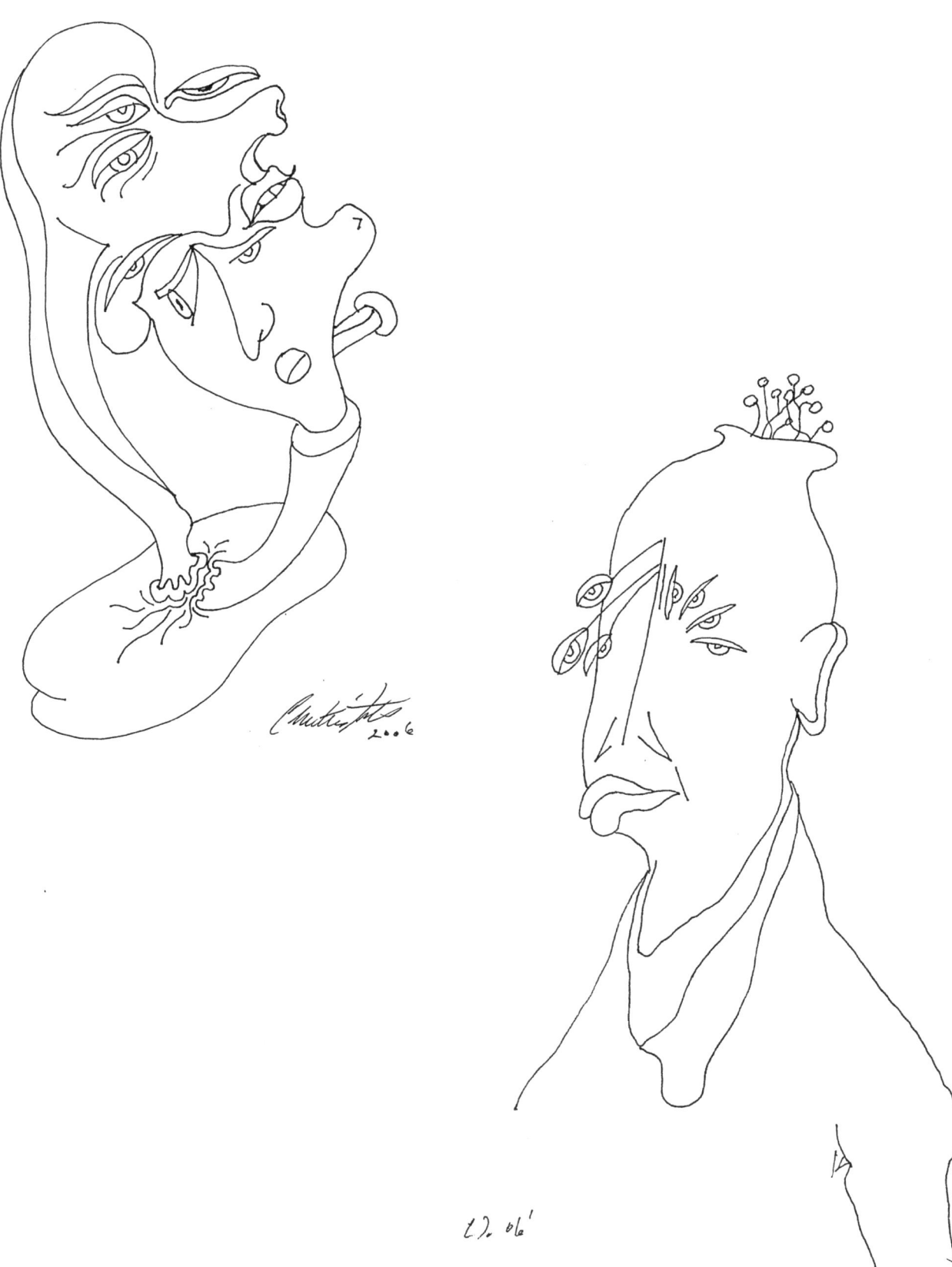

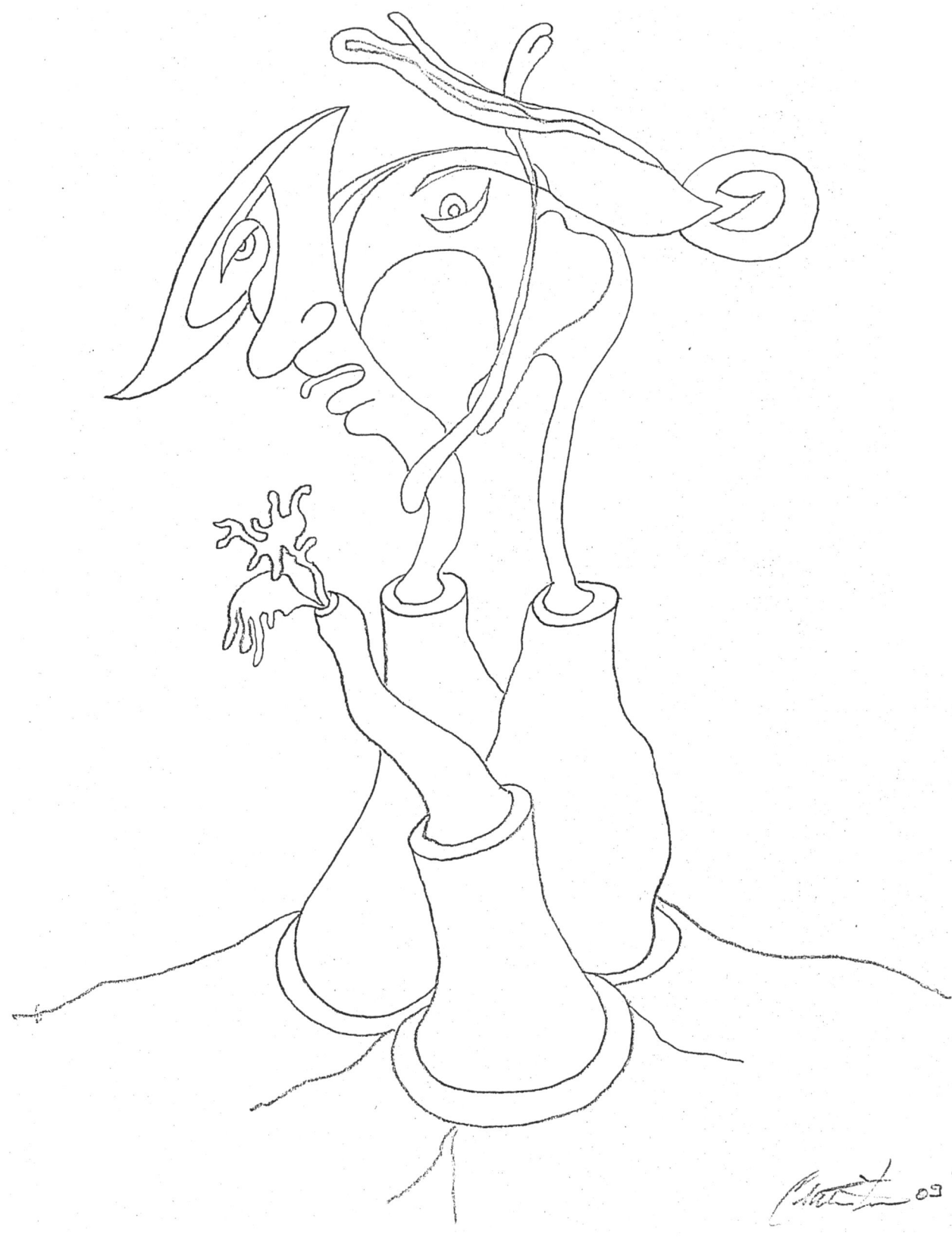

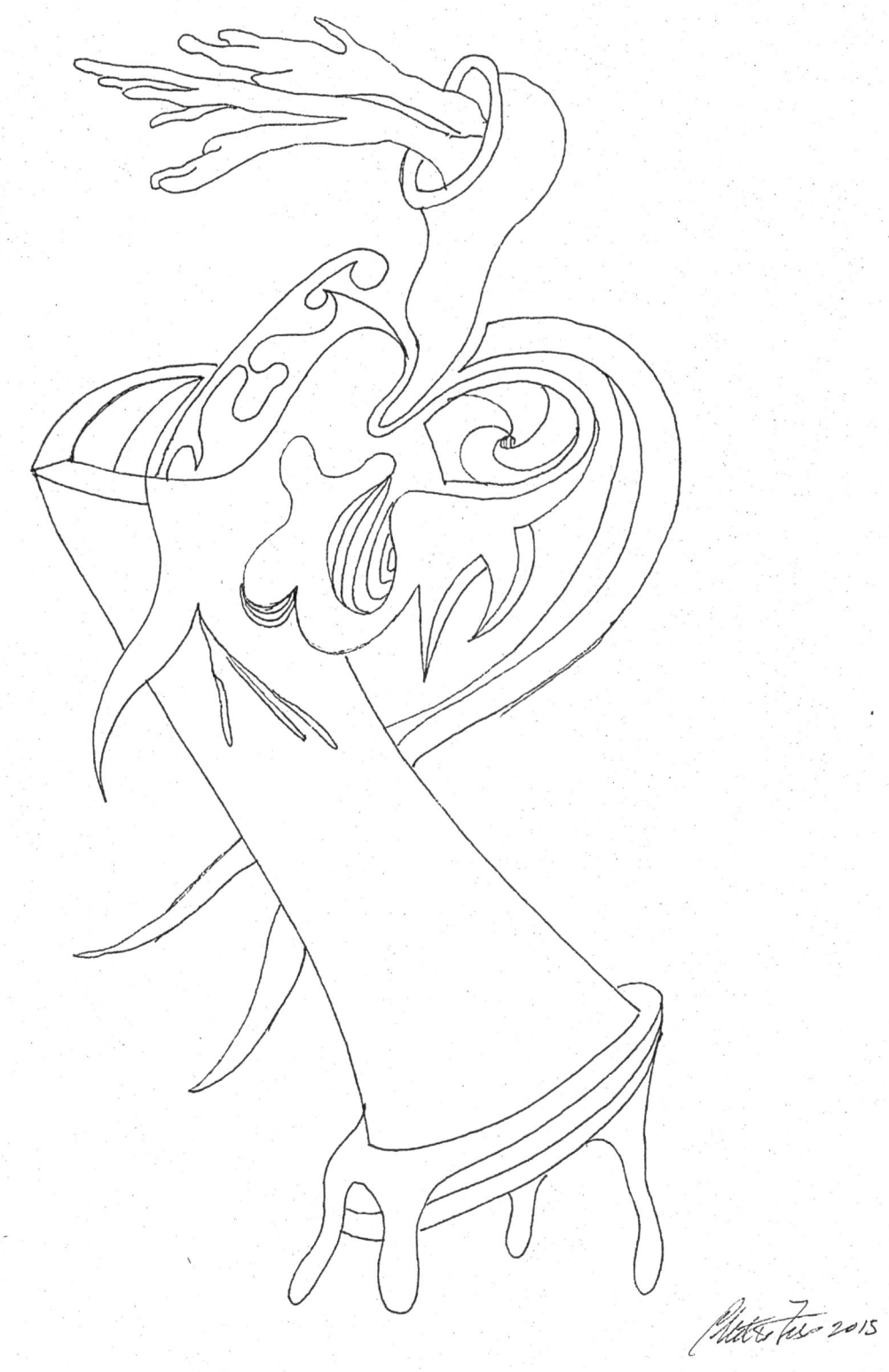

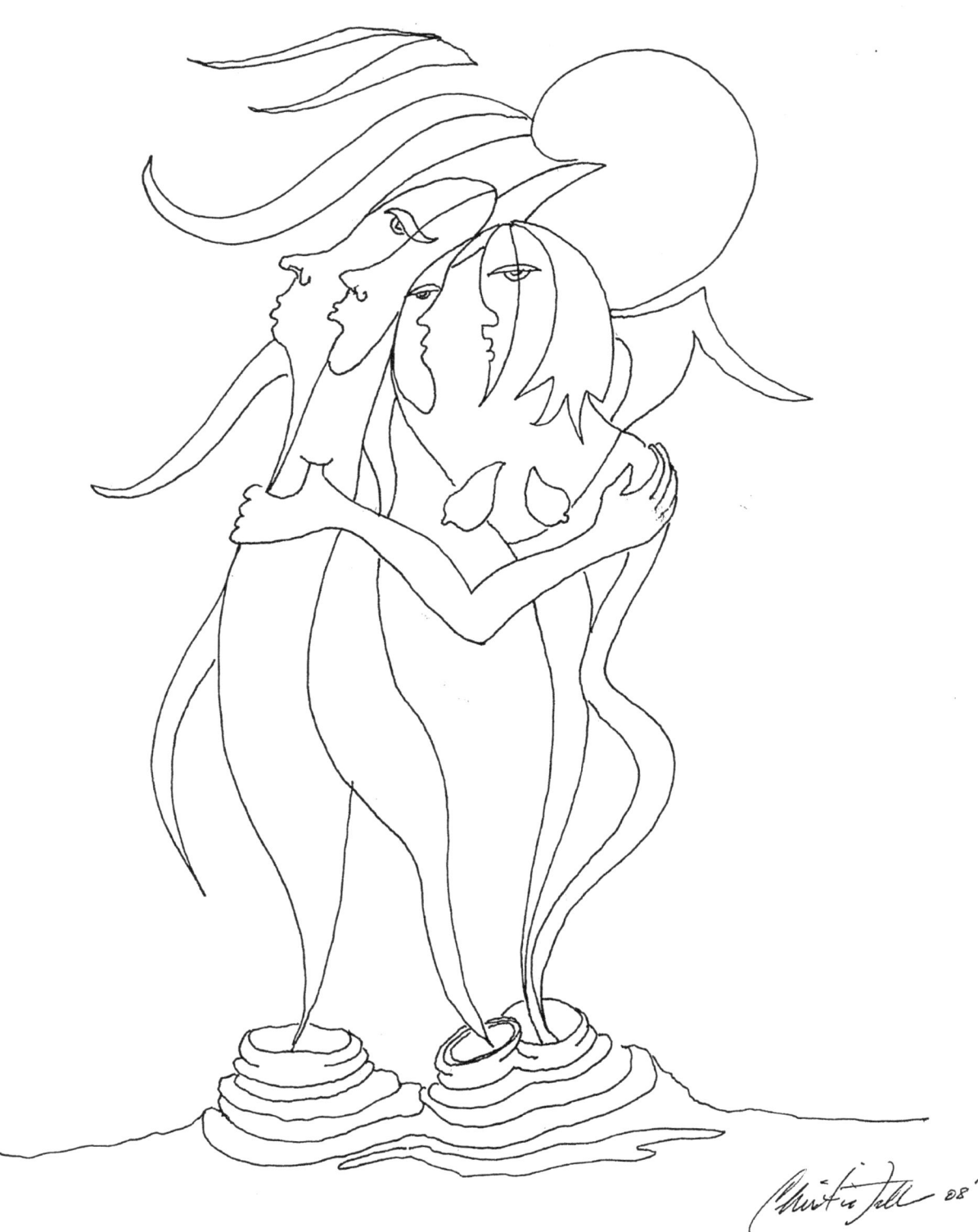

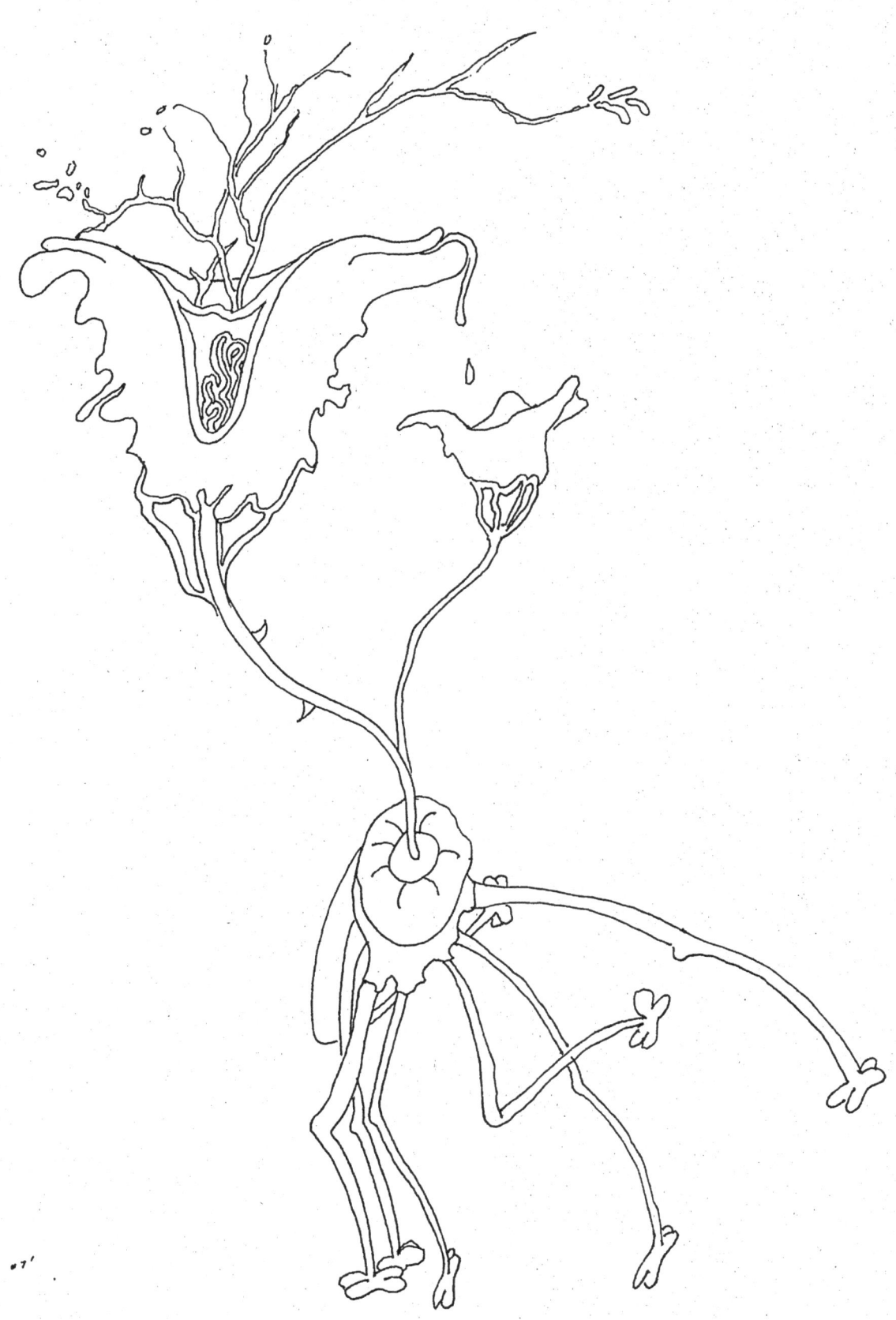

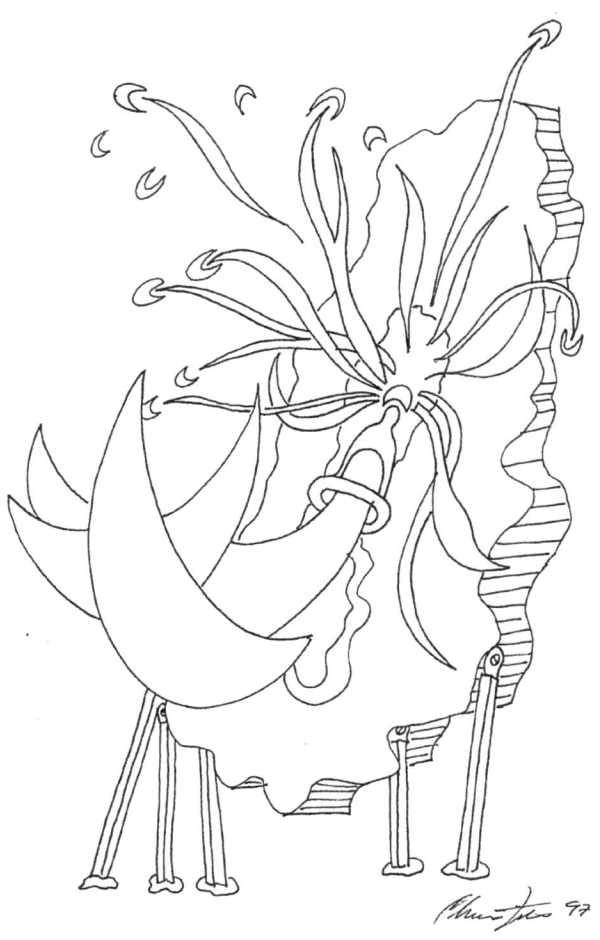

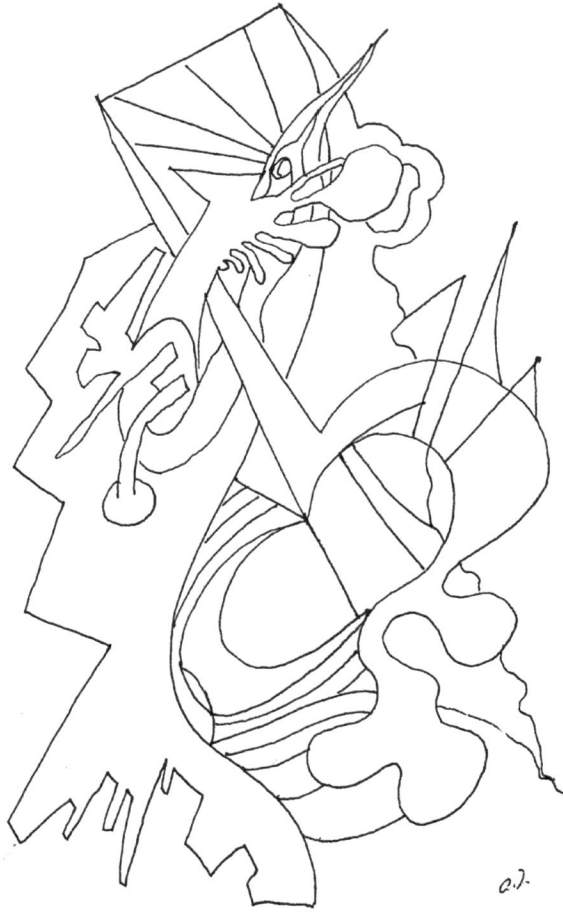

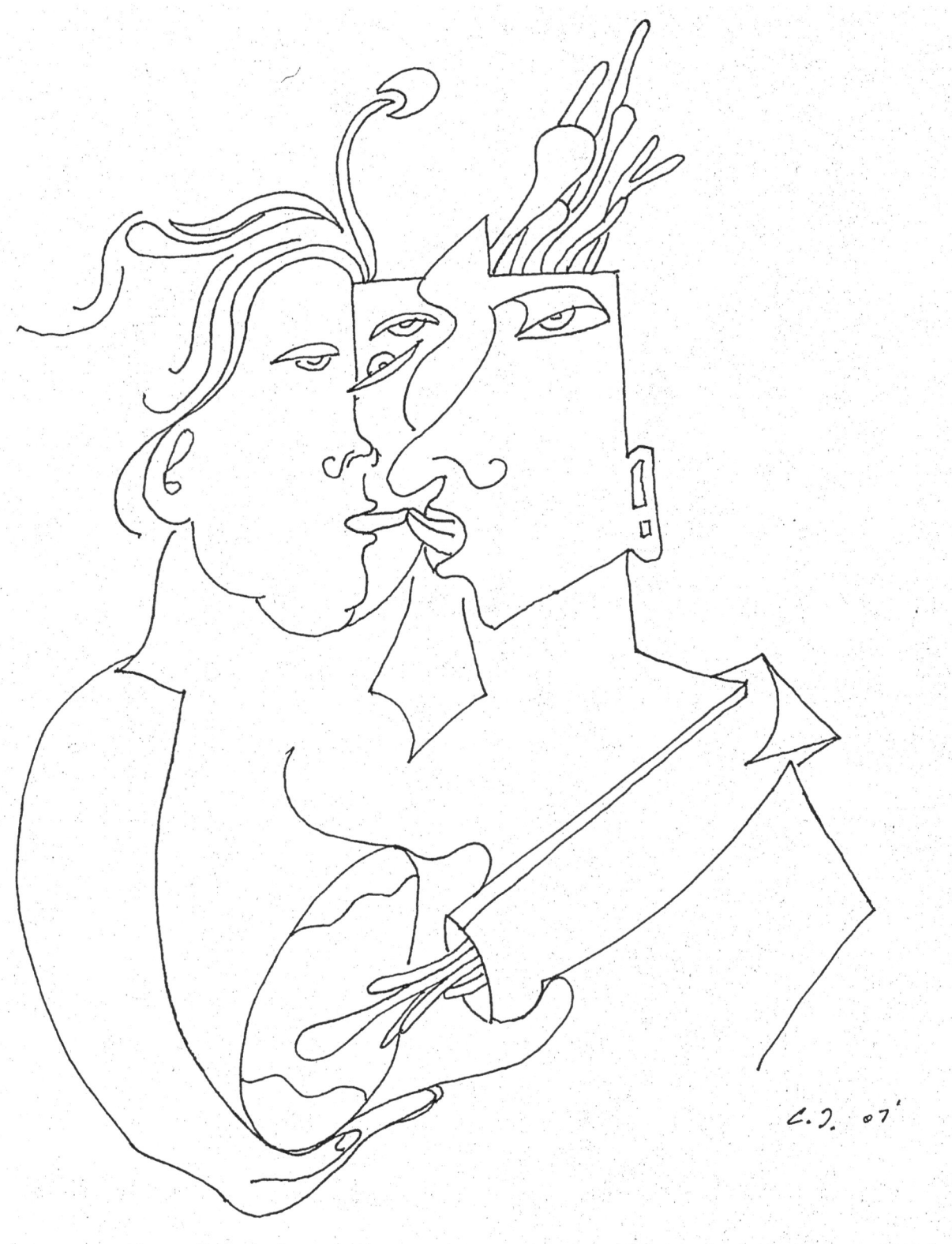

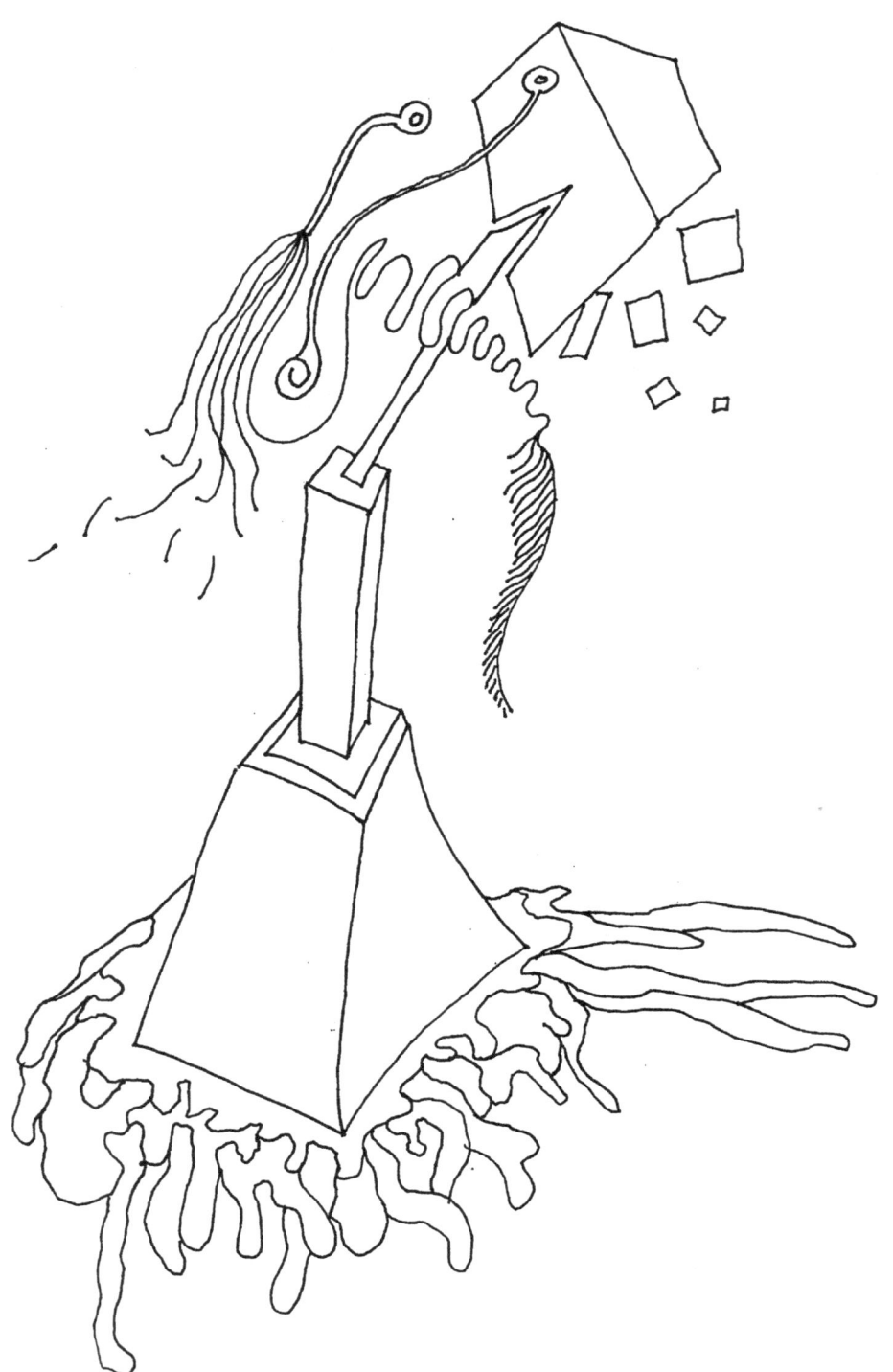

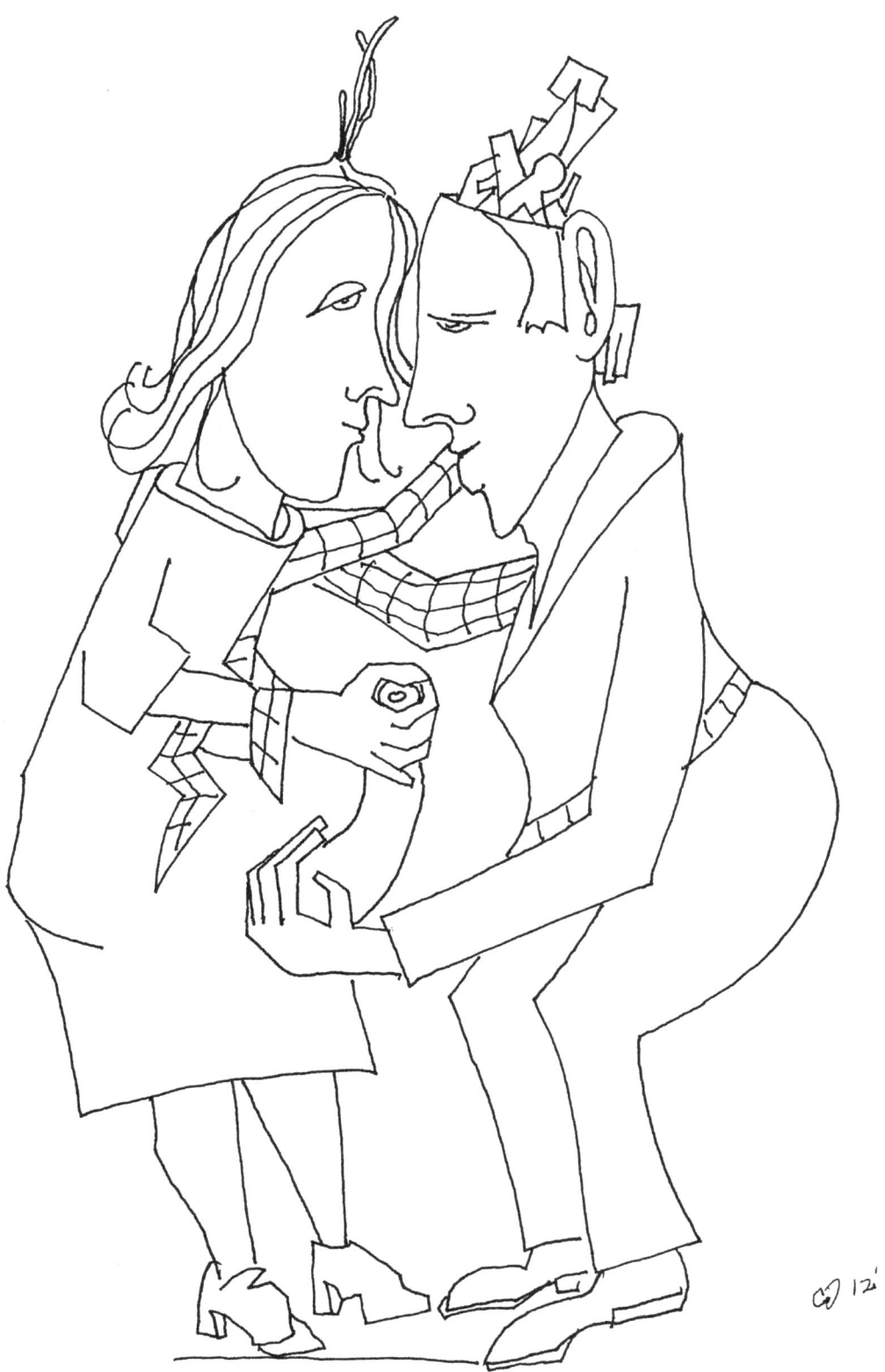

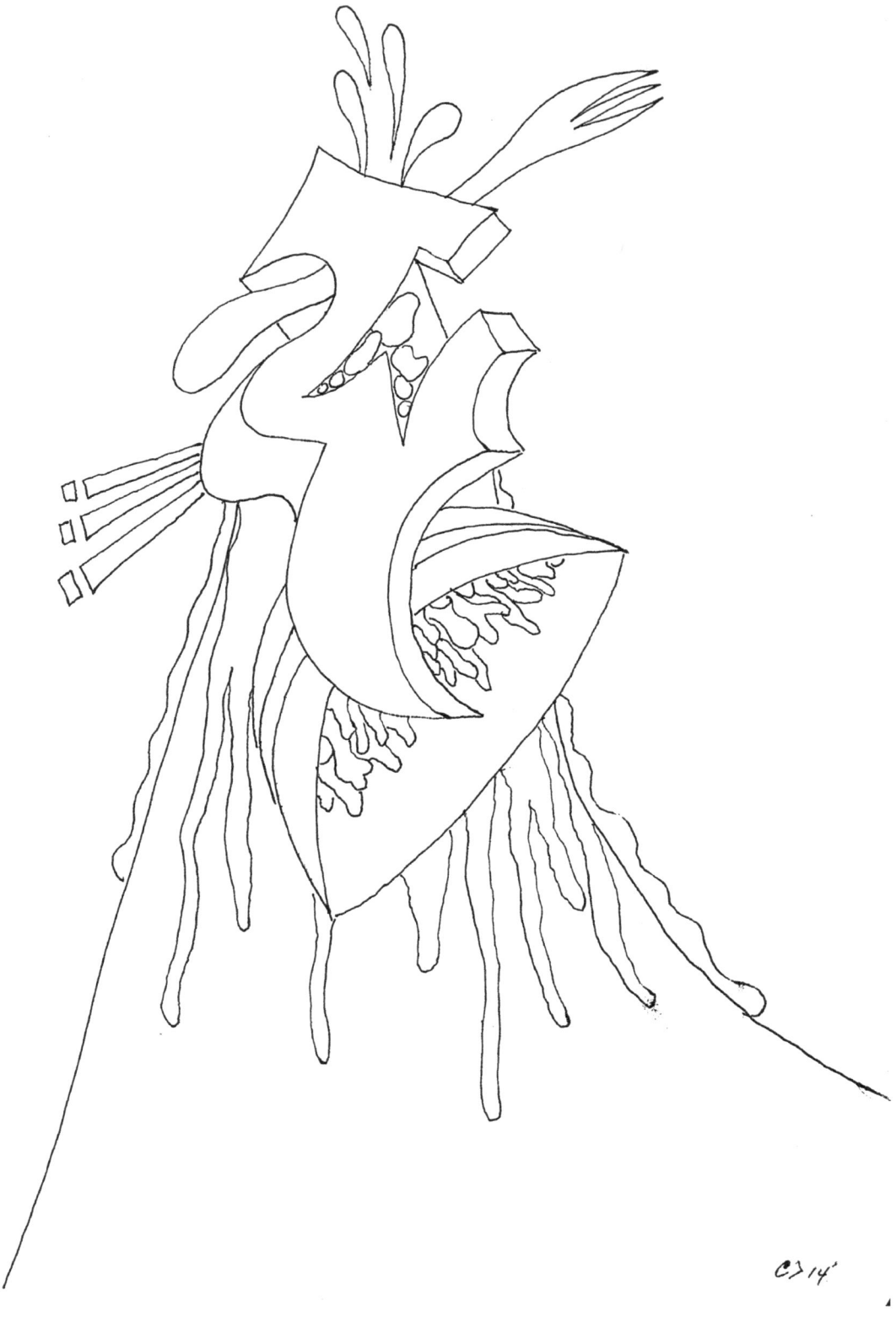

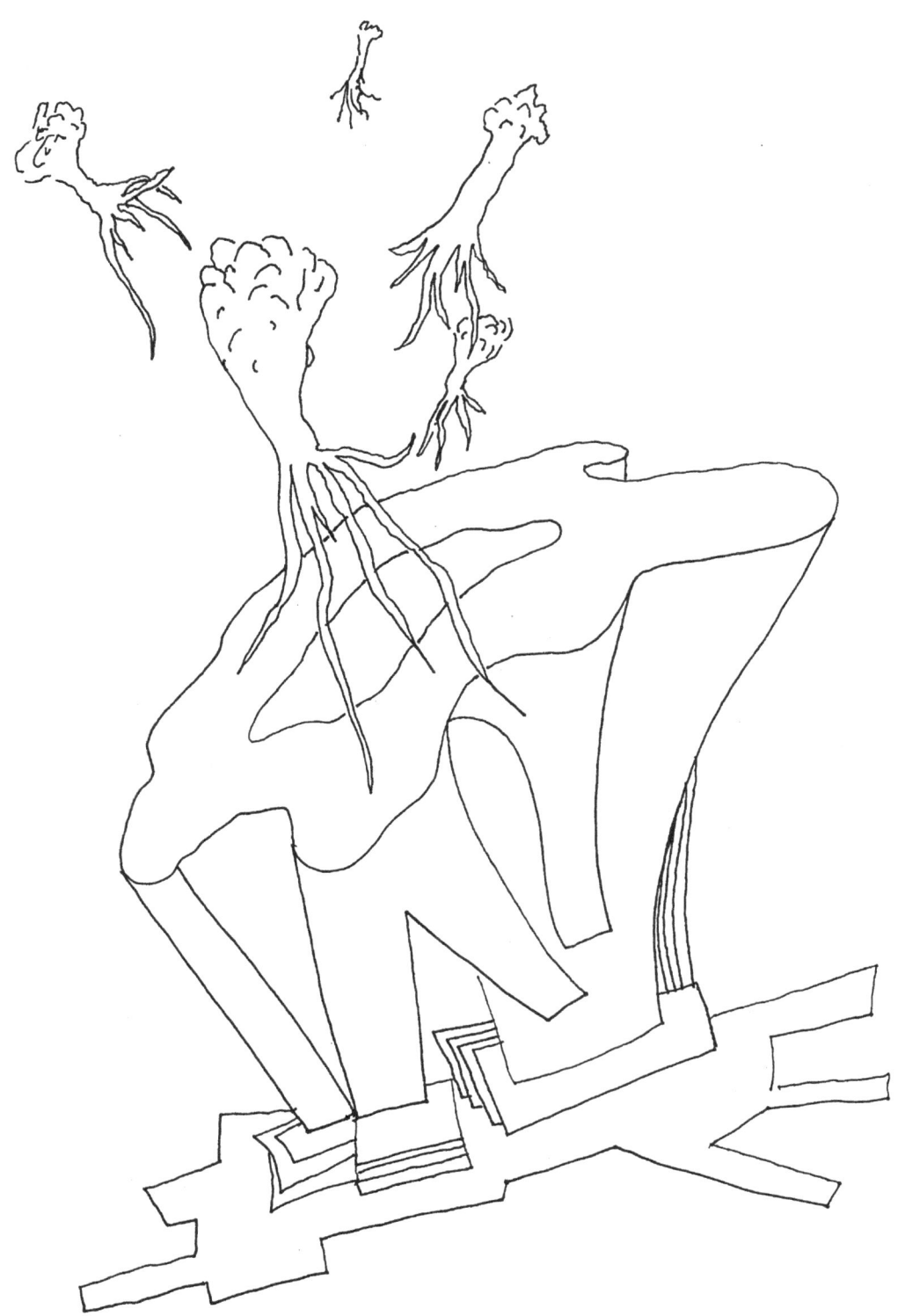

CJ 2012 NZ

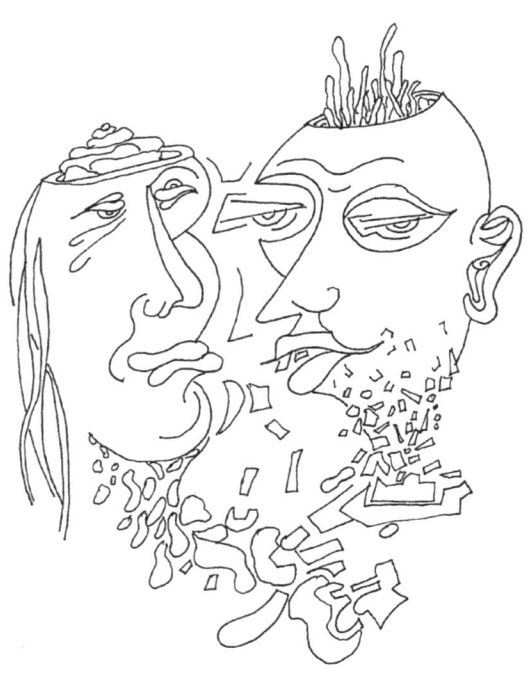

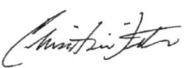

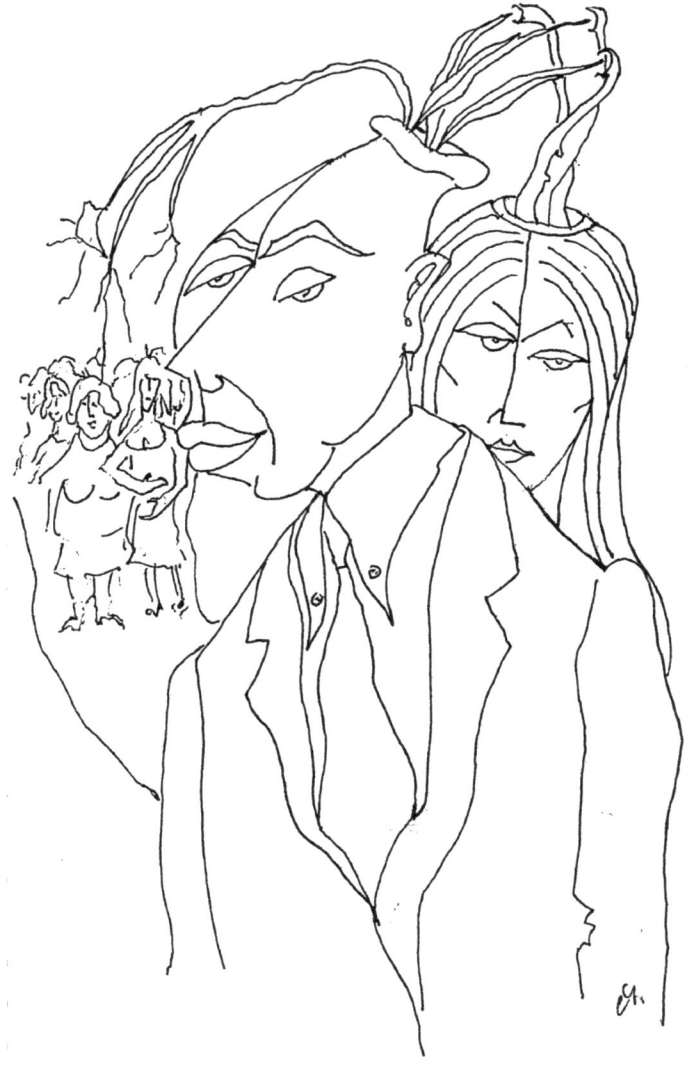

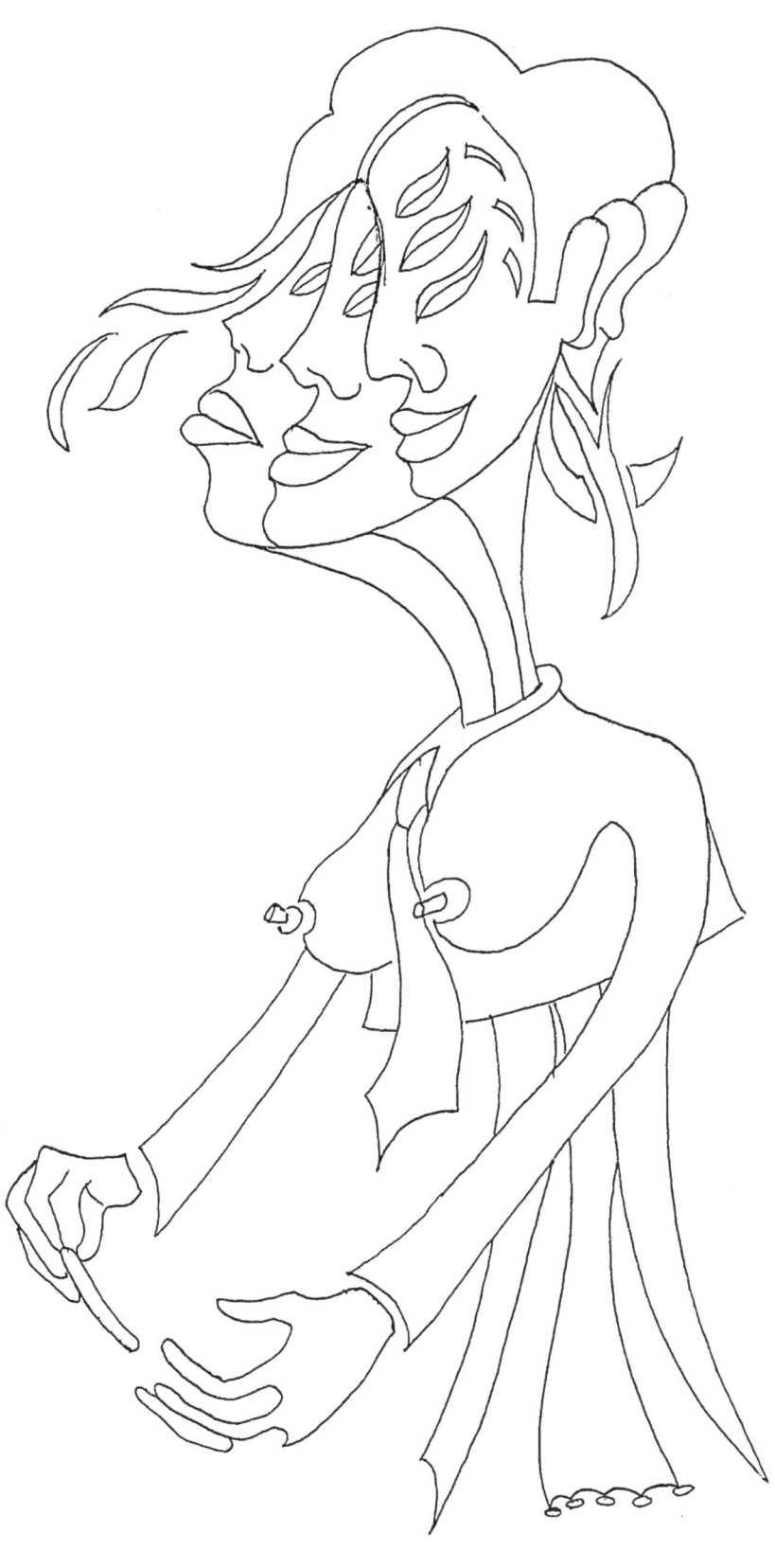

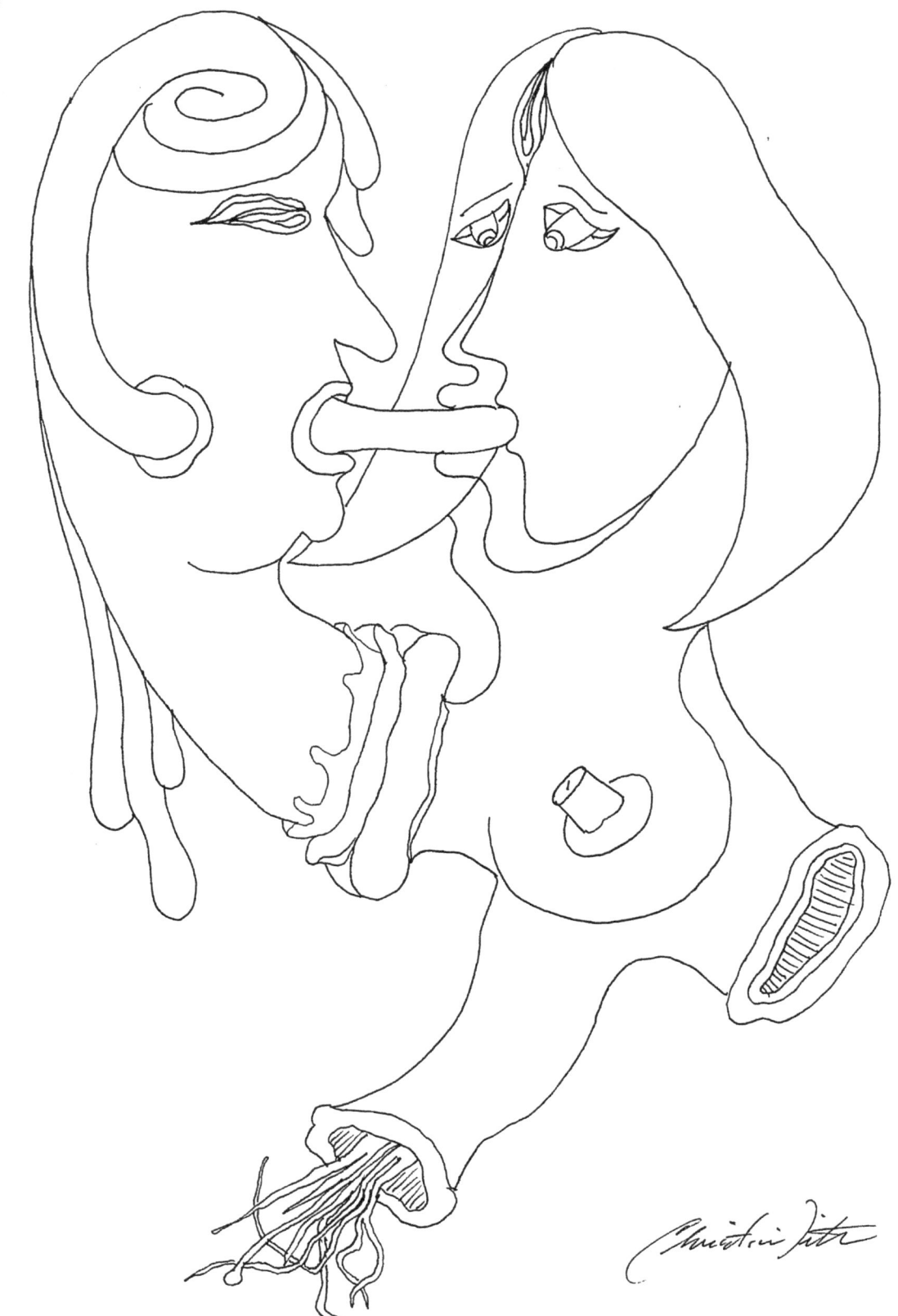

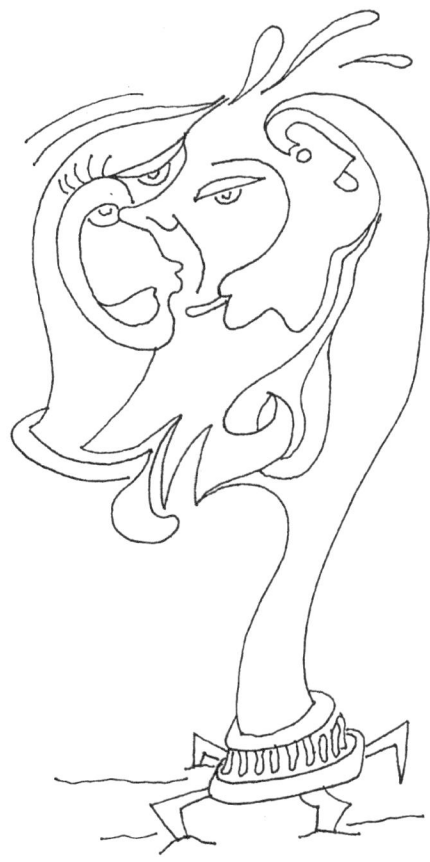

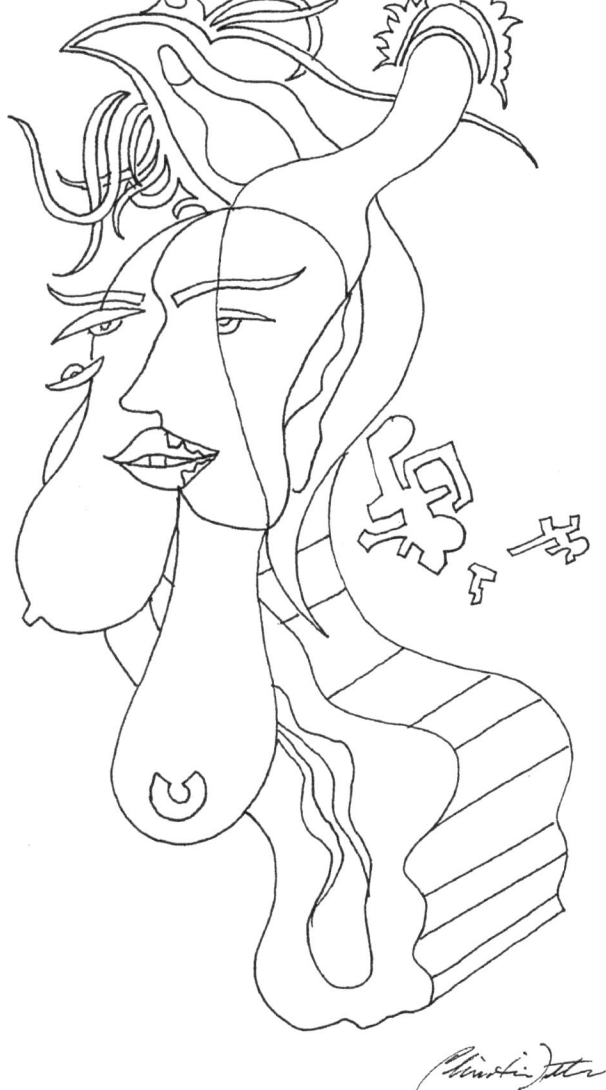

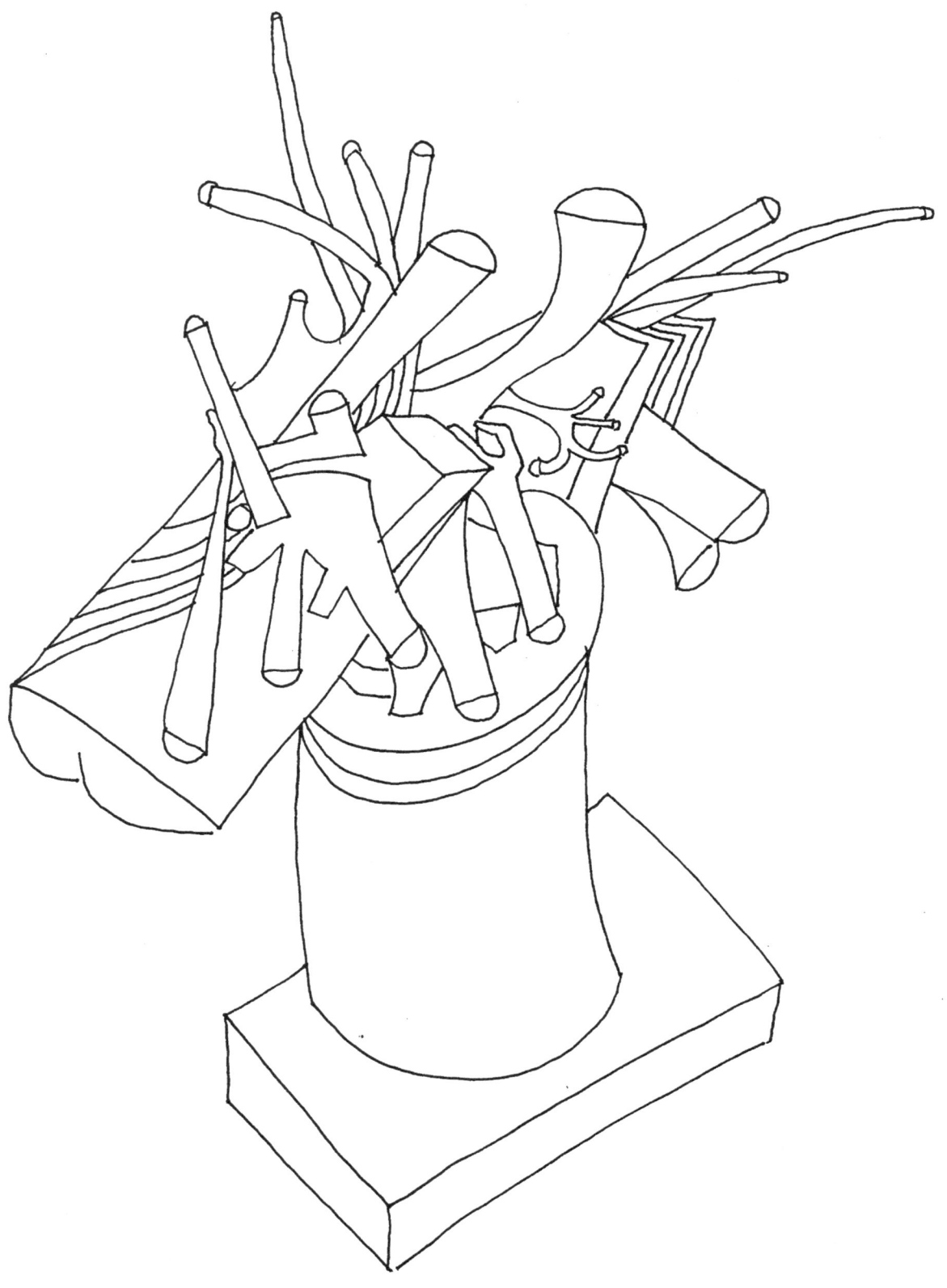

© 2012 NZ
ROUND ENDS

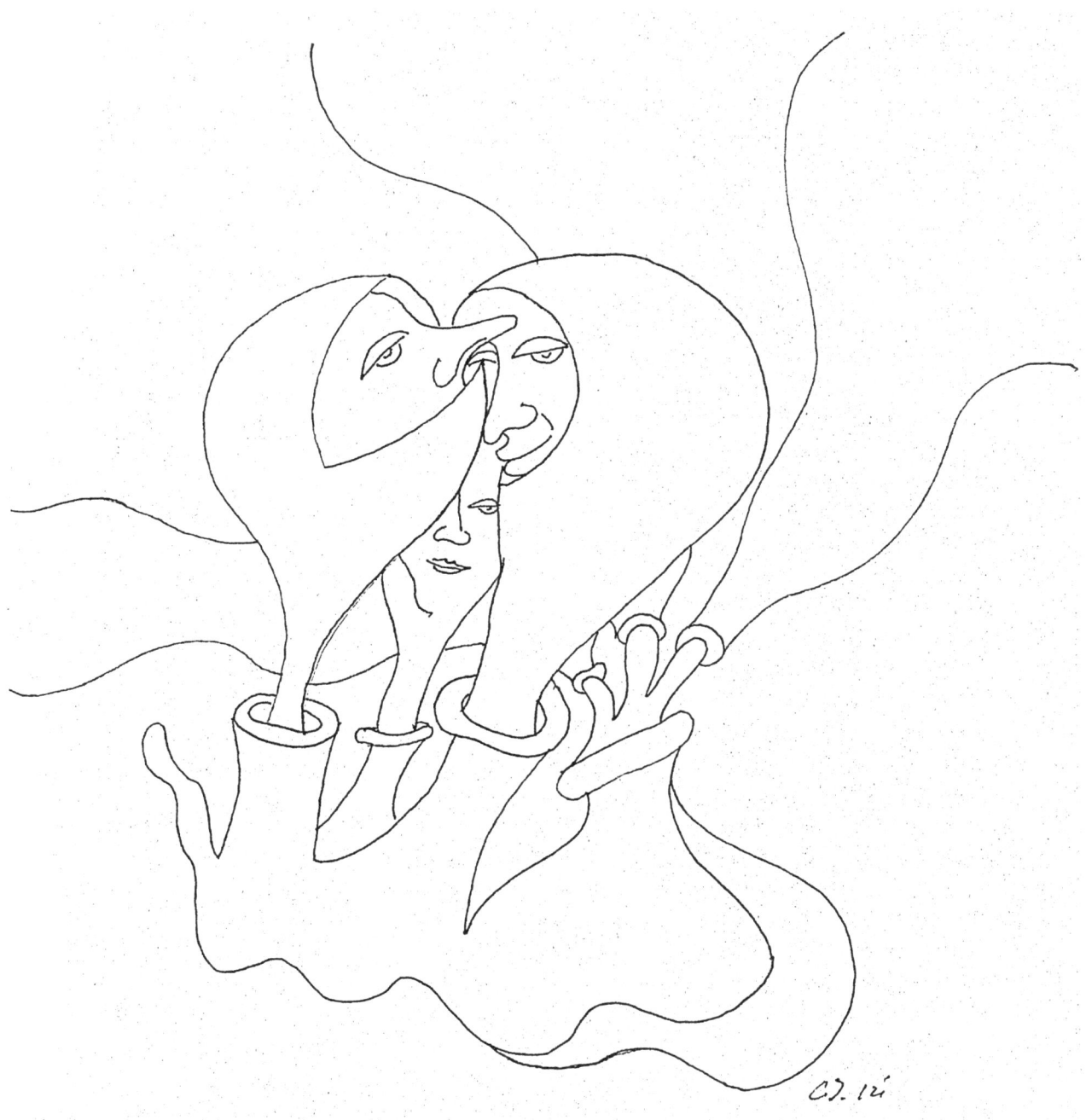

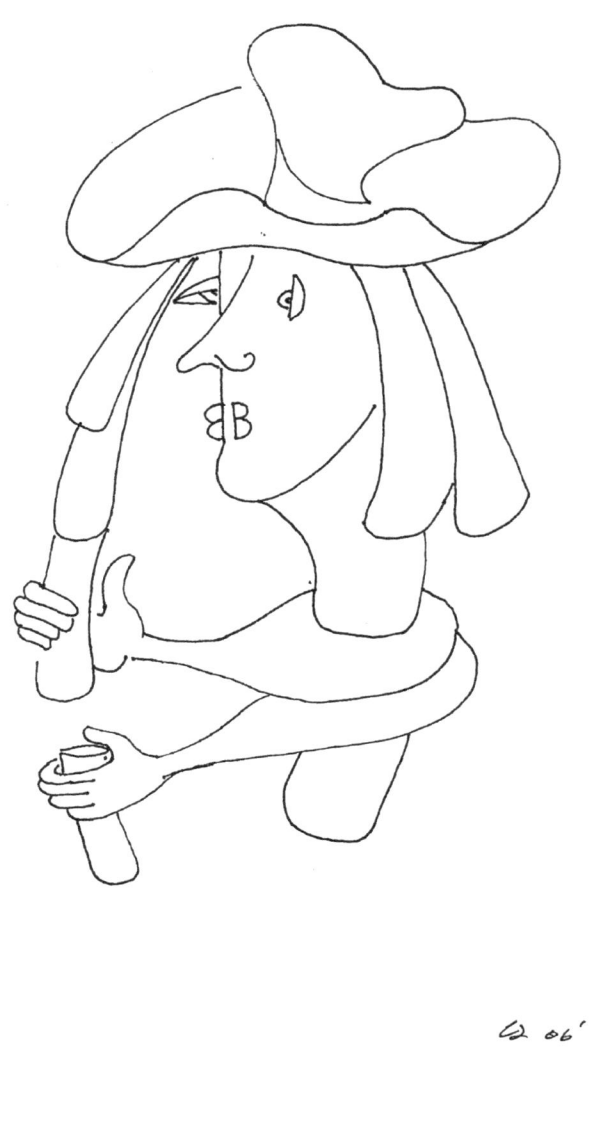

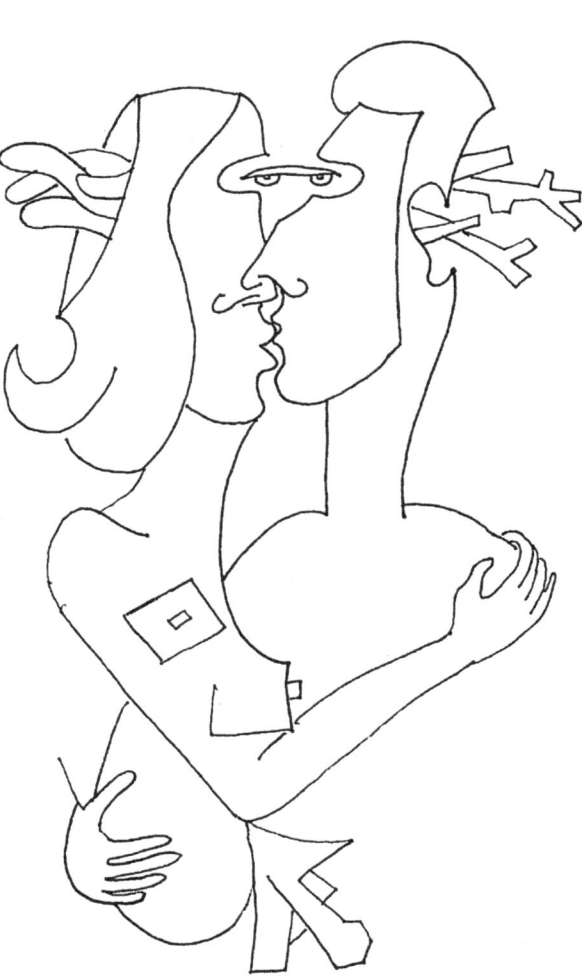

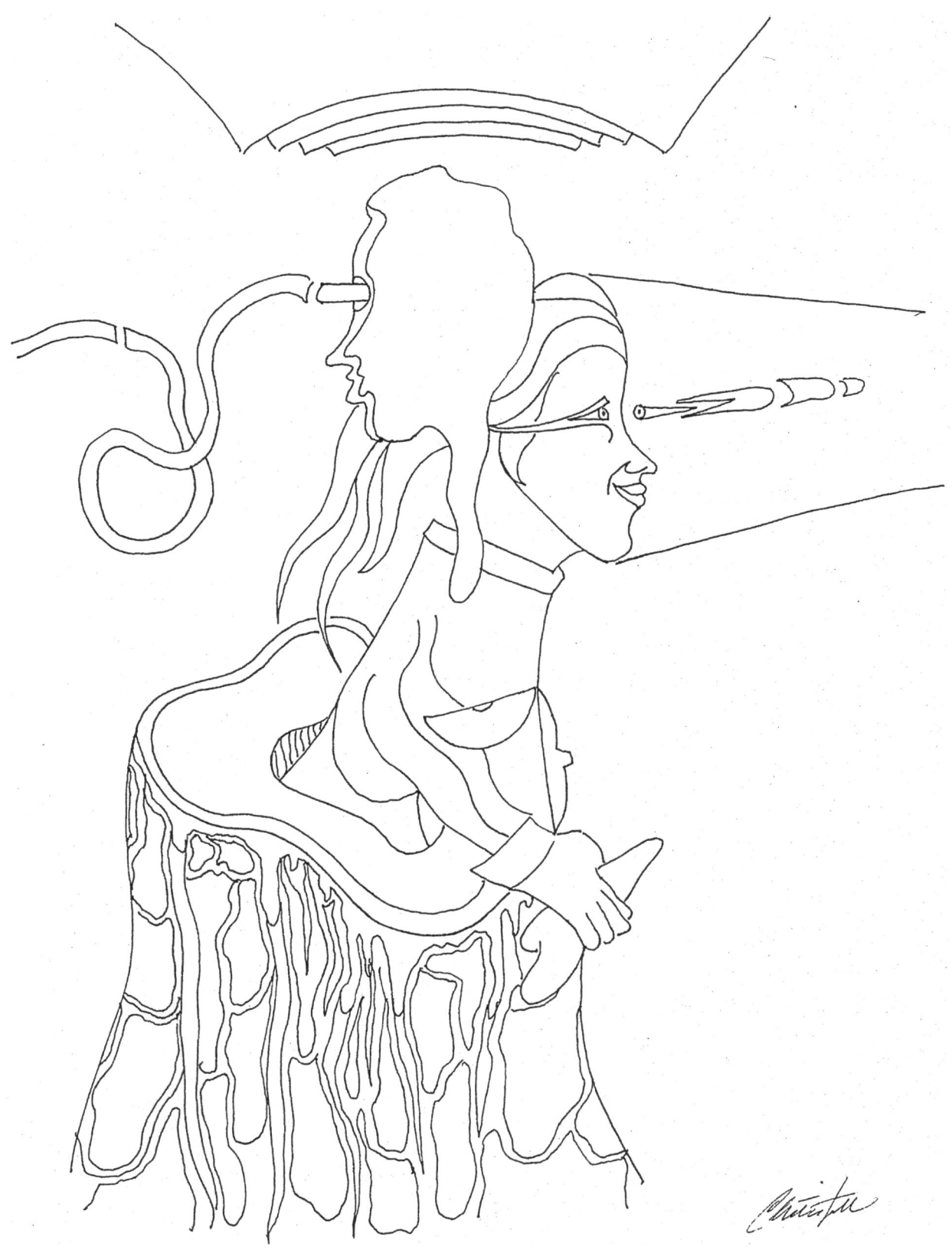

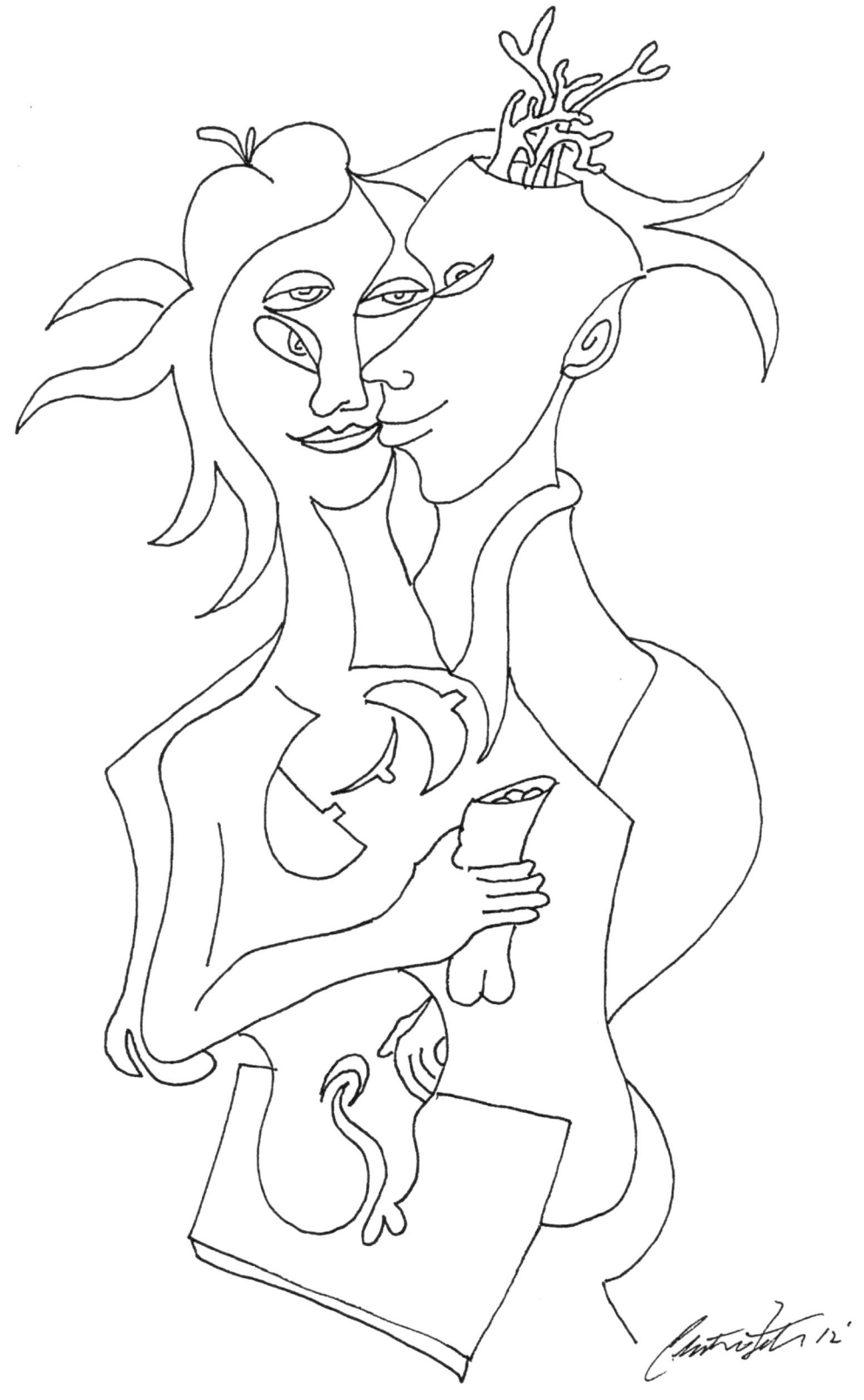

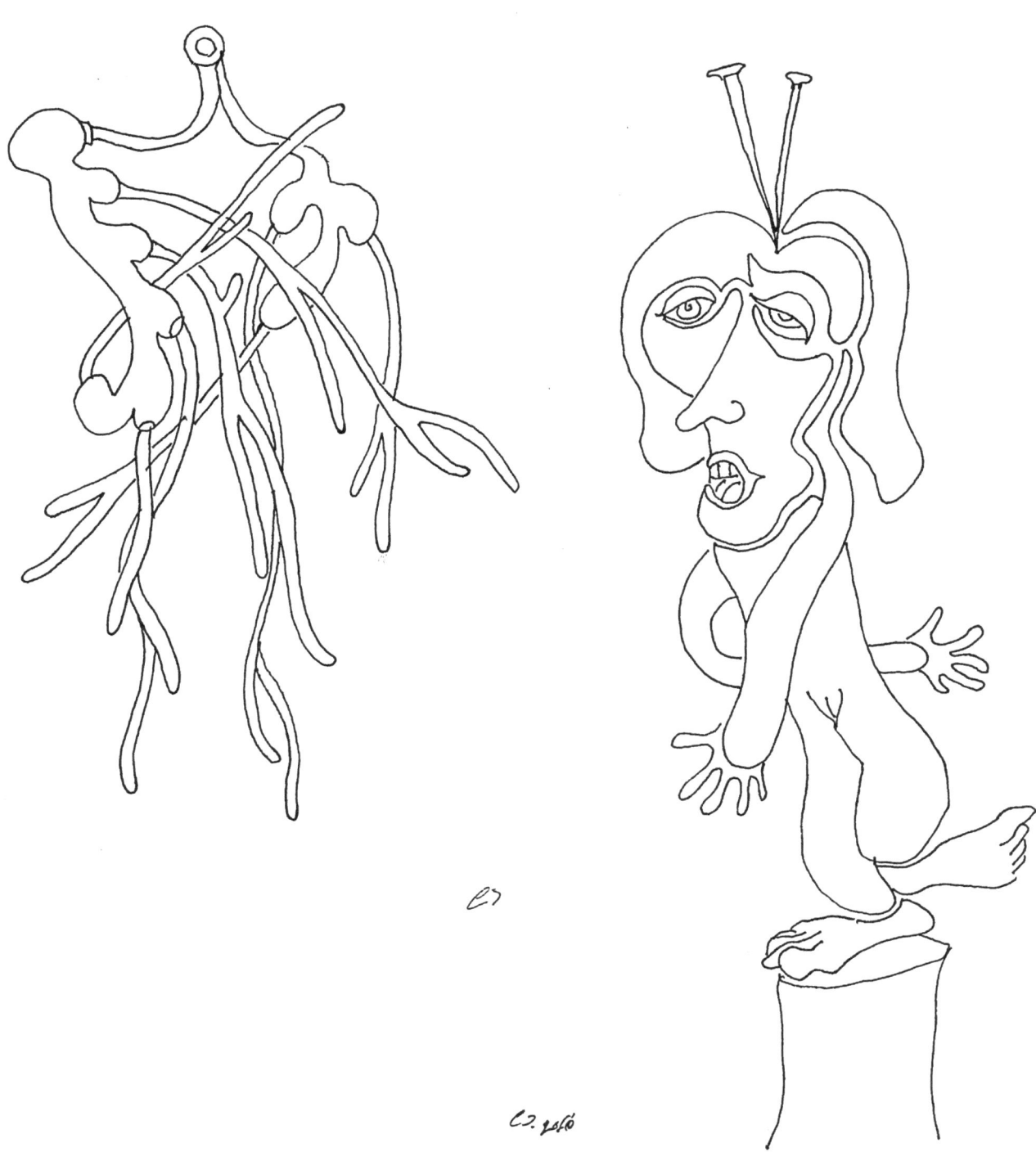

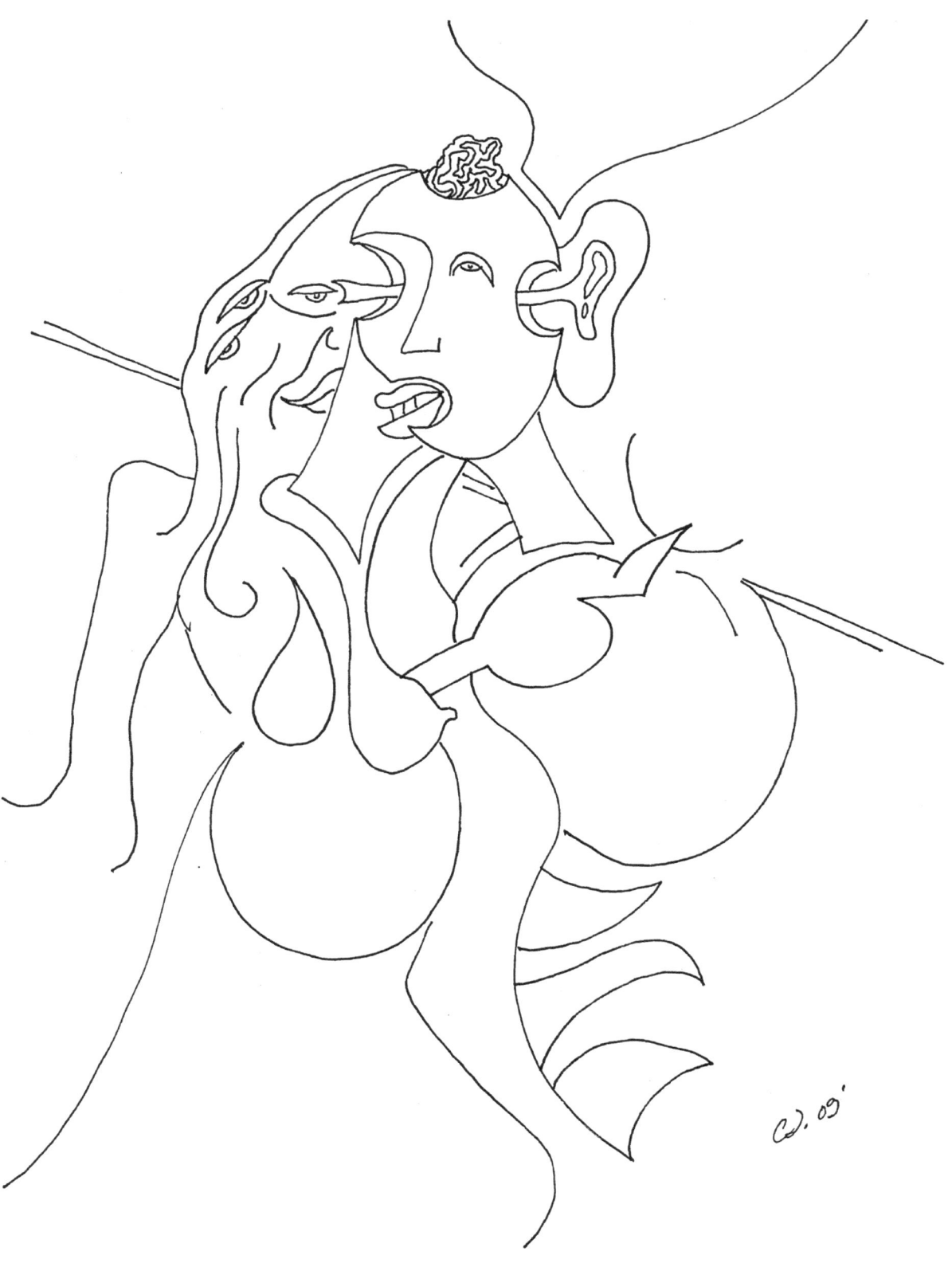

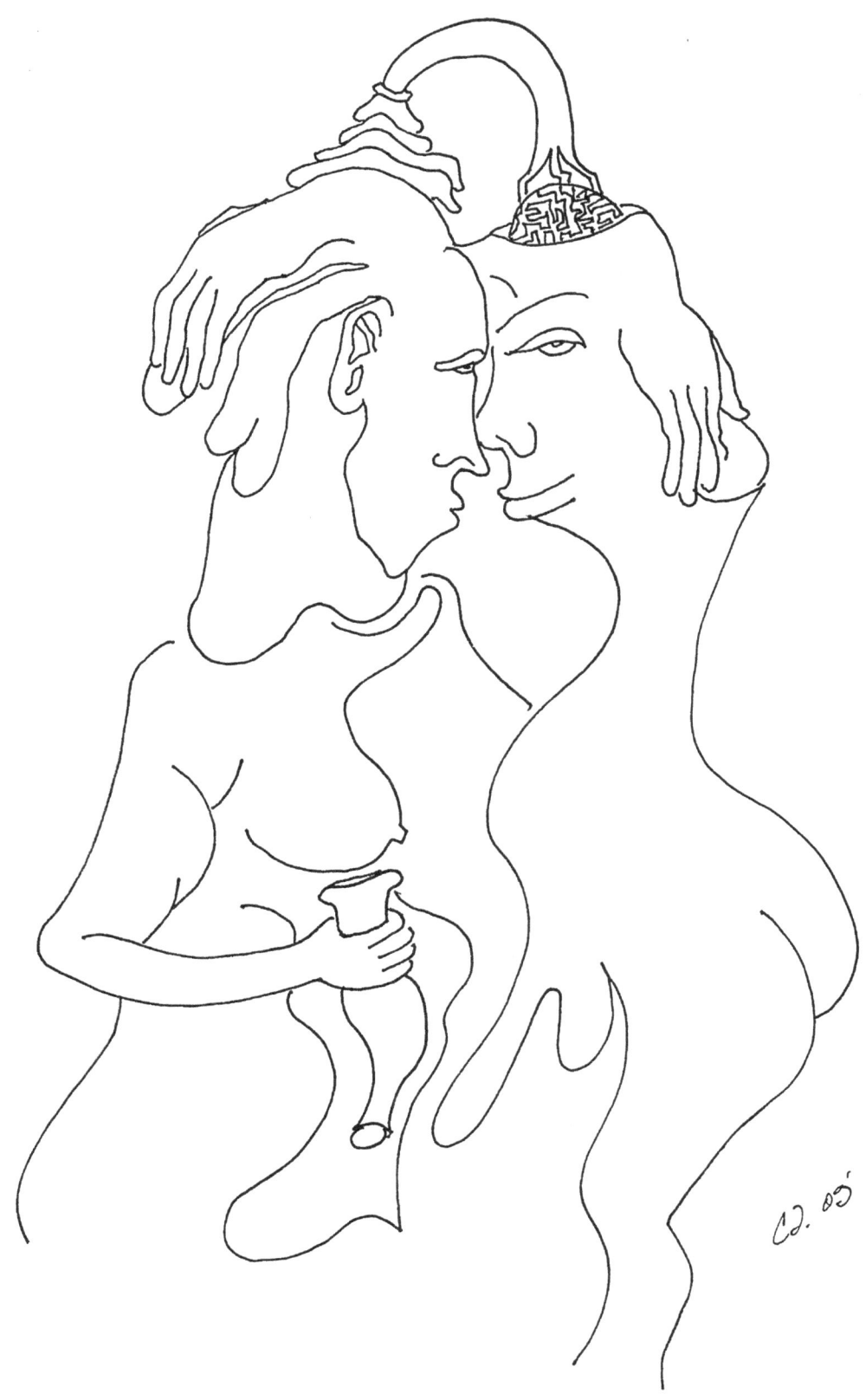

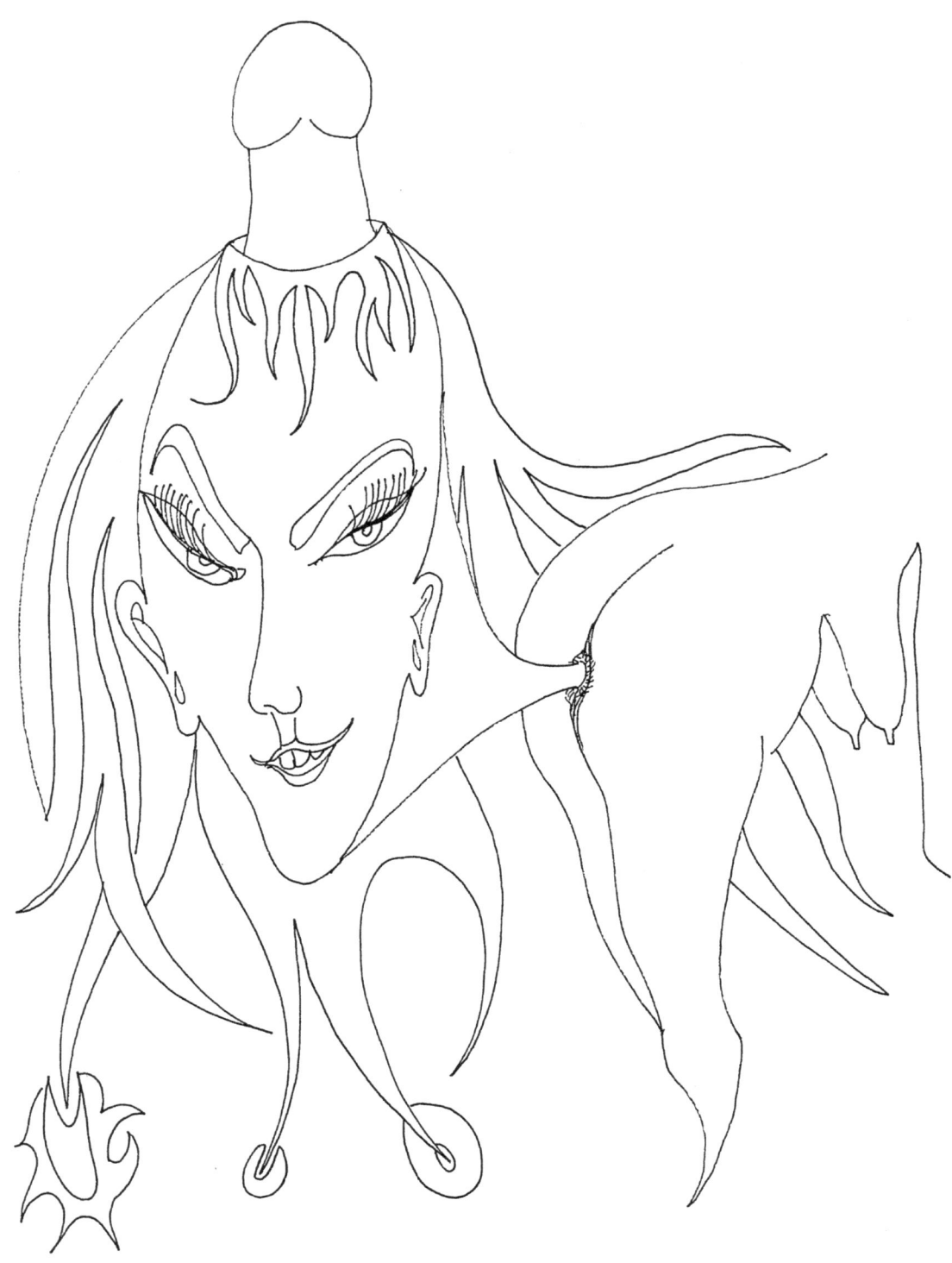

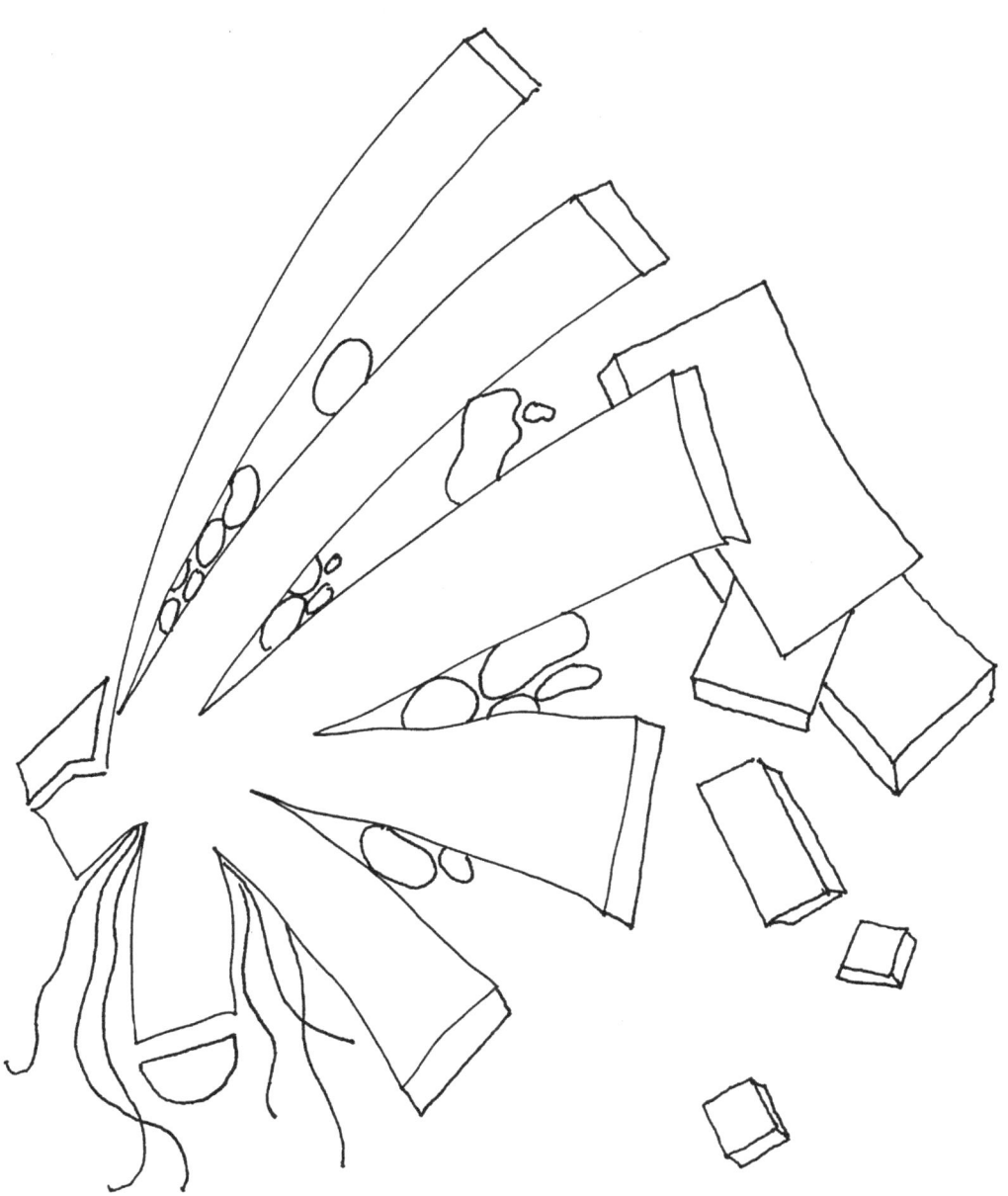

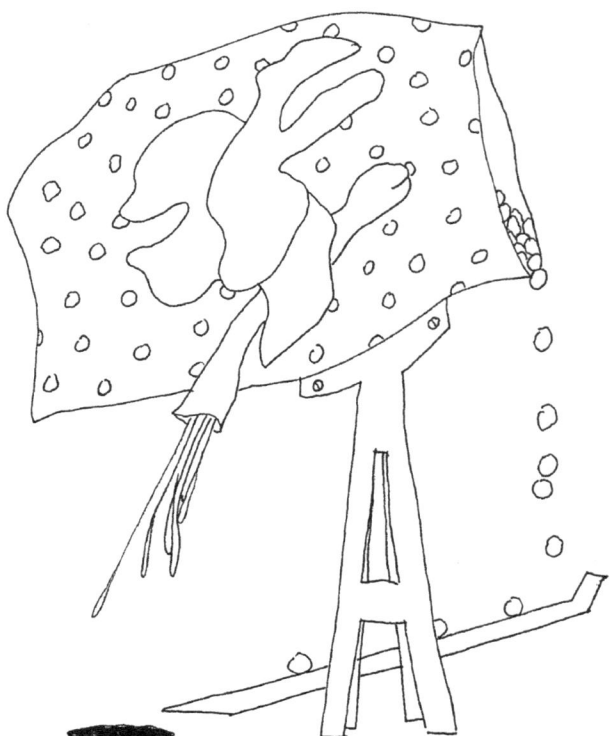

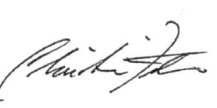

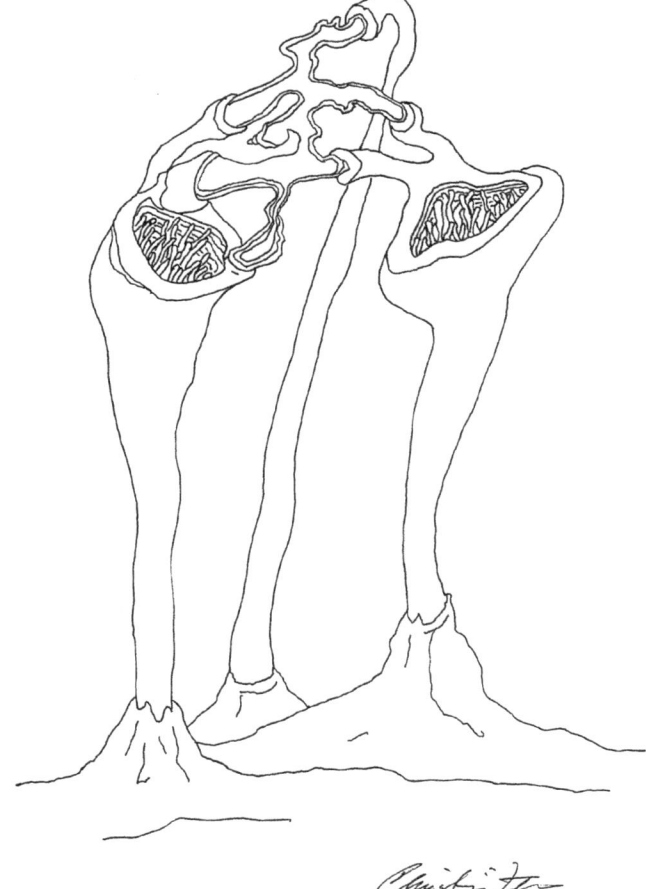

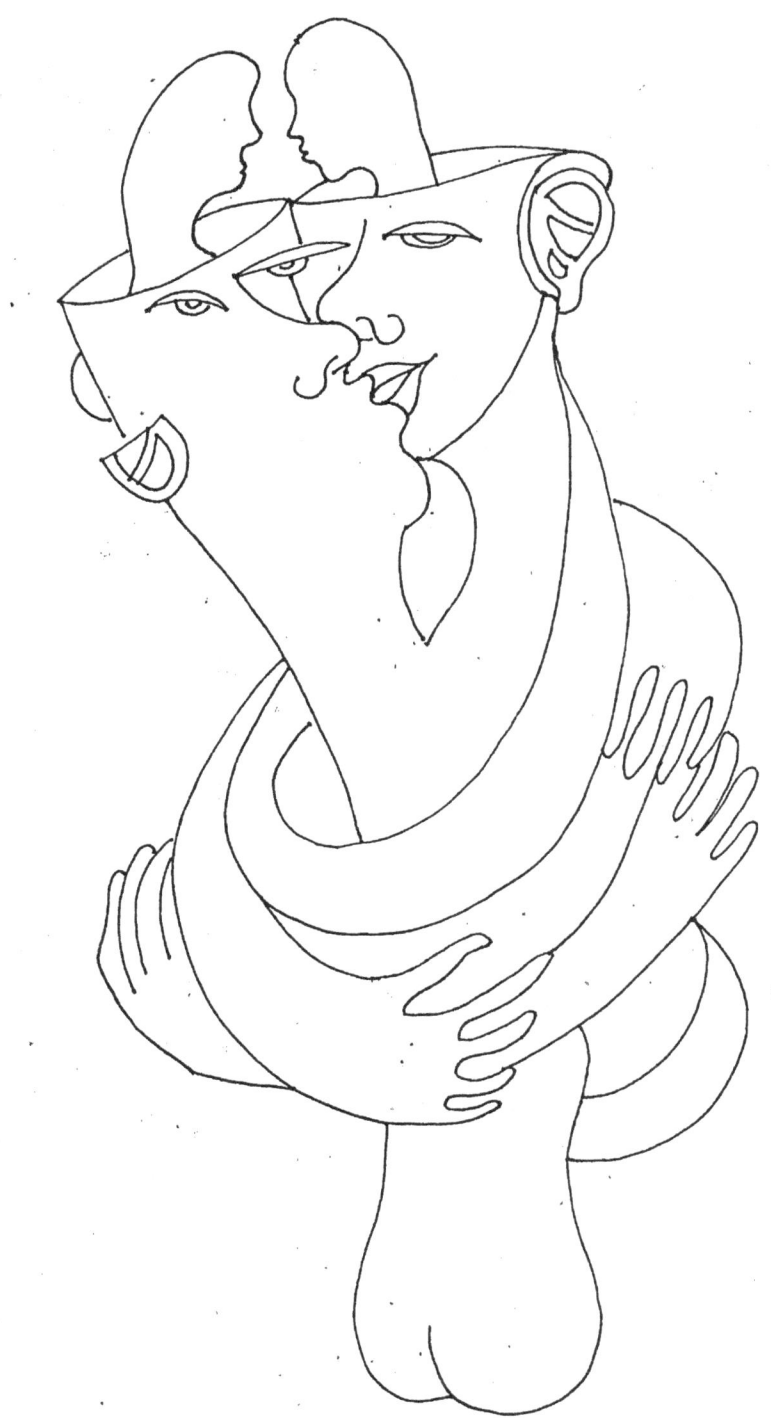

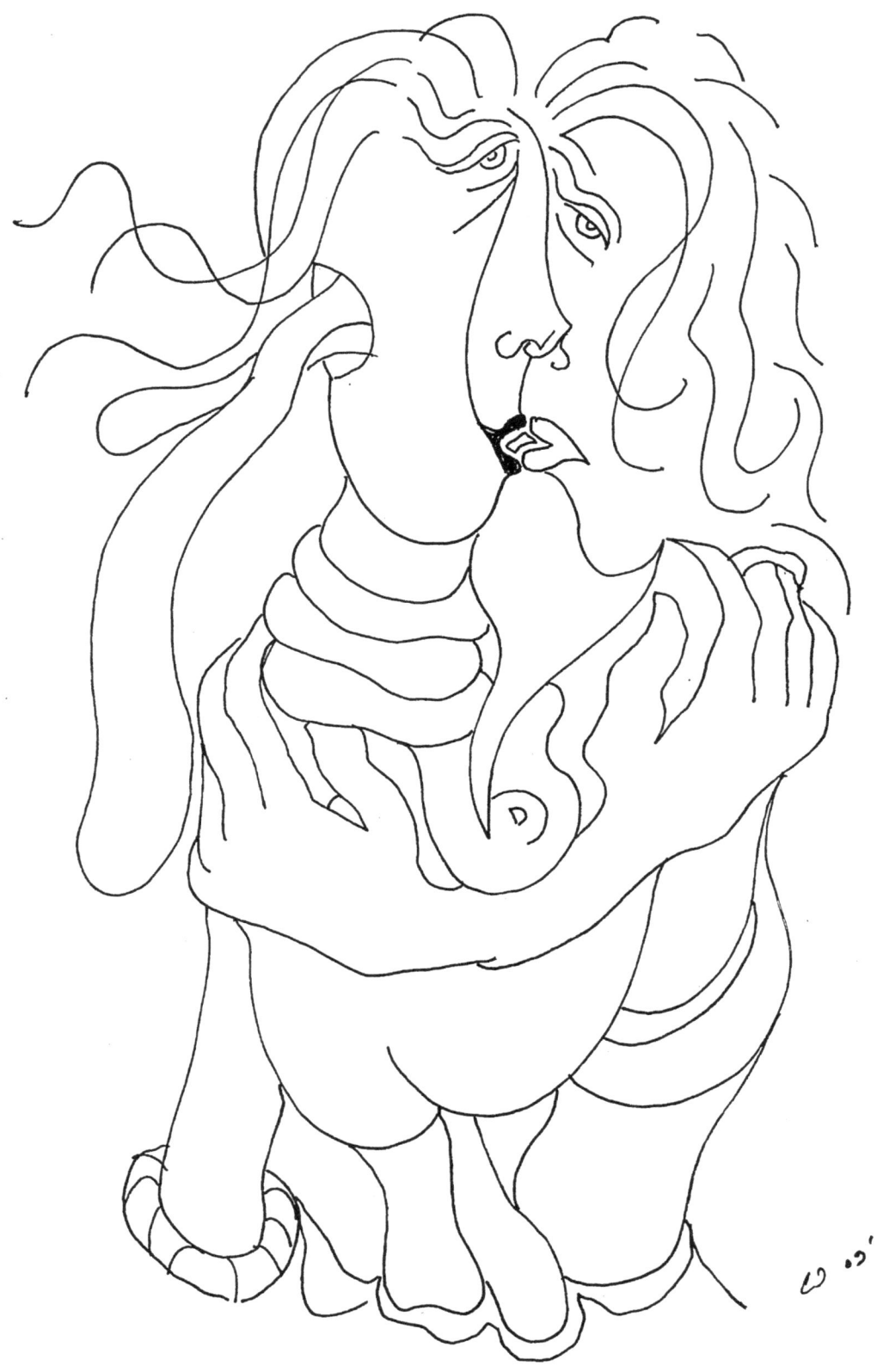

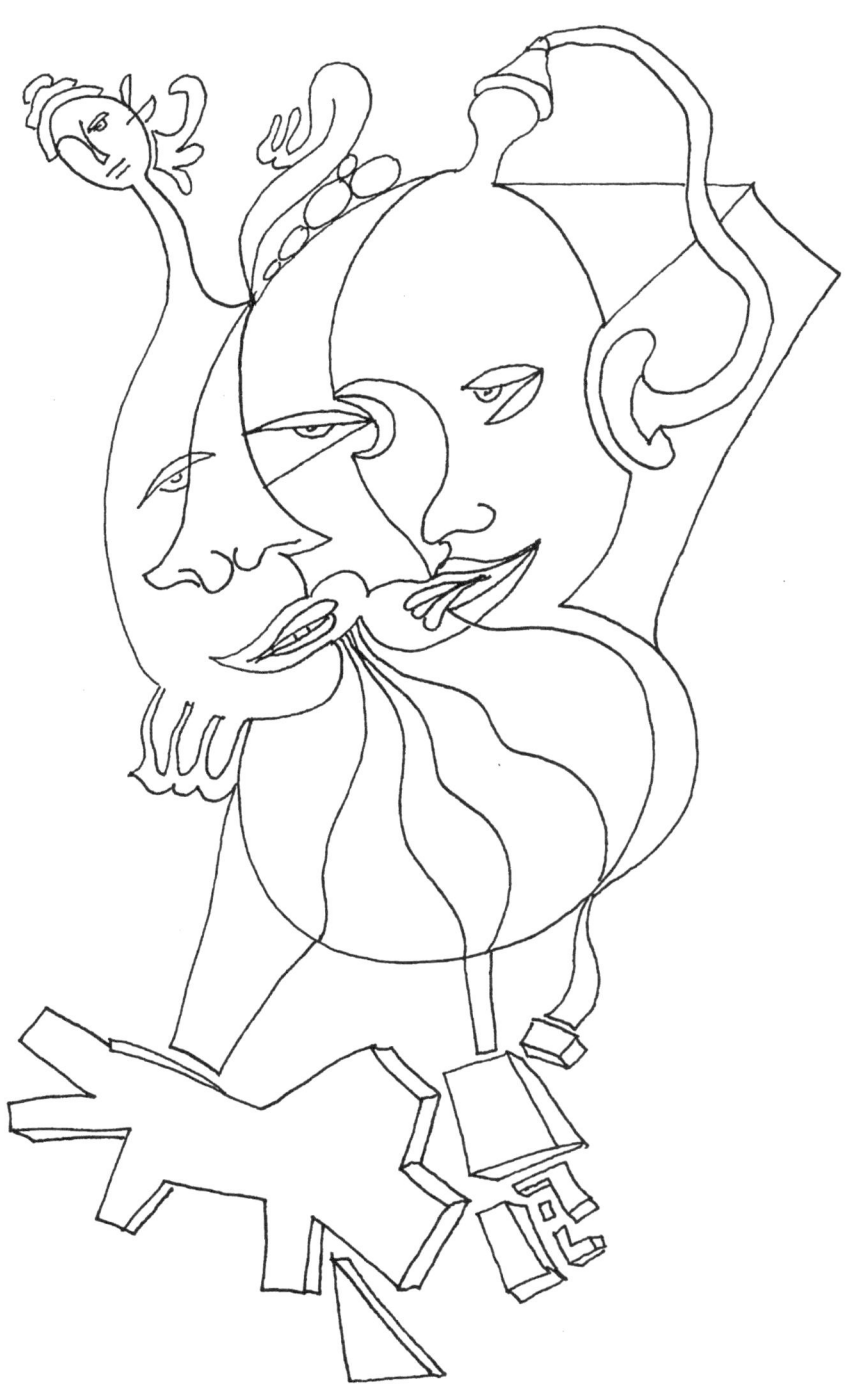

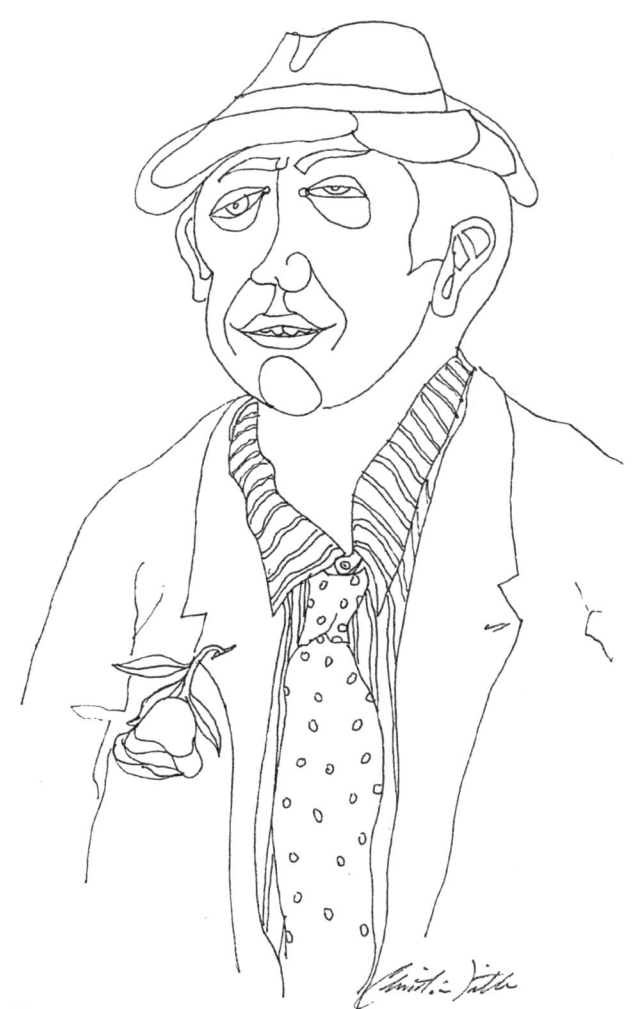

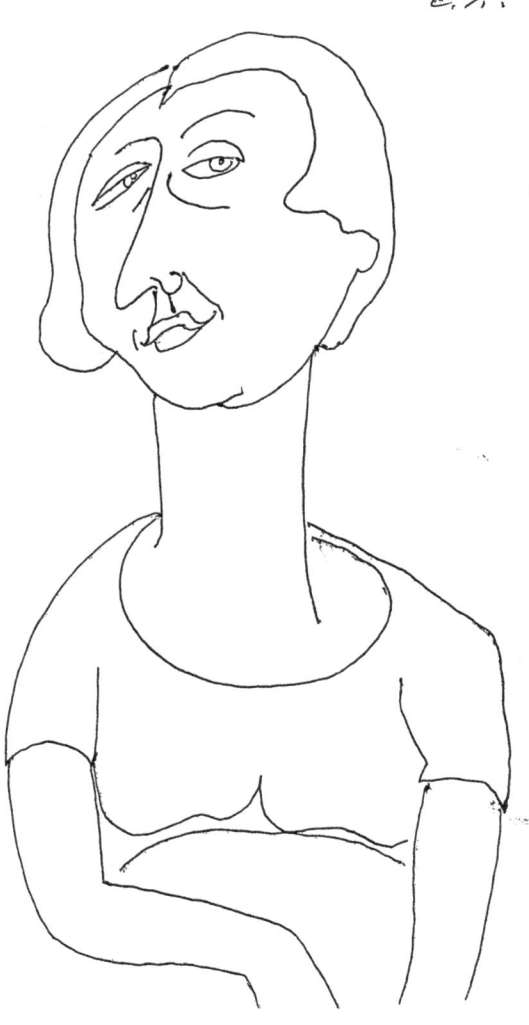

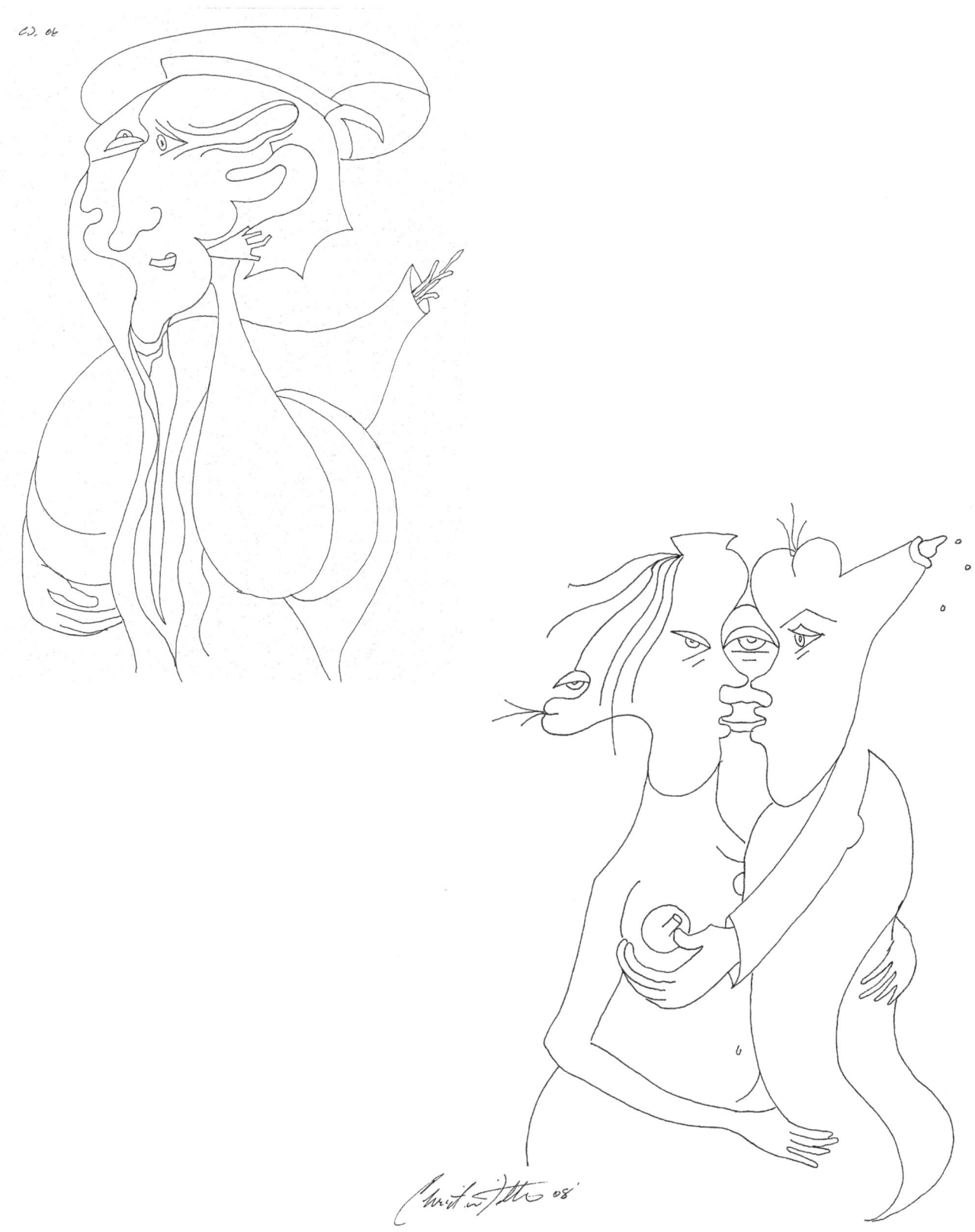

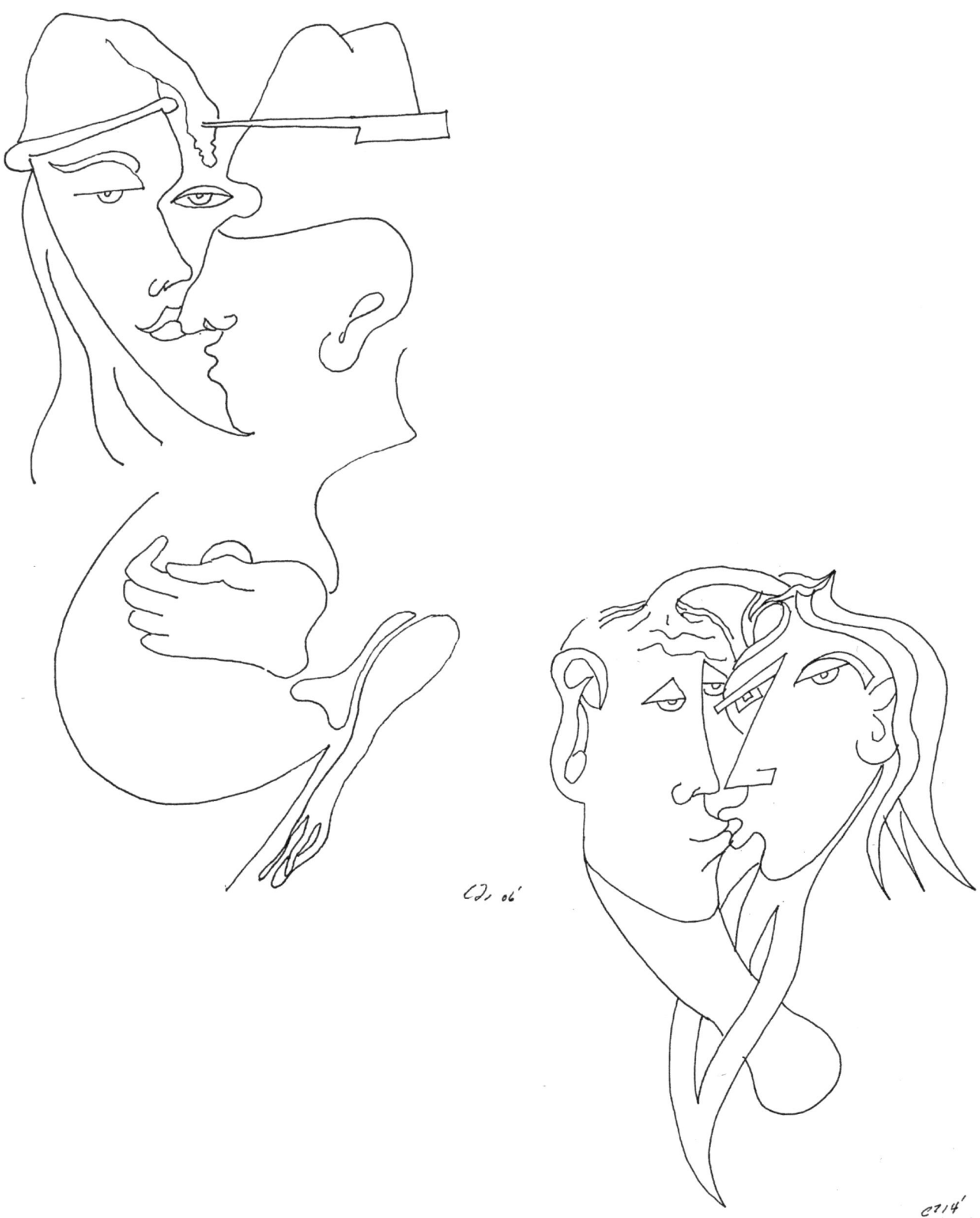

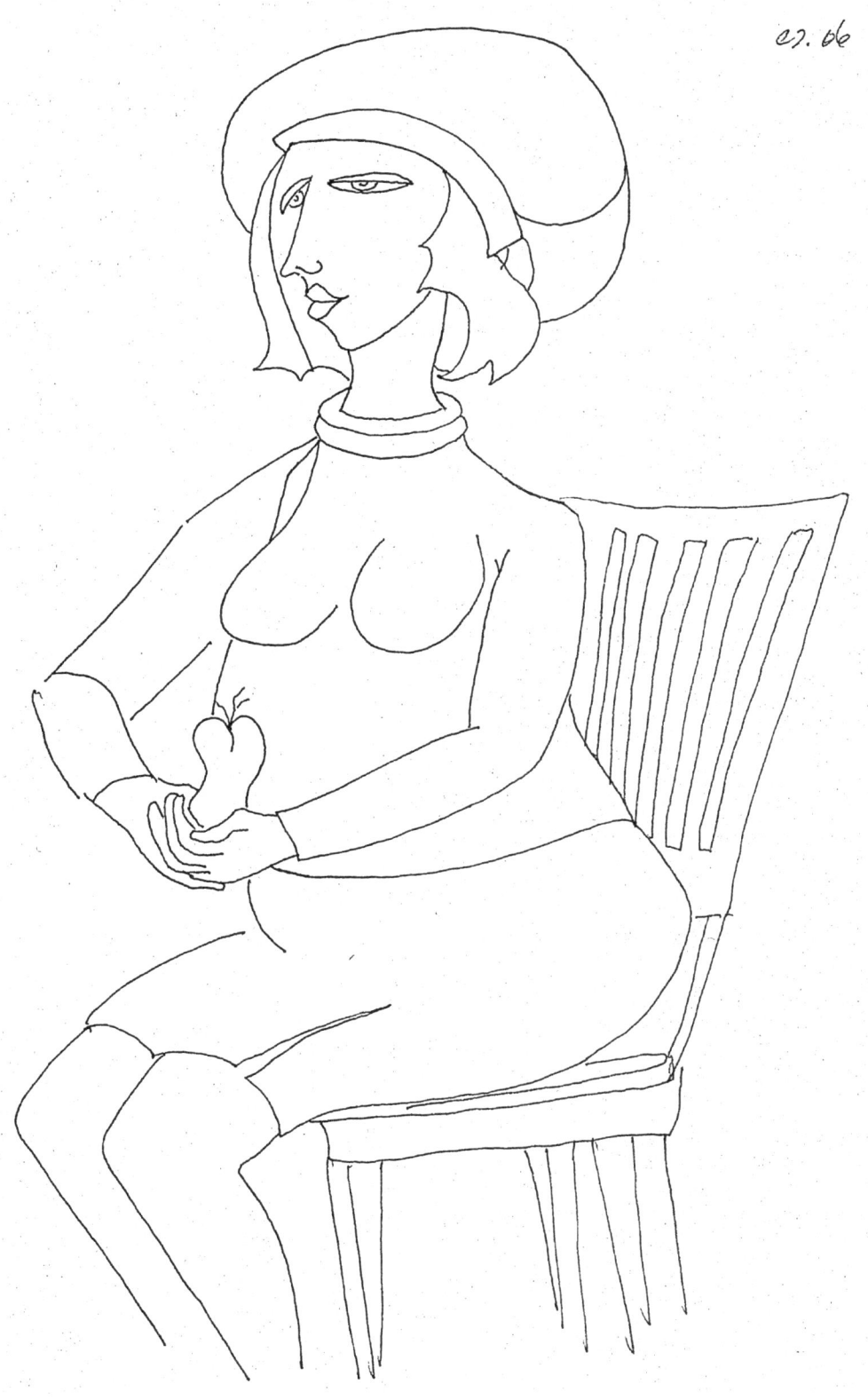

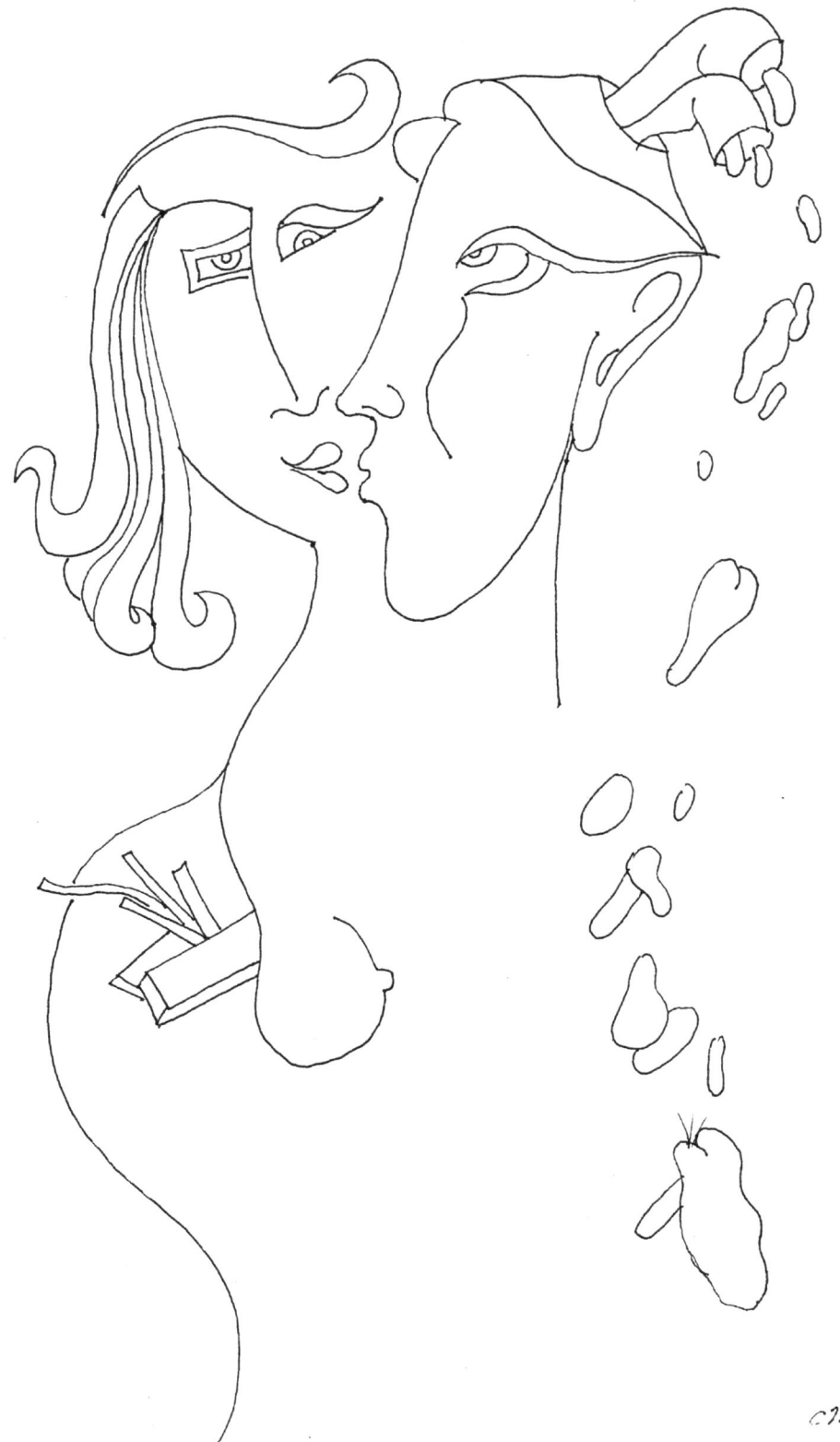

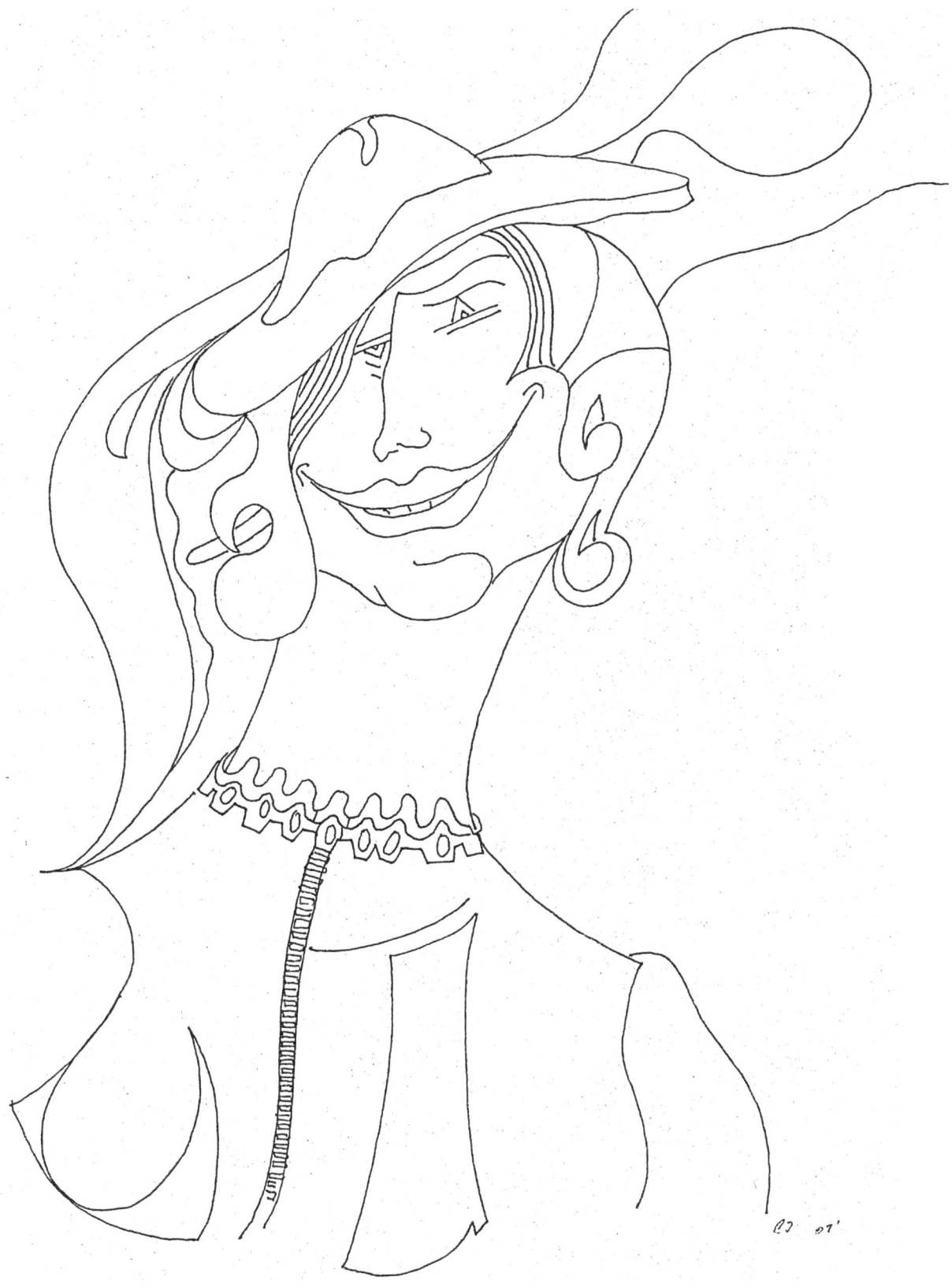

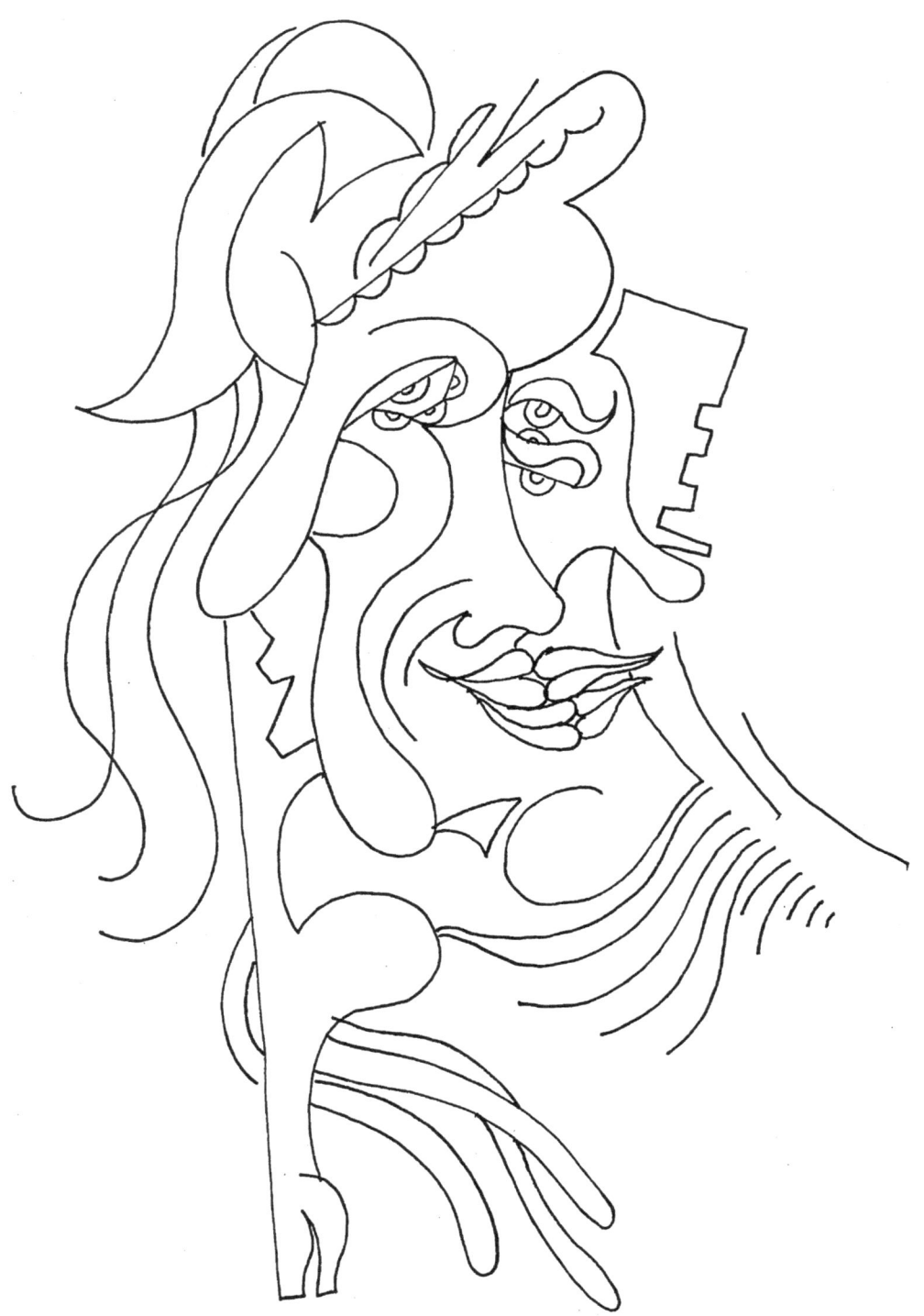

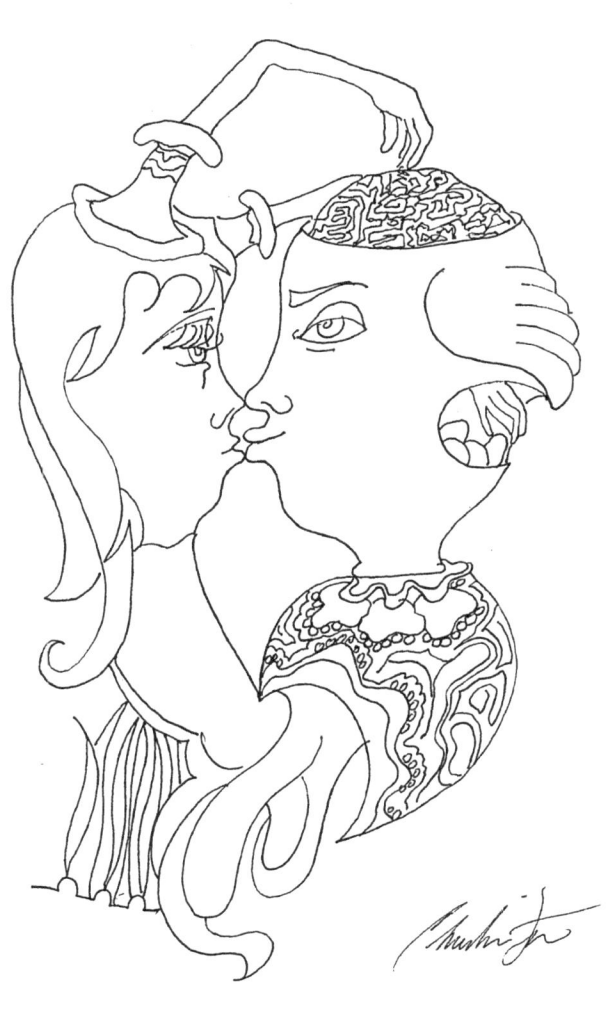

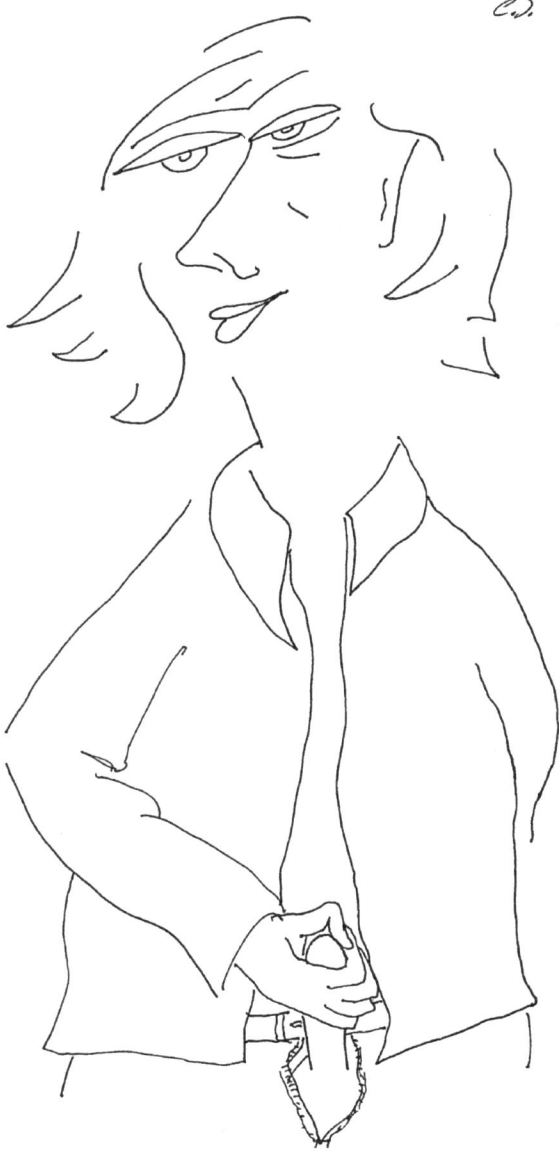

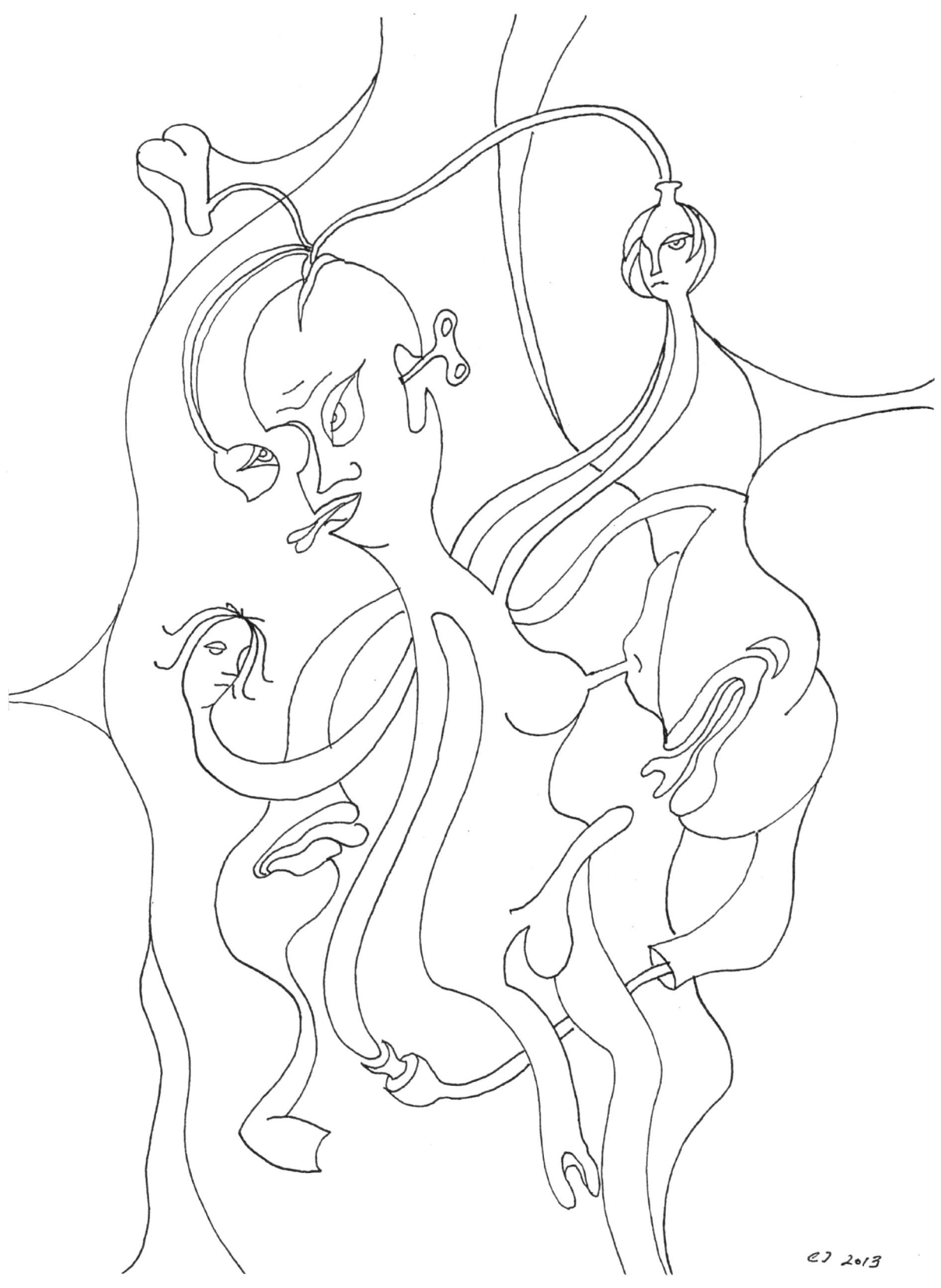

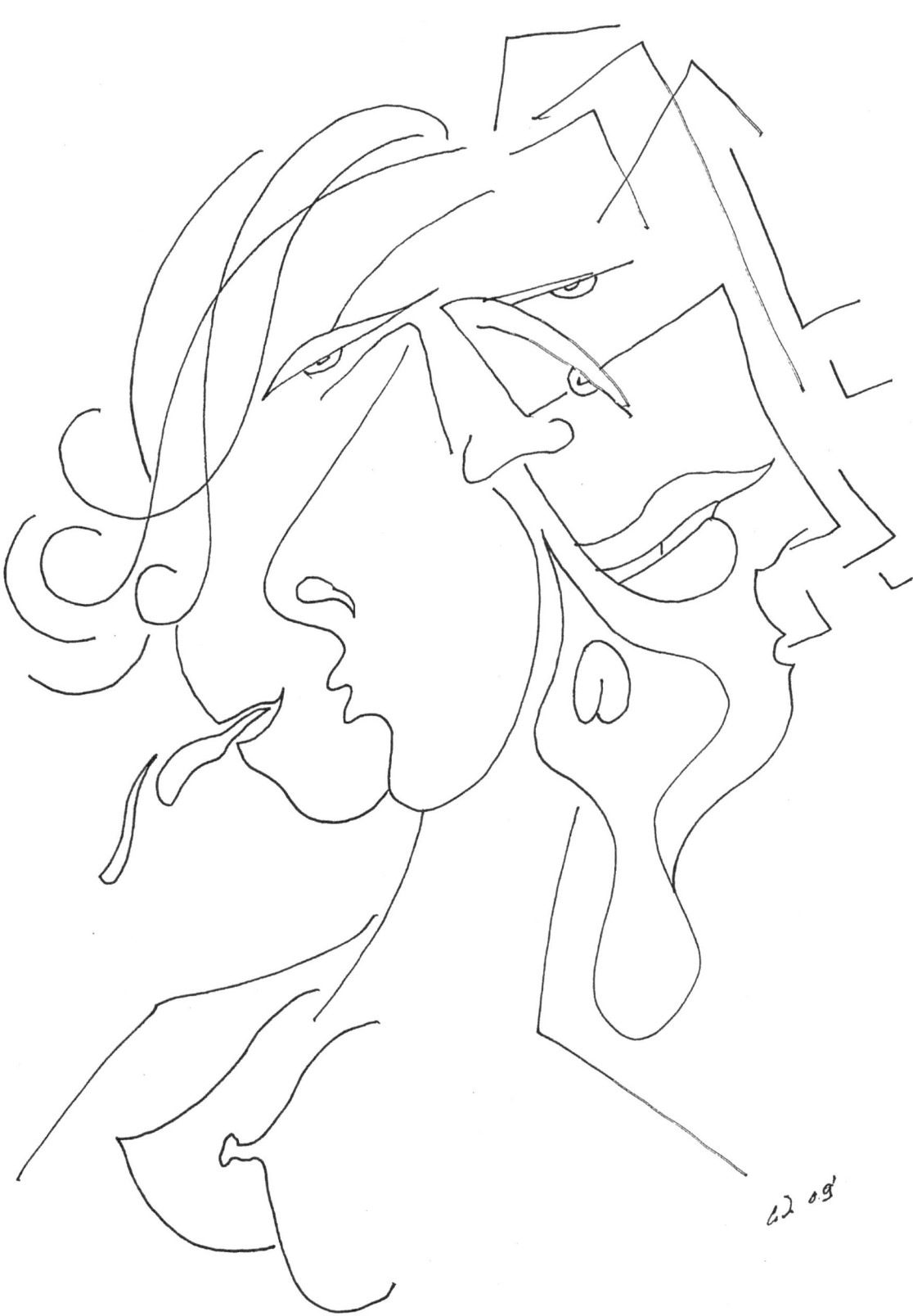

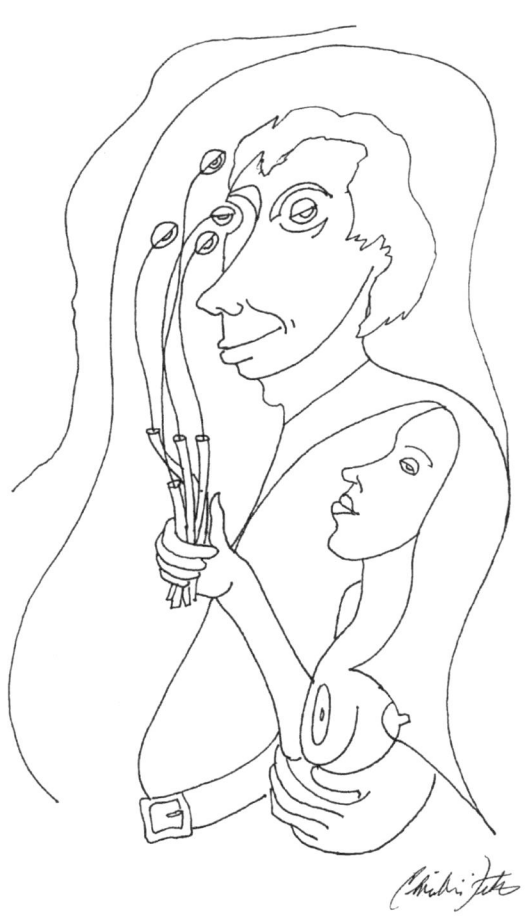

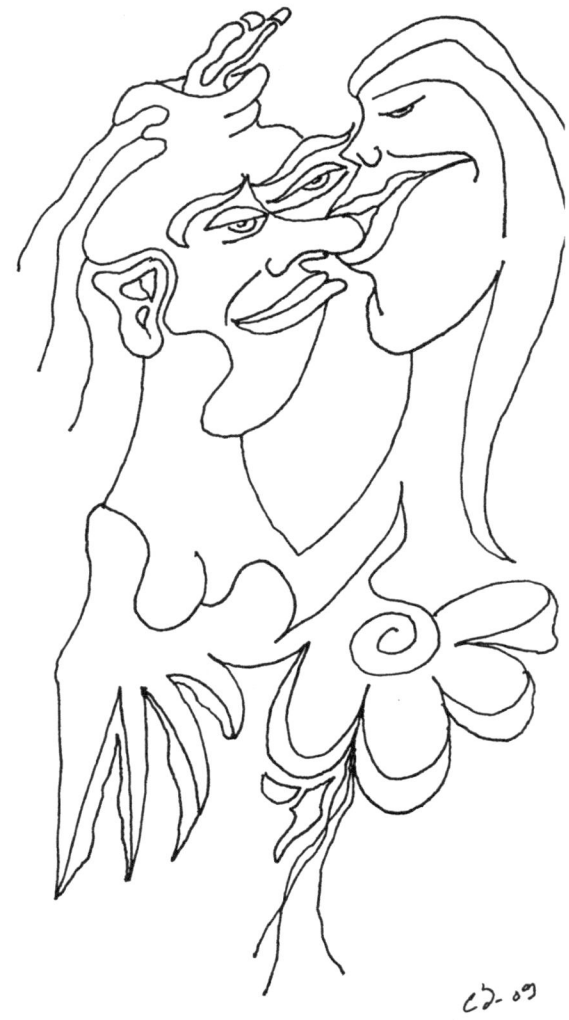

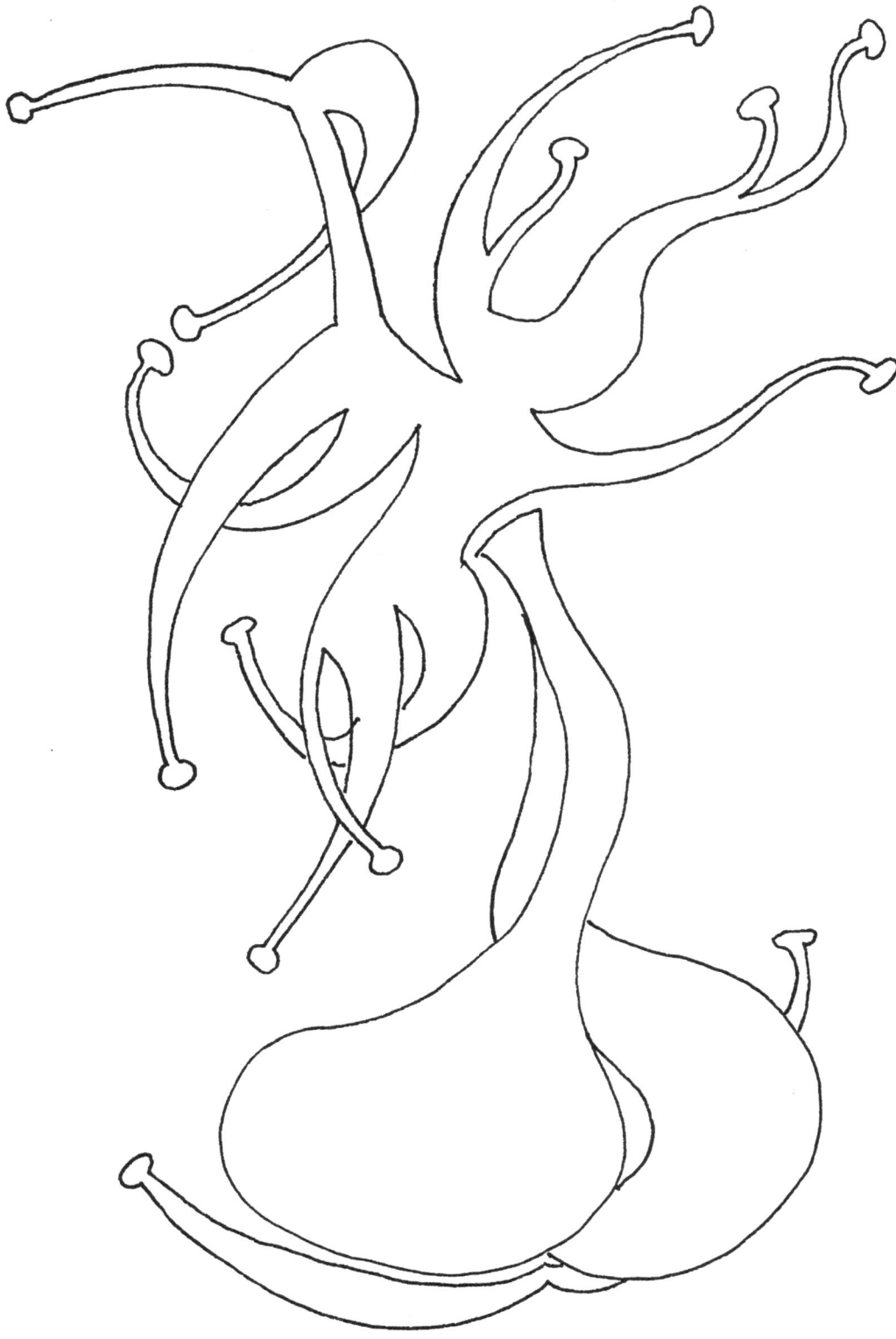

CJ 2015

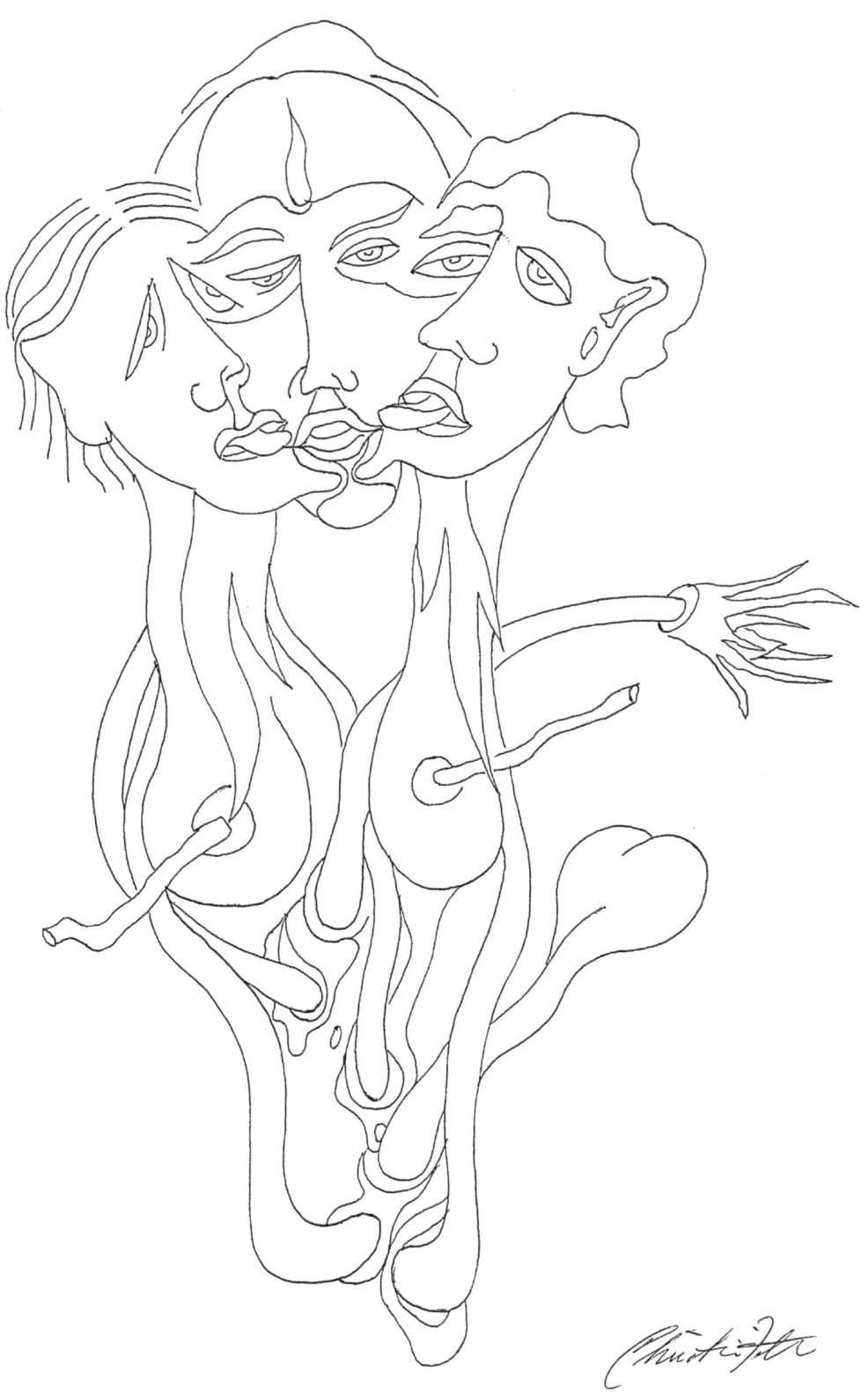

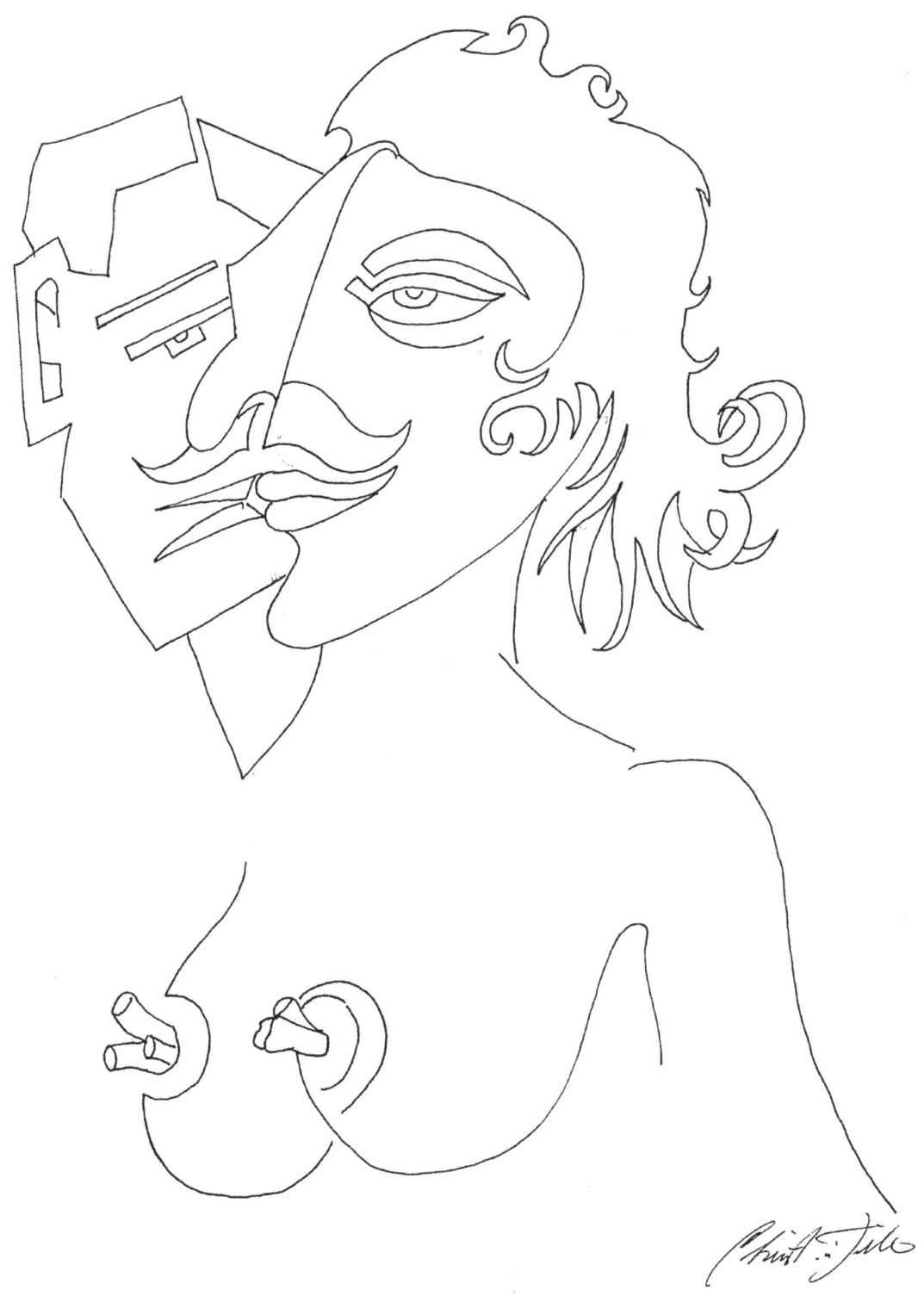

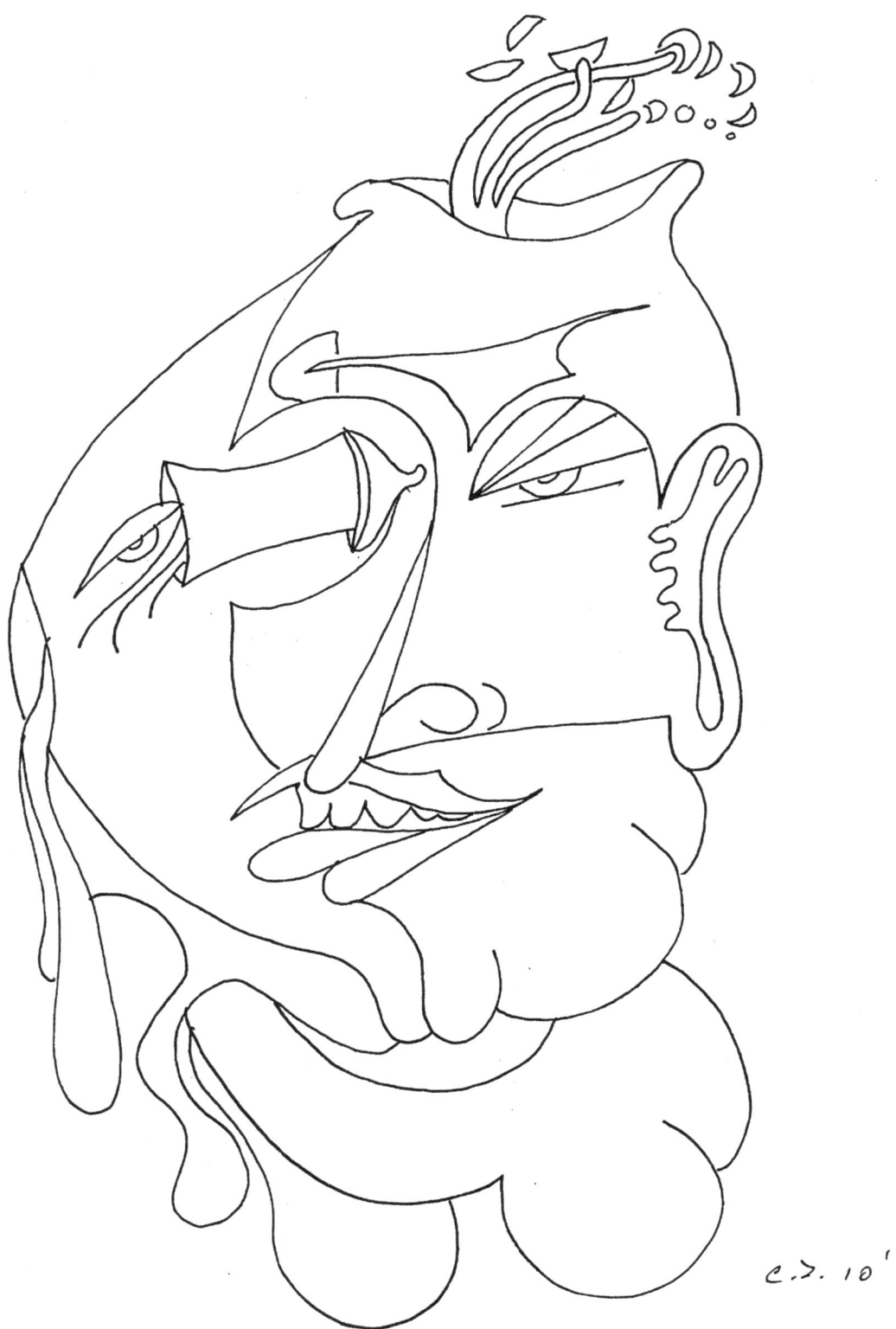

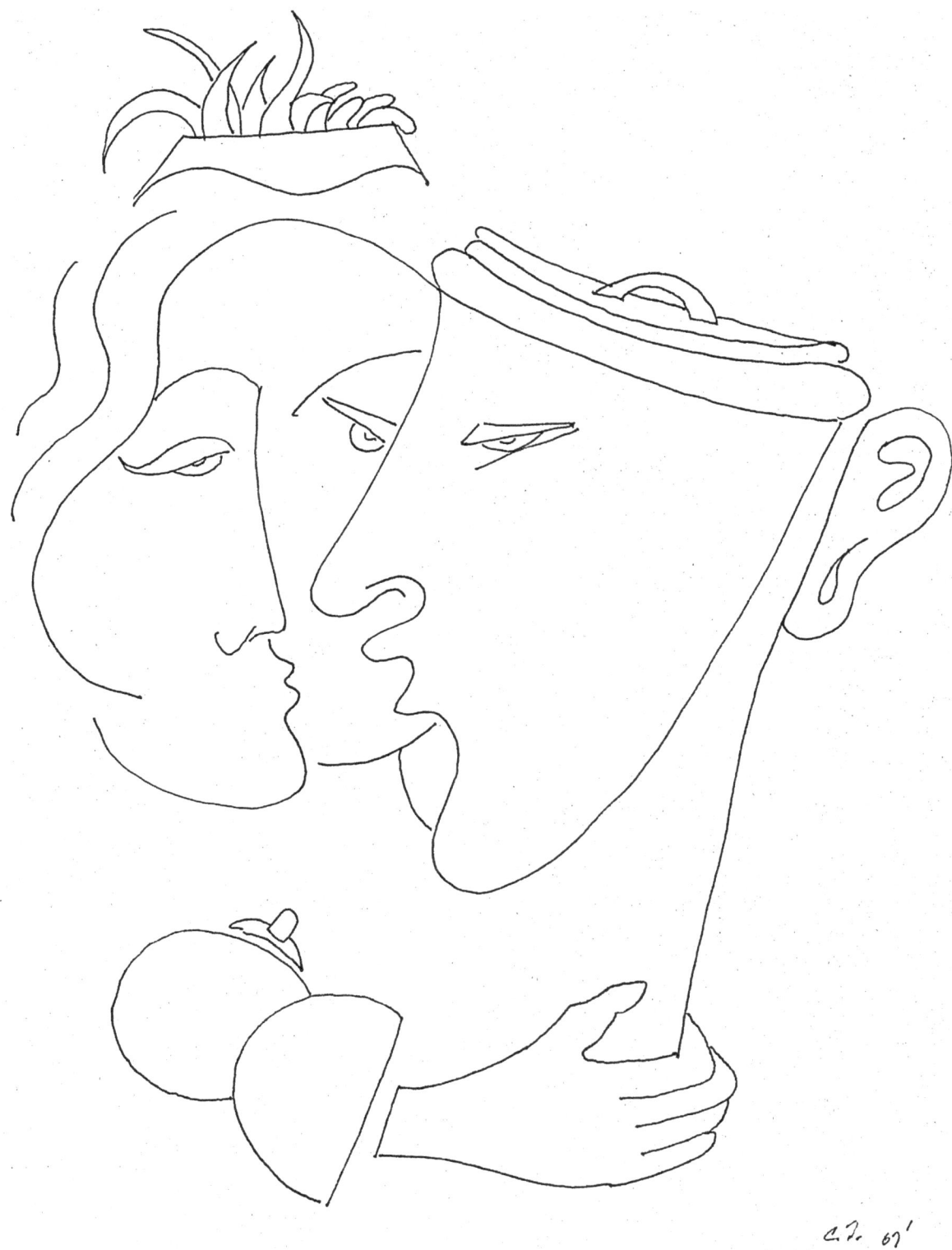

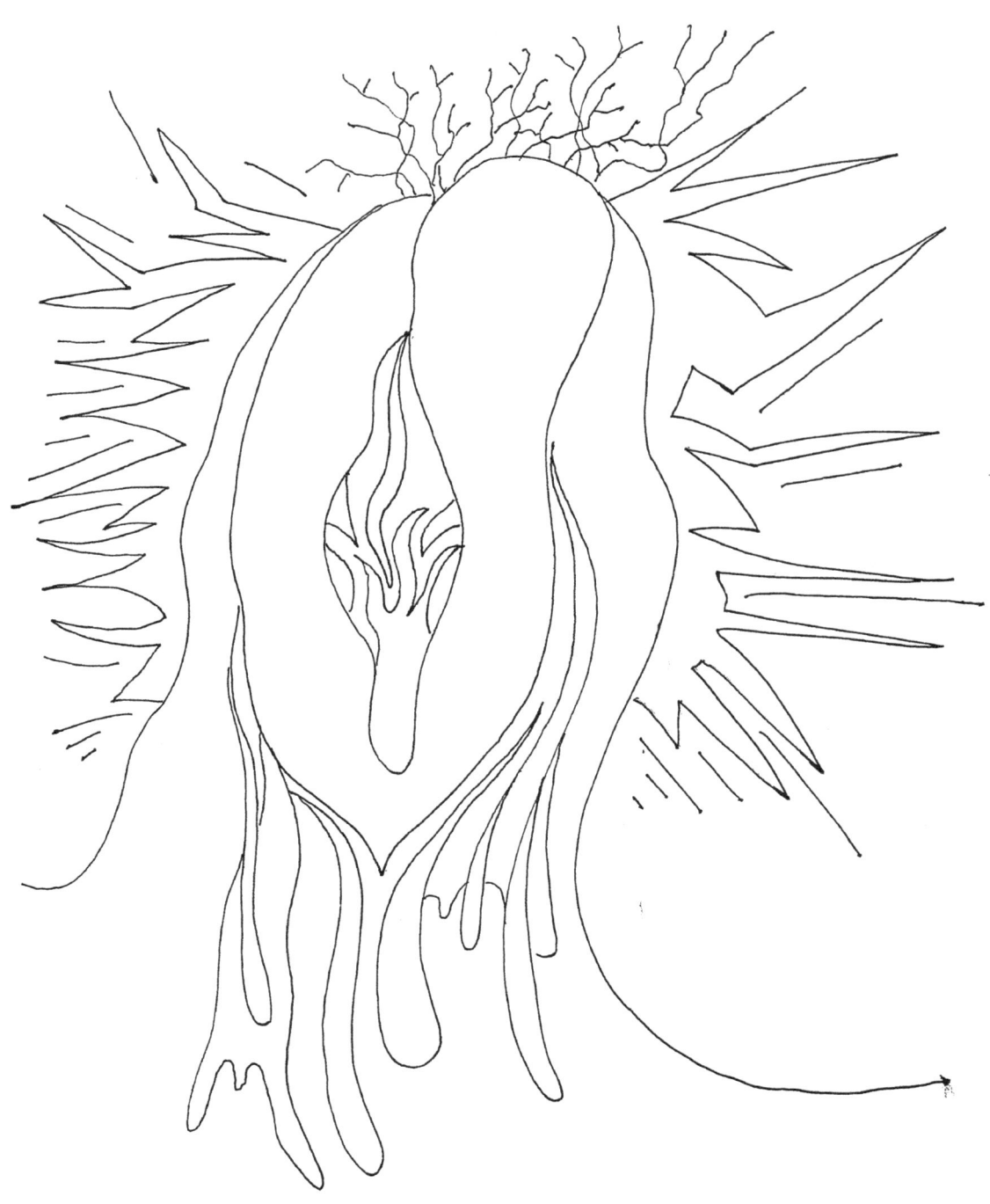

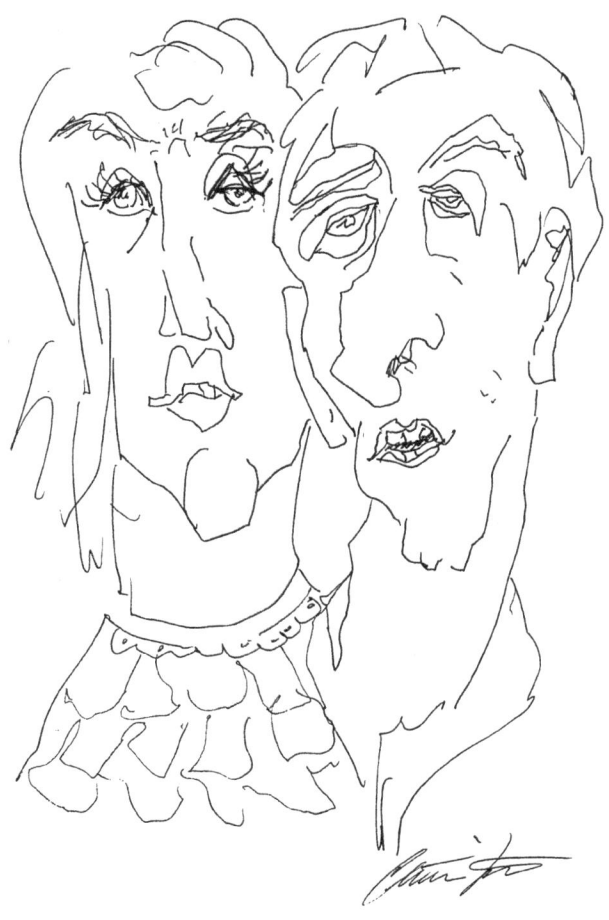

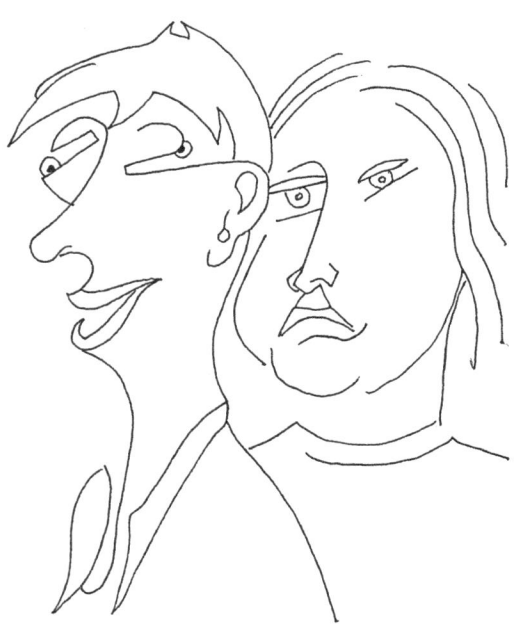

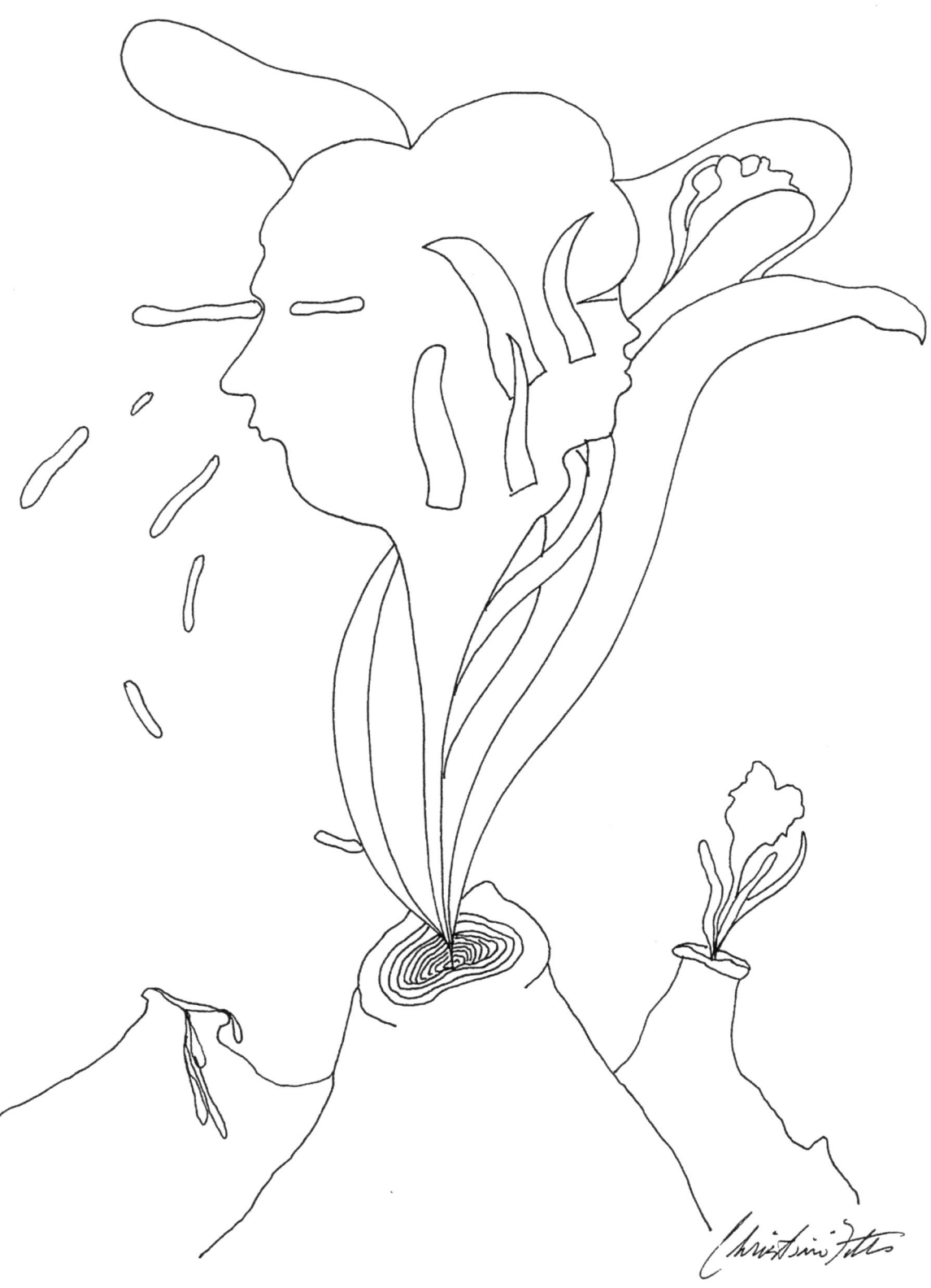

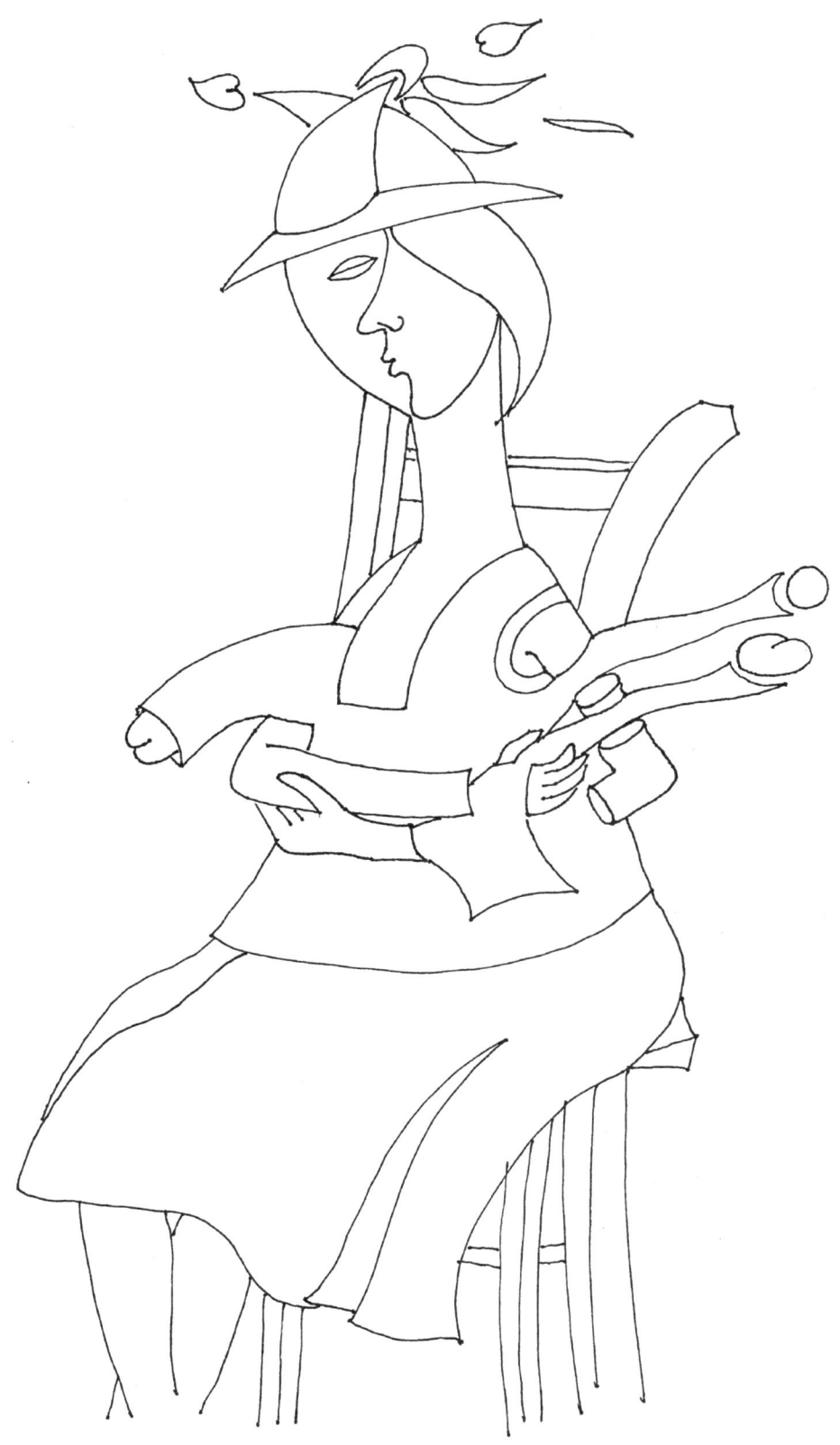

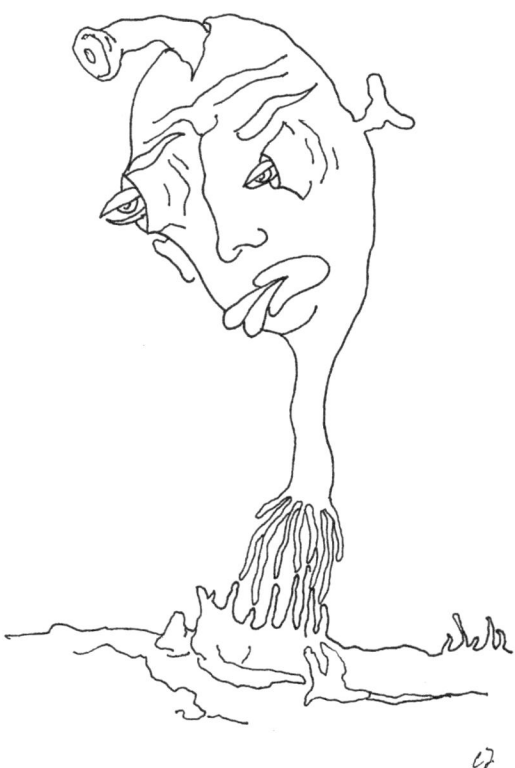

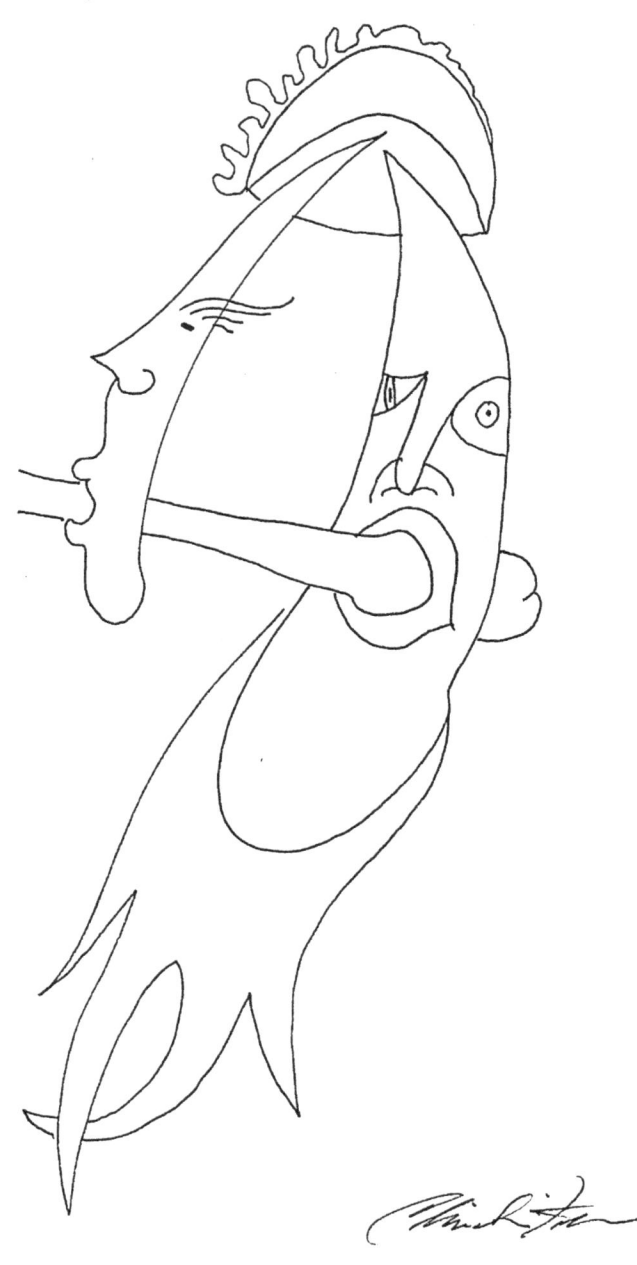

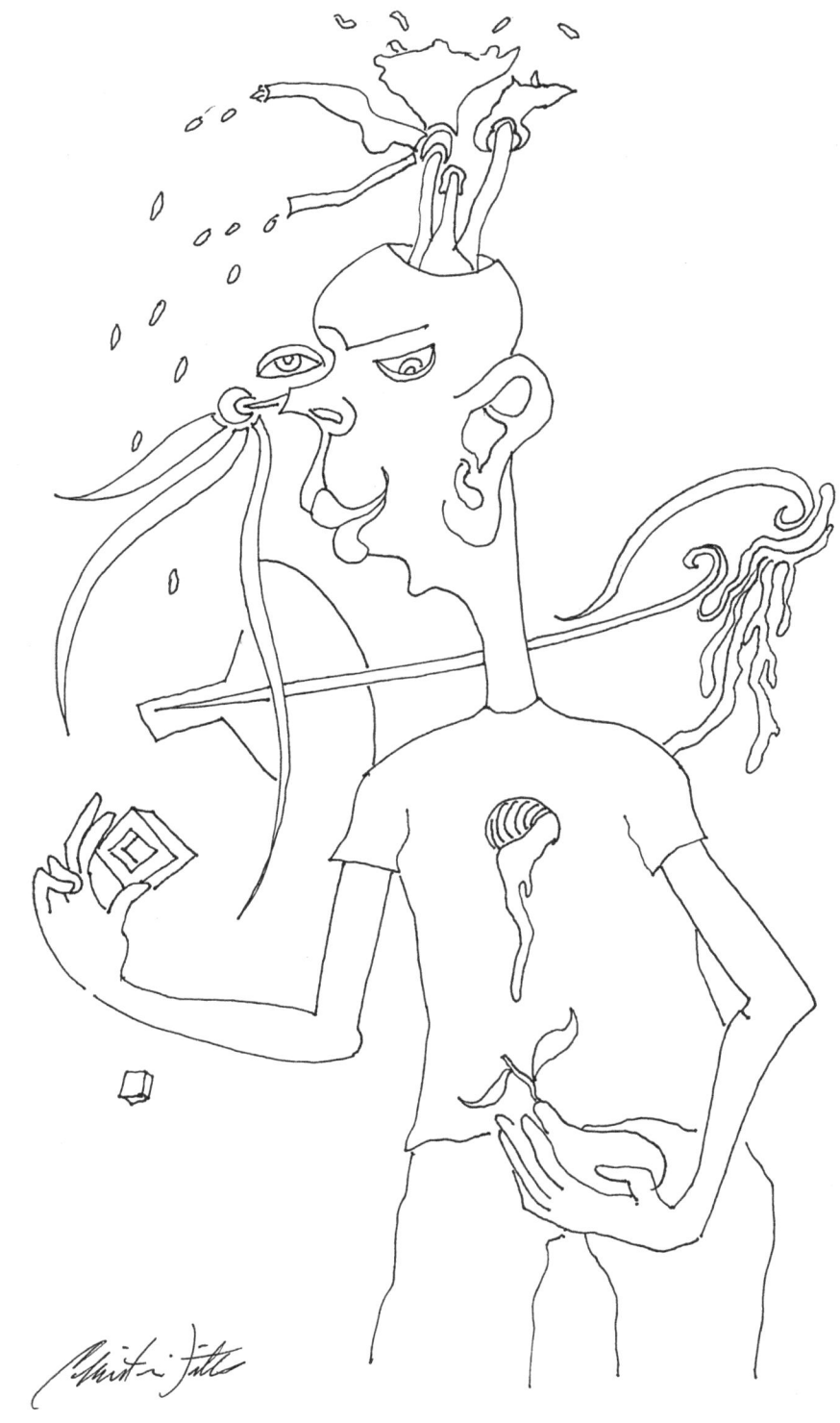

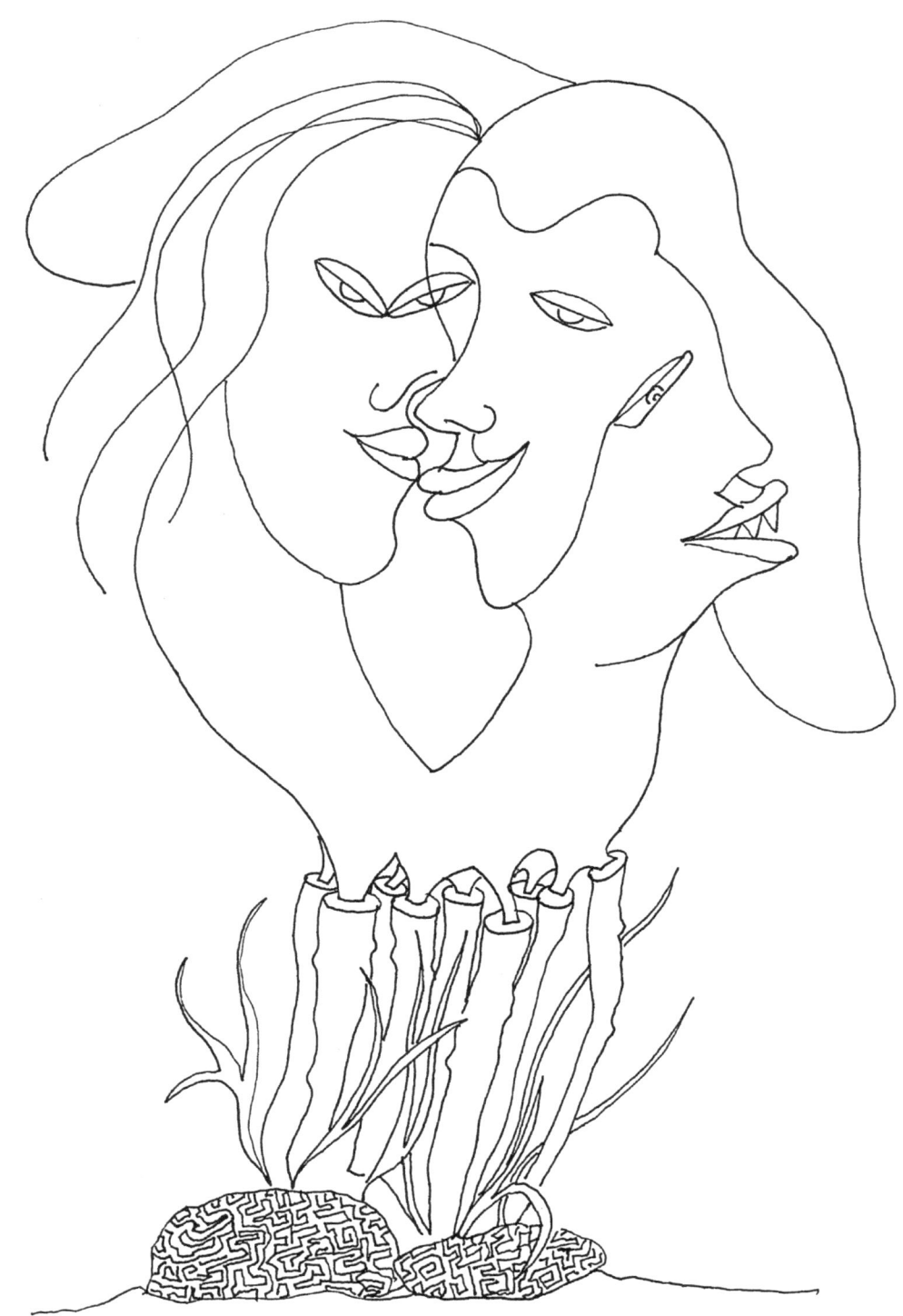

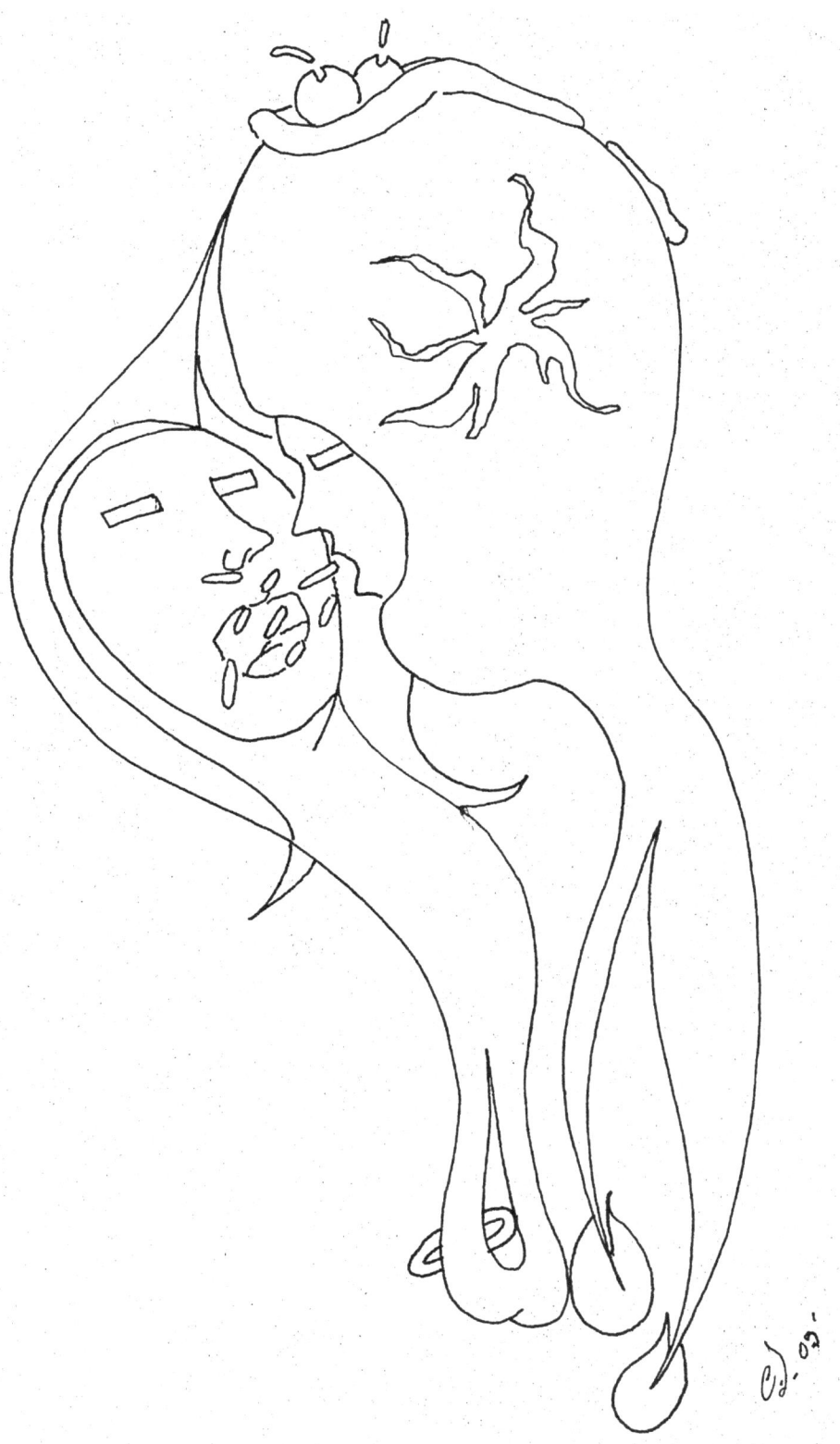

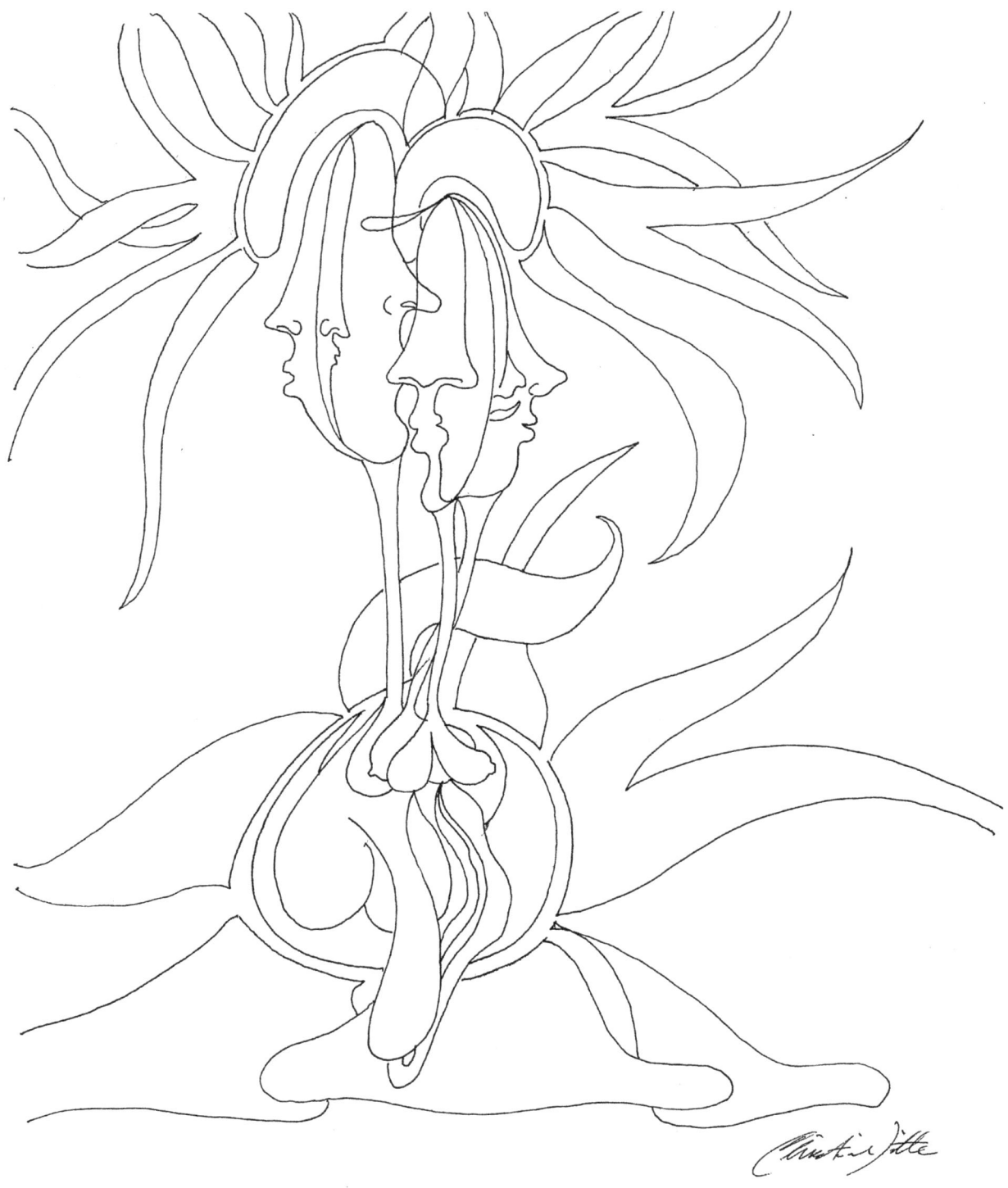

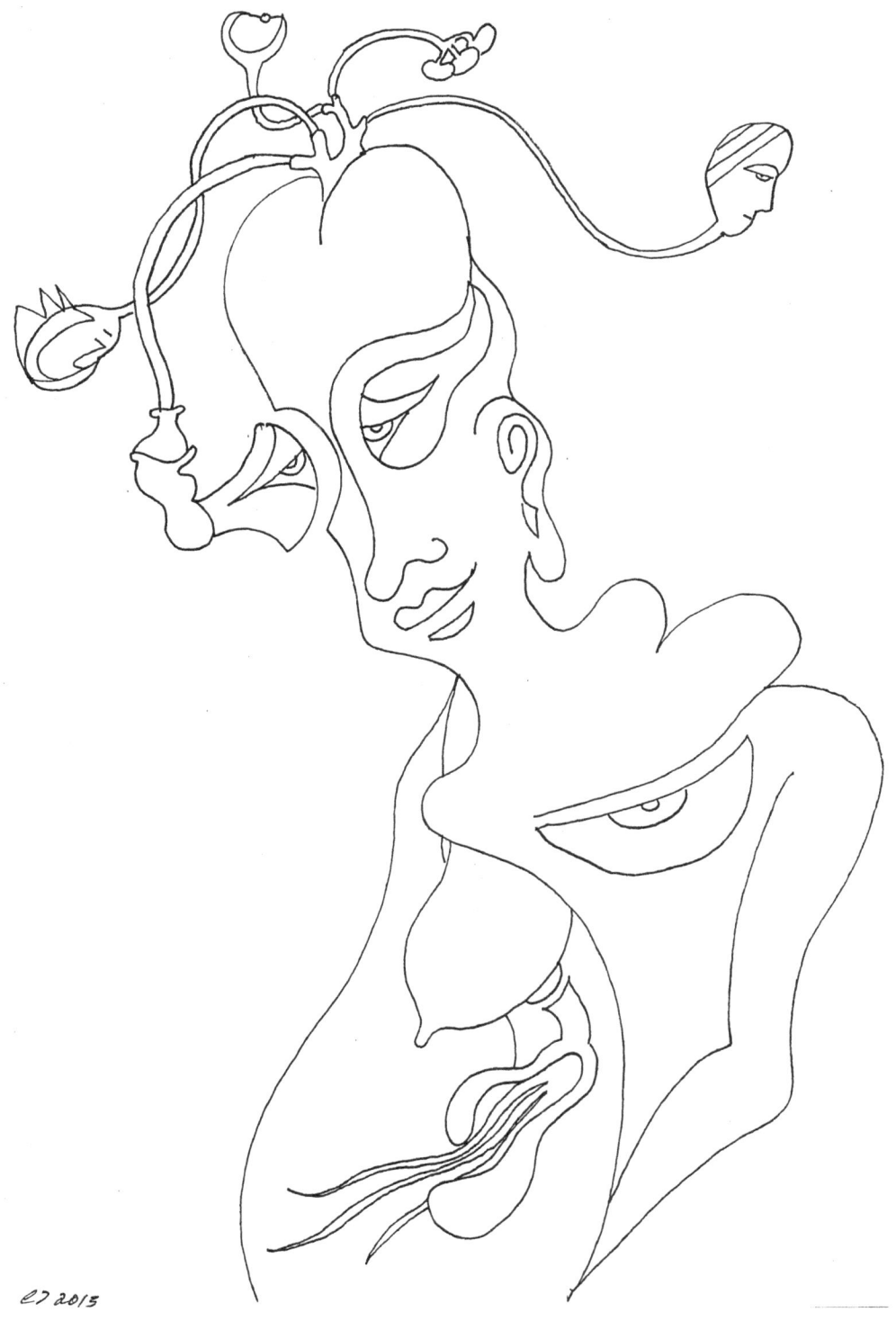

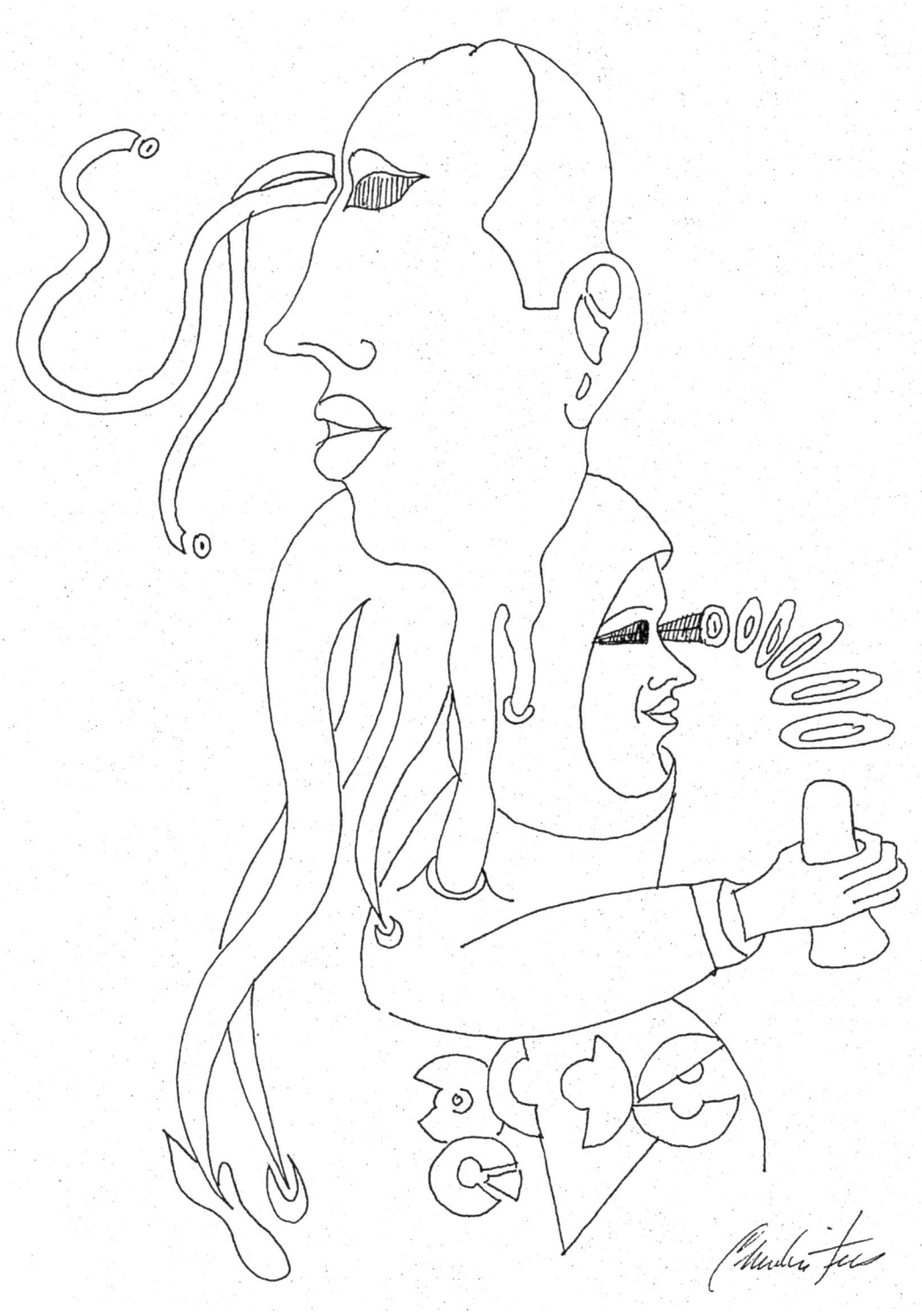

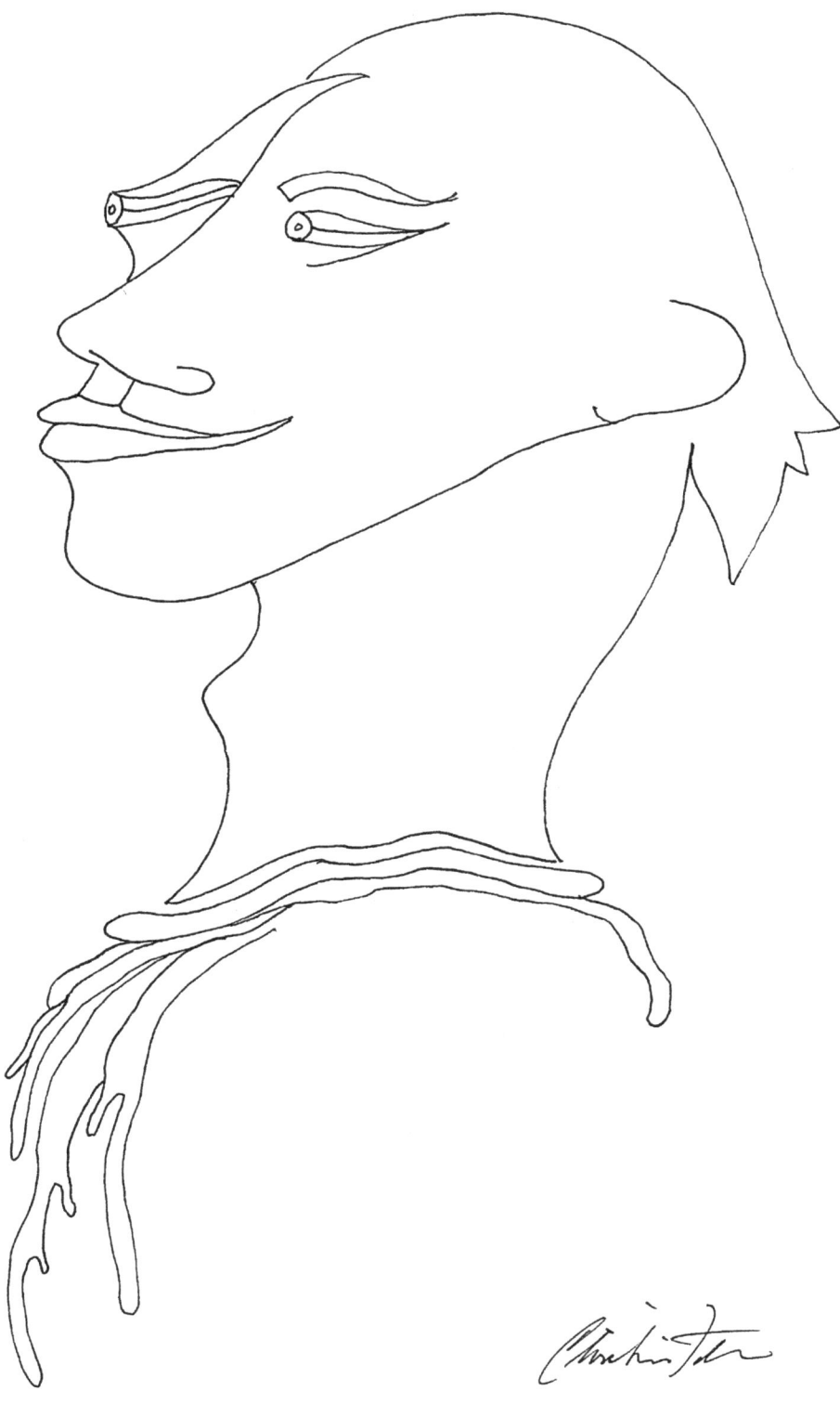

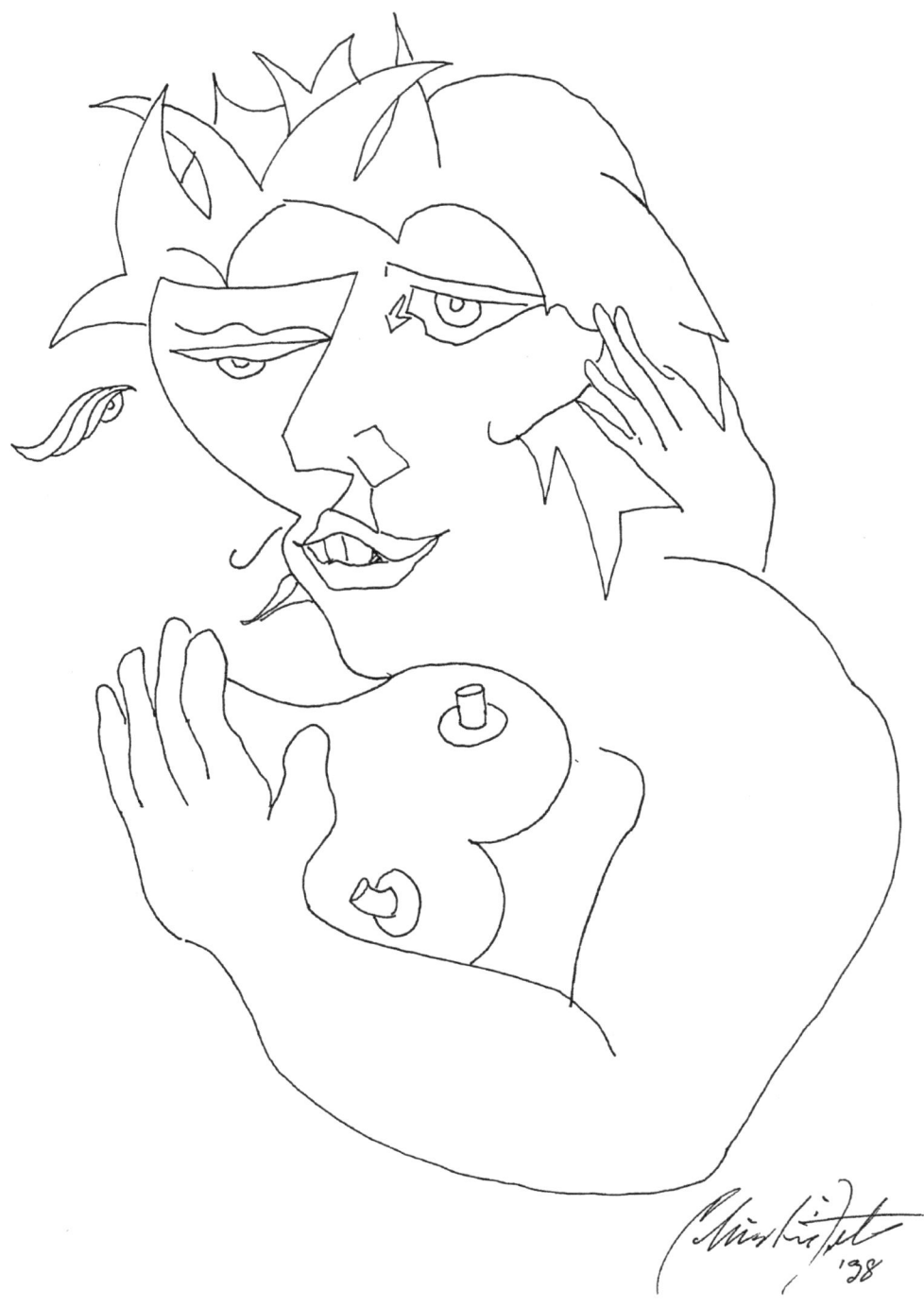

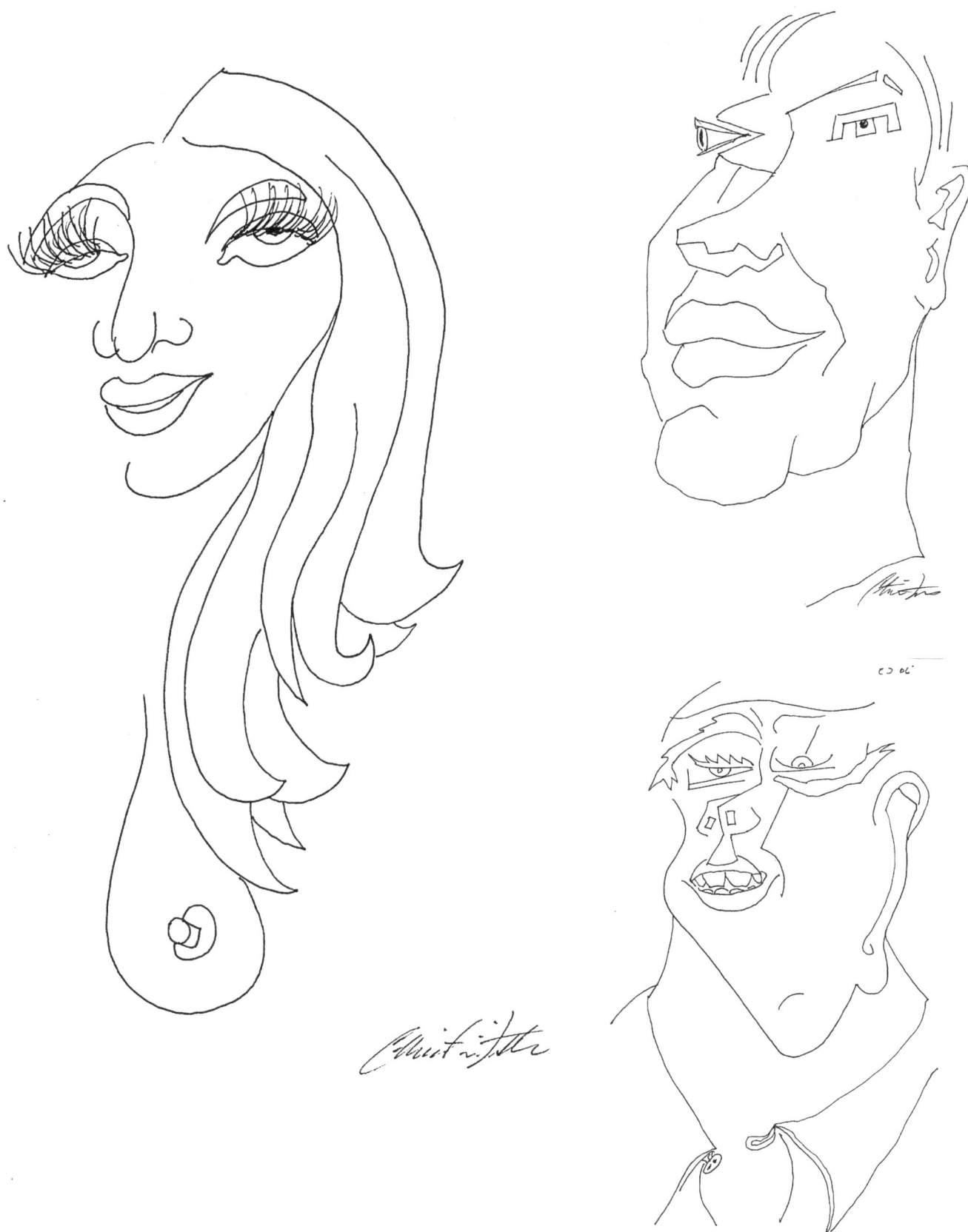

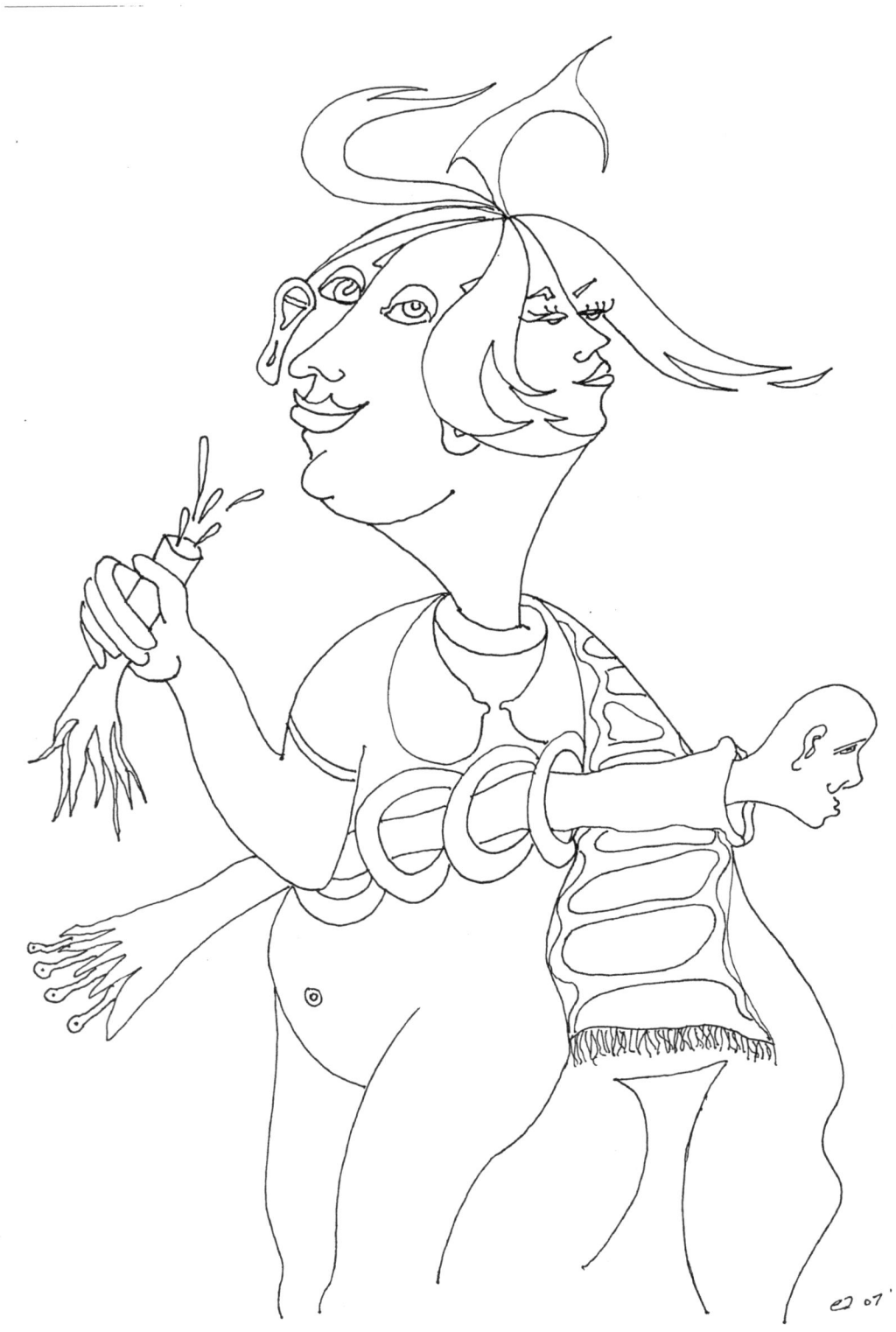

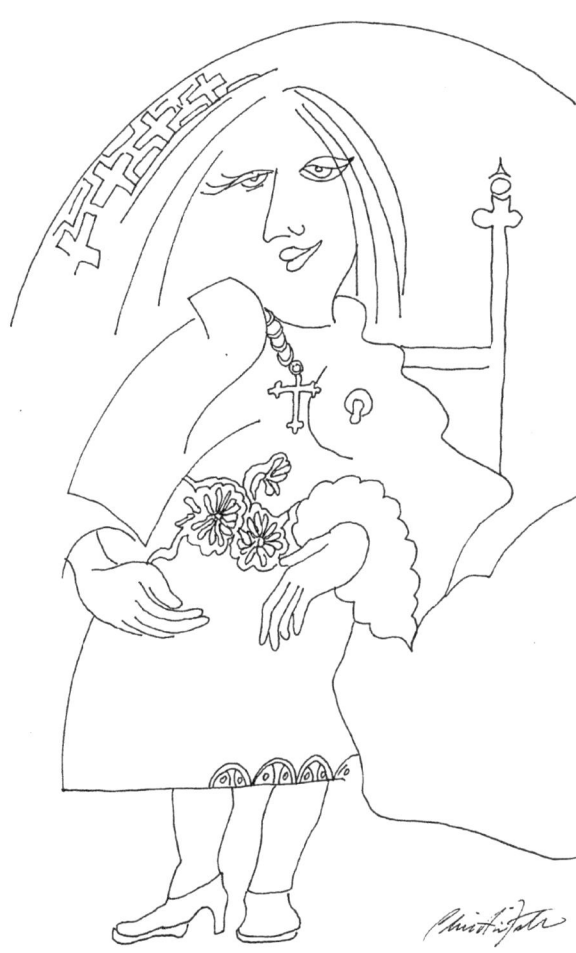

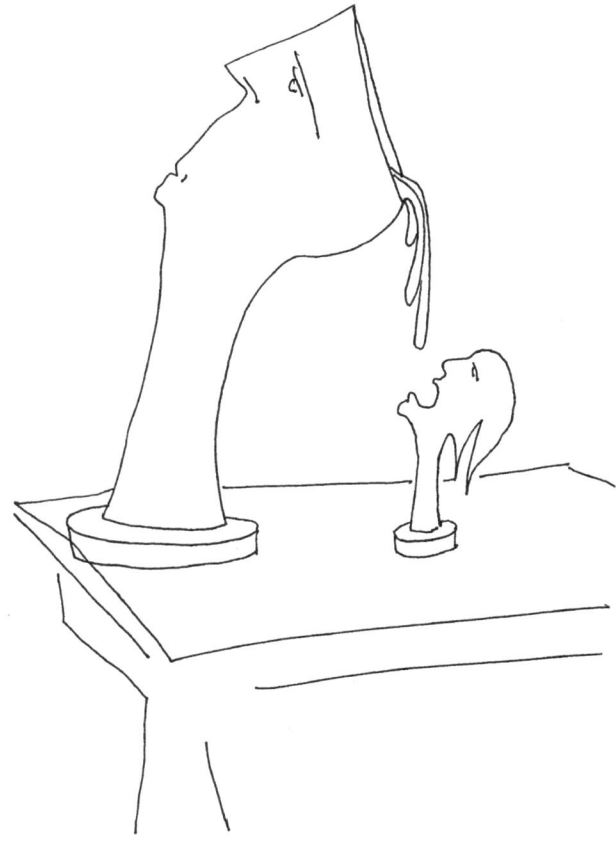

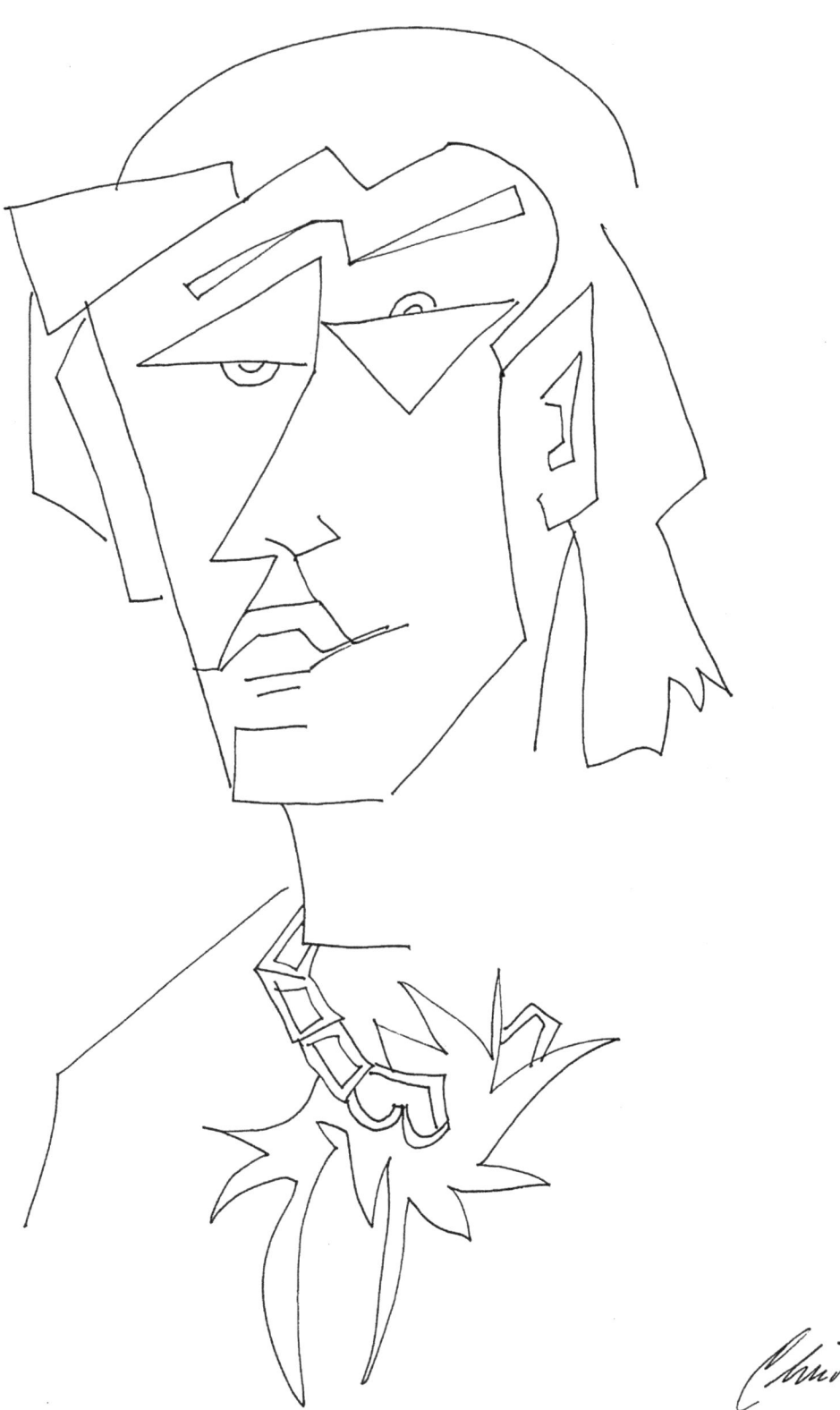

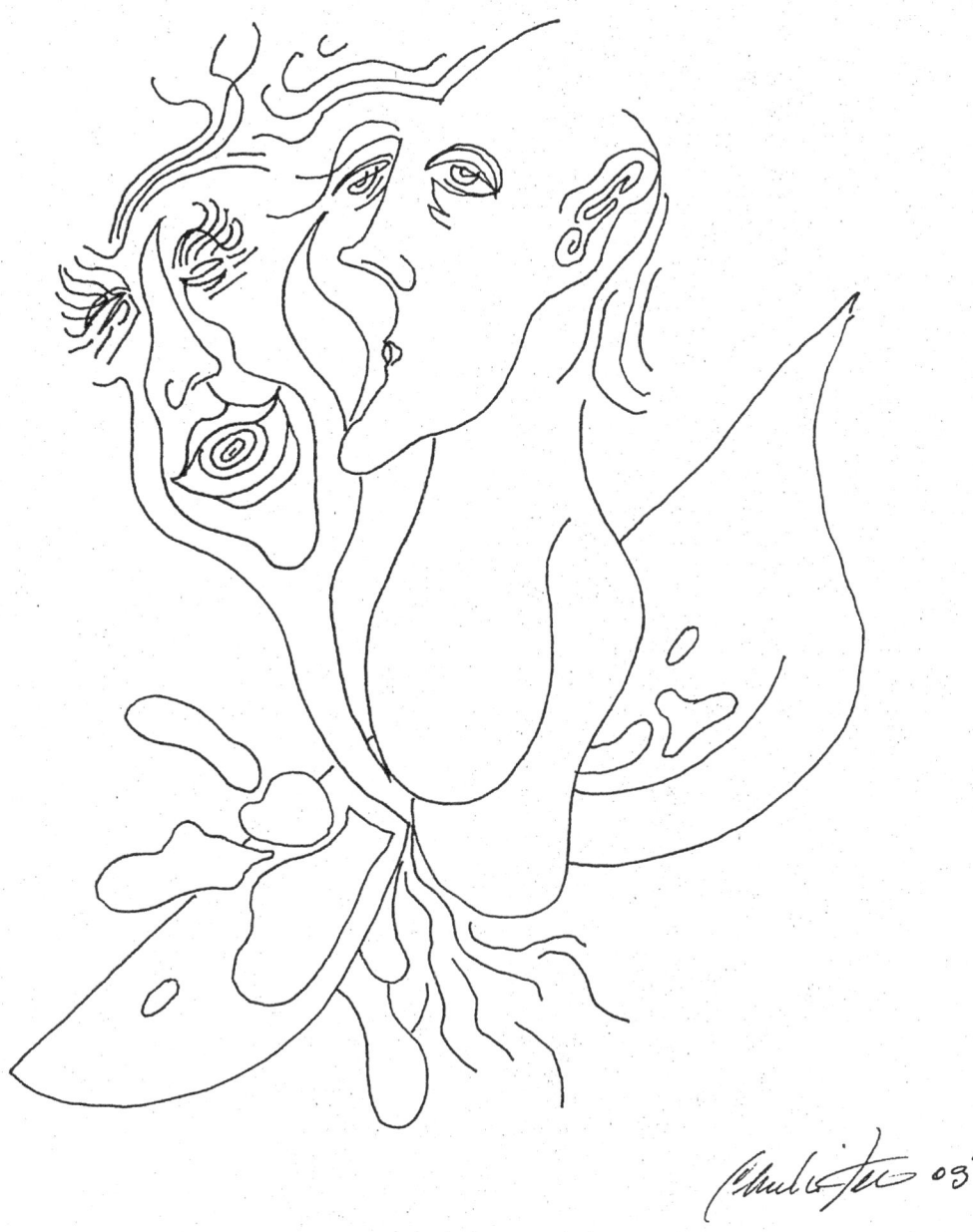

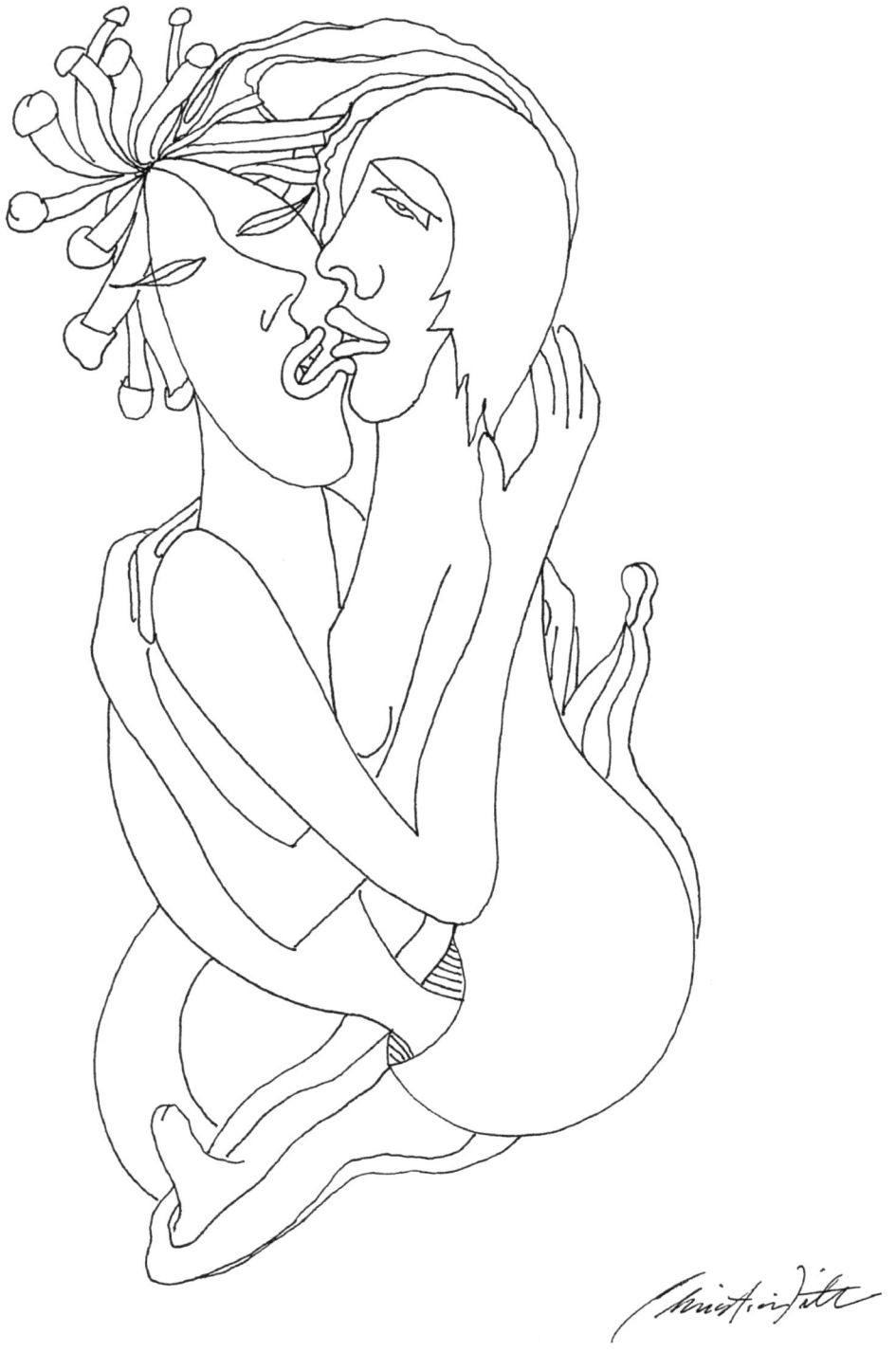

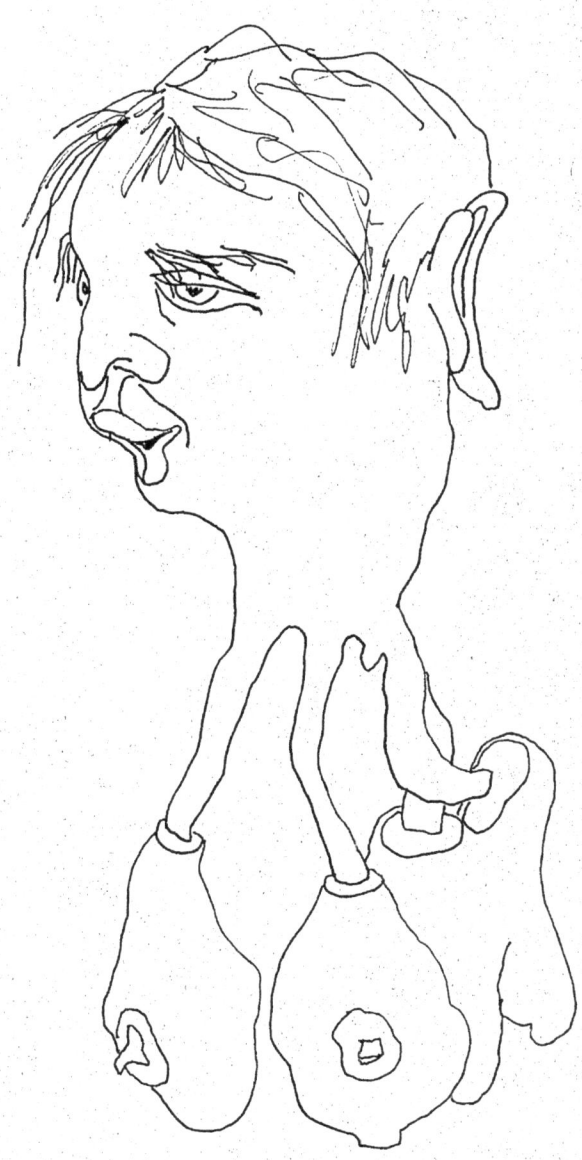

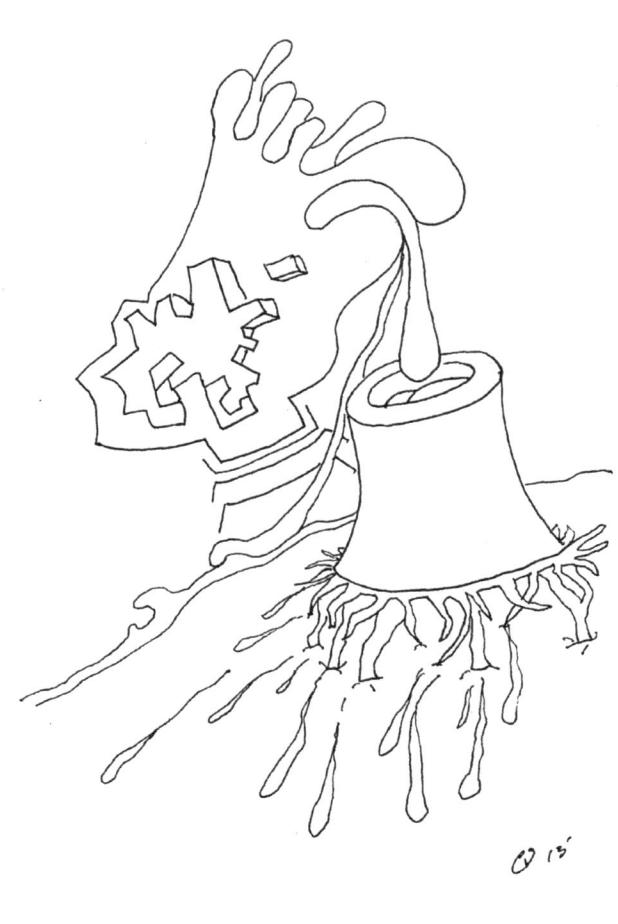

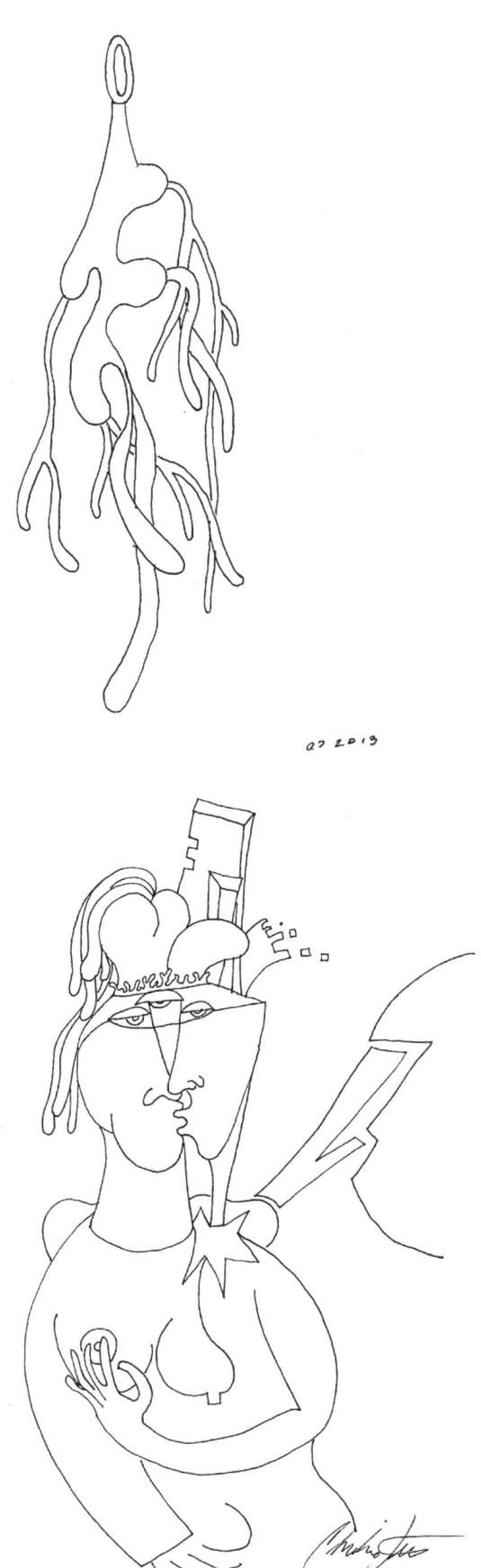

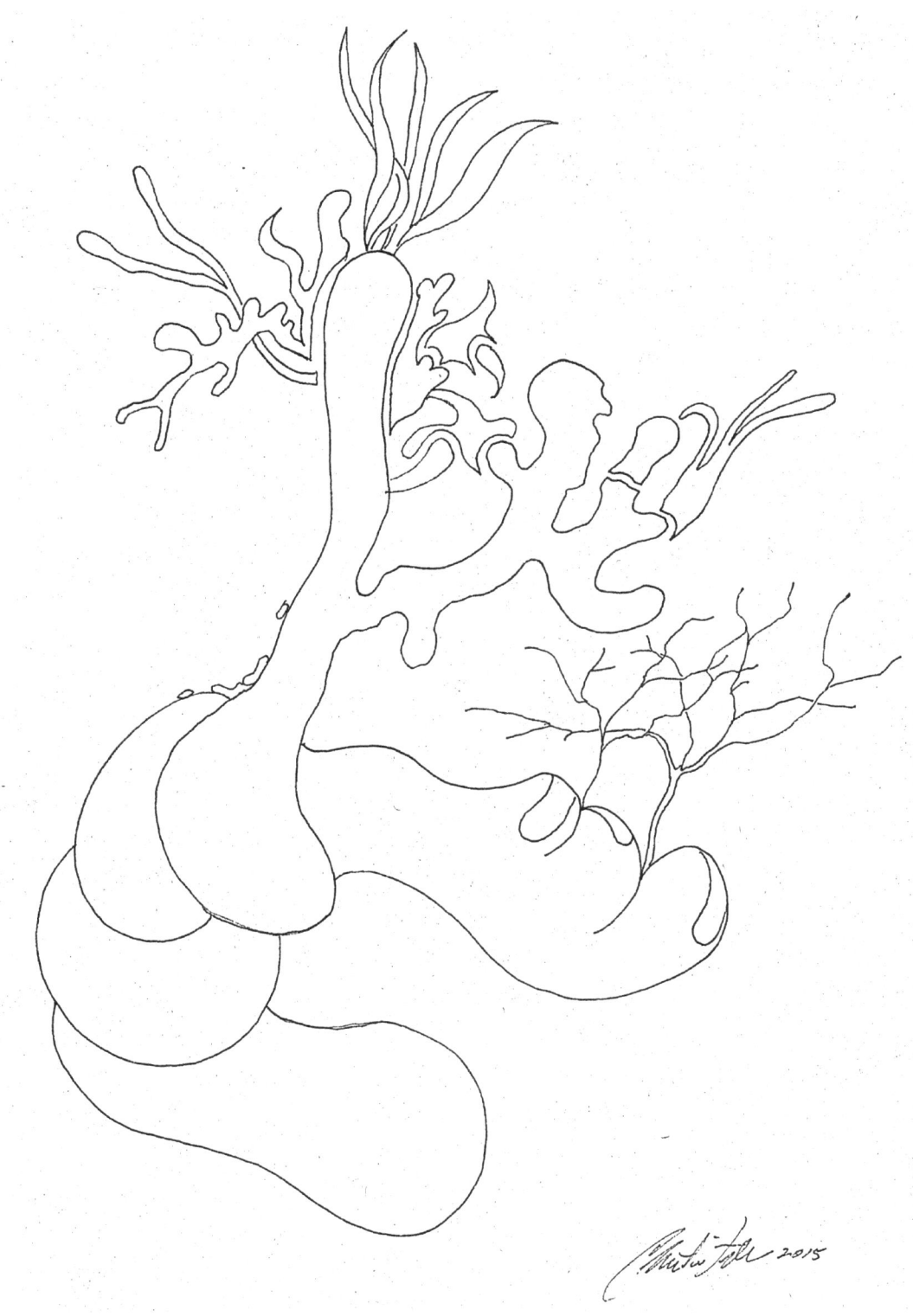

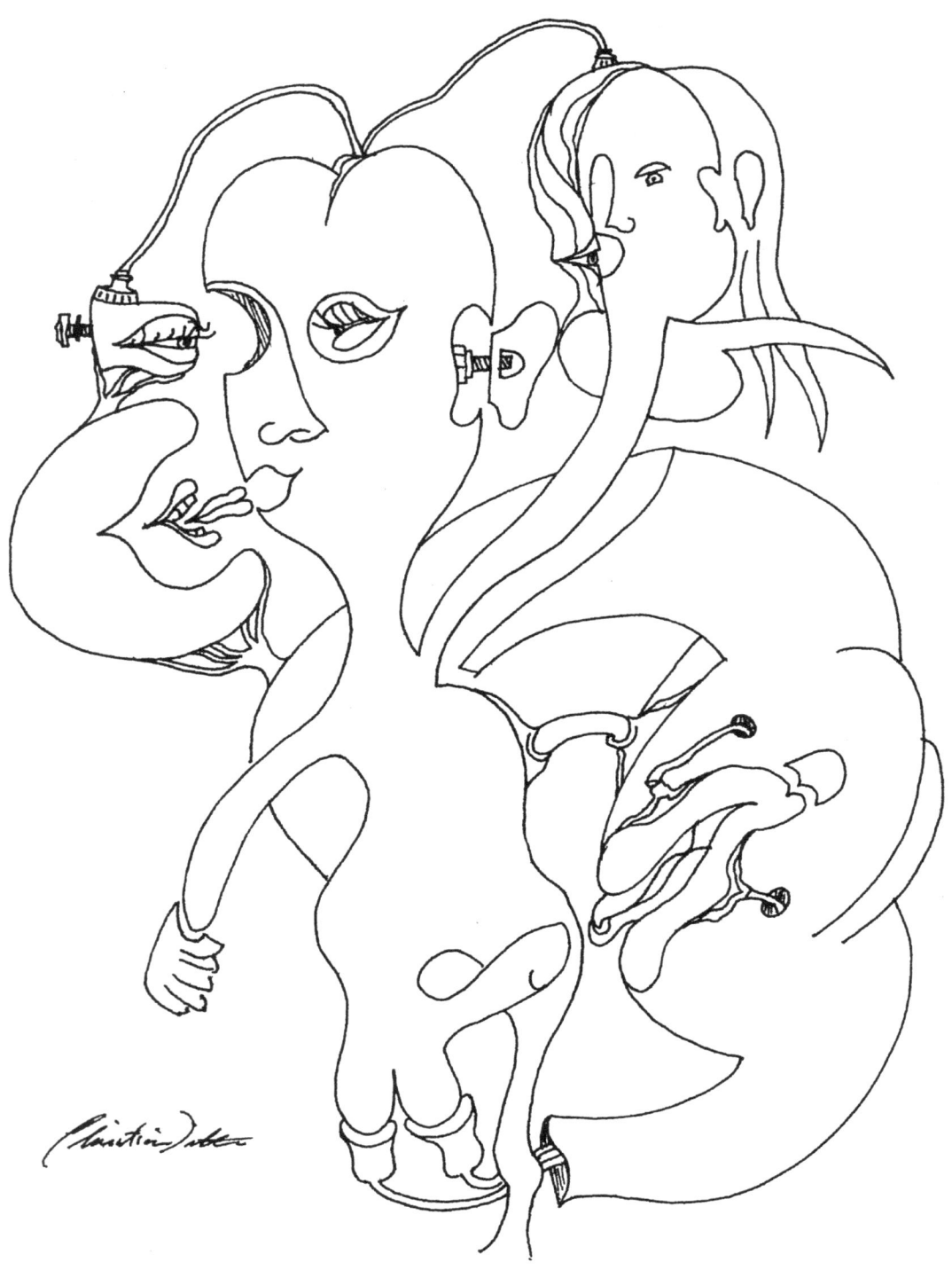

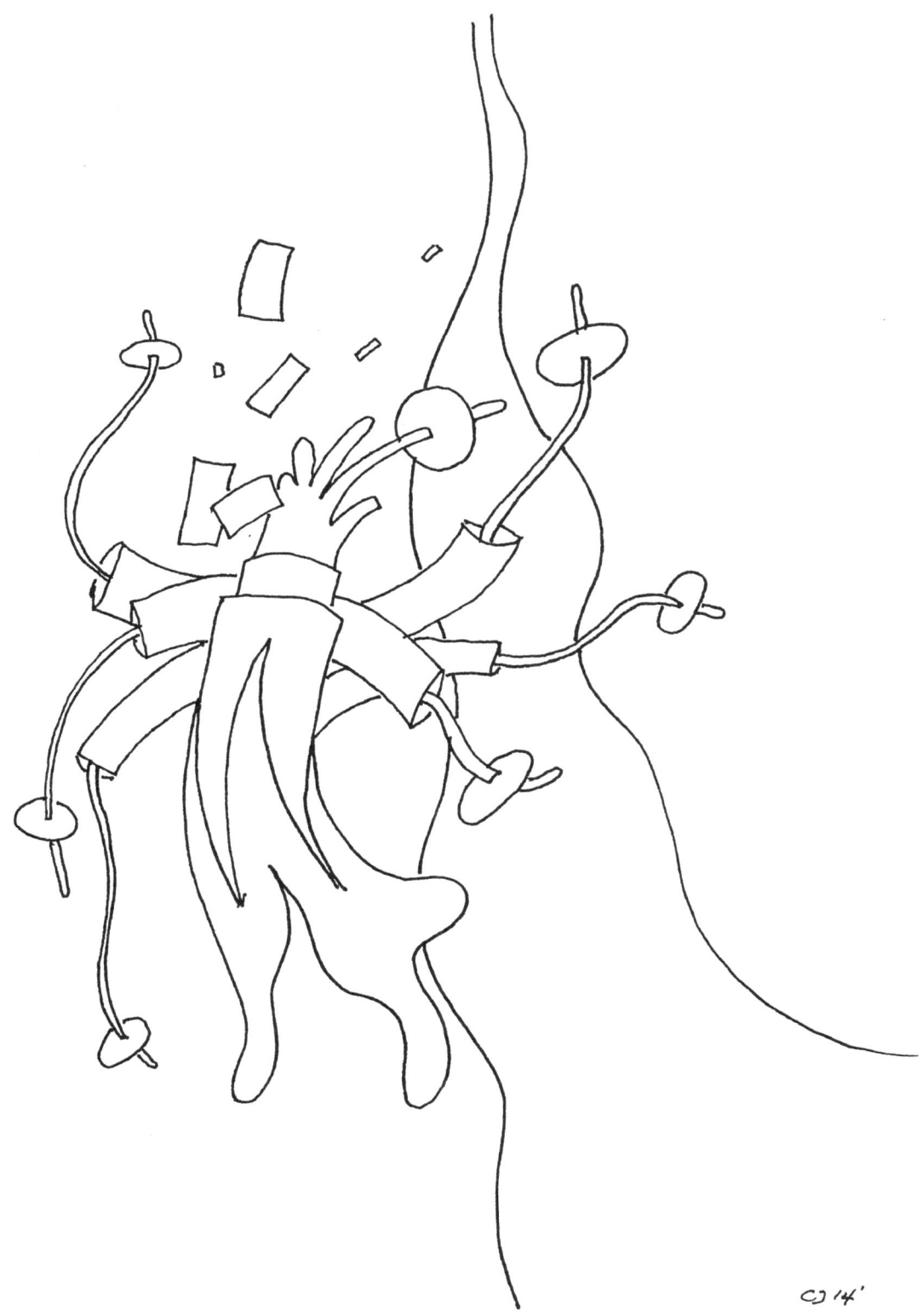

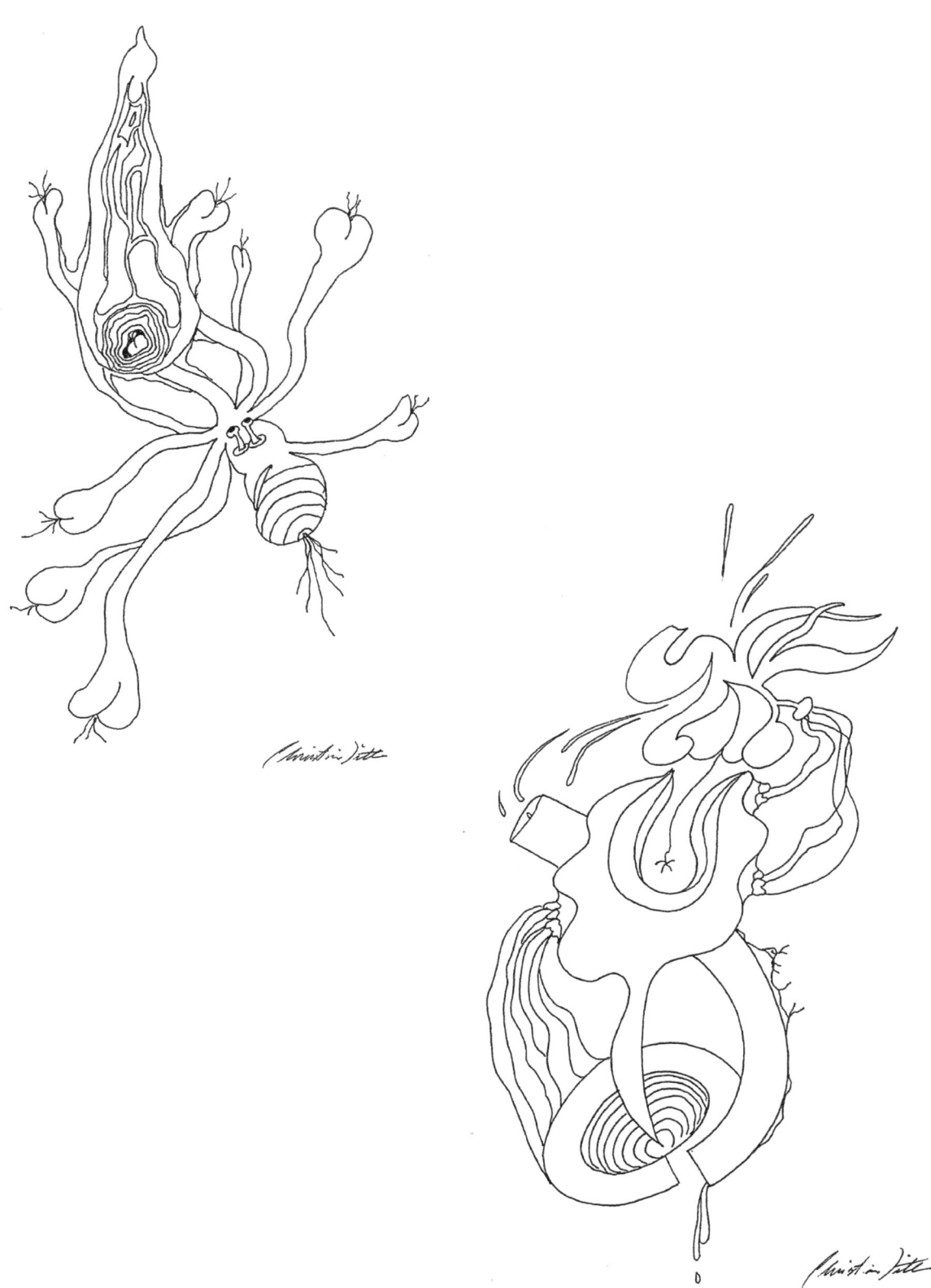

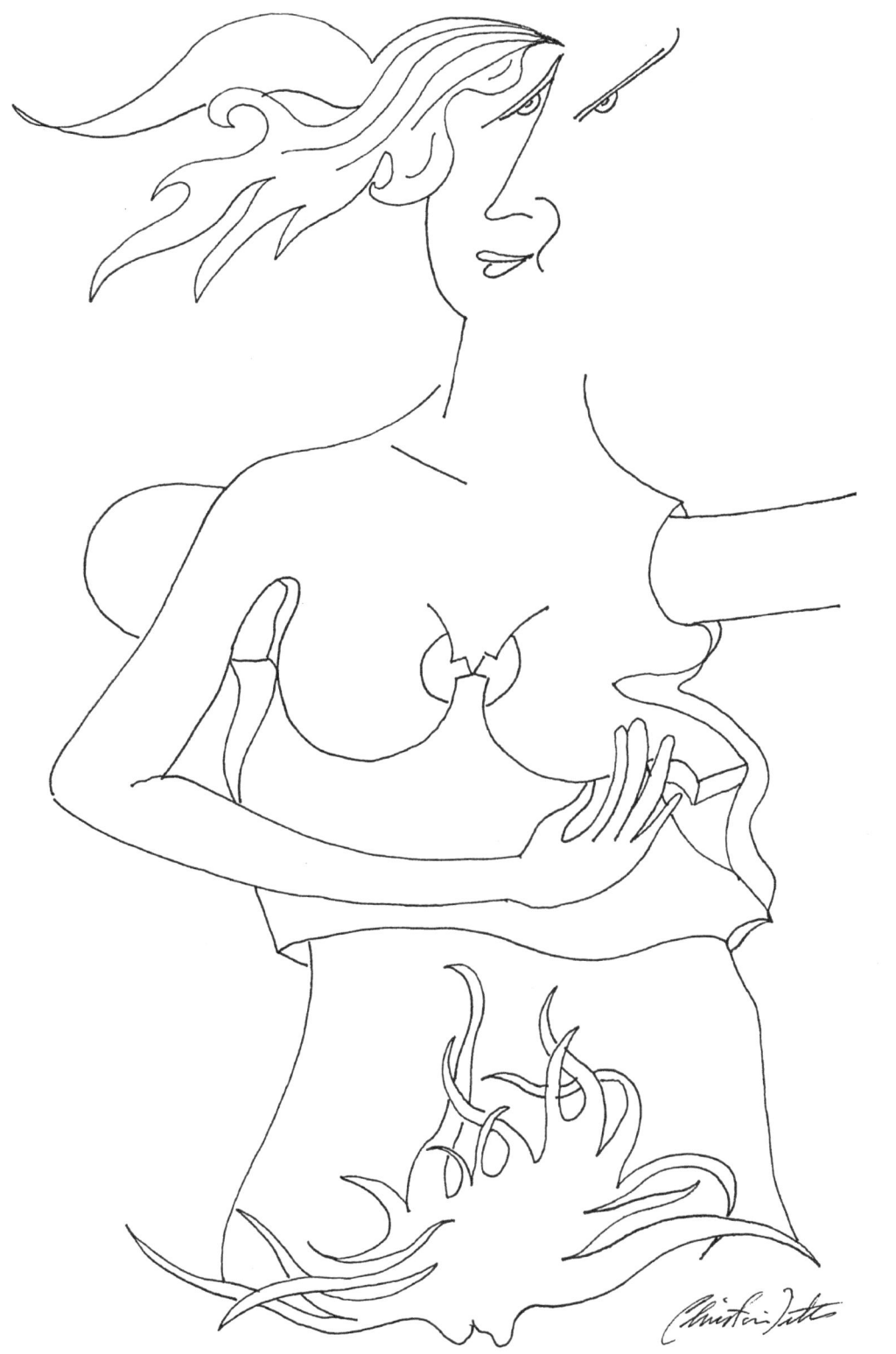

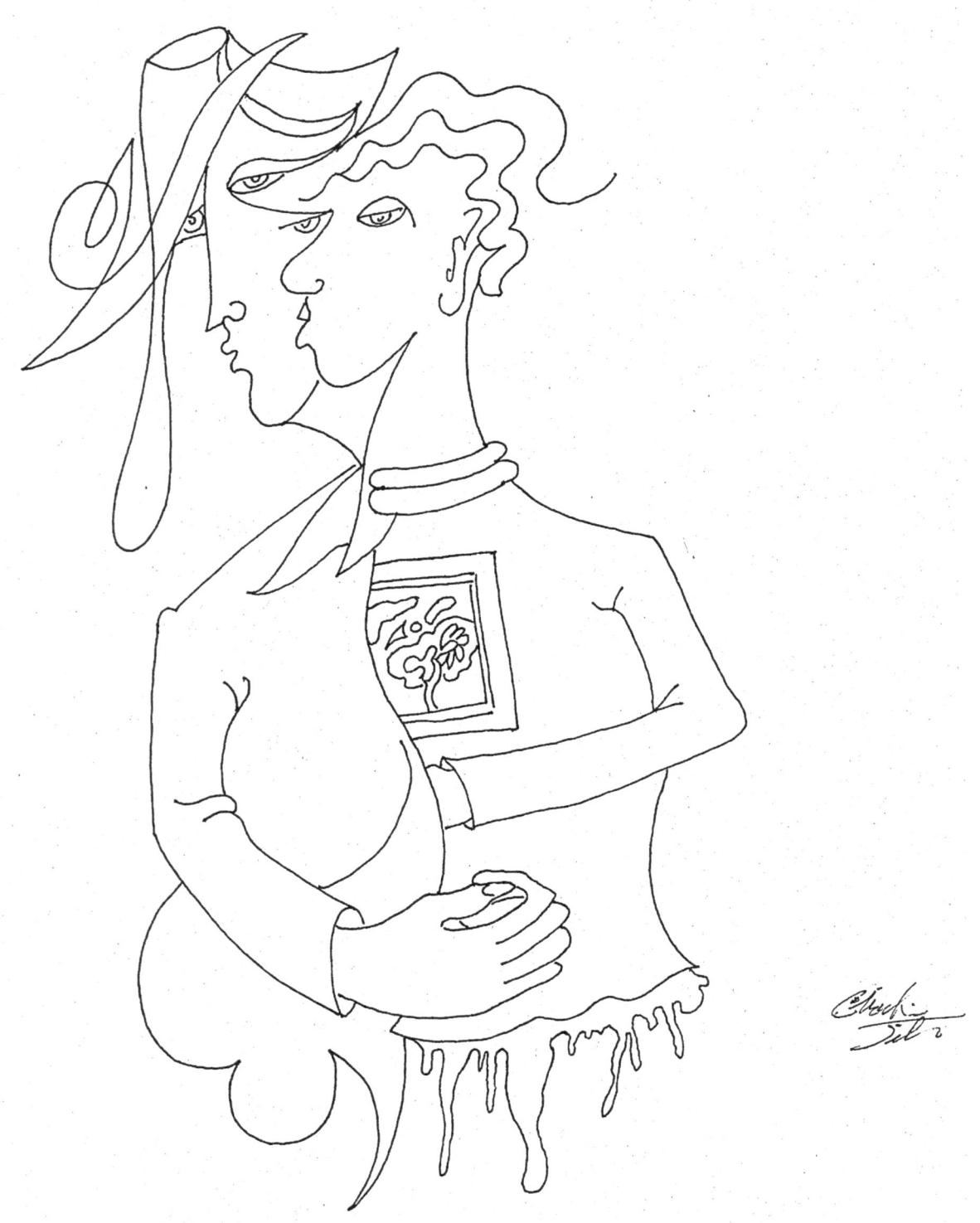

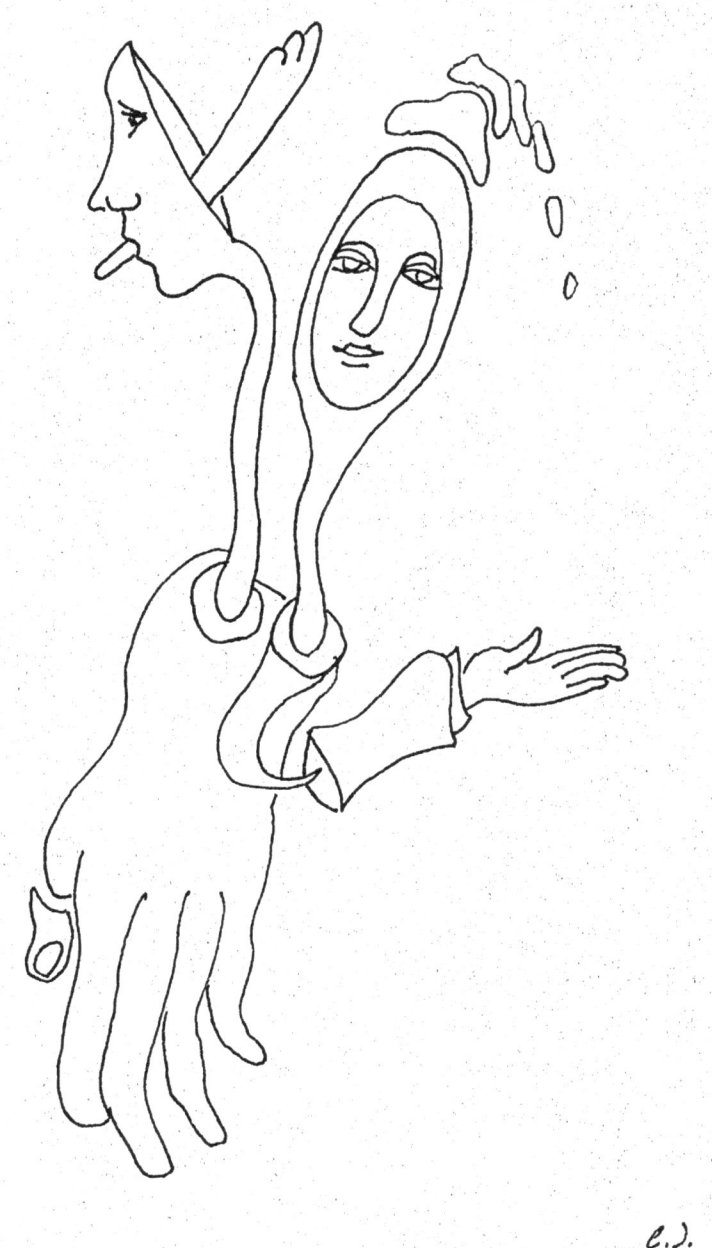

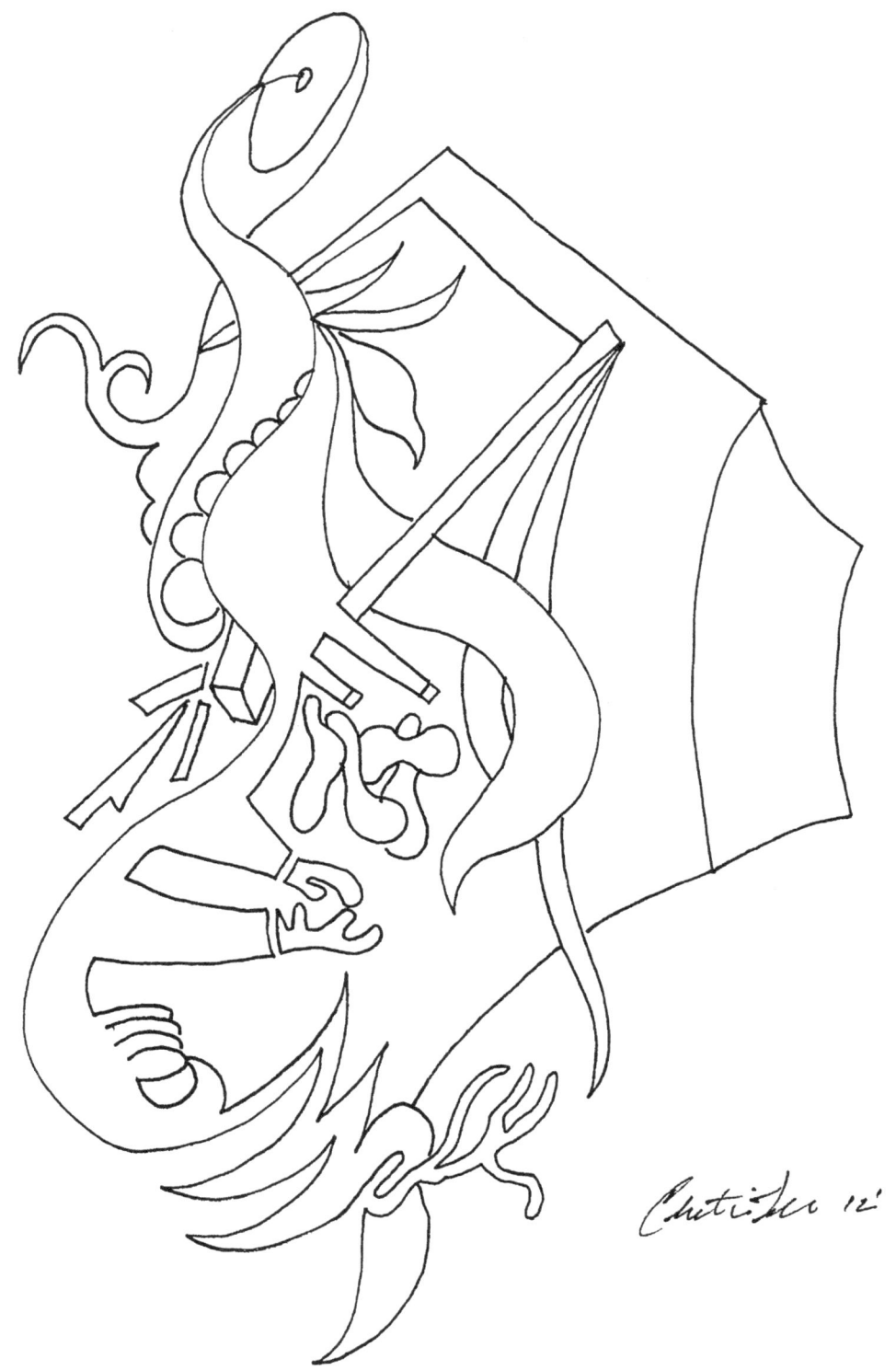

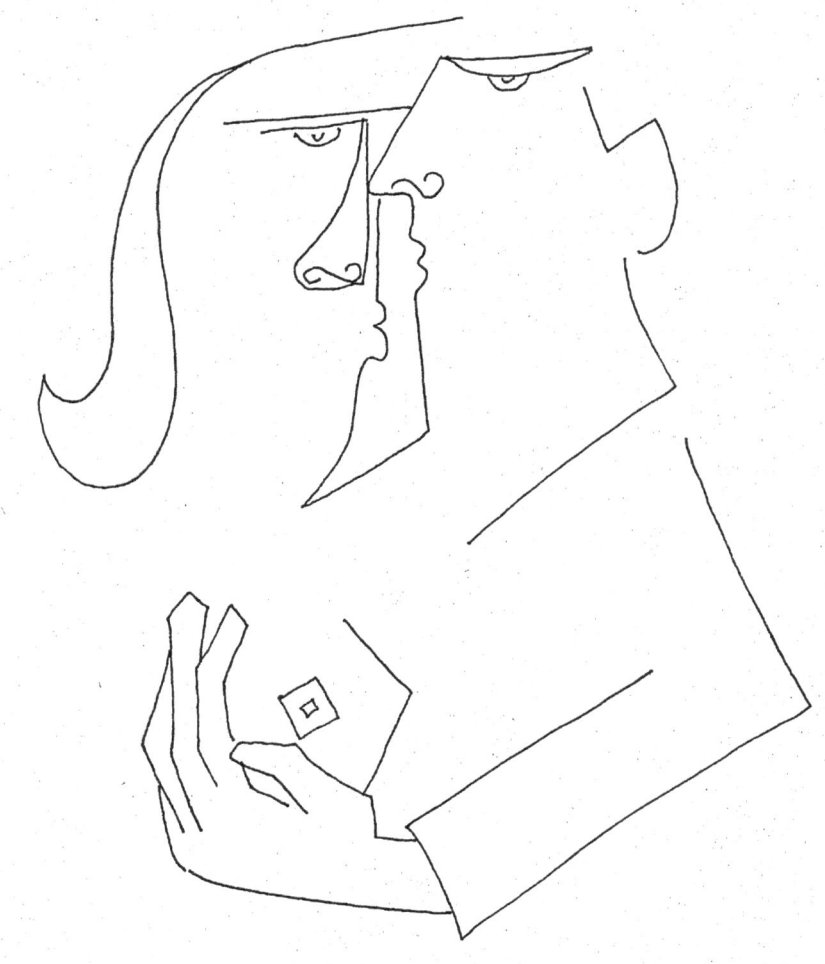

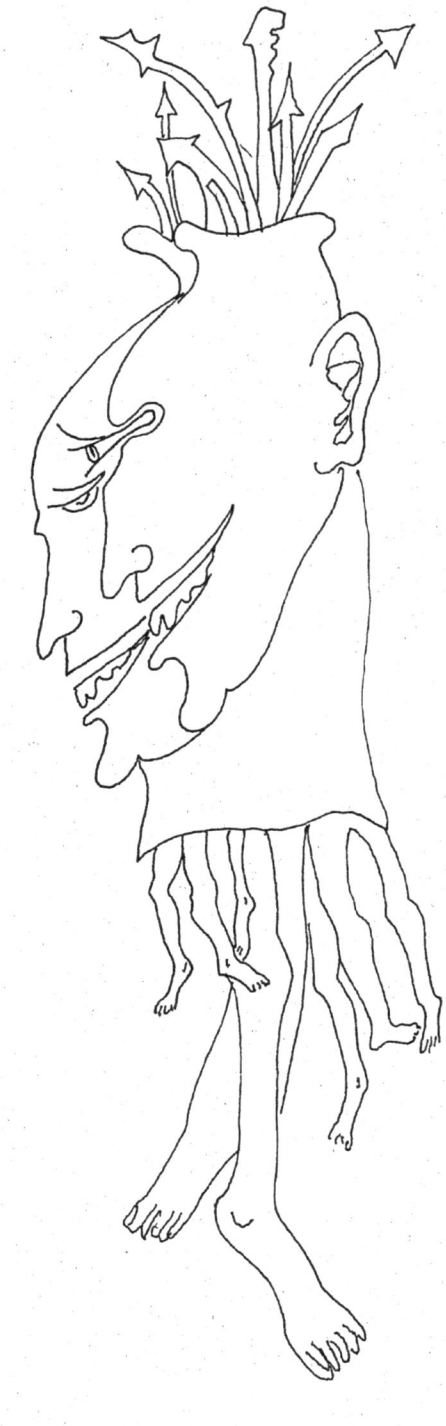

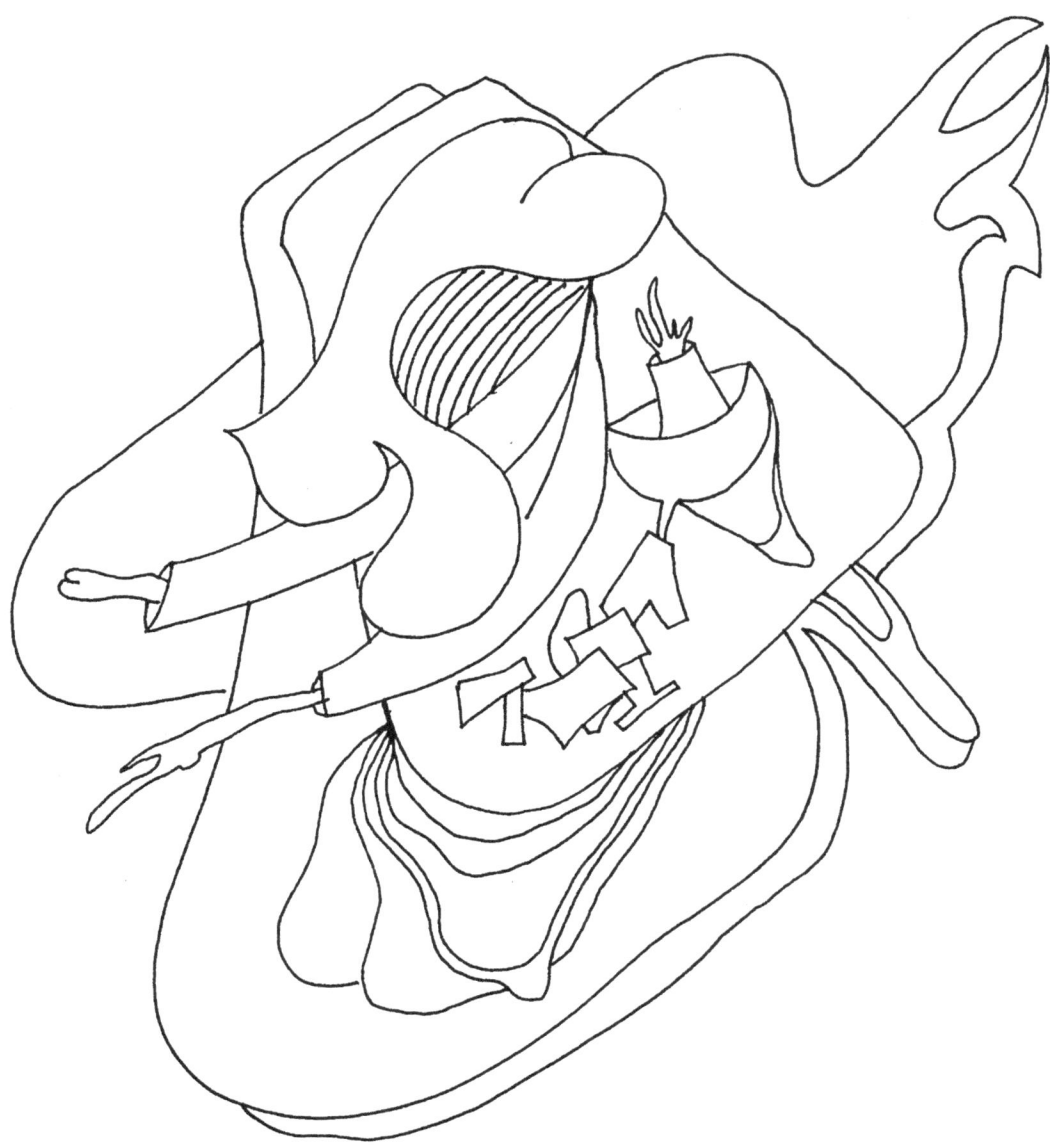

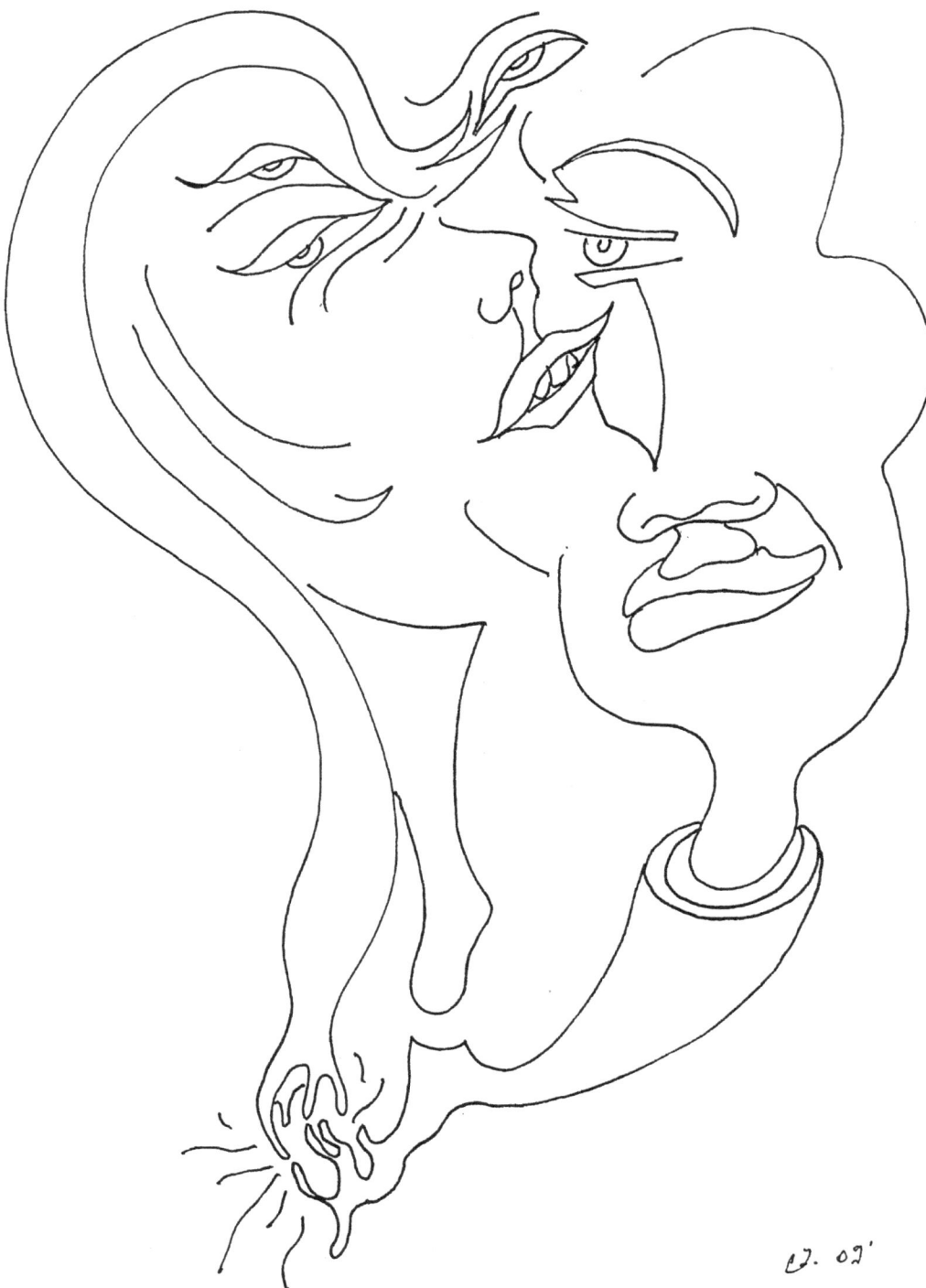

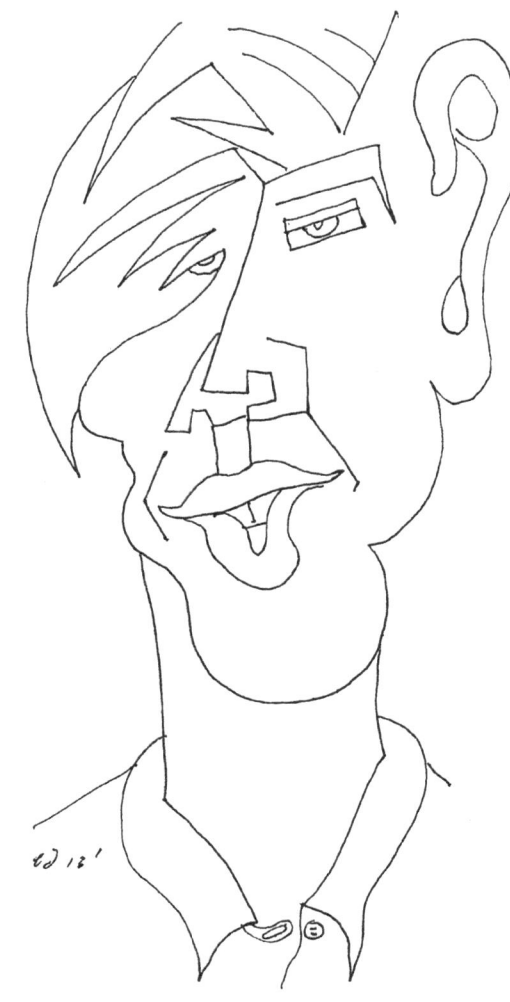

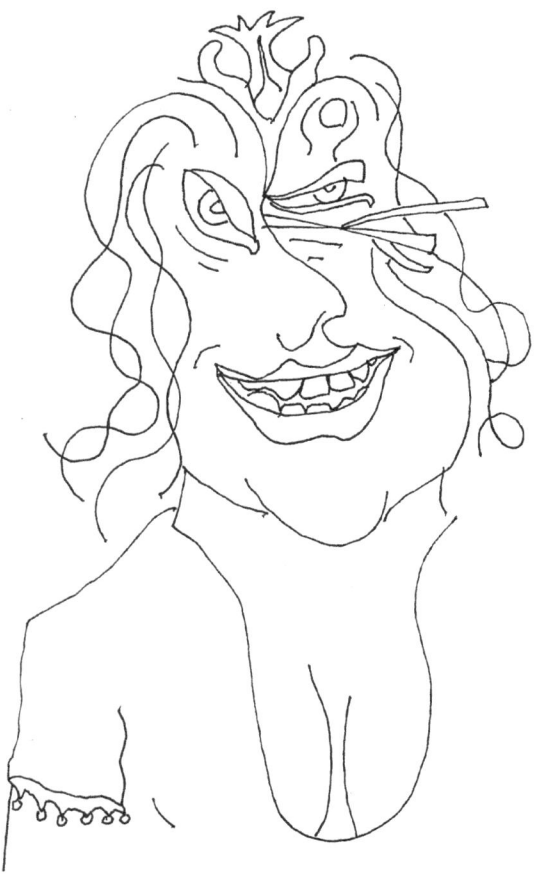

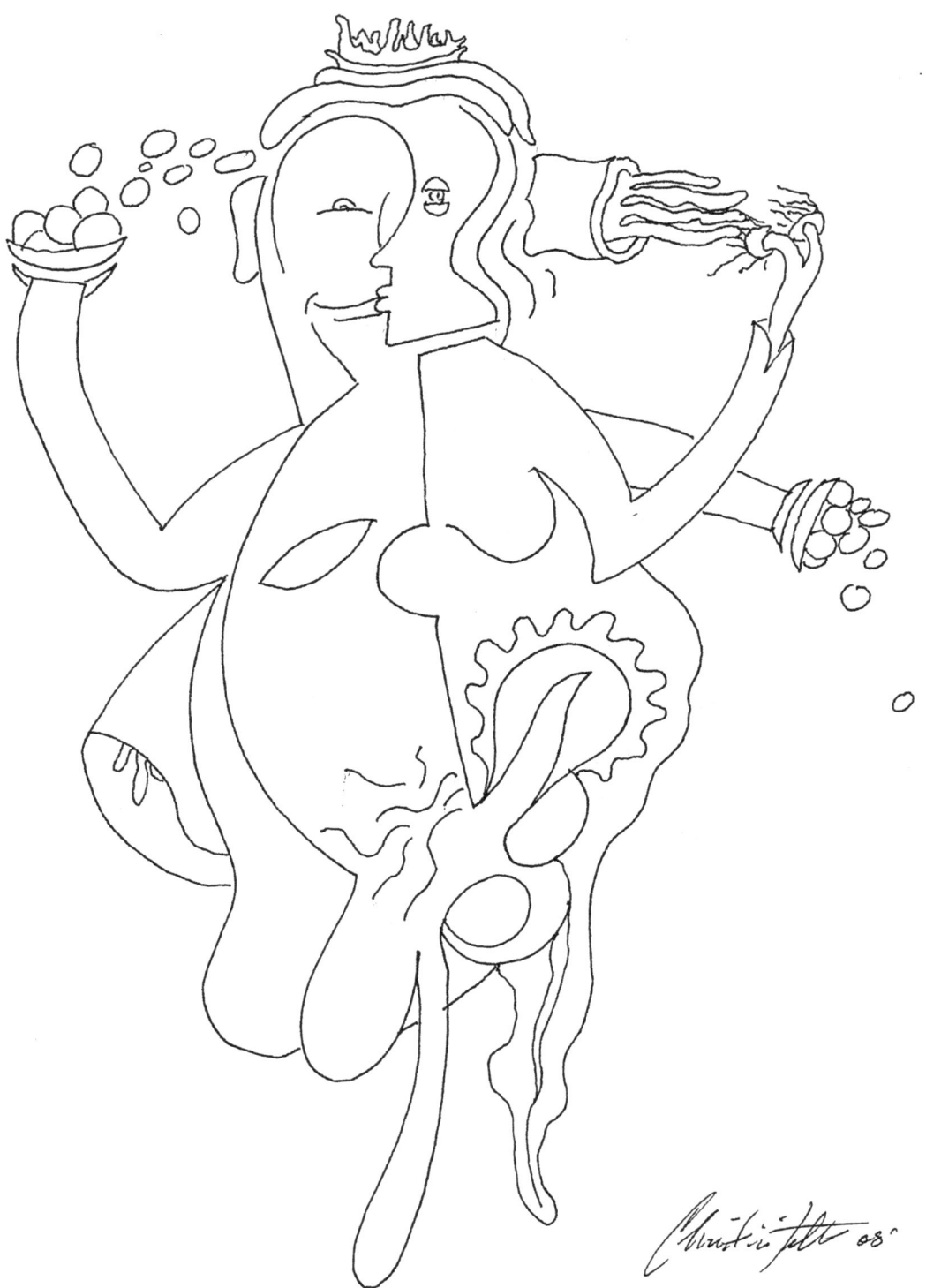

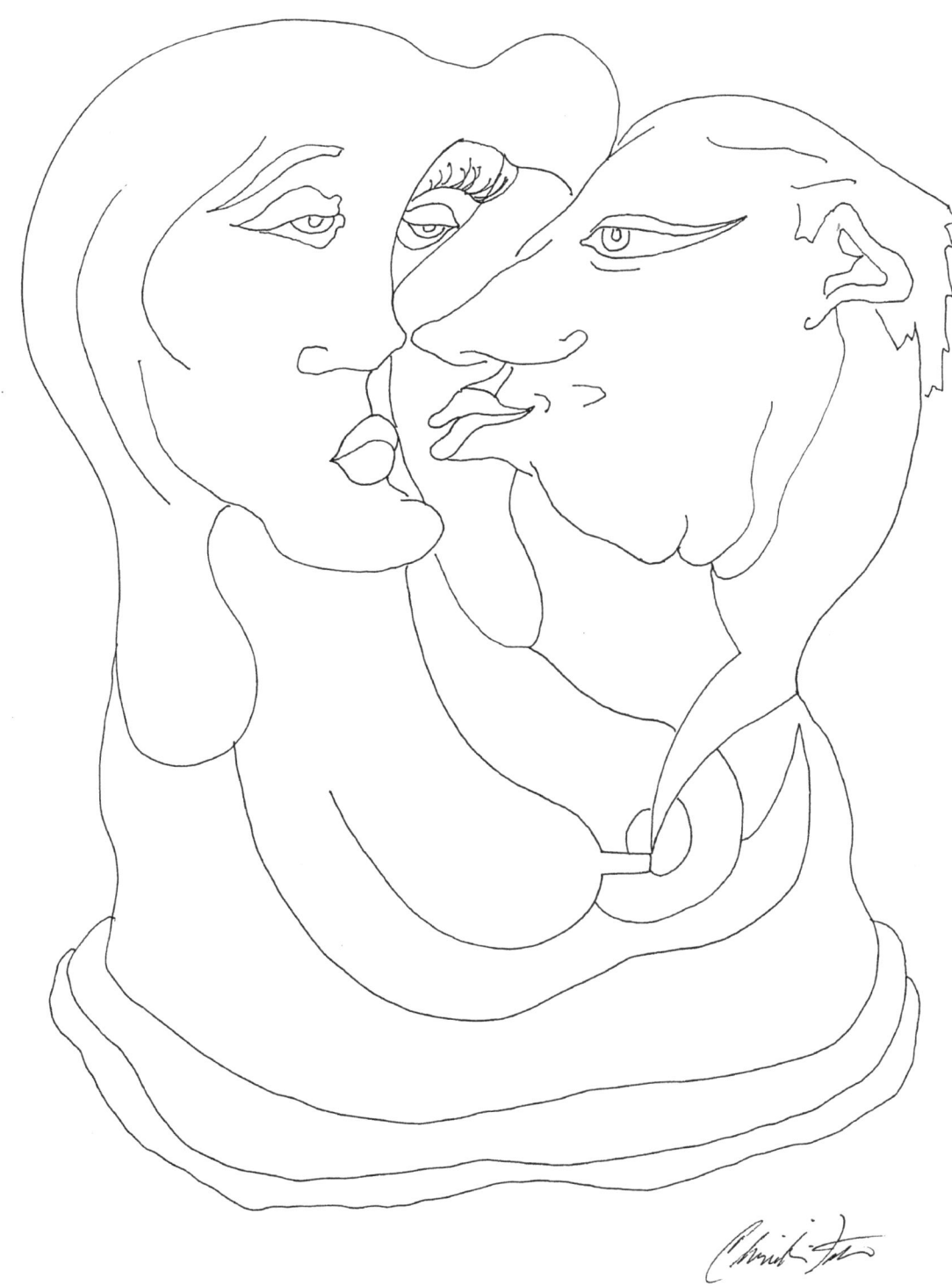

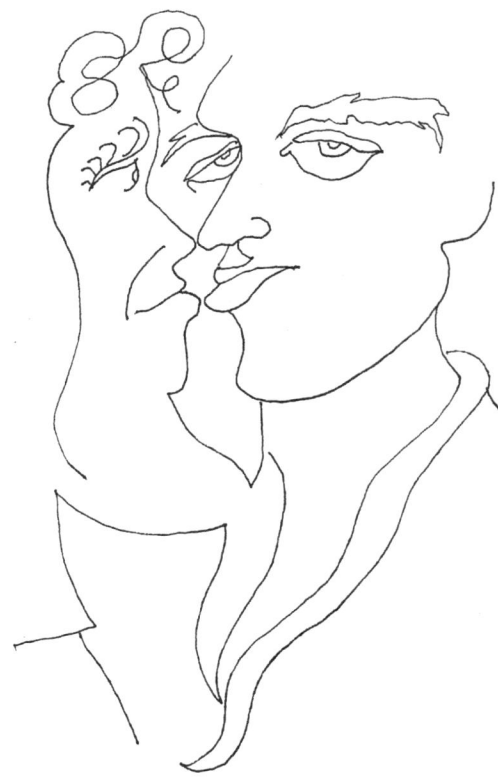

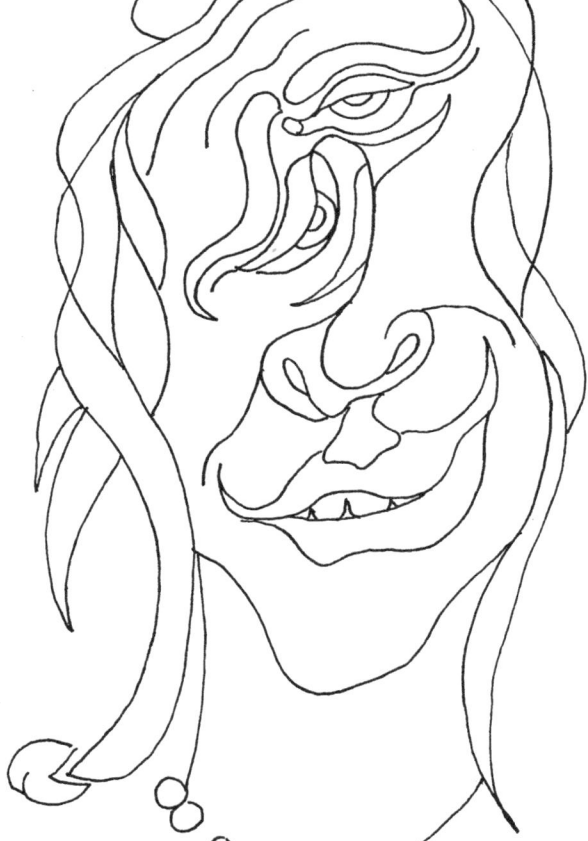

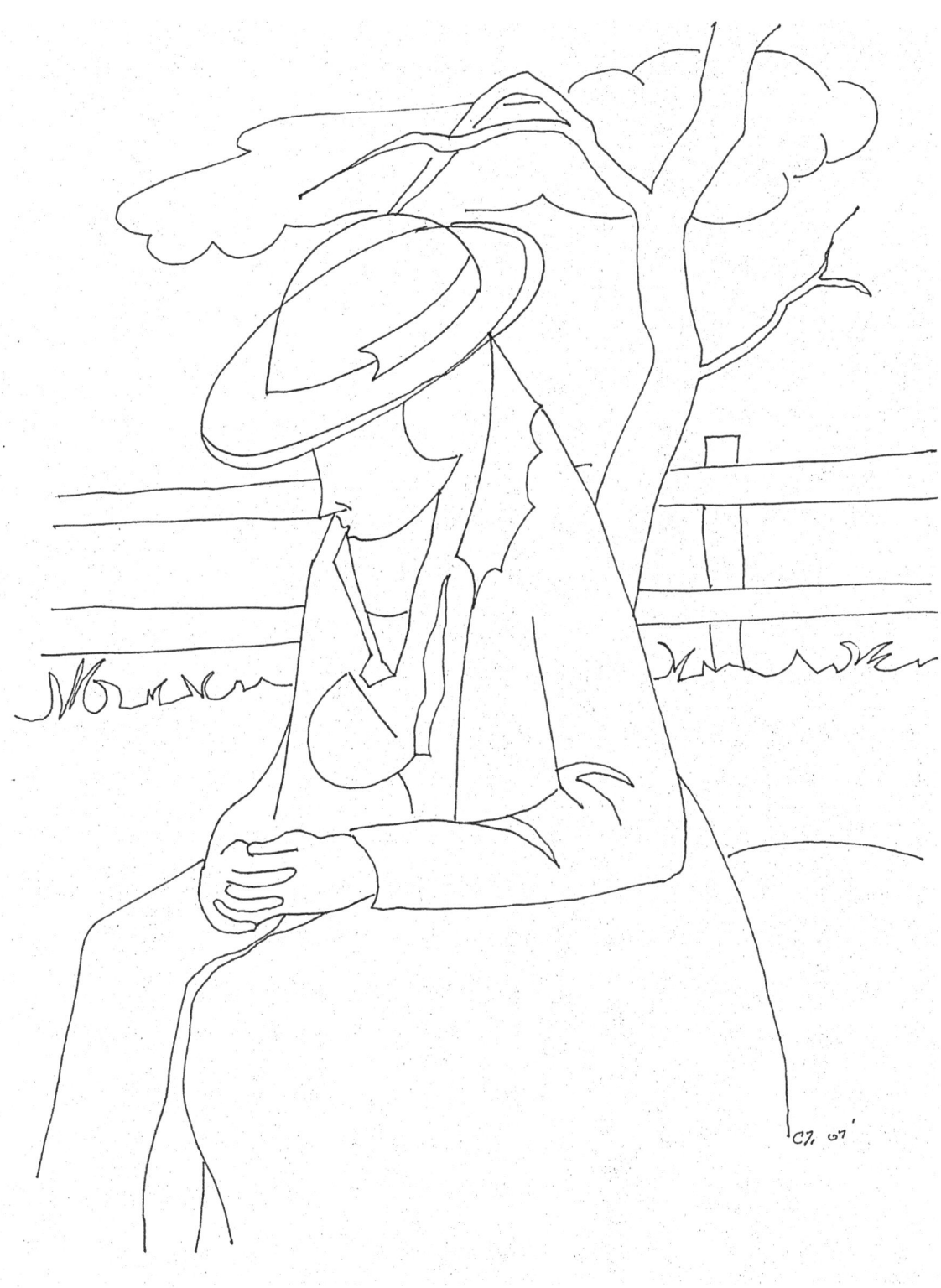

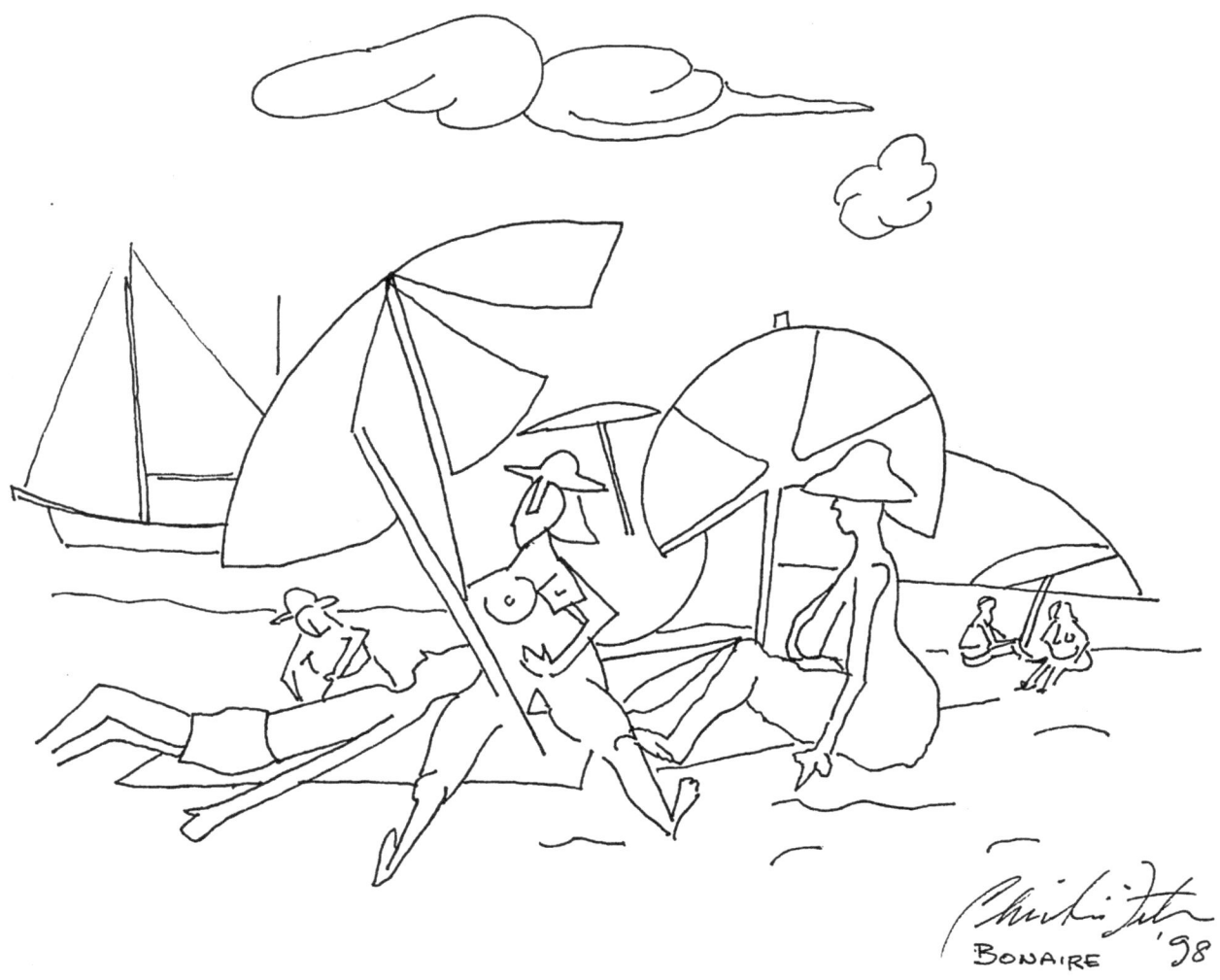

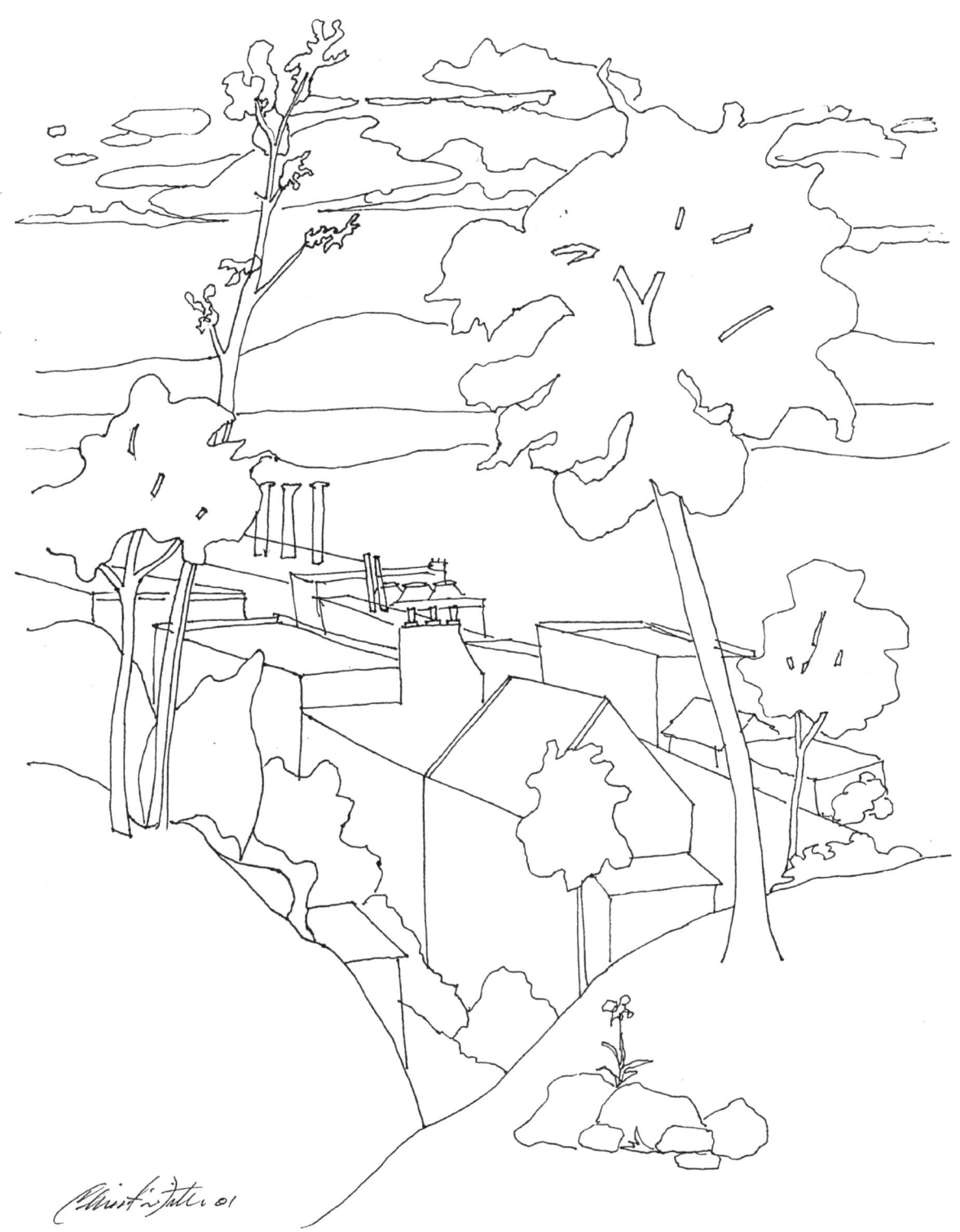

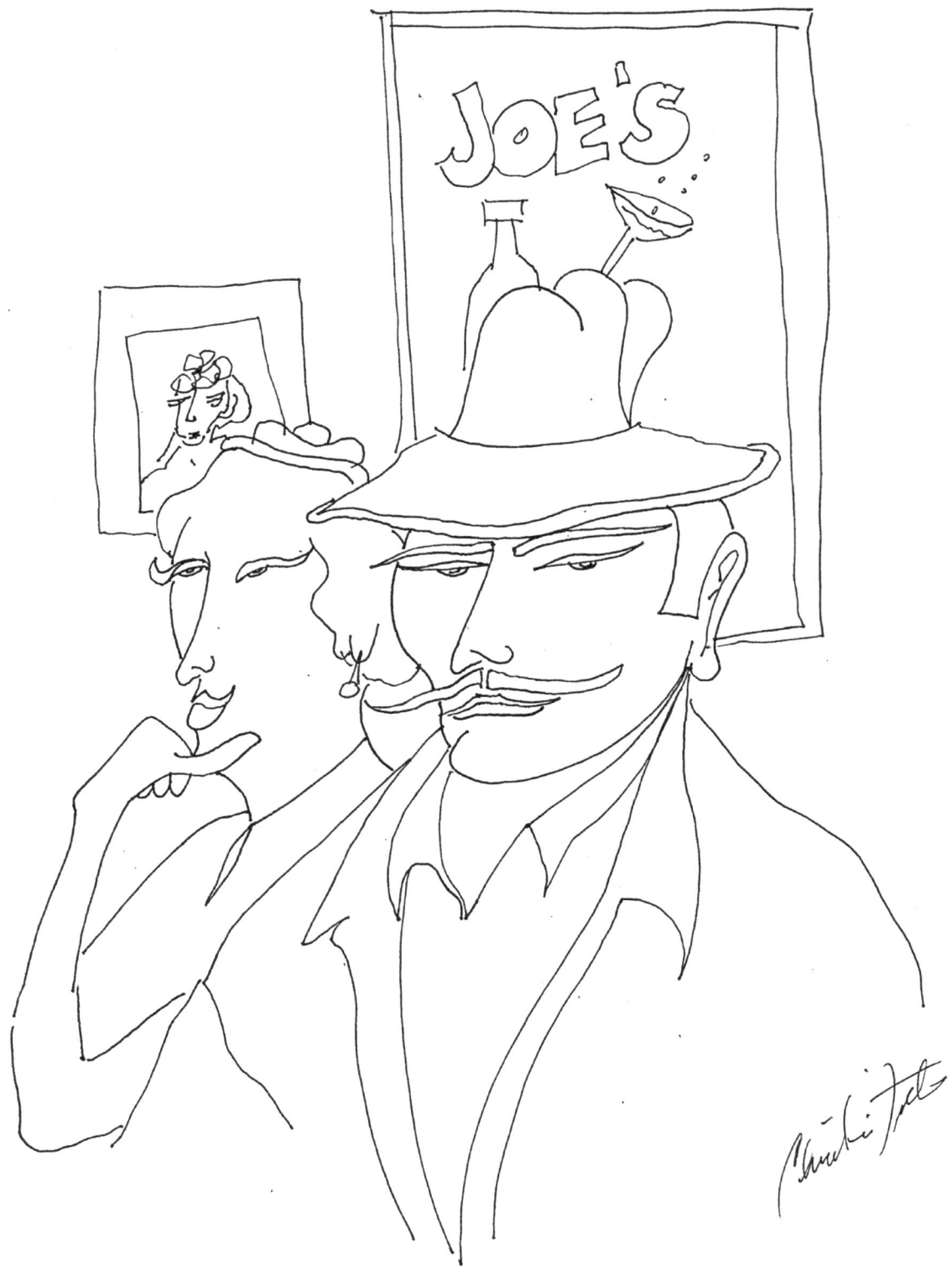

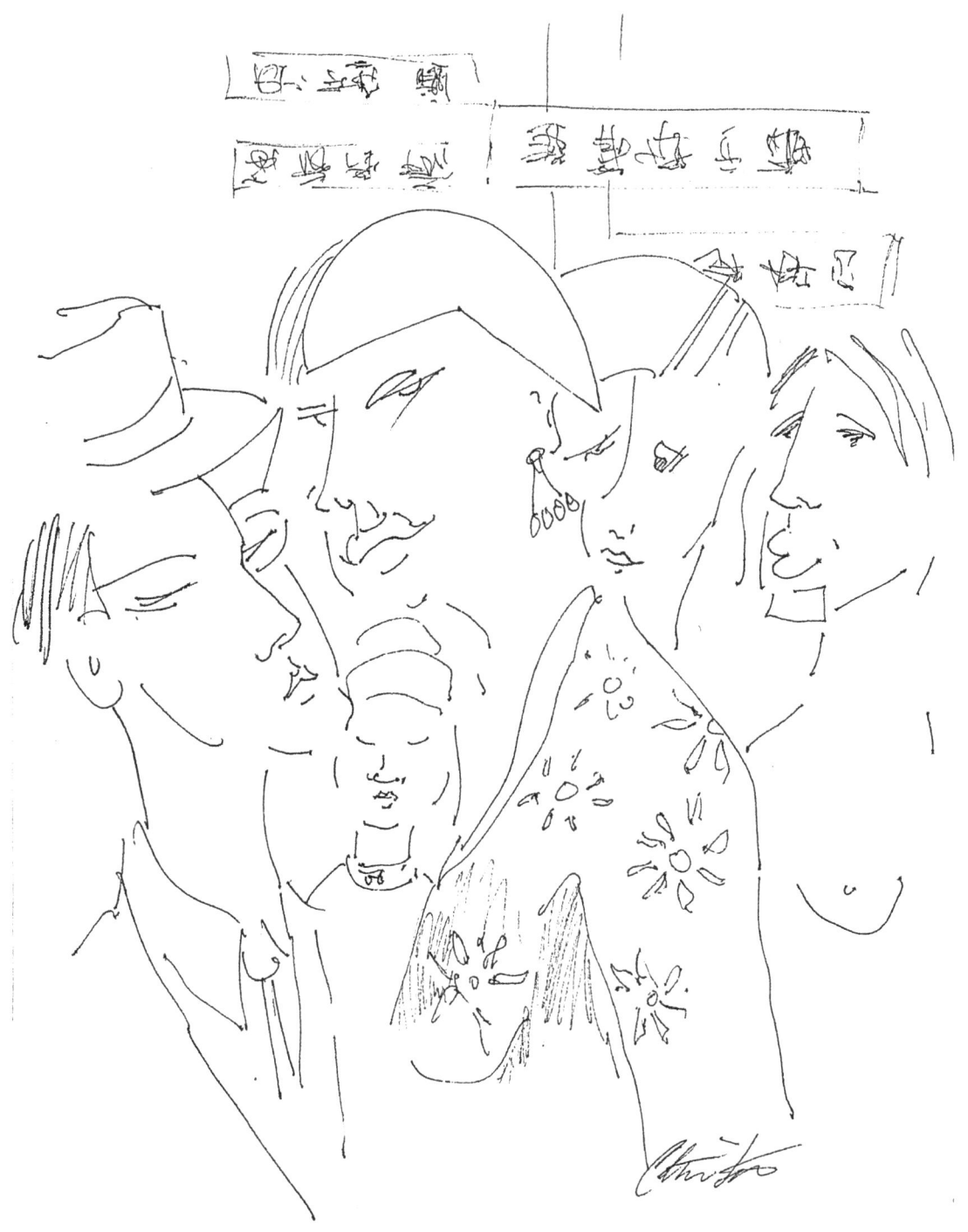

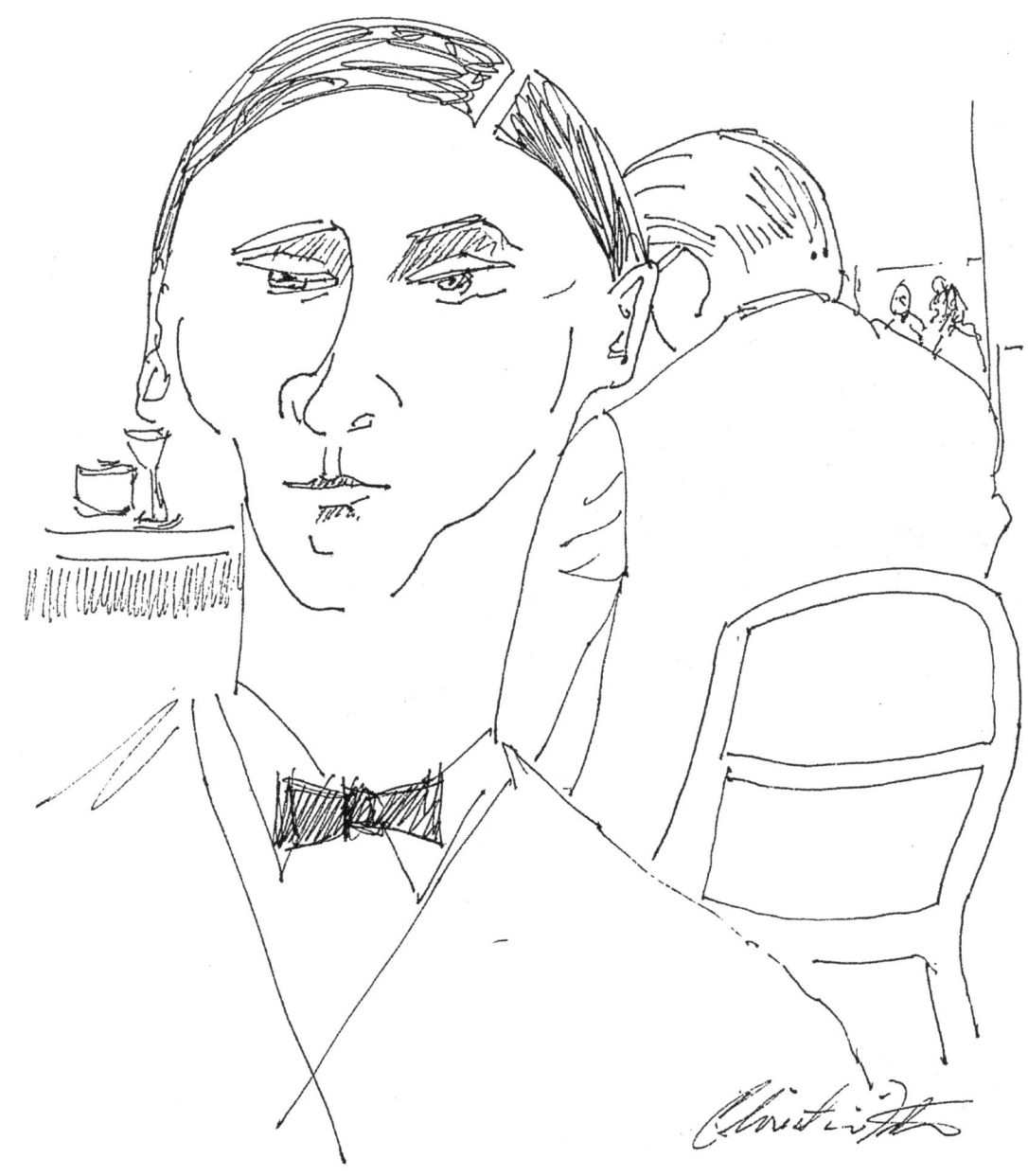

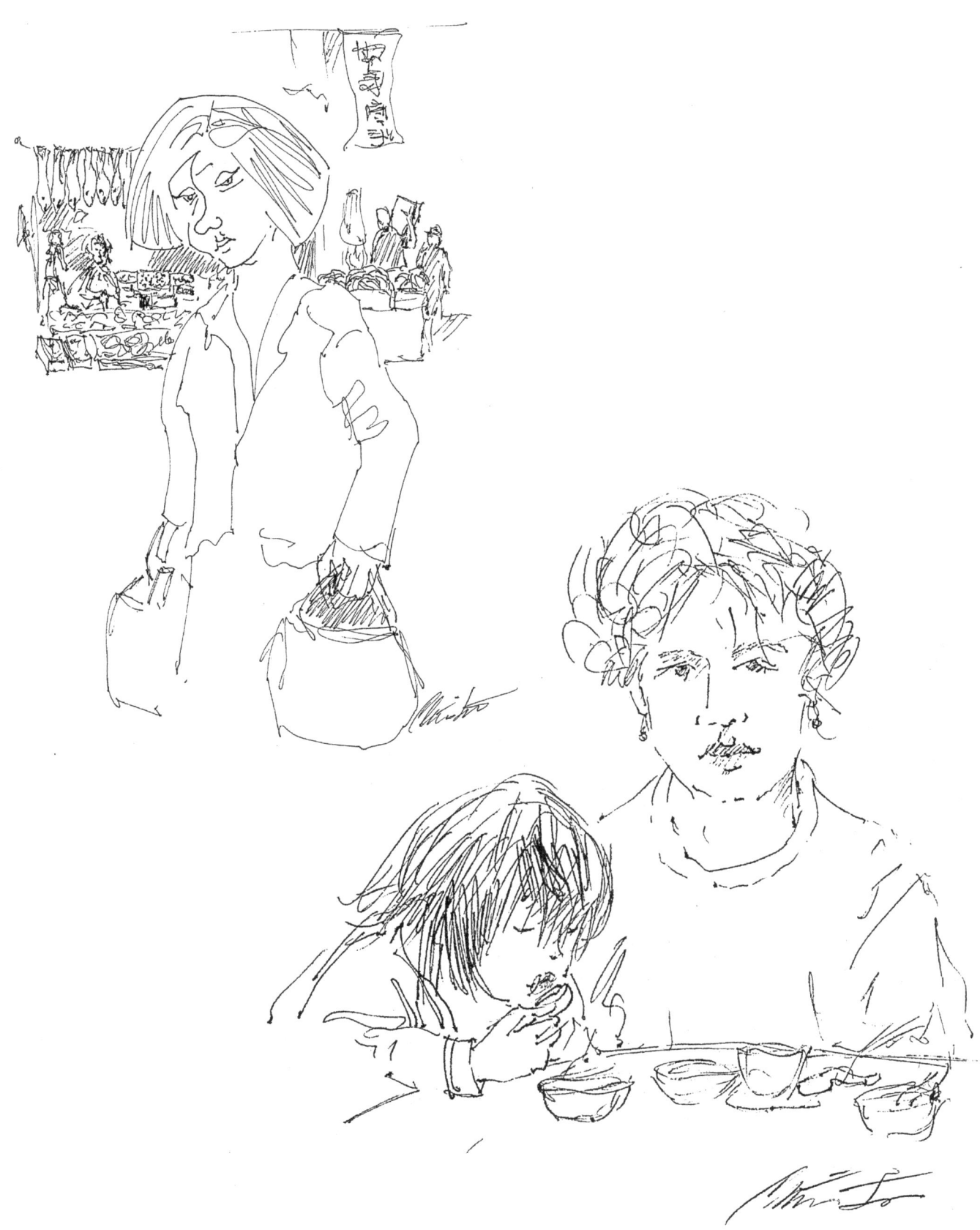

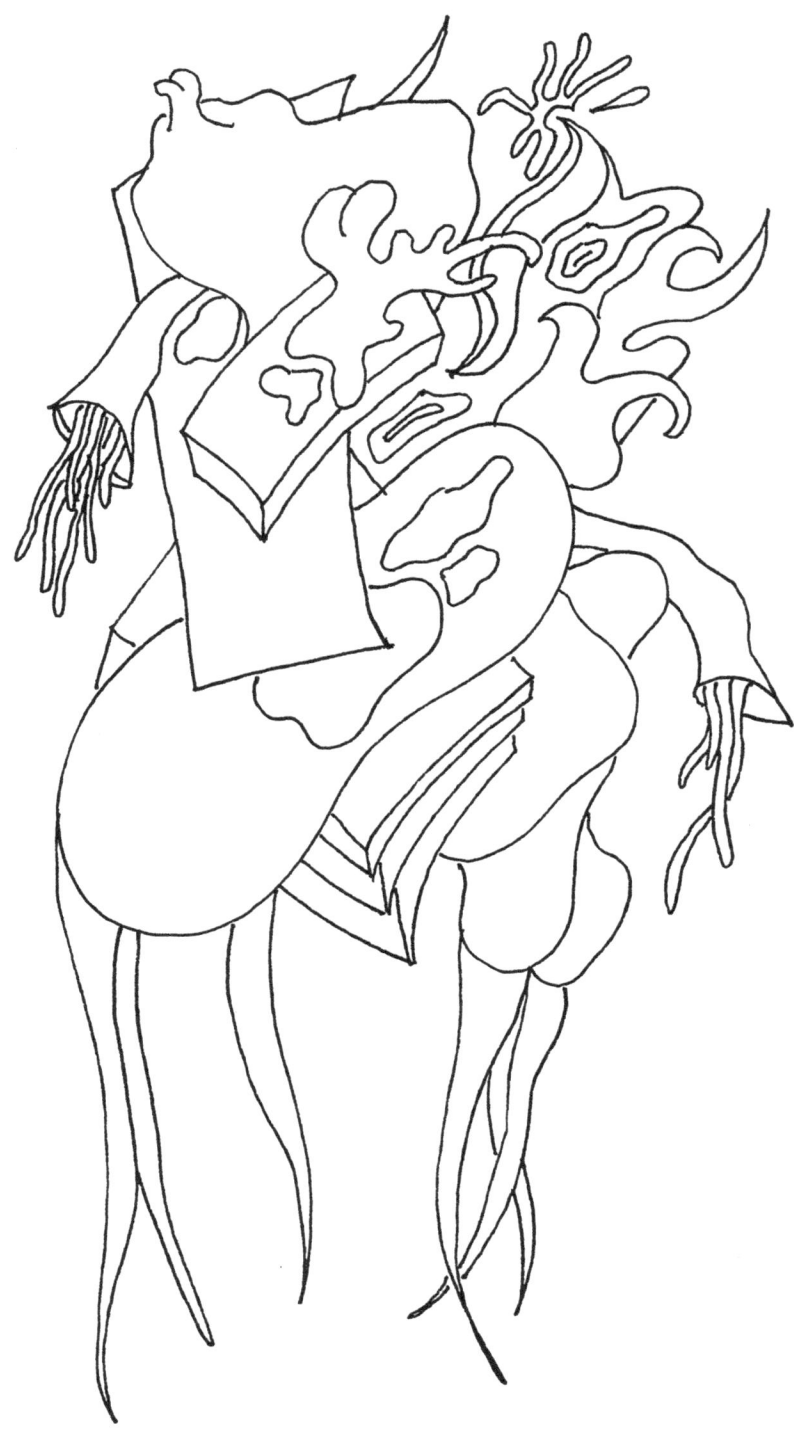

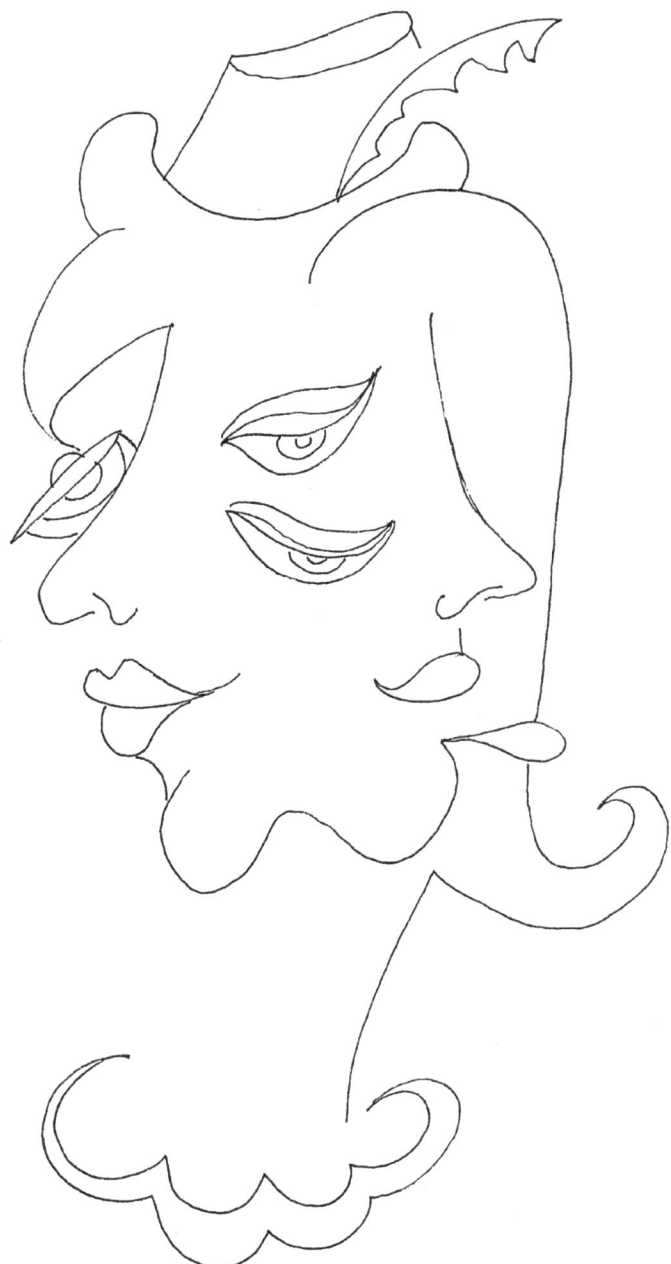

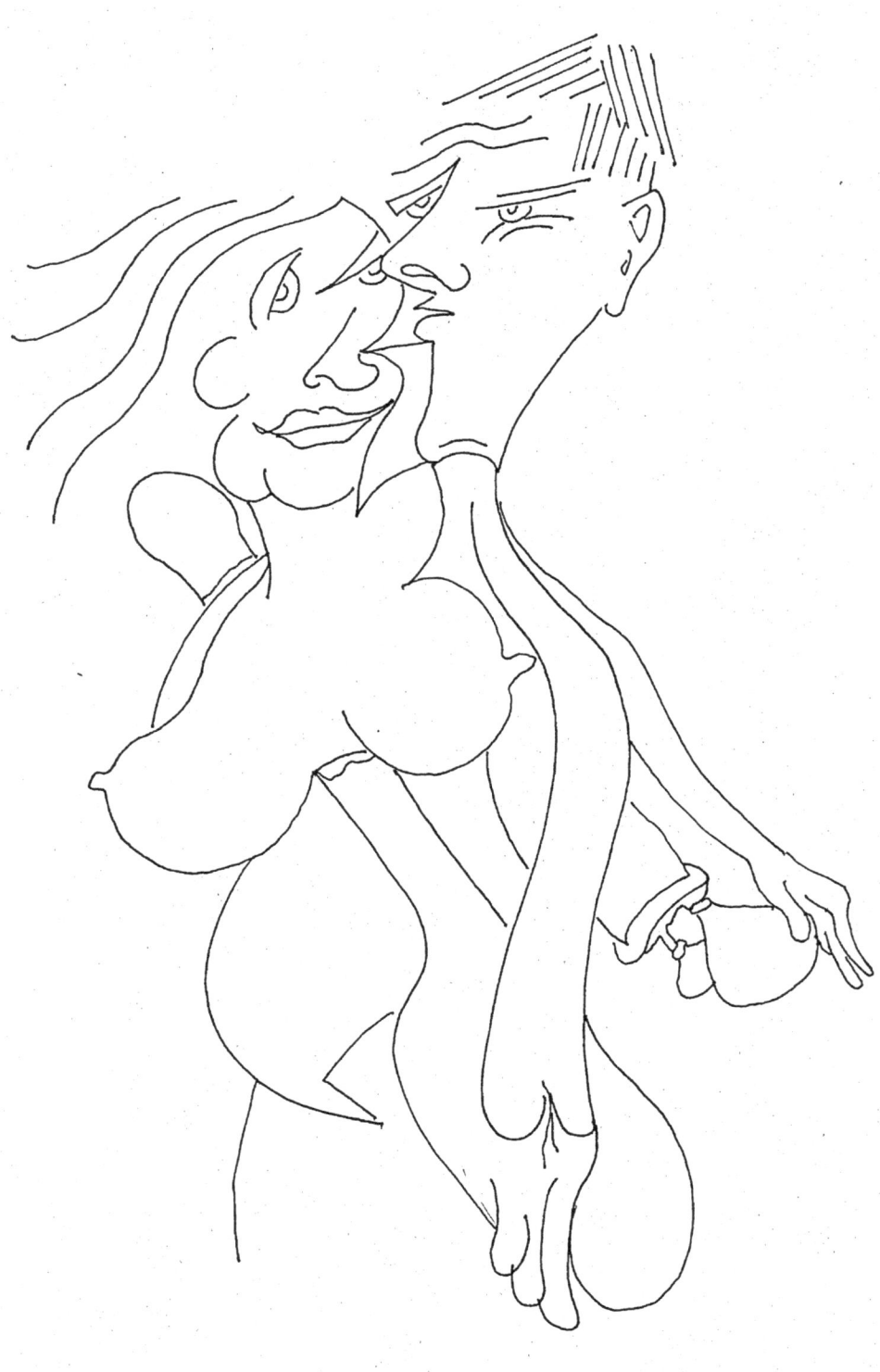

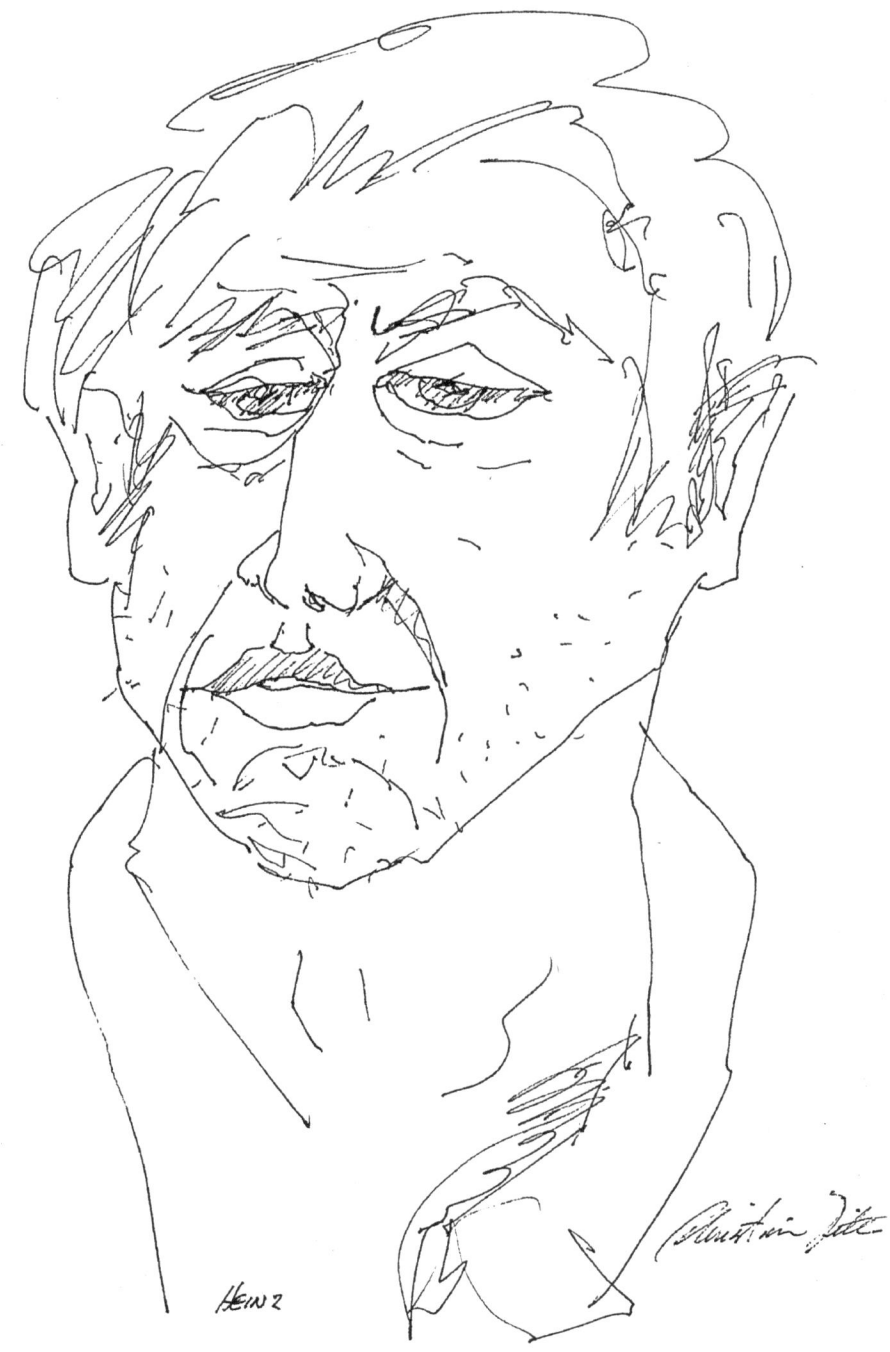

HEINZ

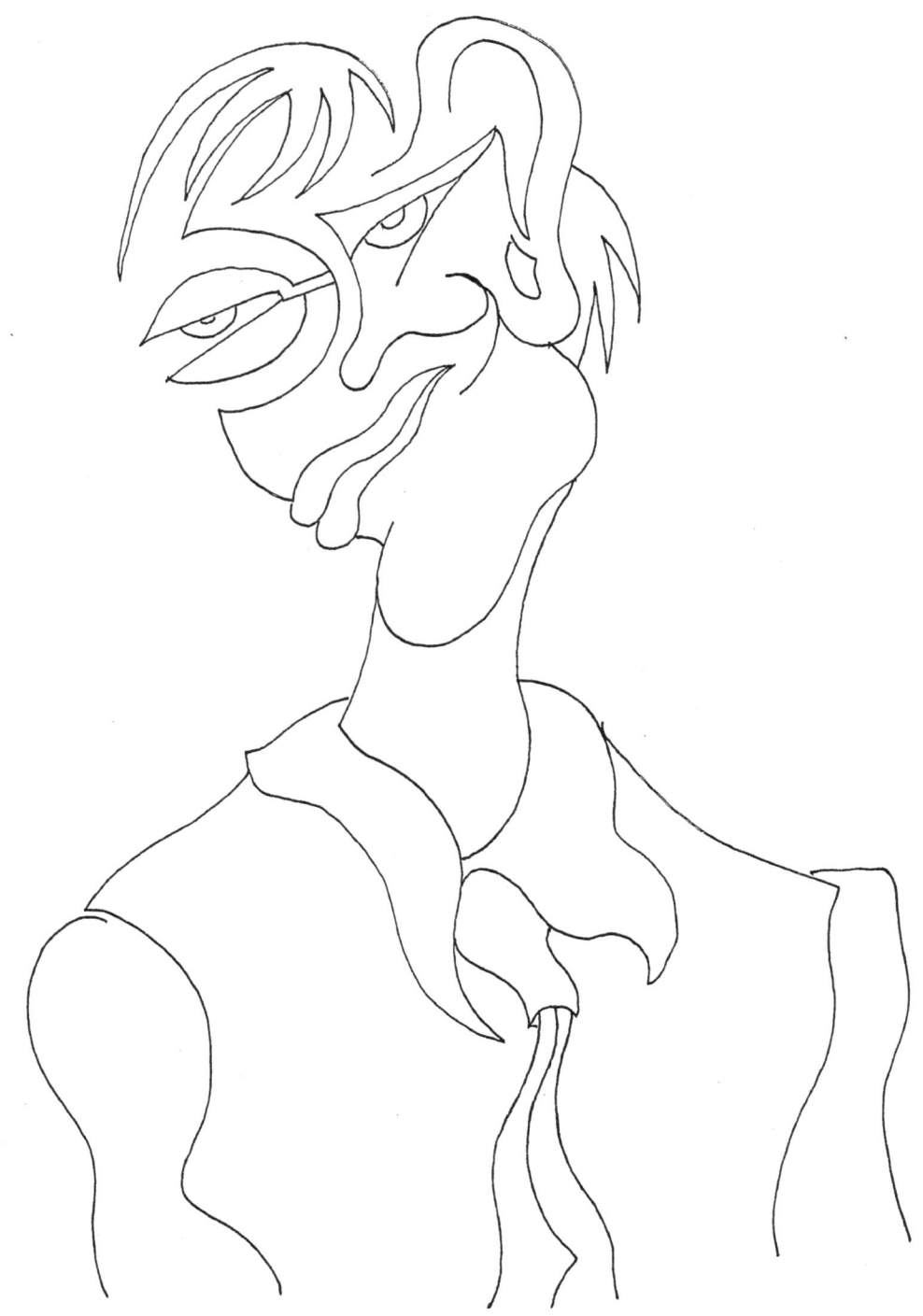

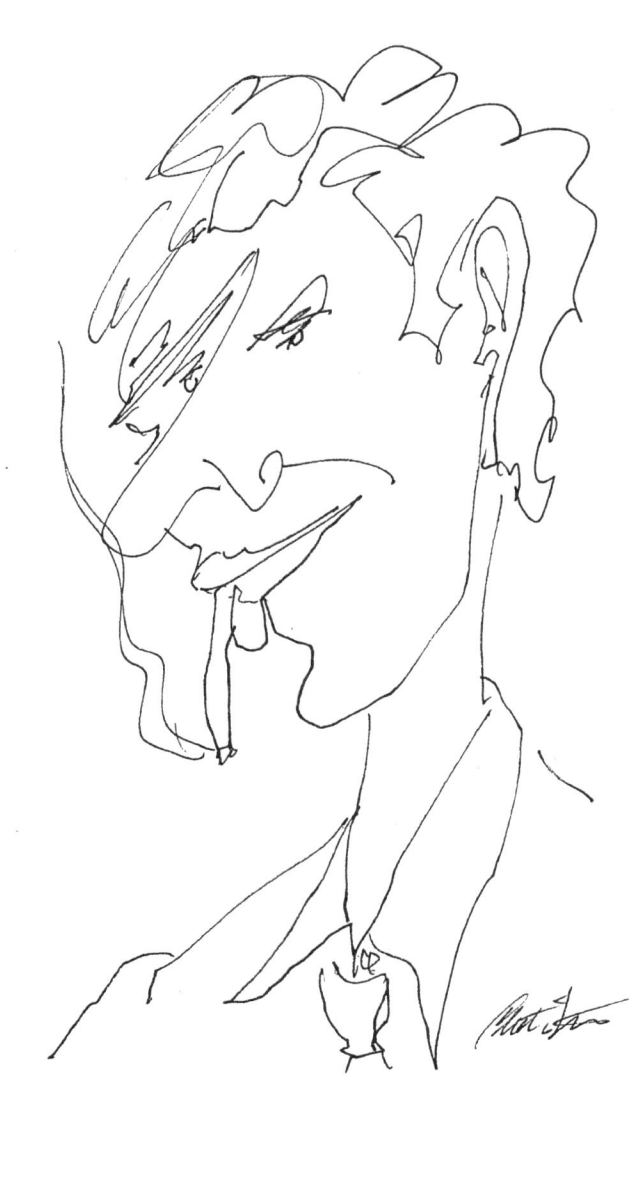

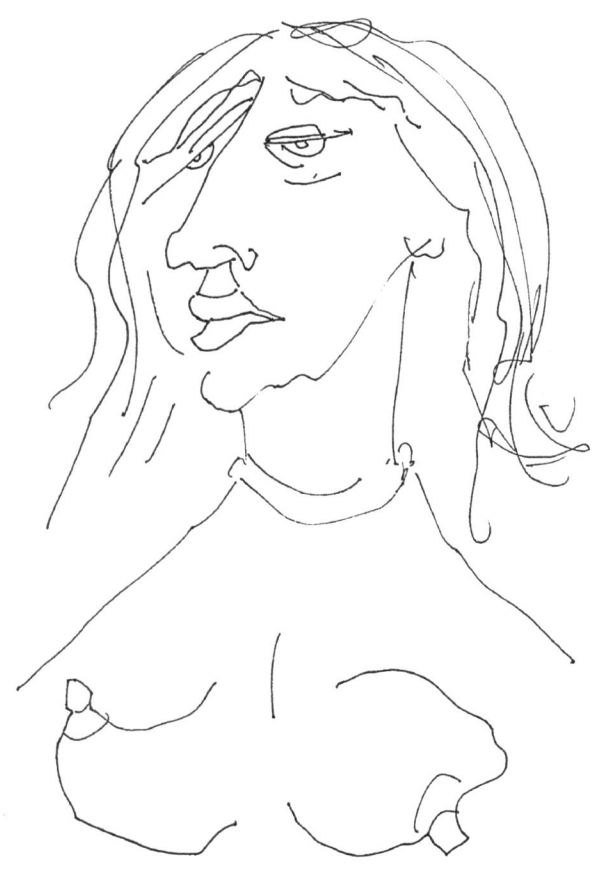

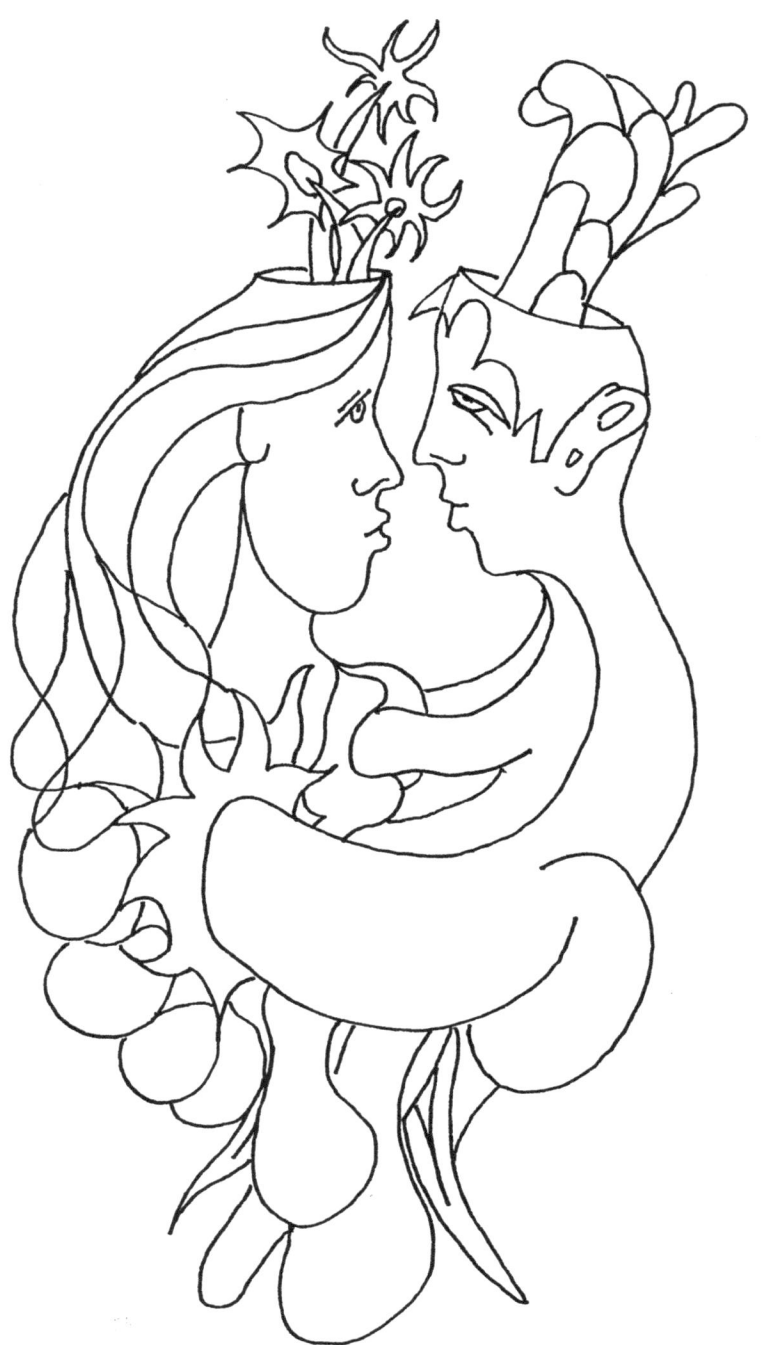

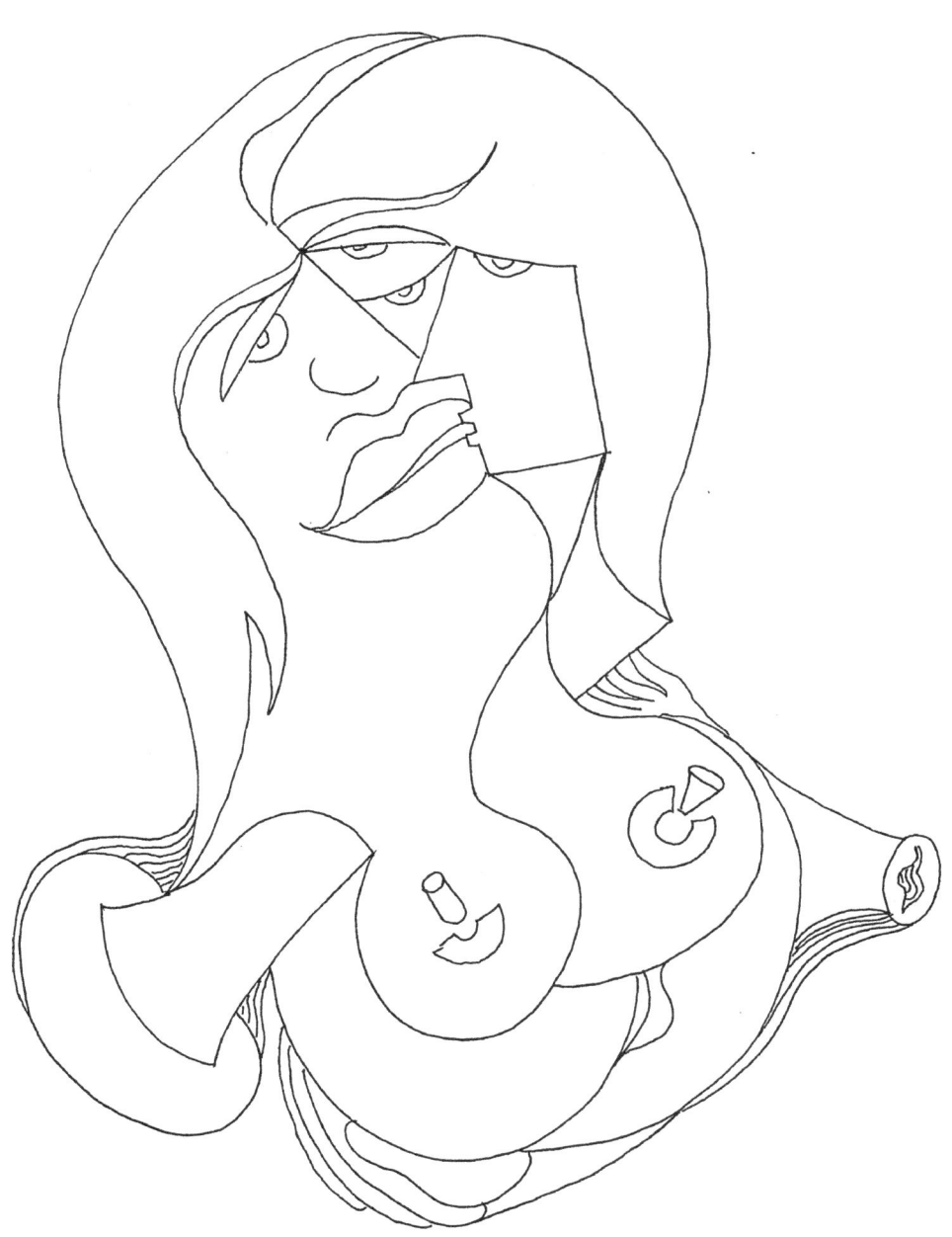

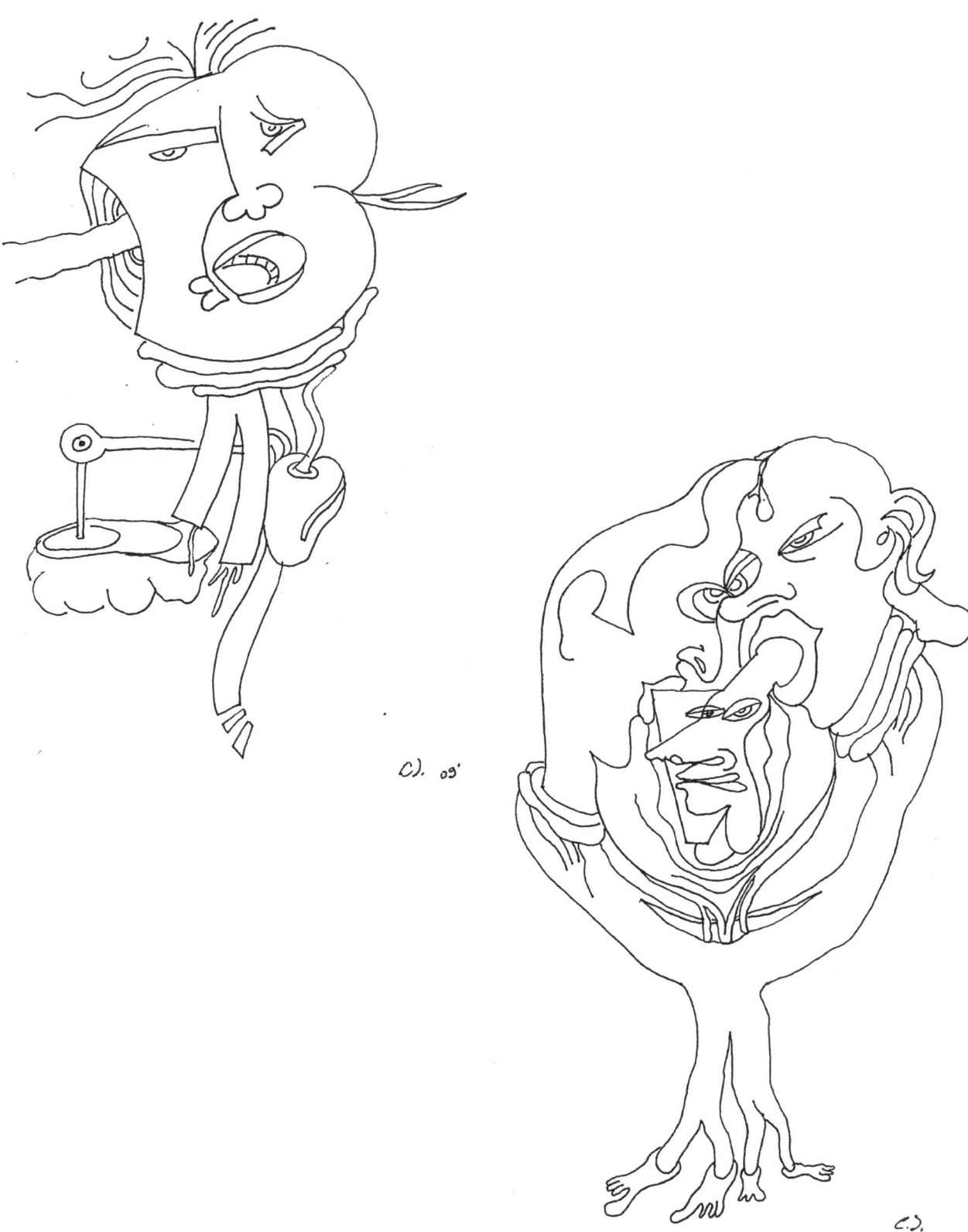

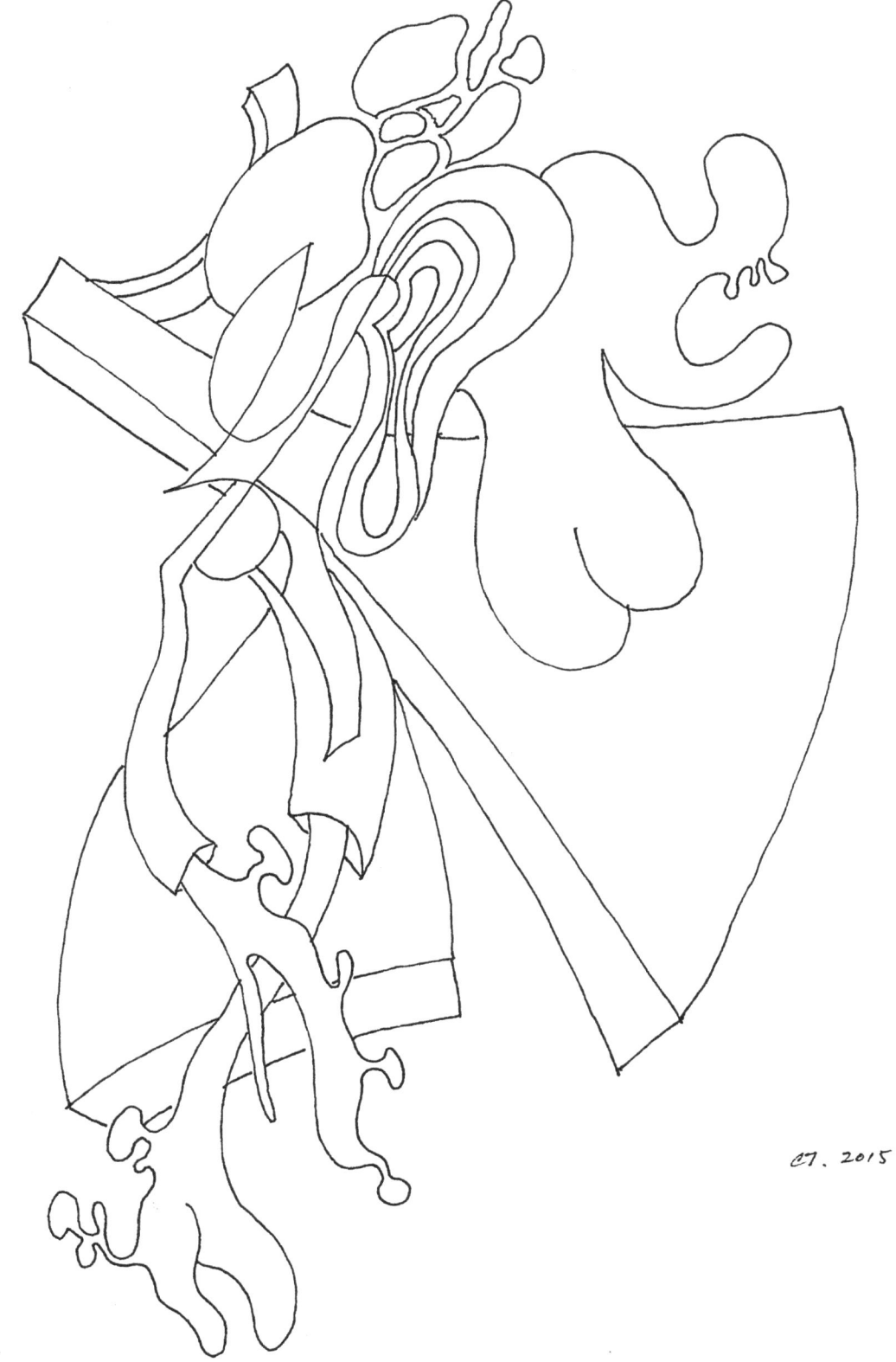

CT. 2015

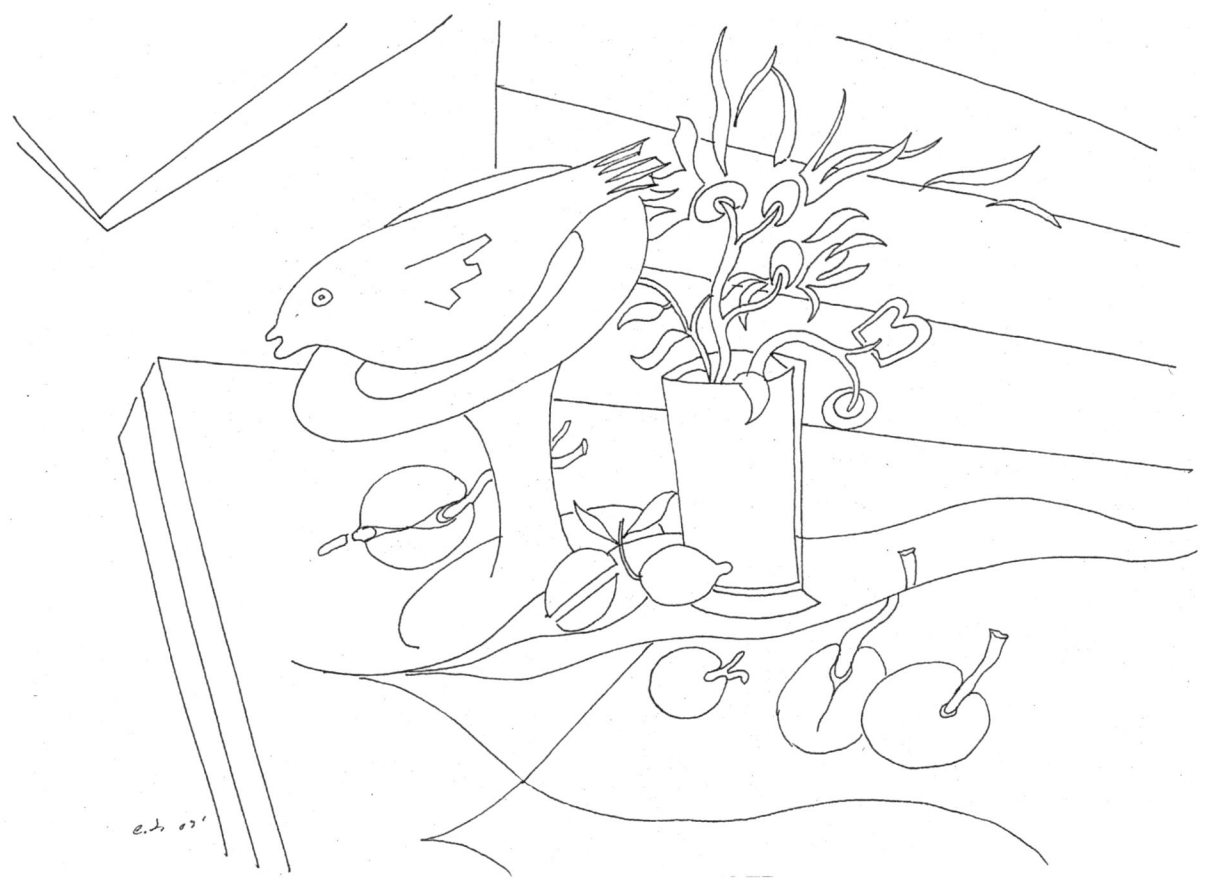

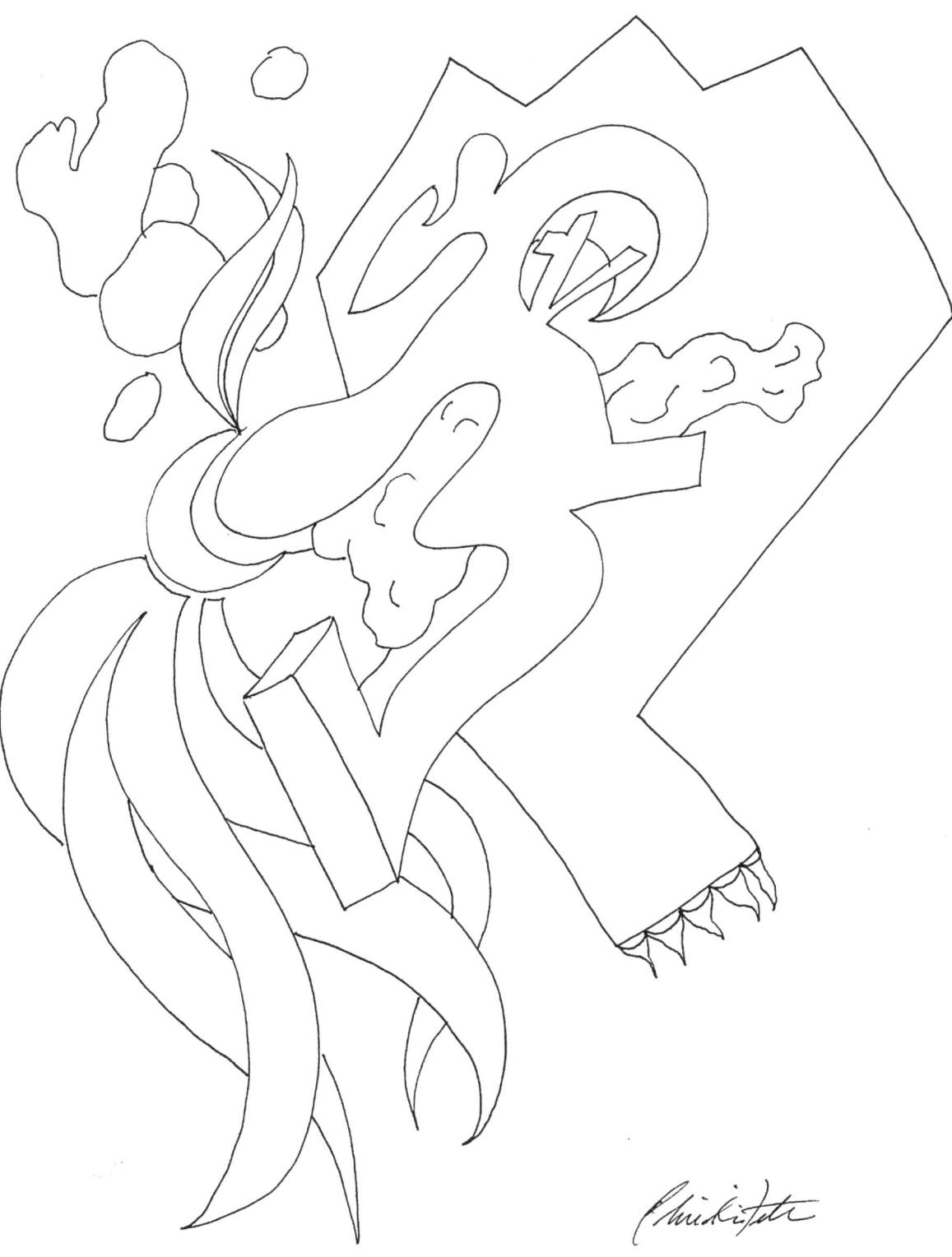

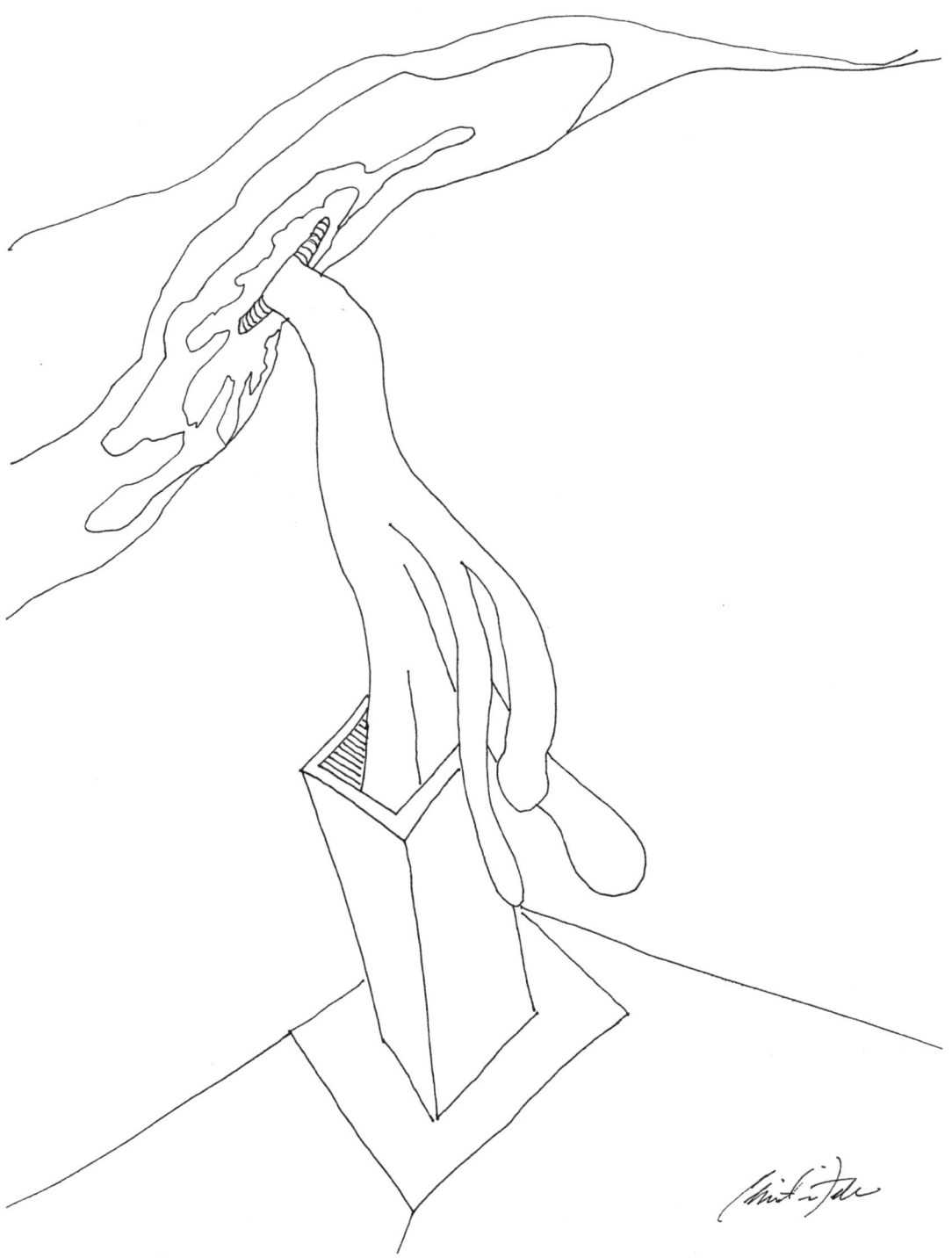

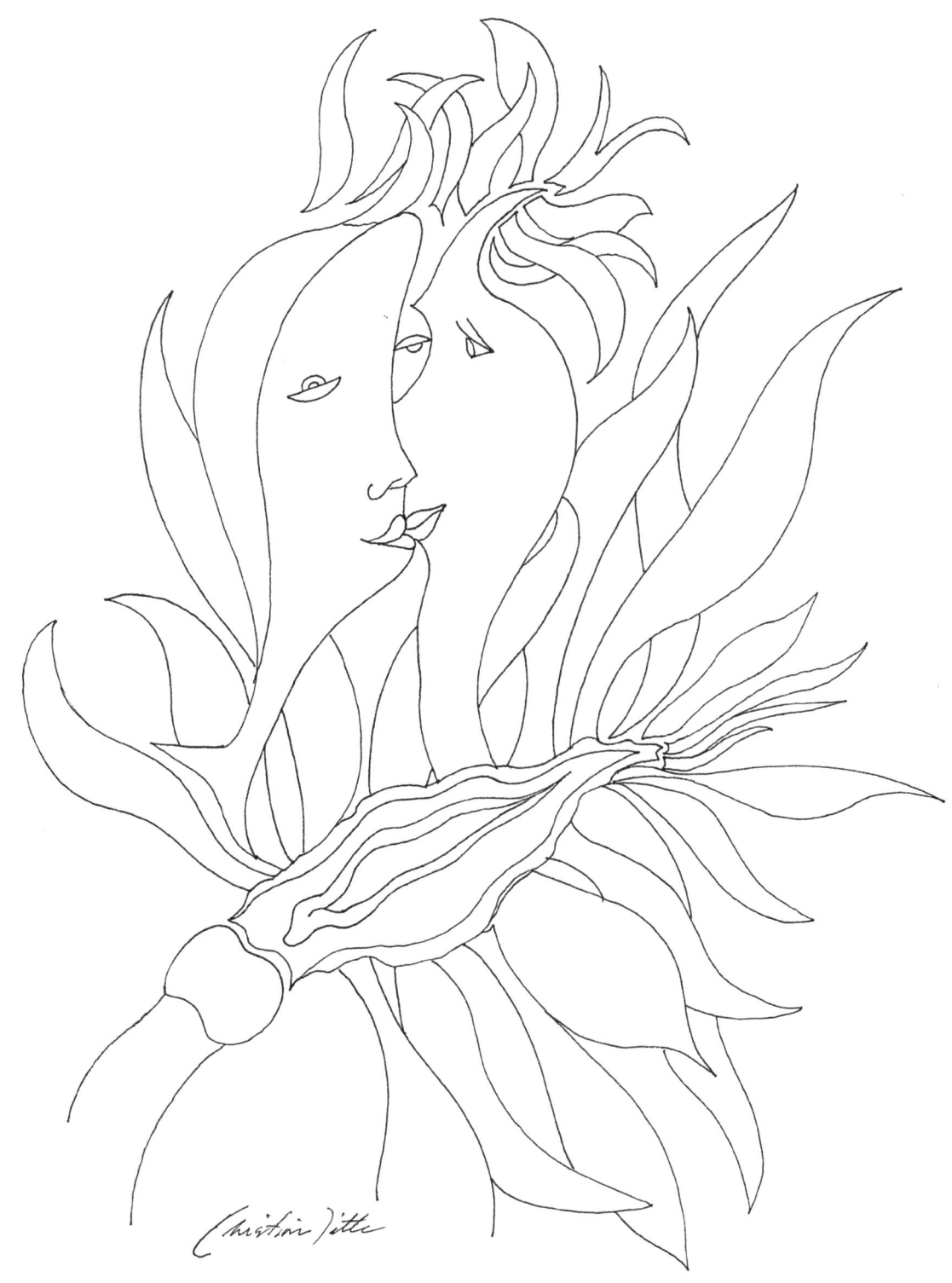

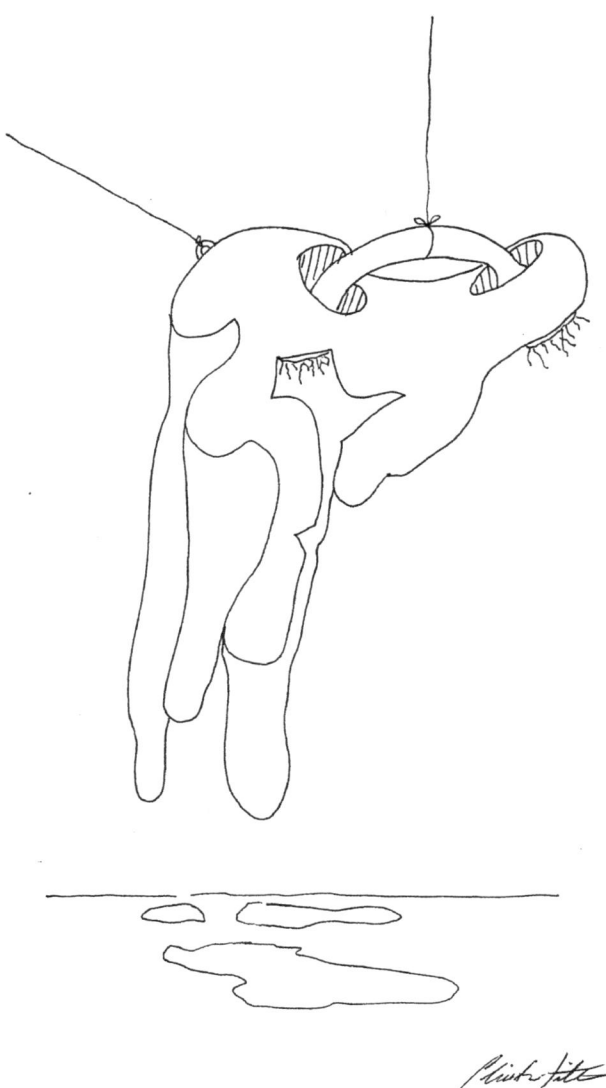

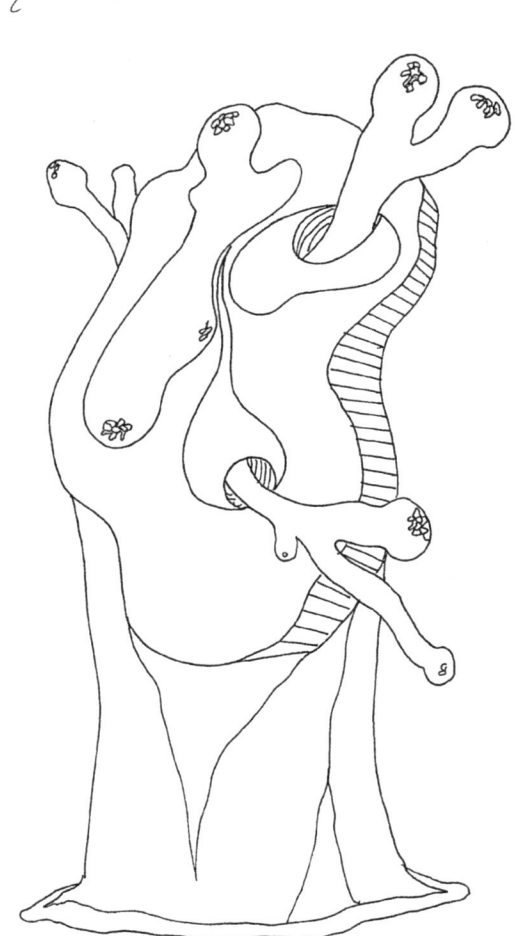

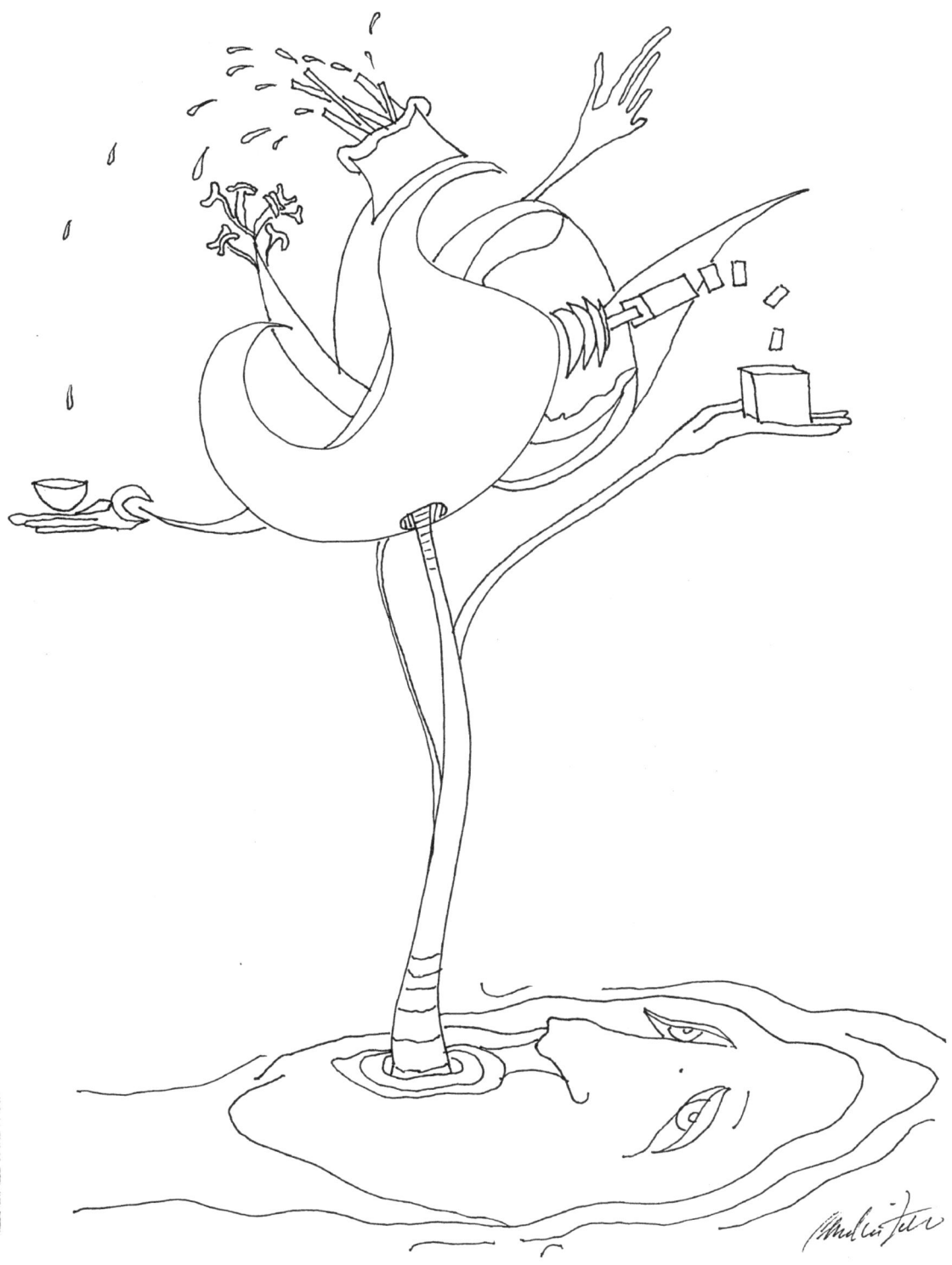

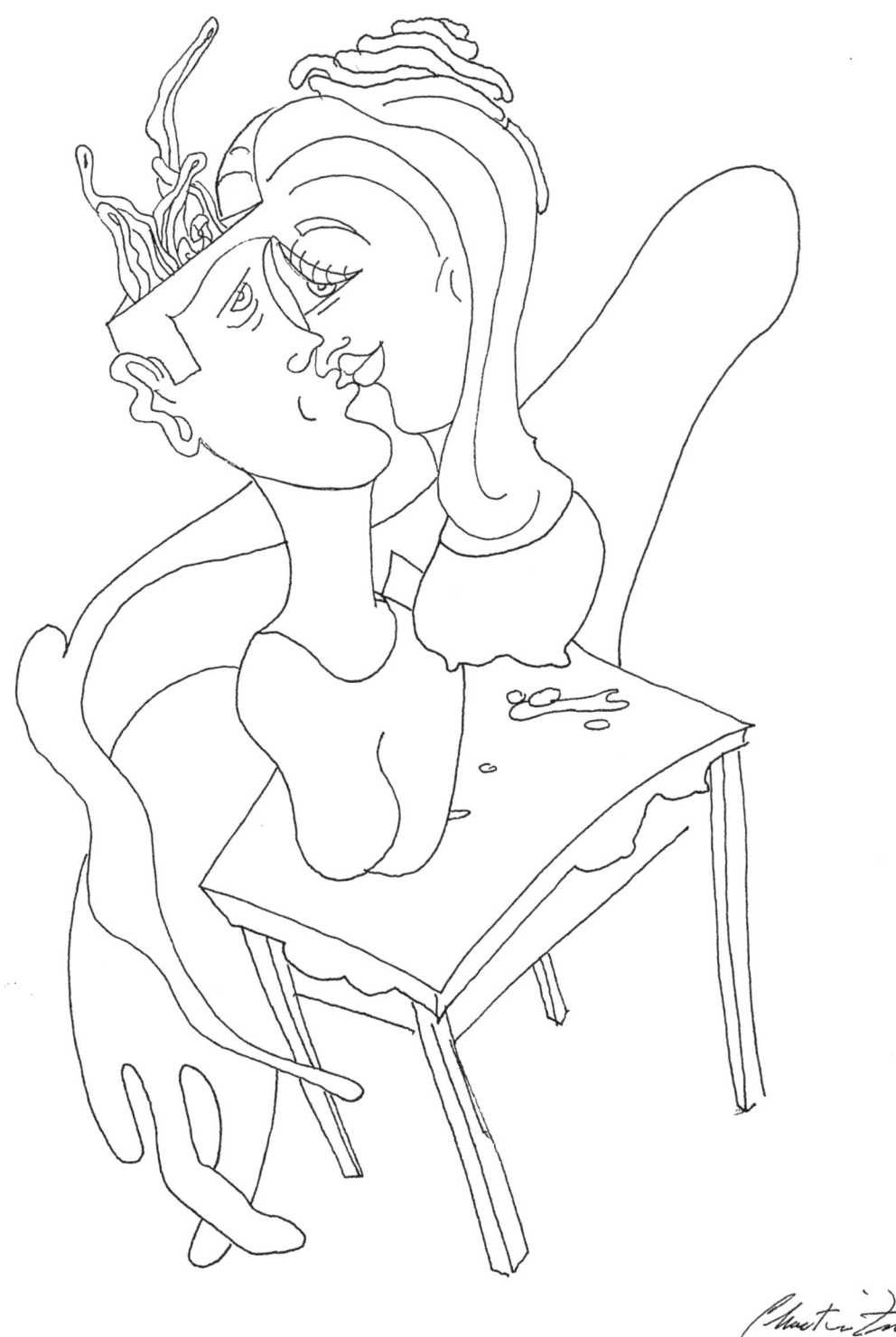

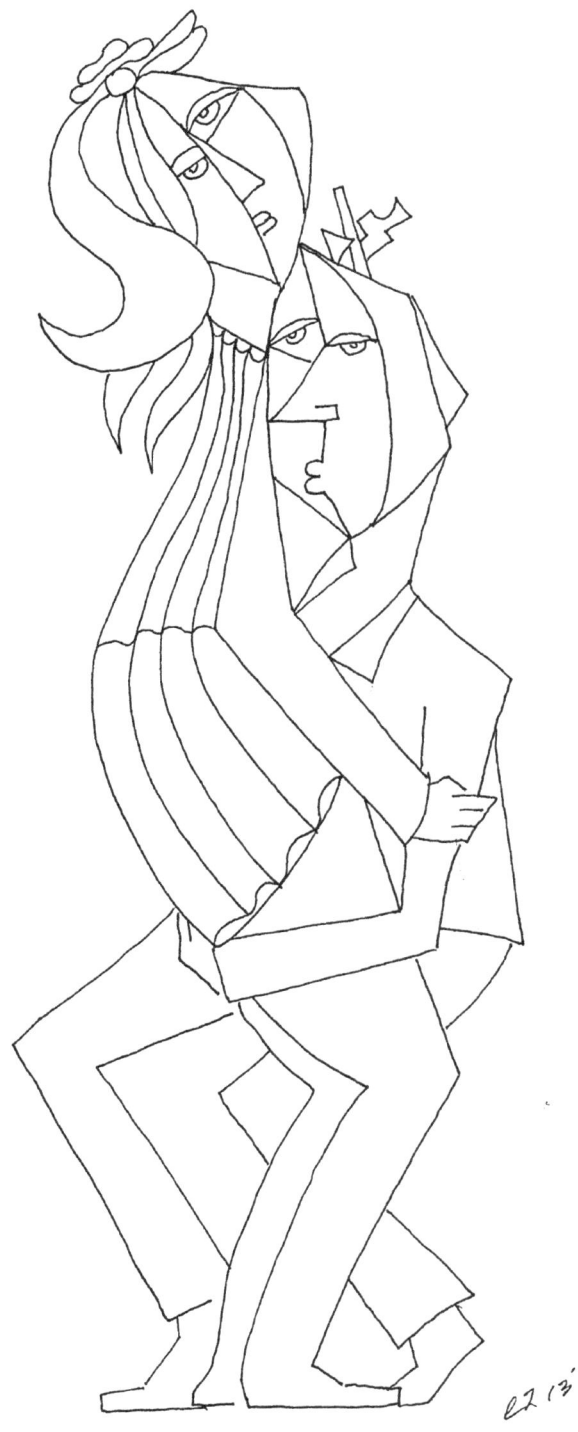

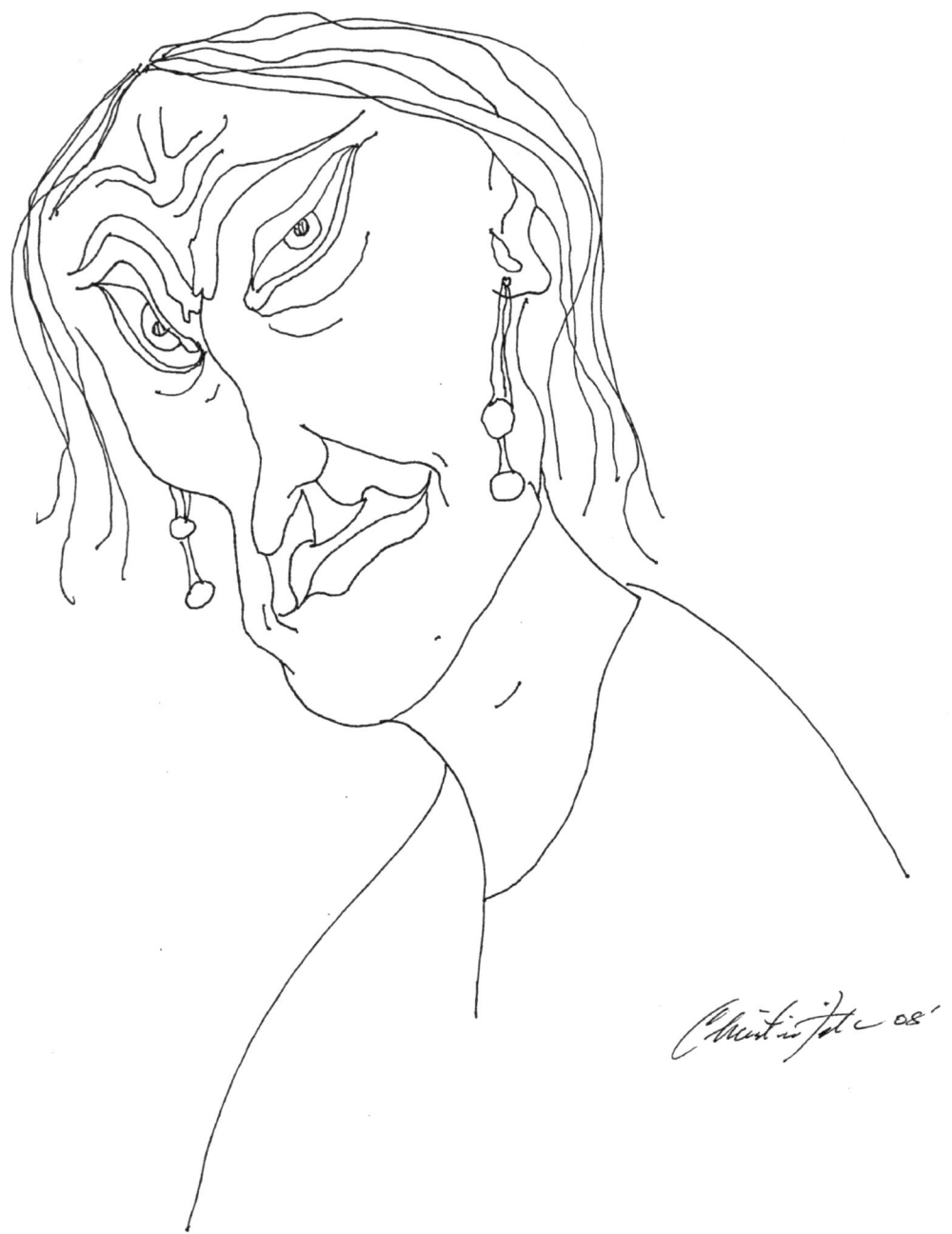

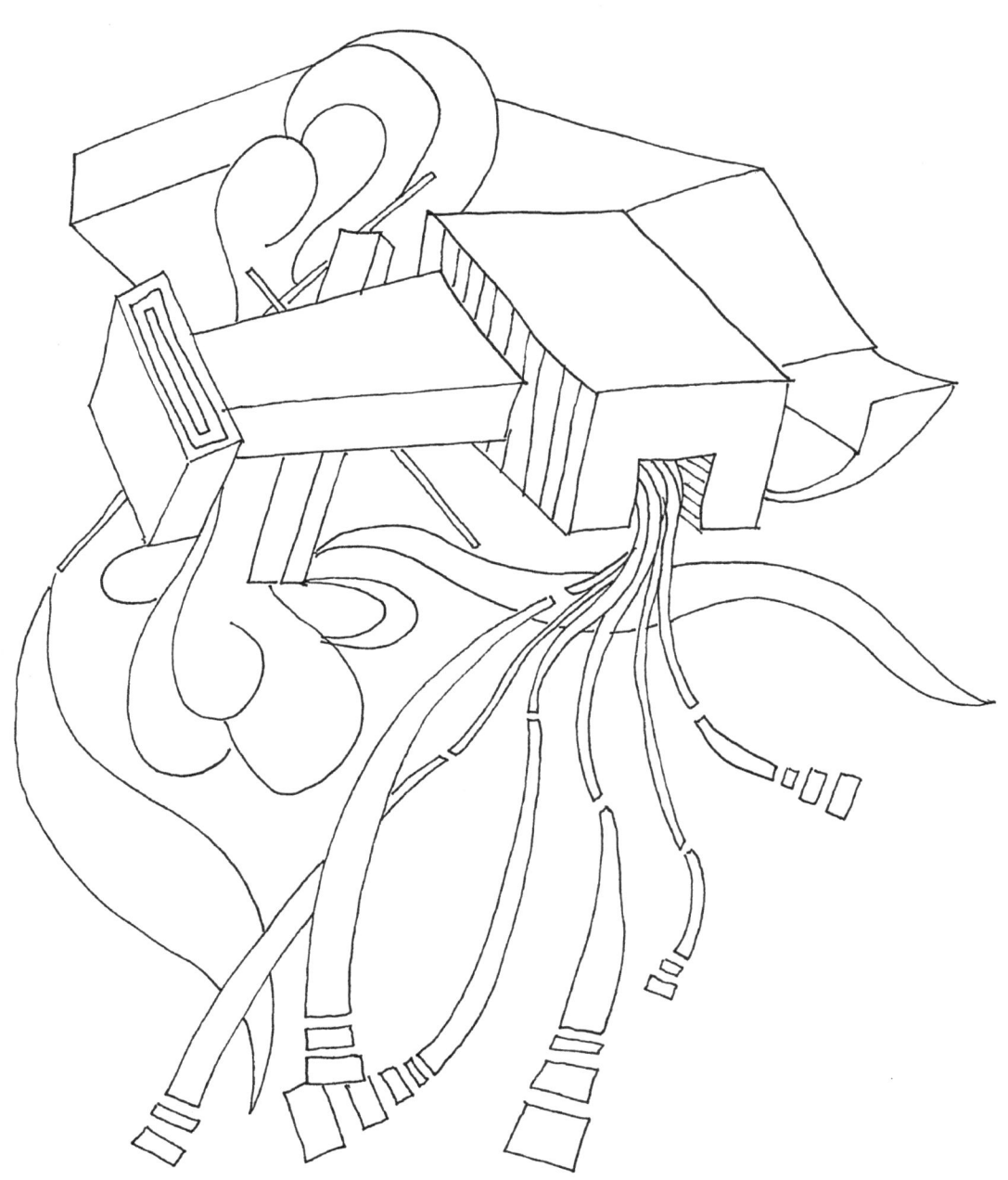

CI 2015

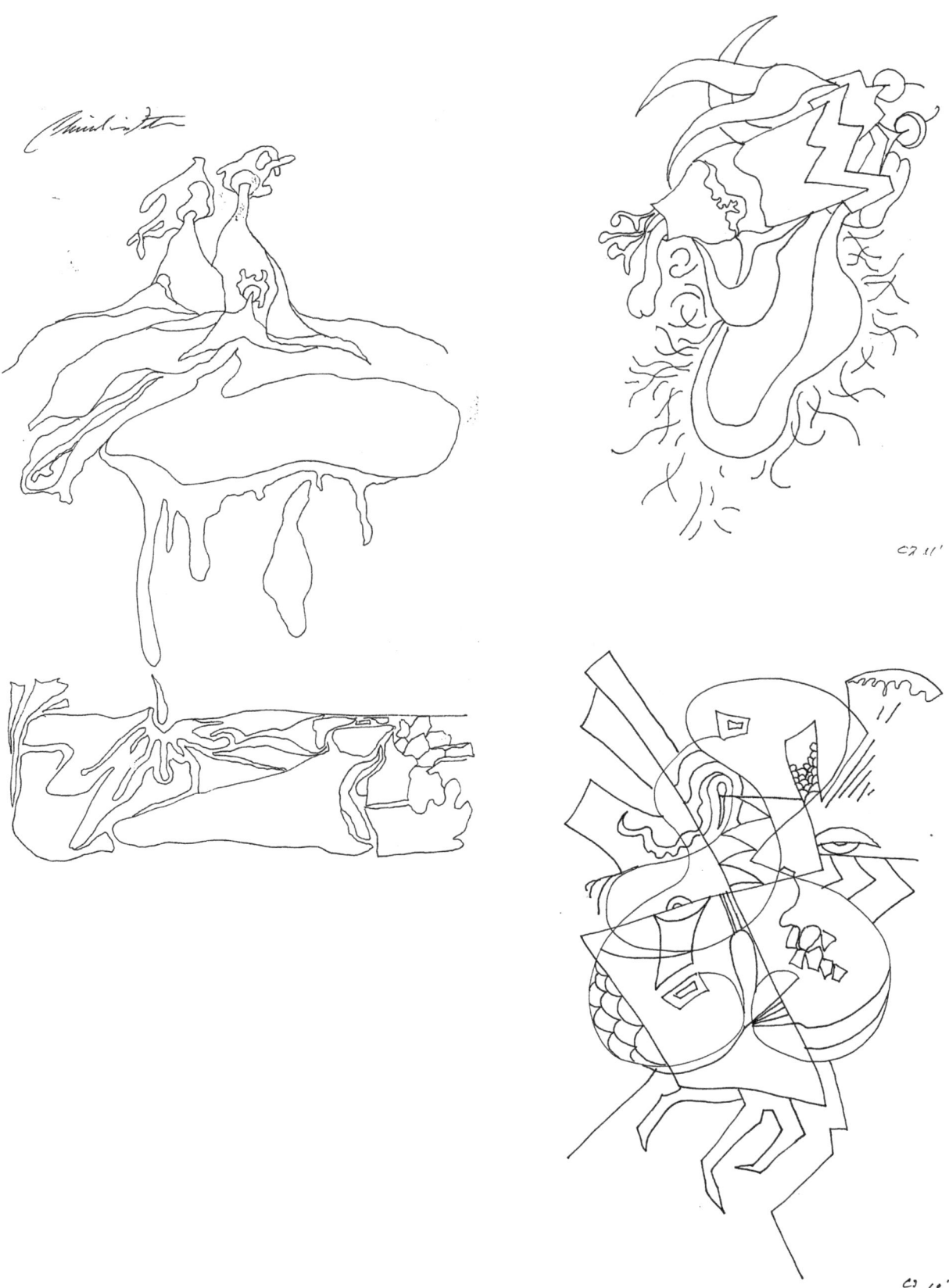

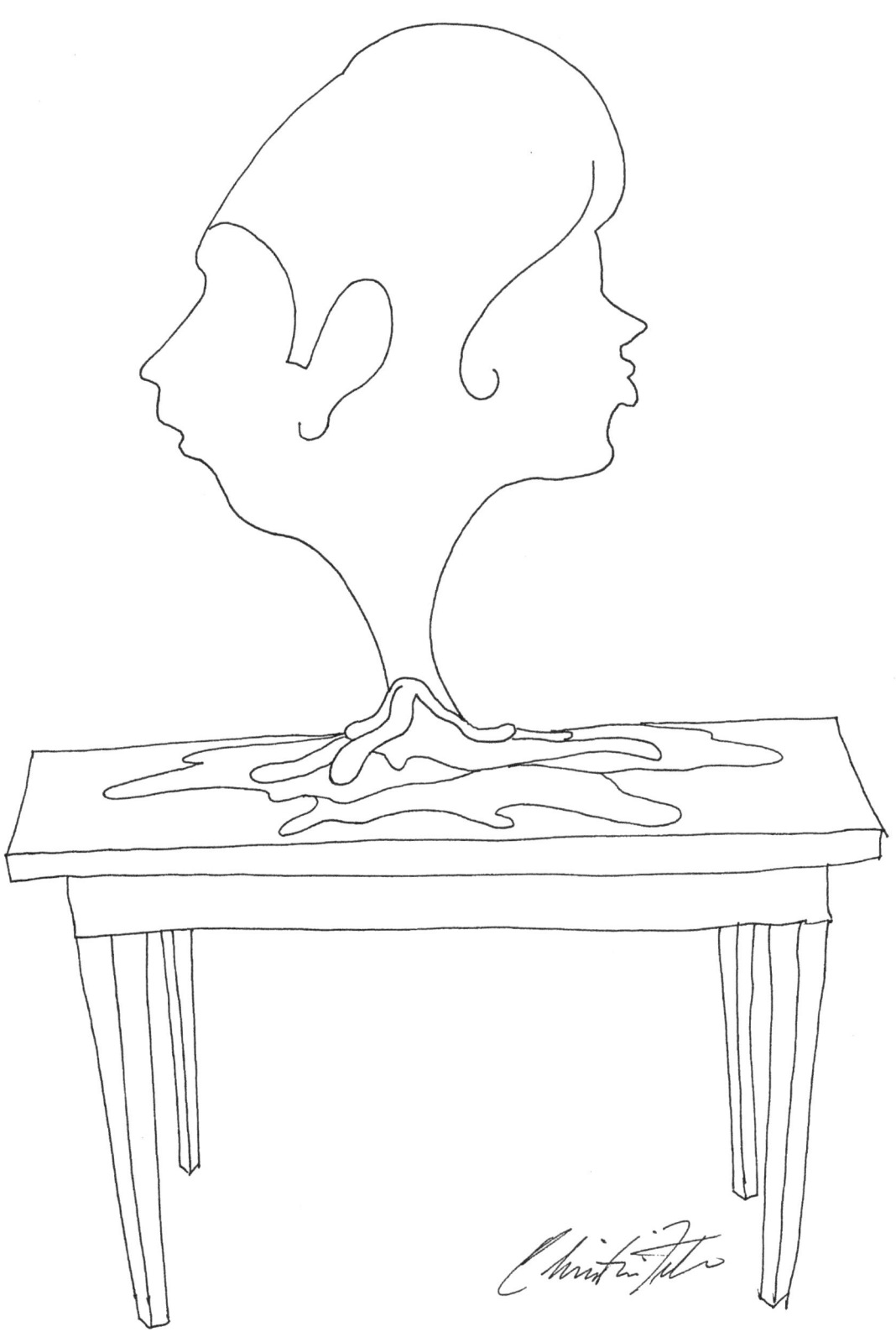

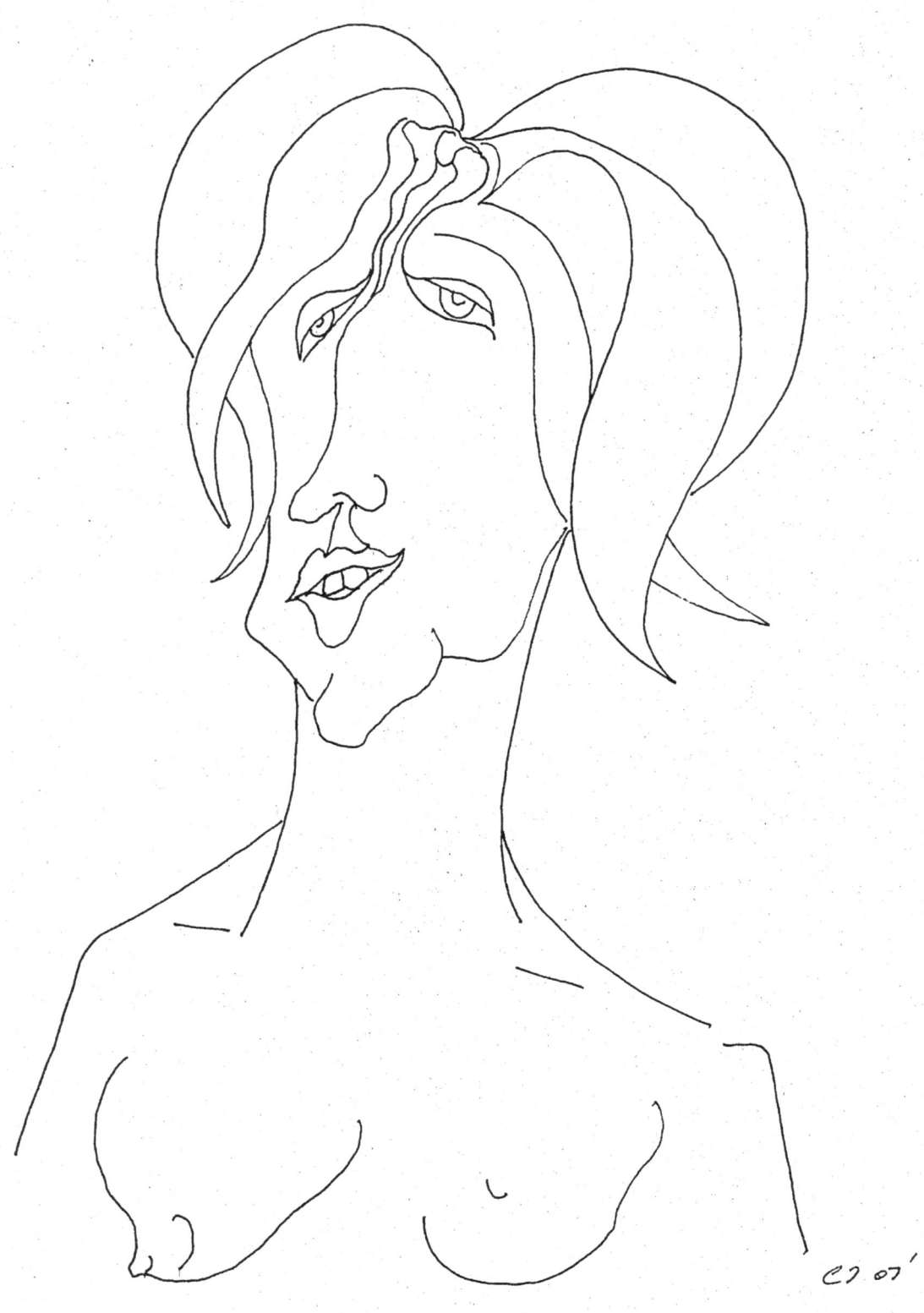

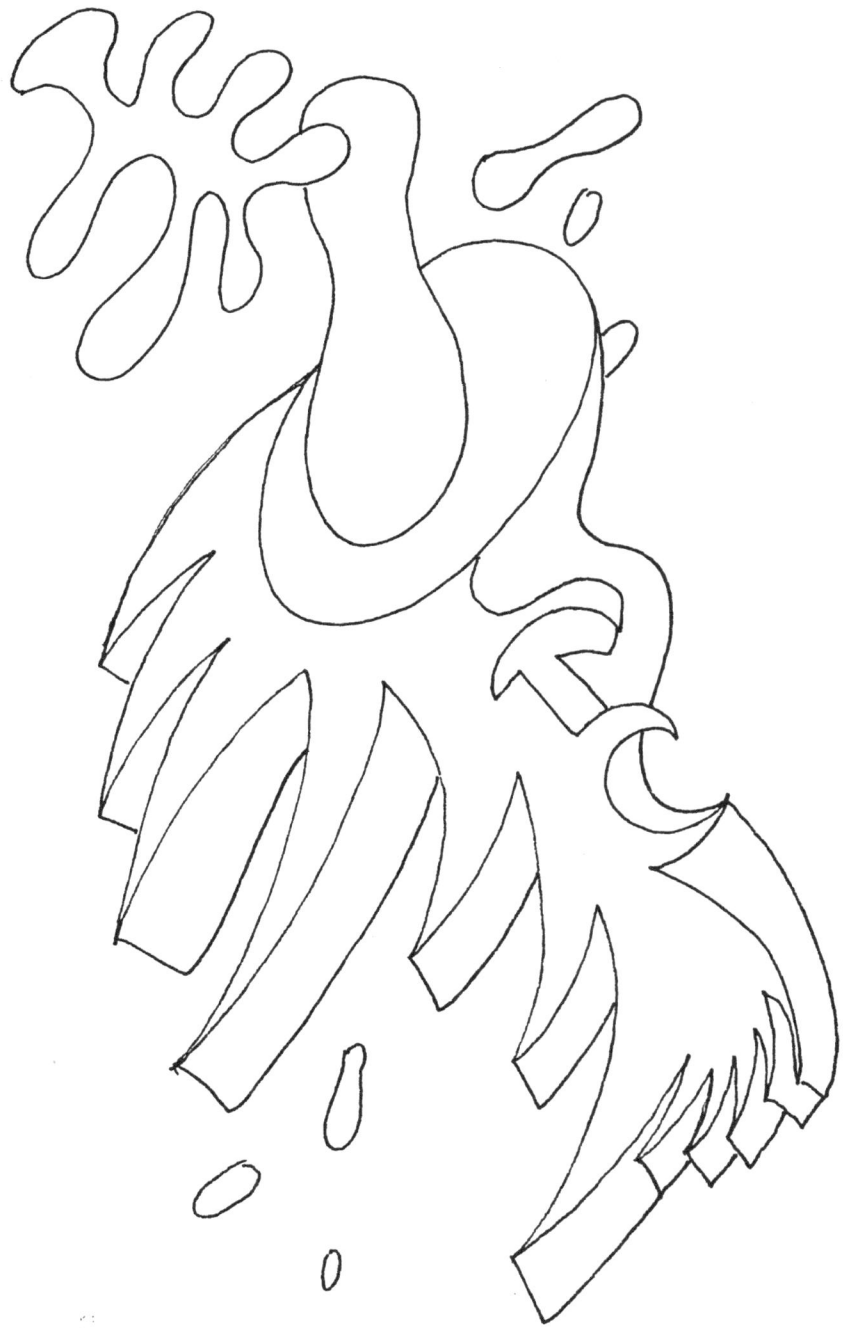

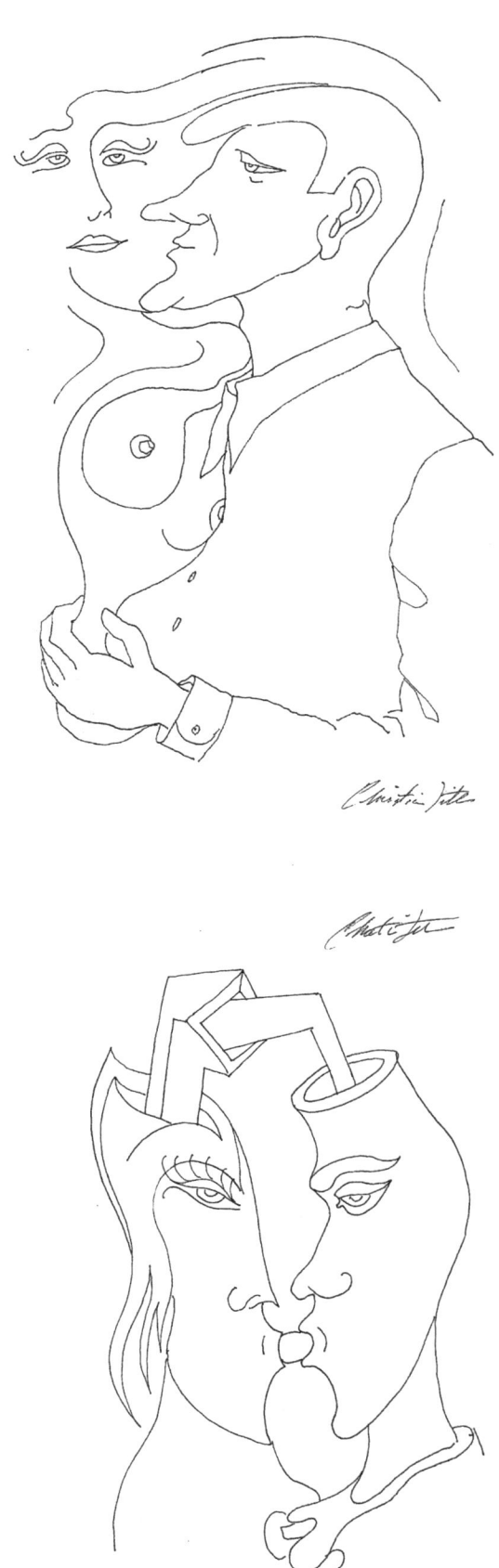

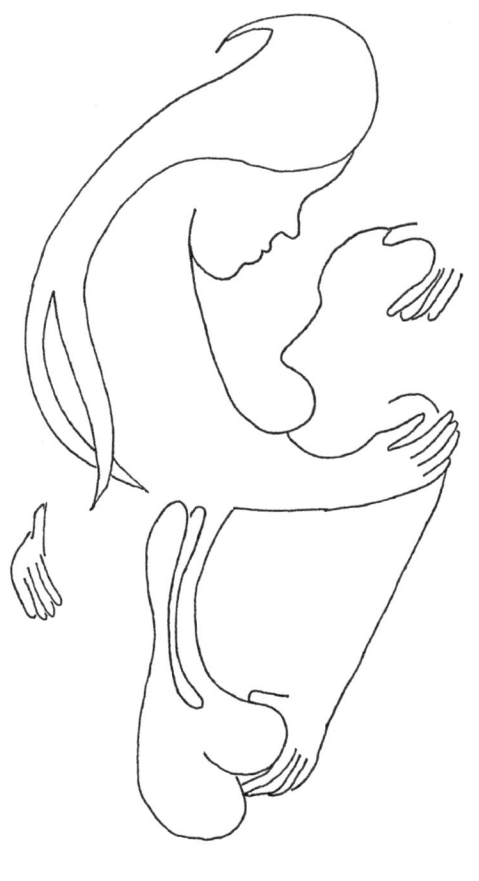

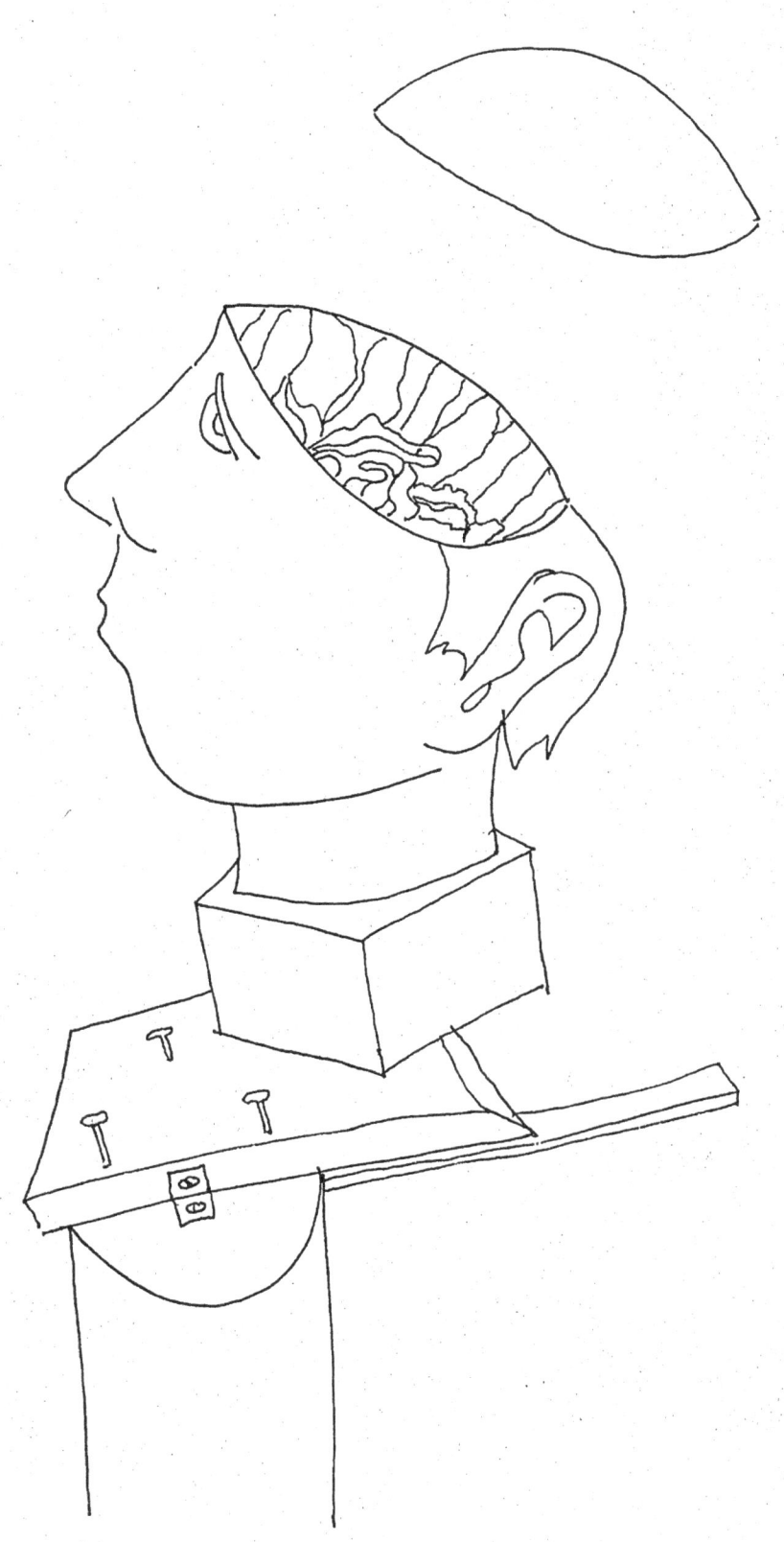

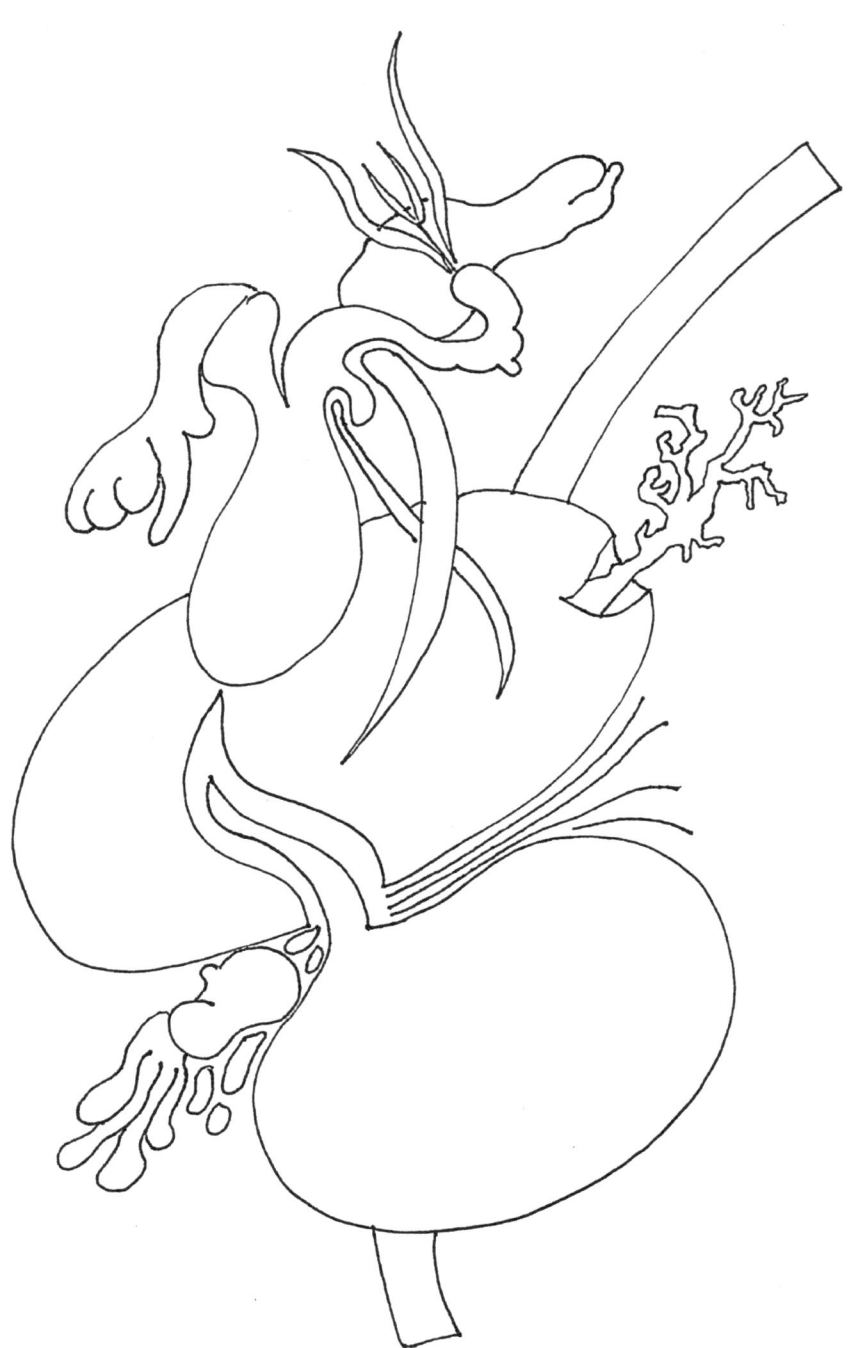

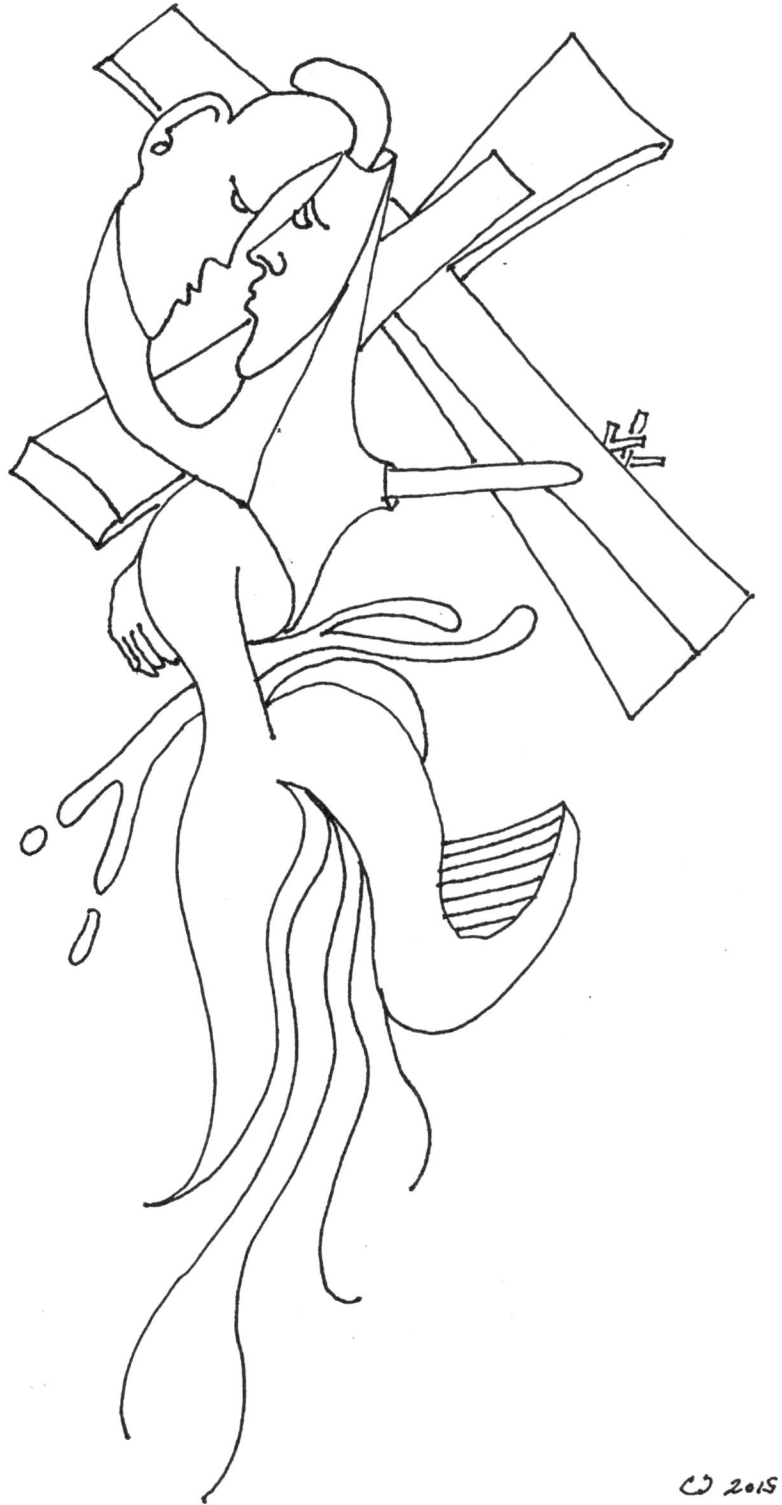

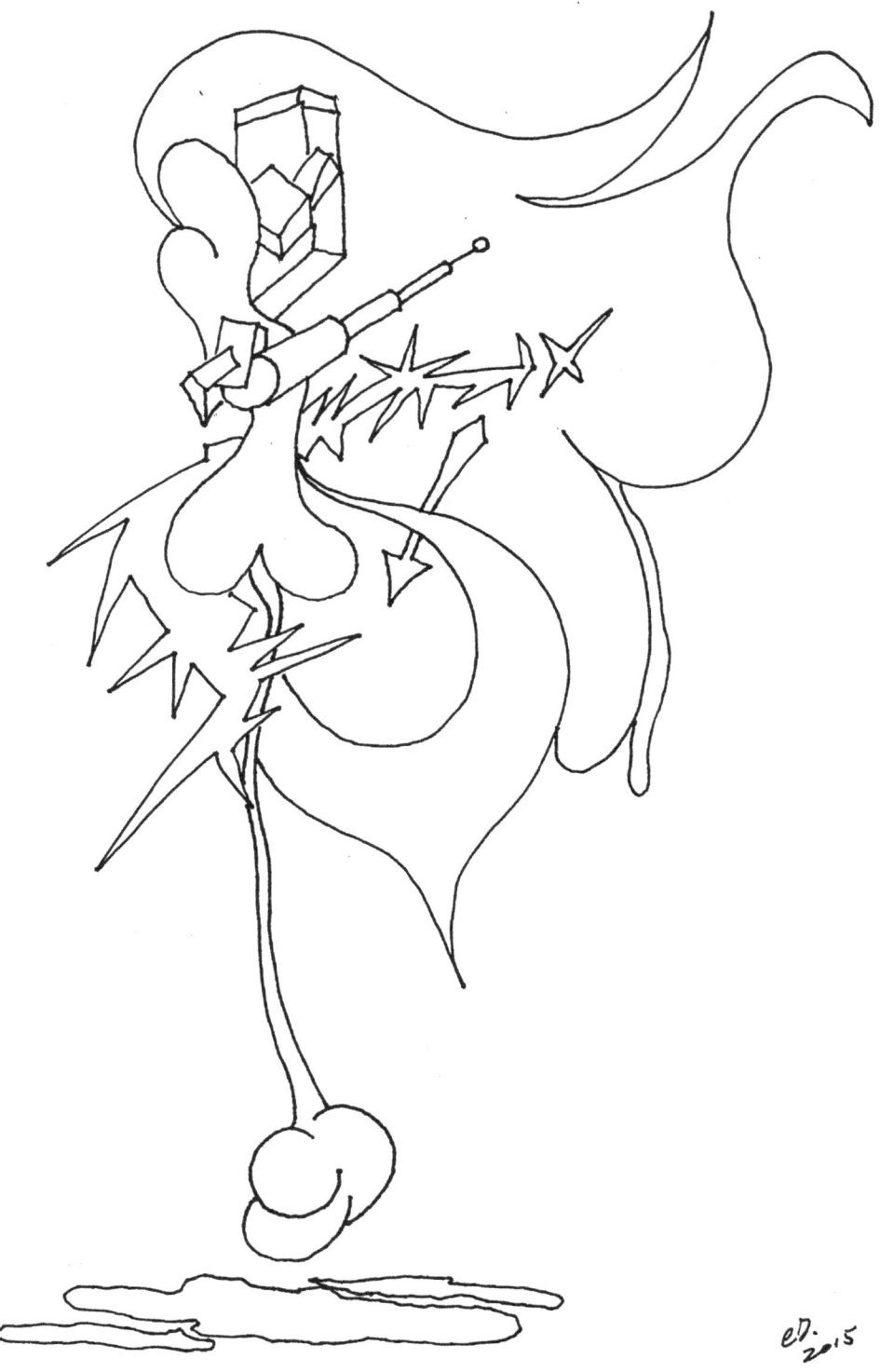

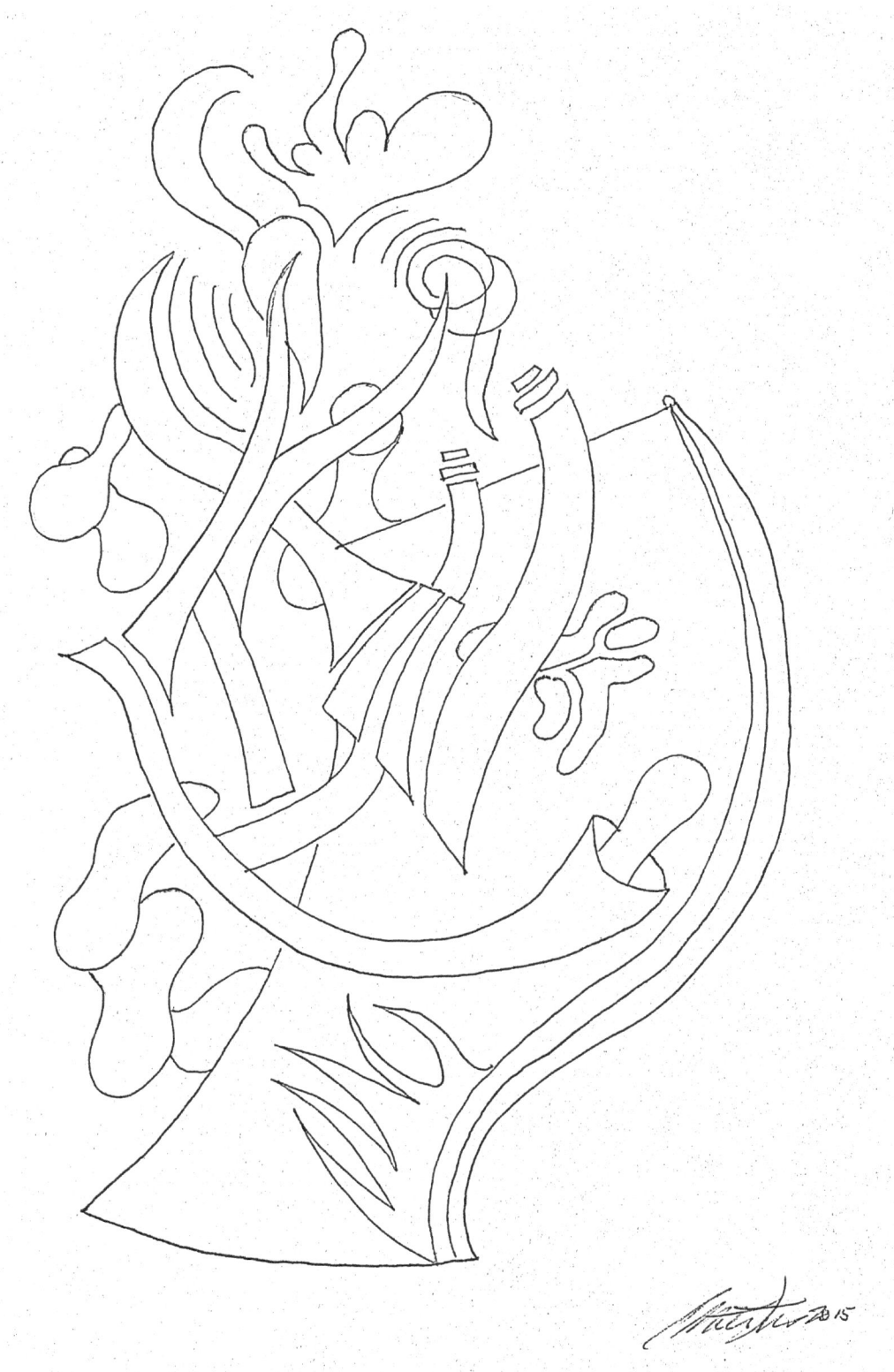

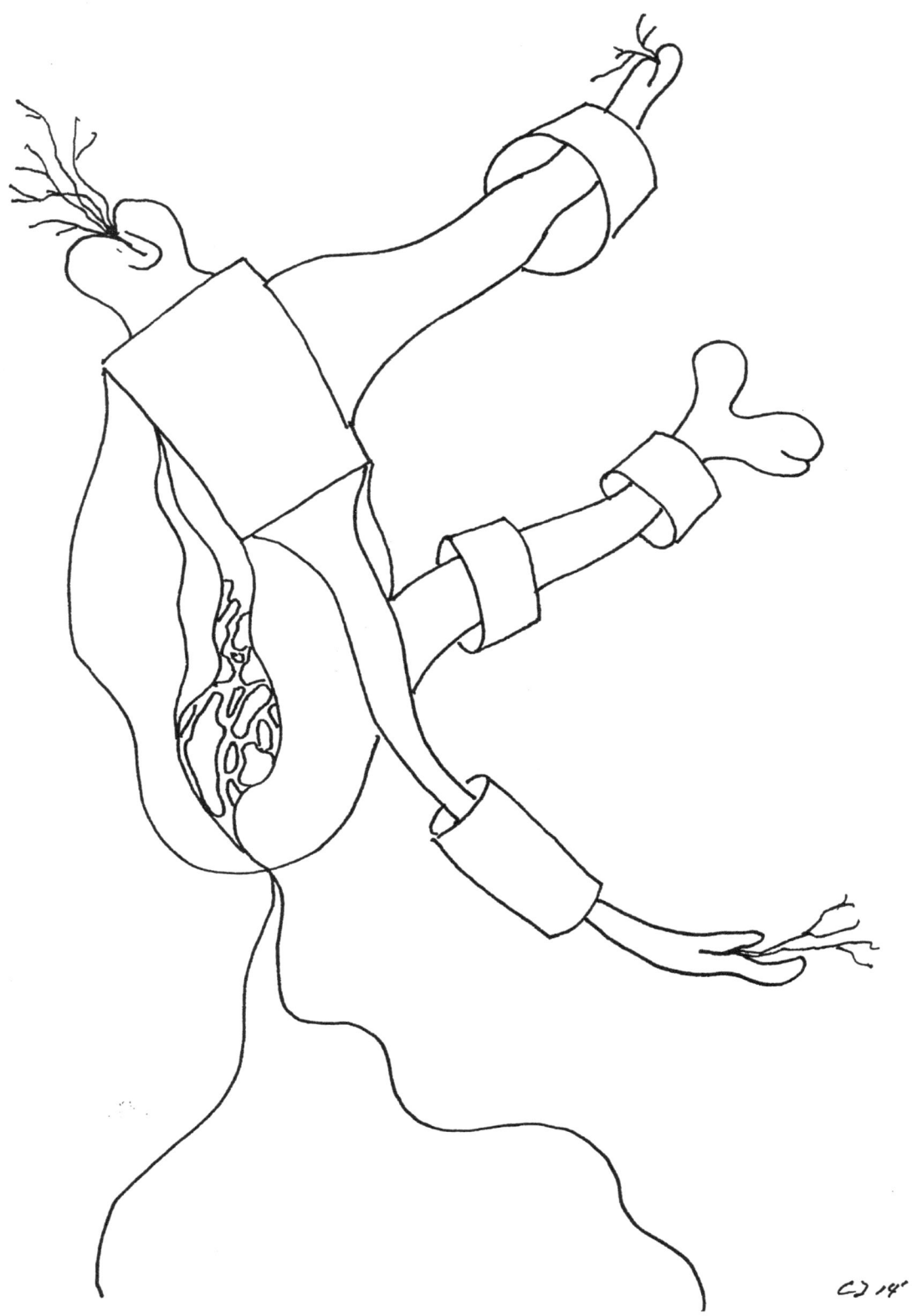

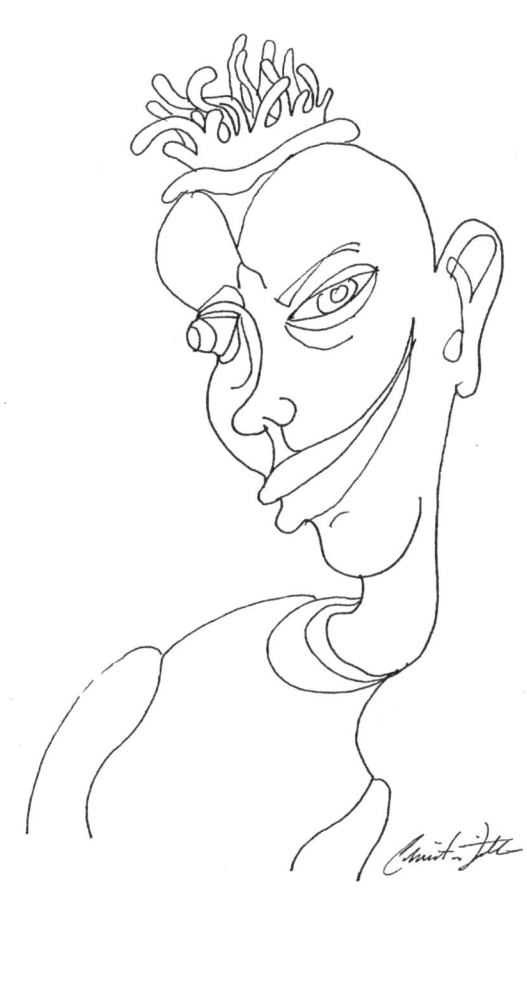

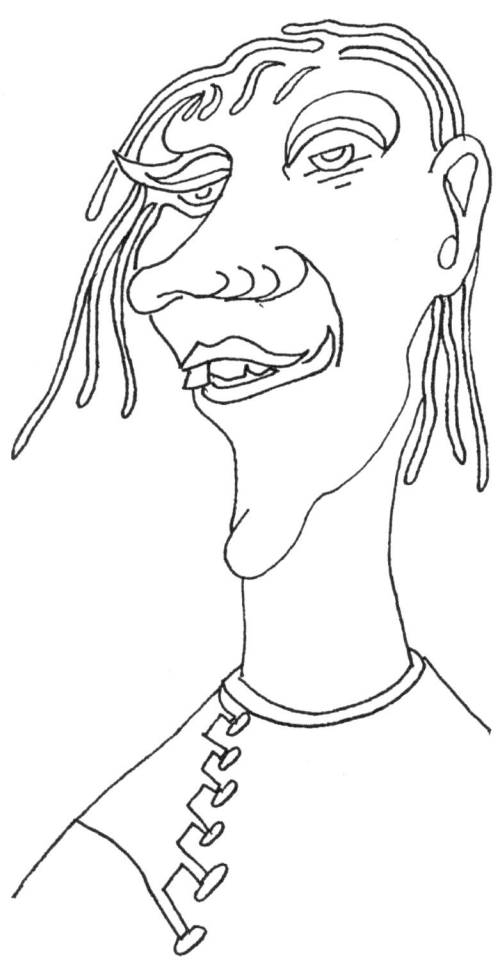

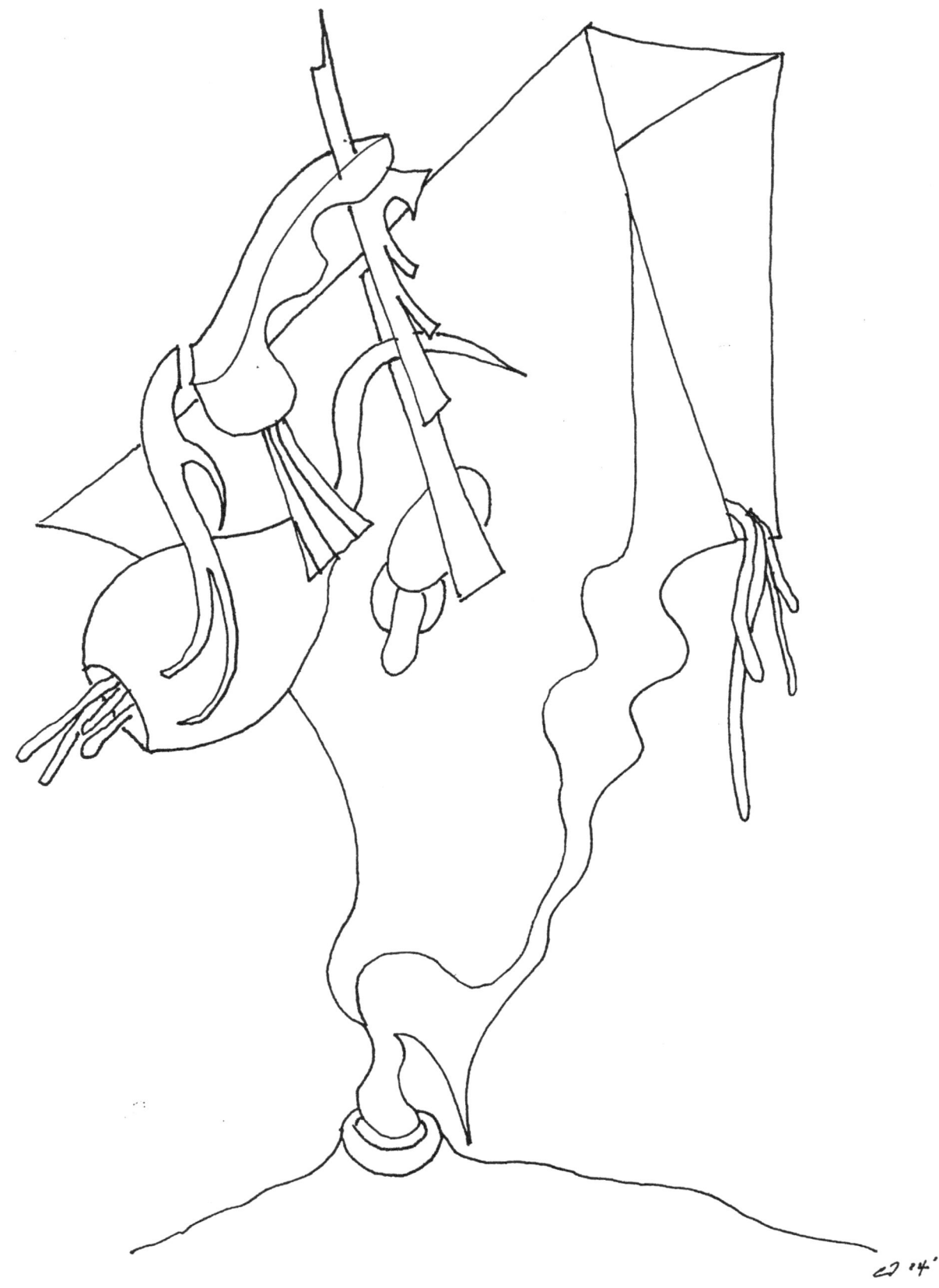

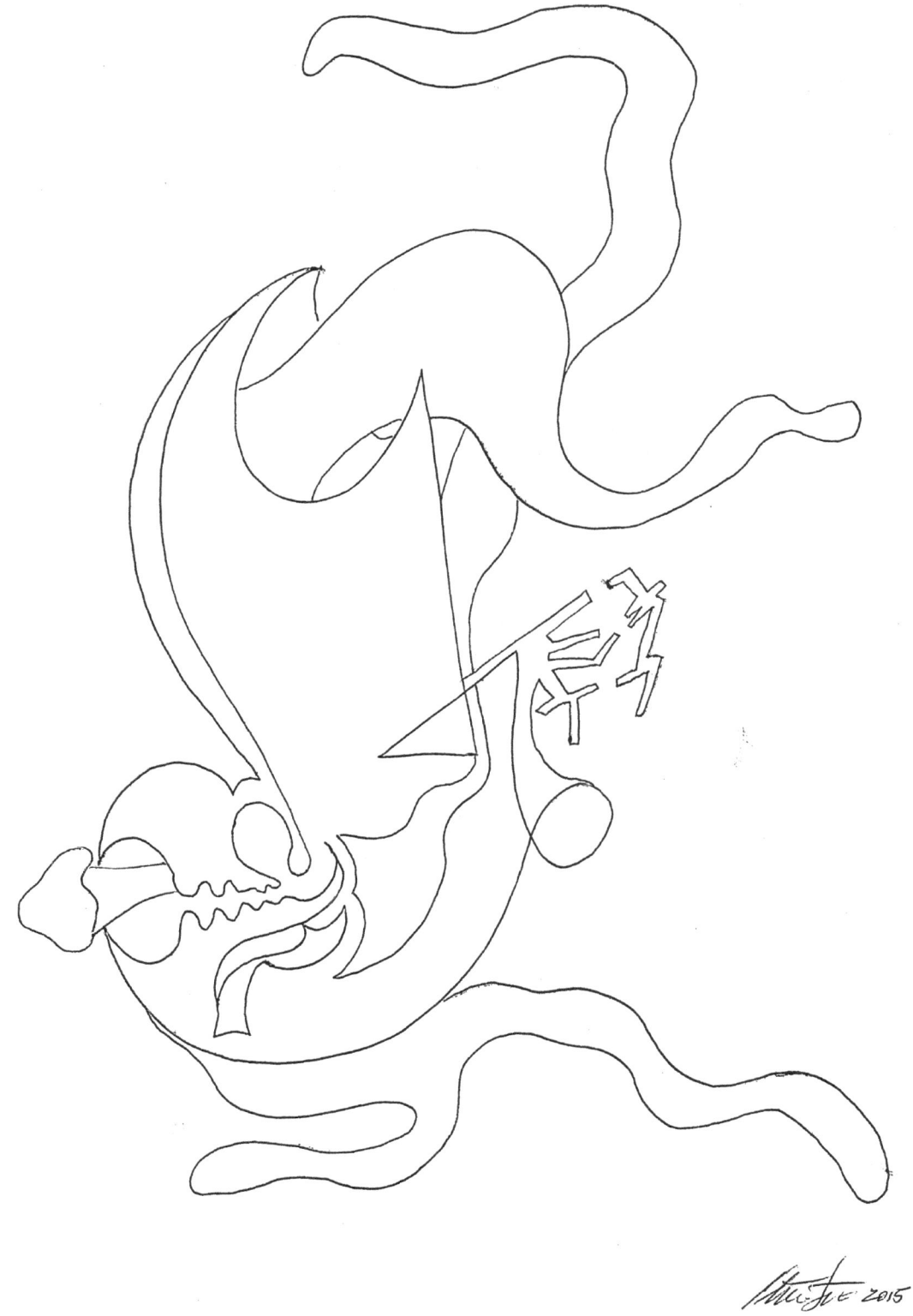

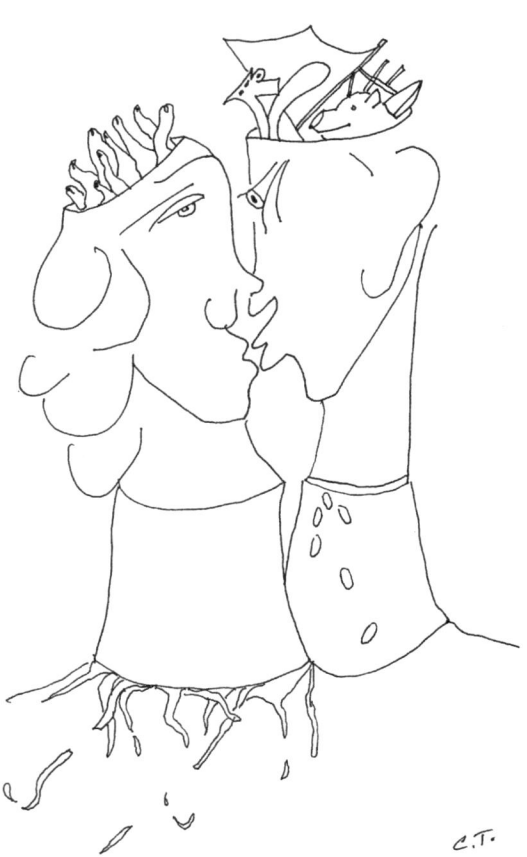

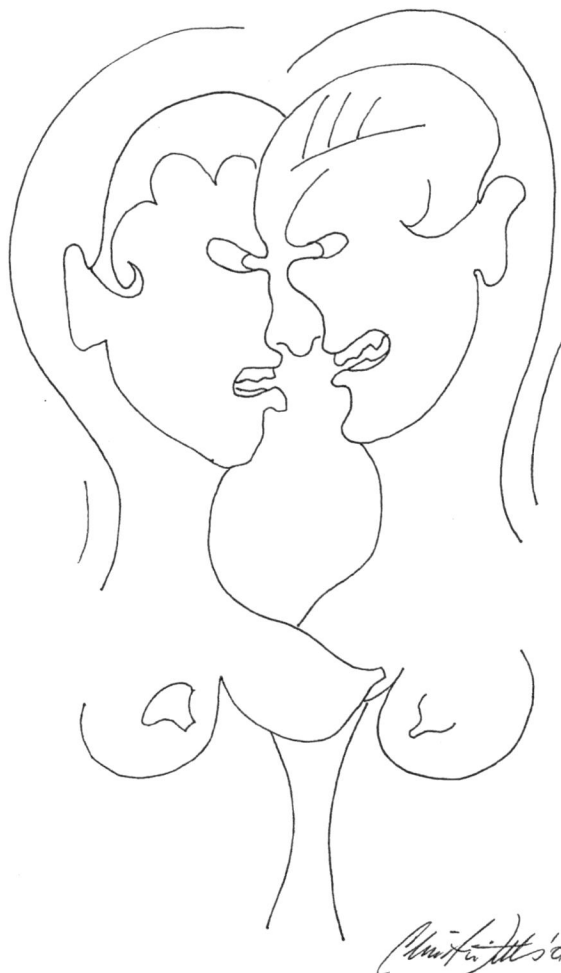

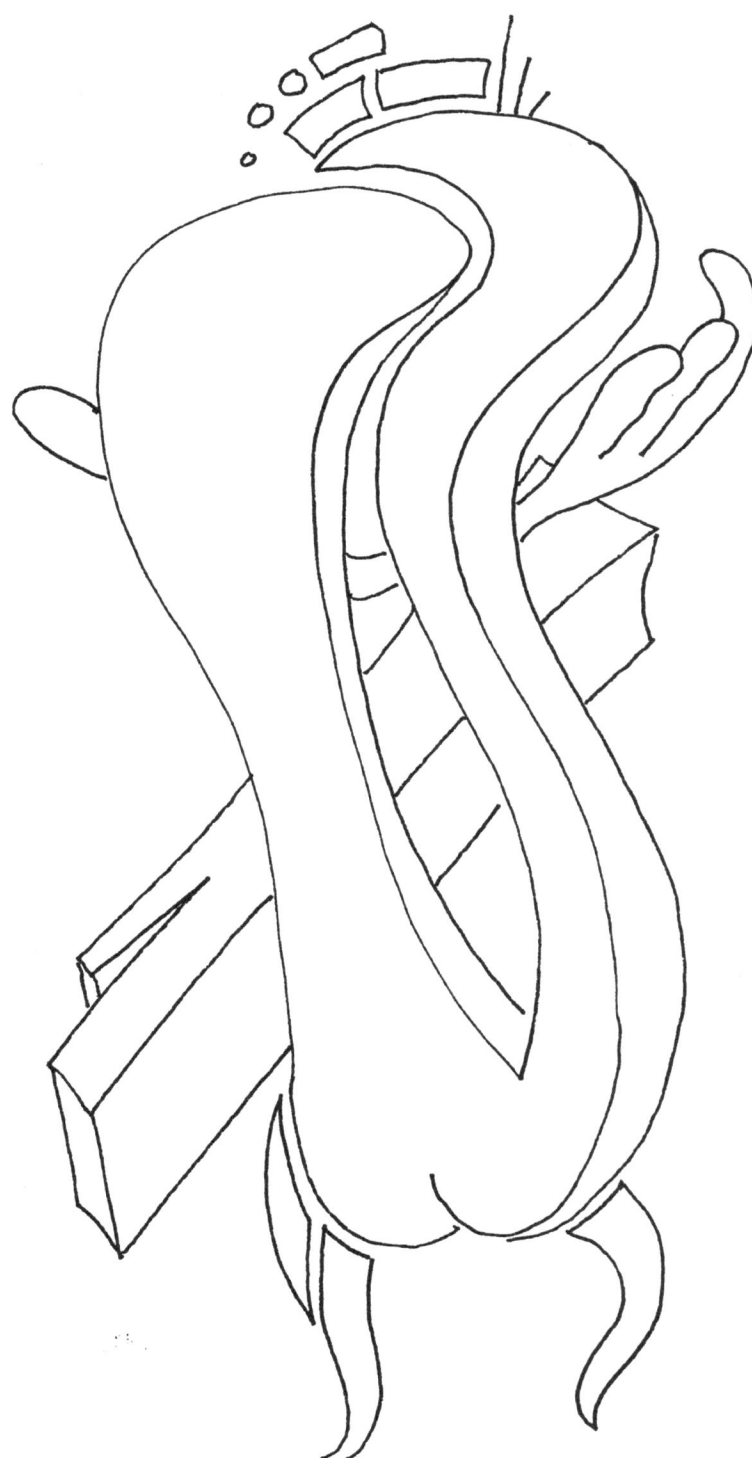

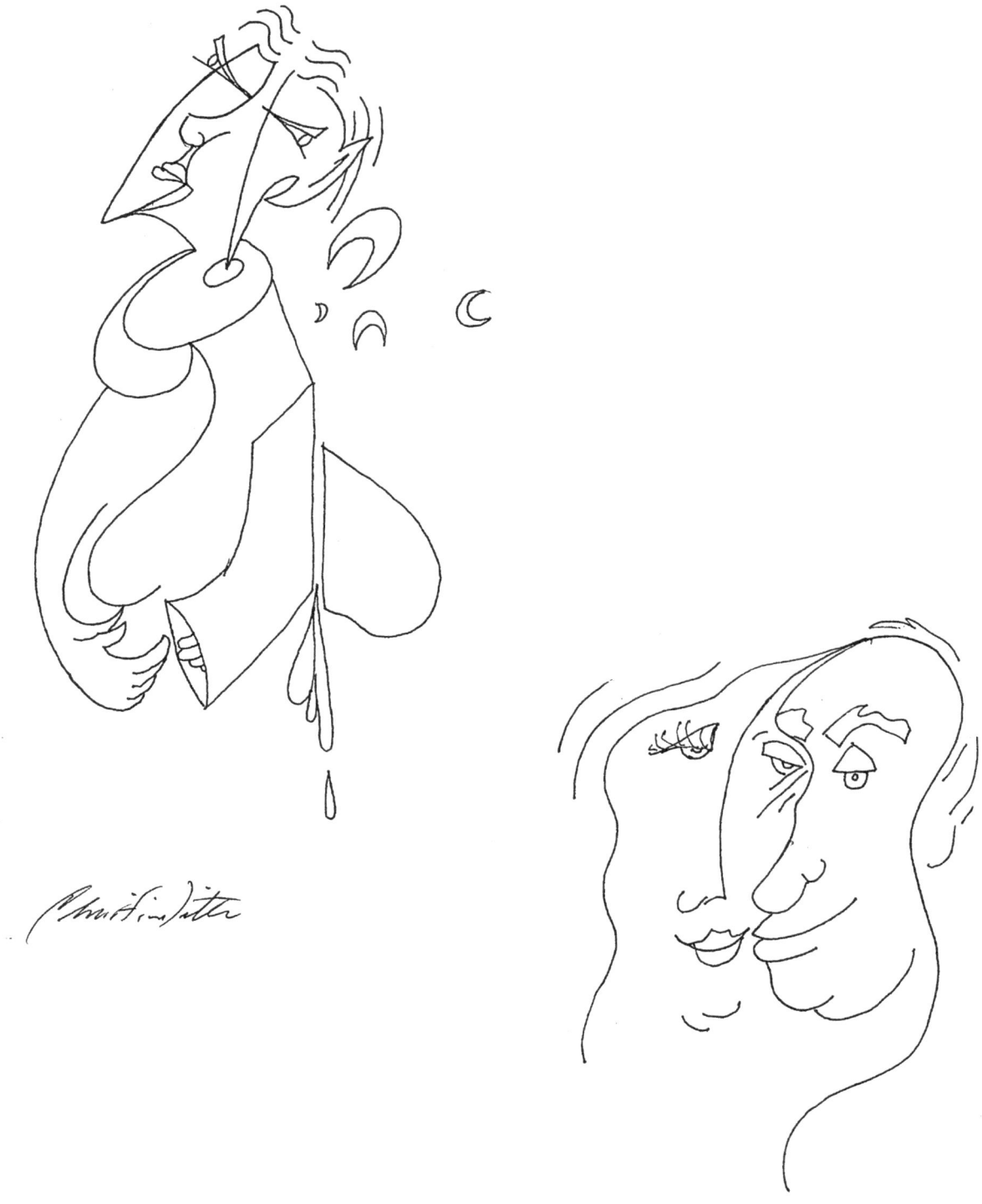

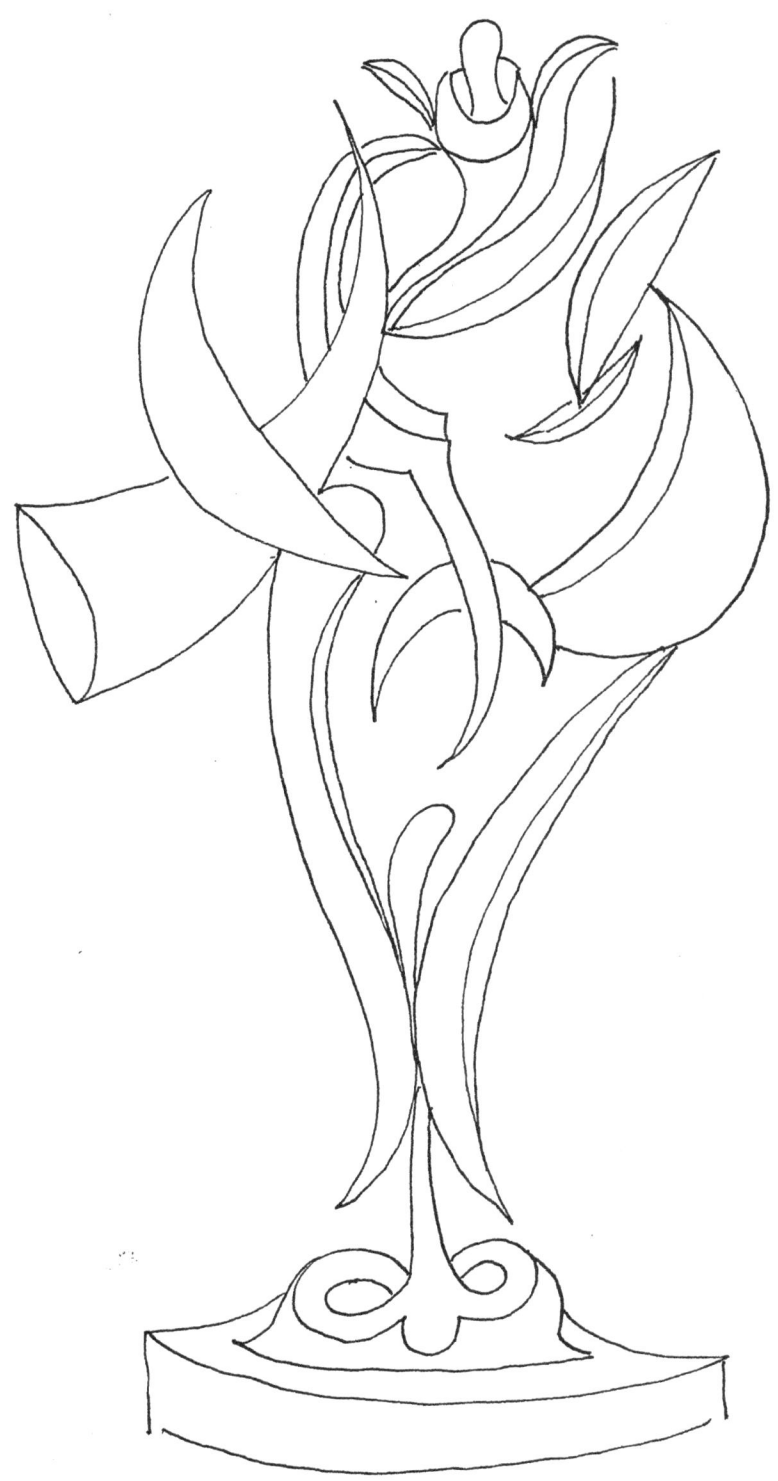

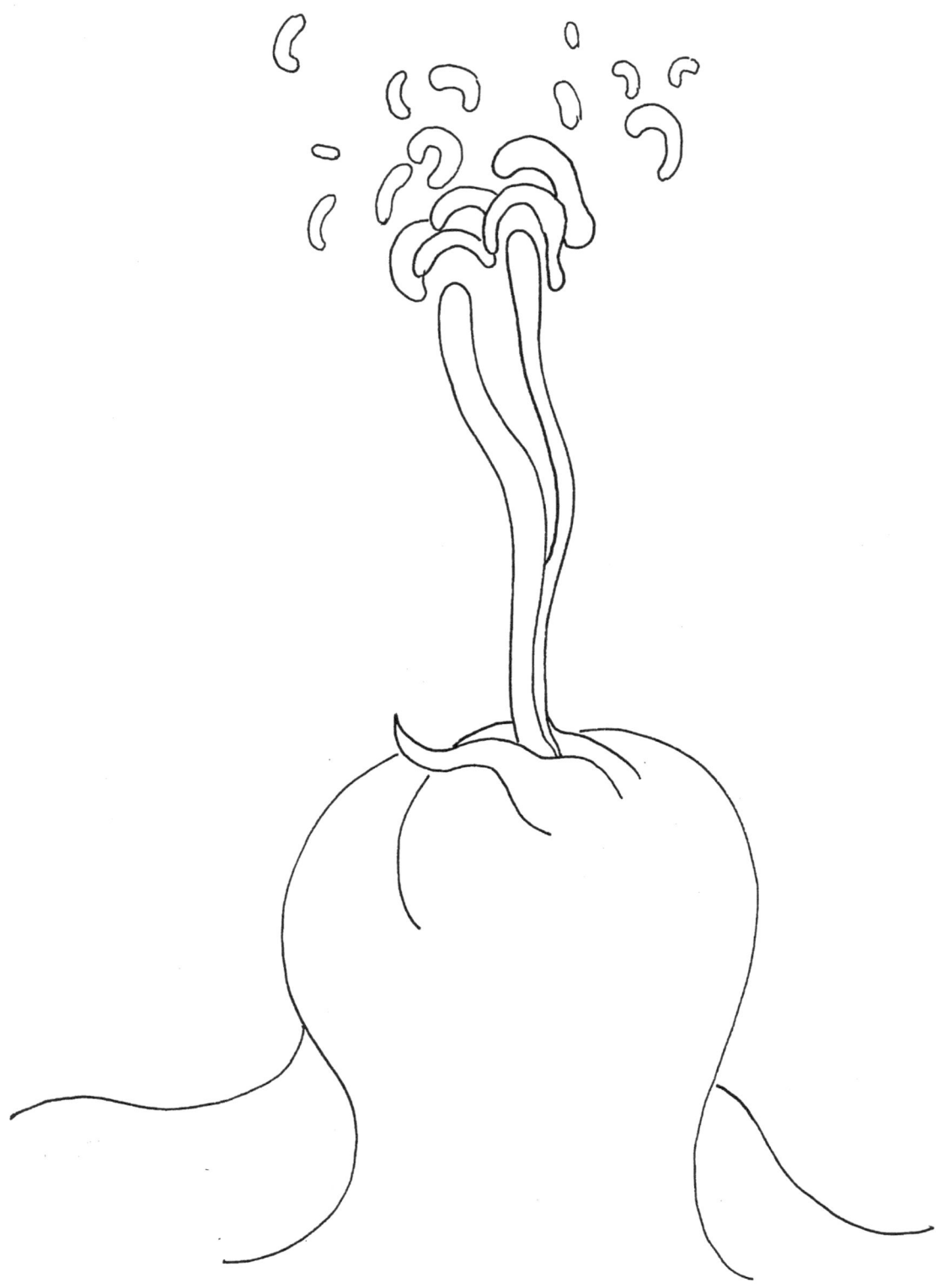

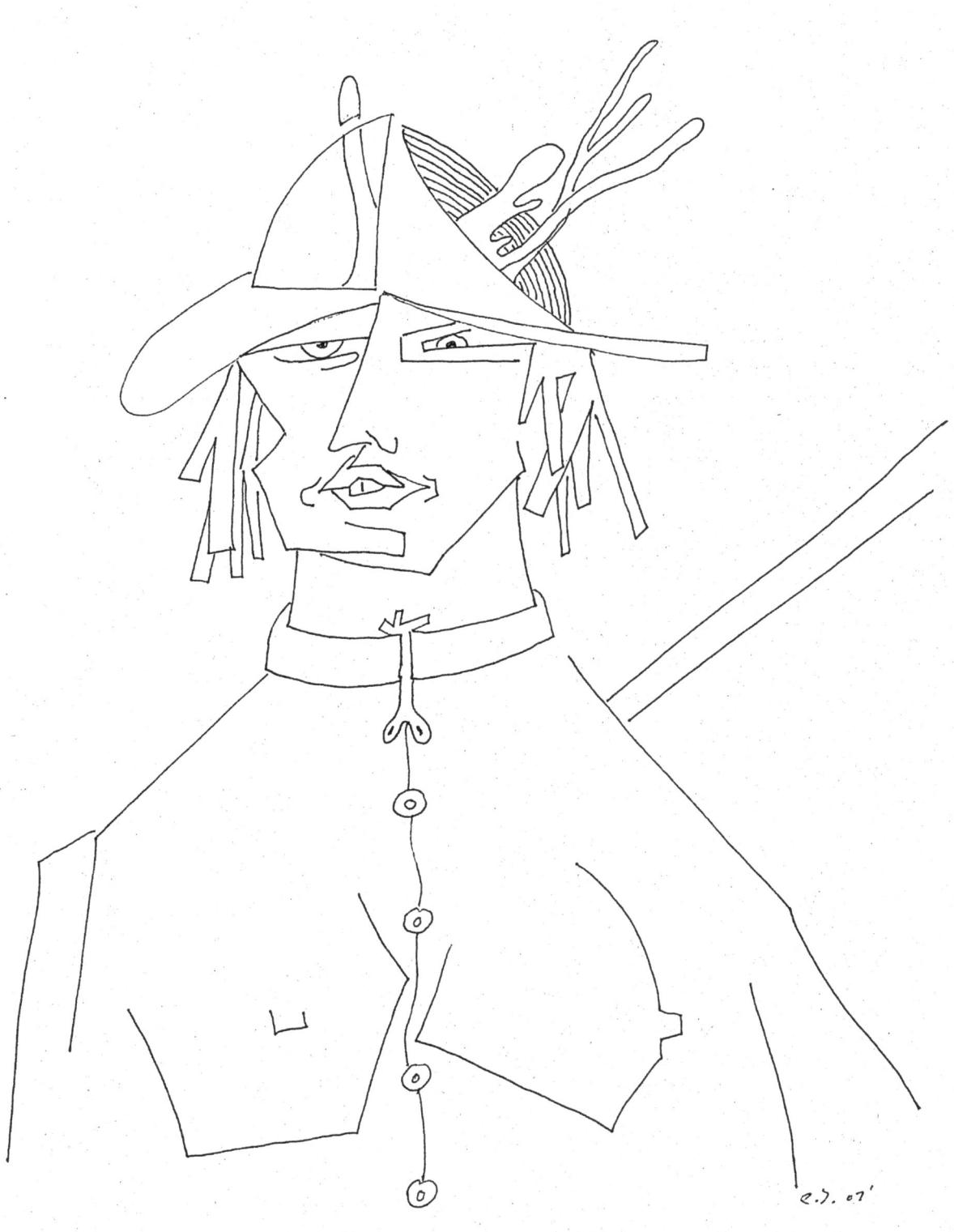

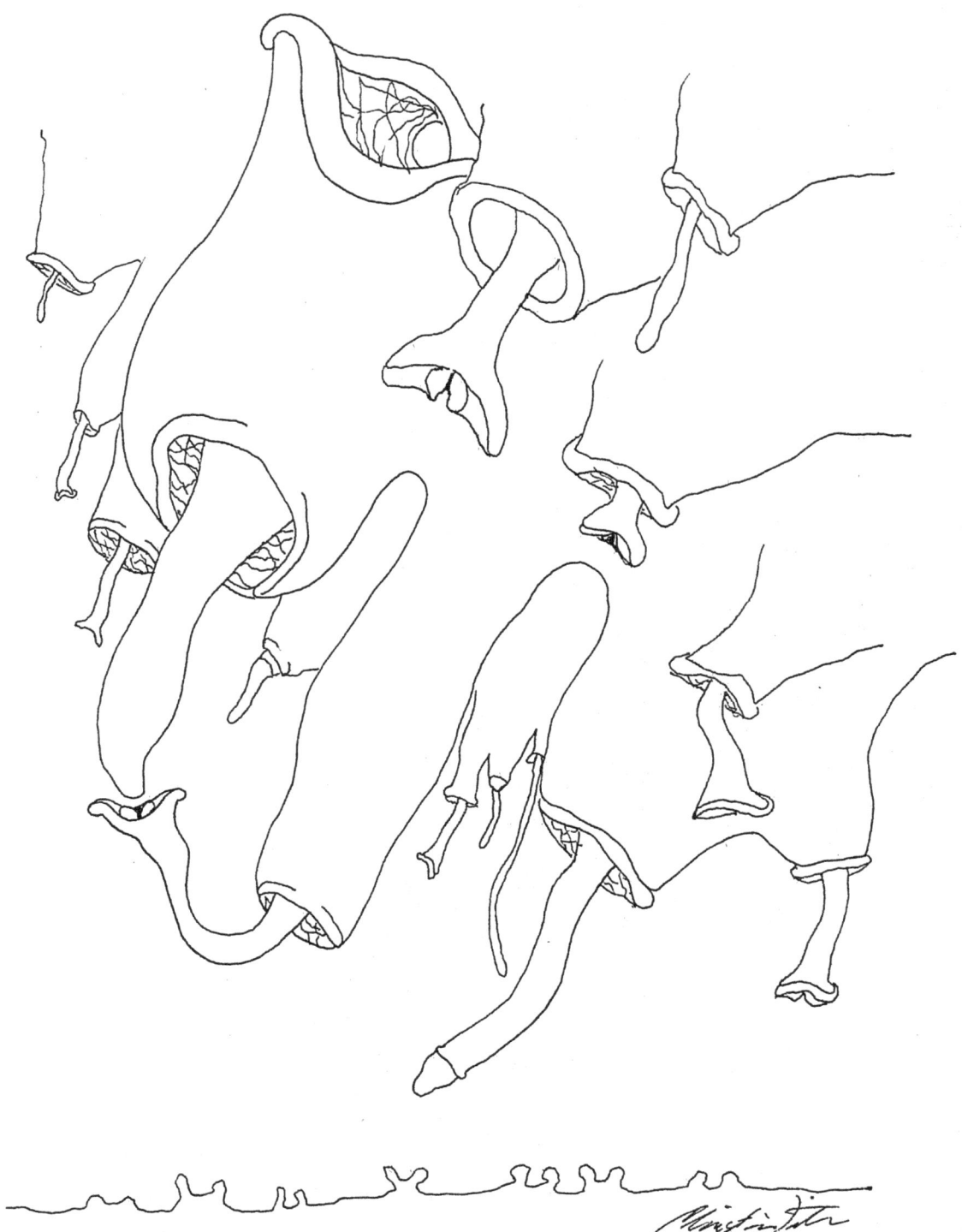

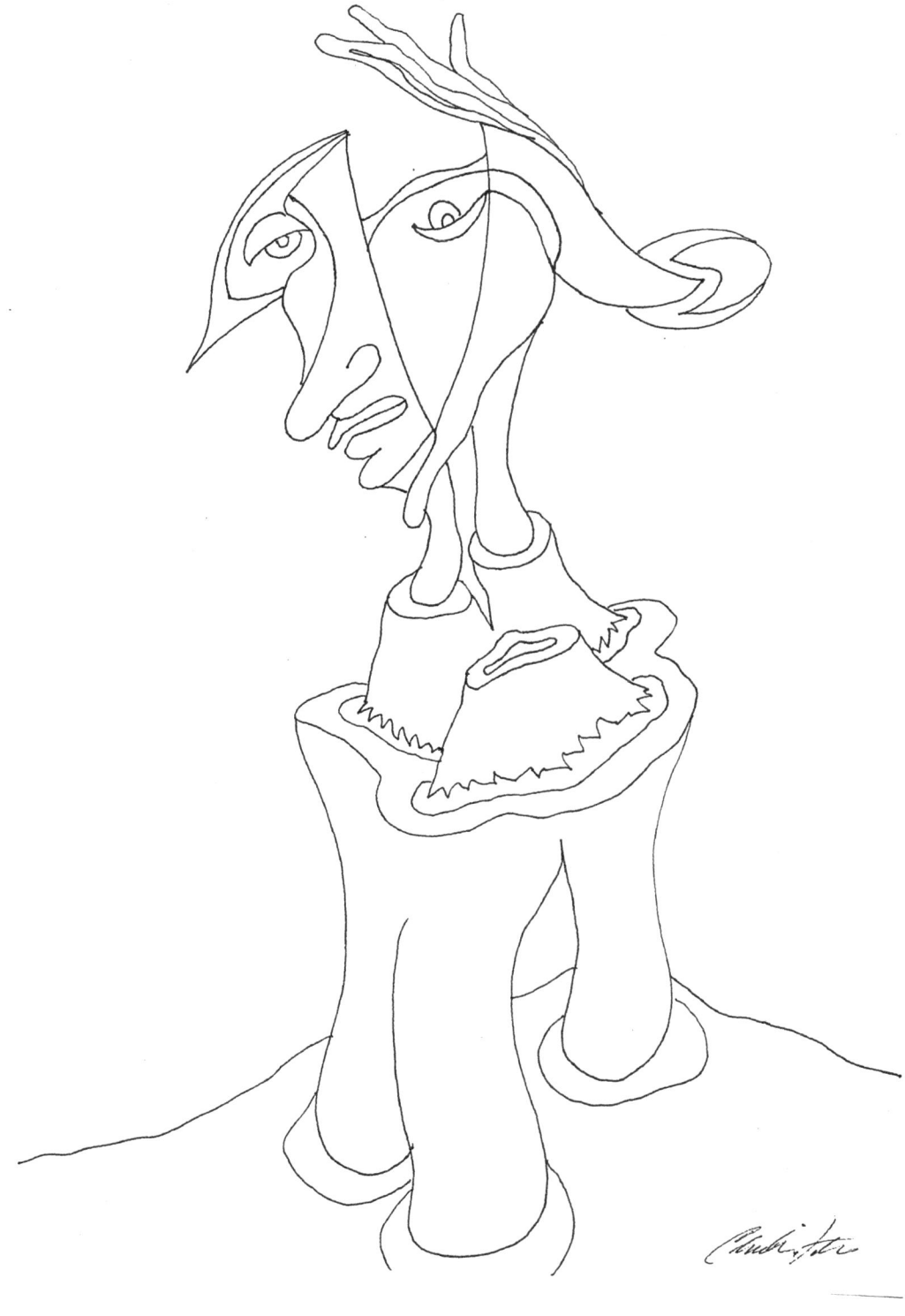

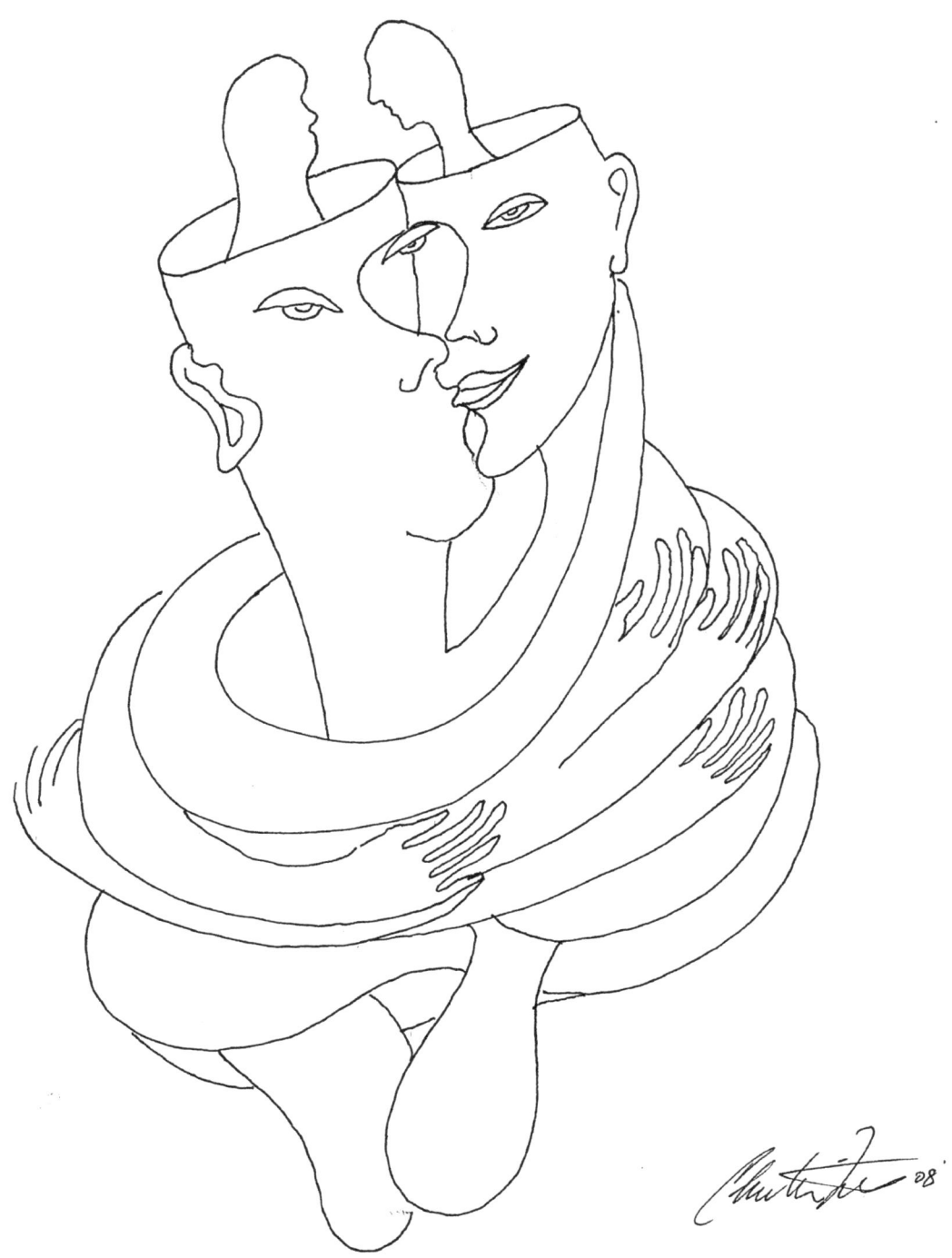

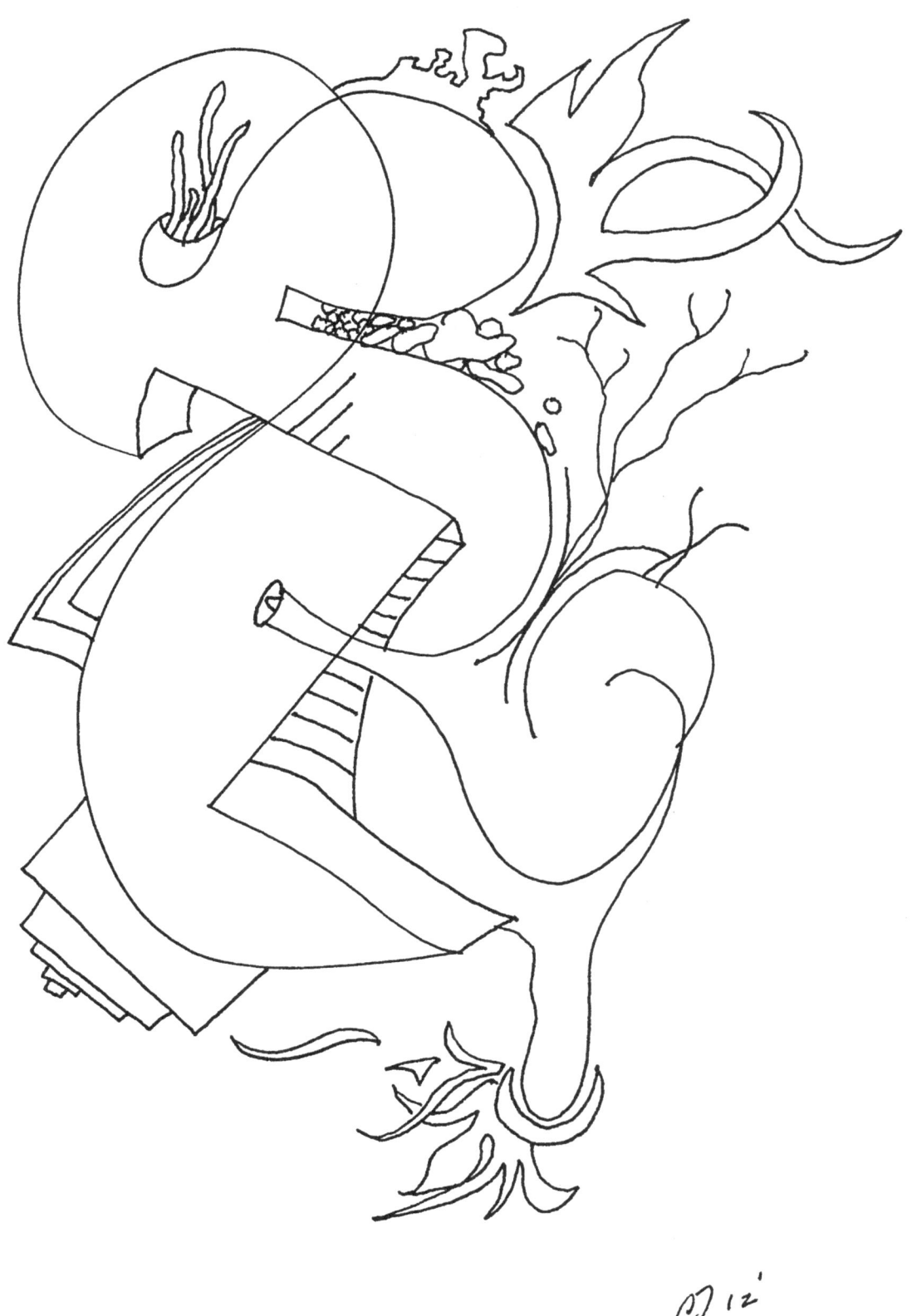

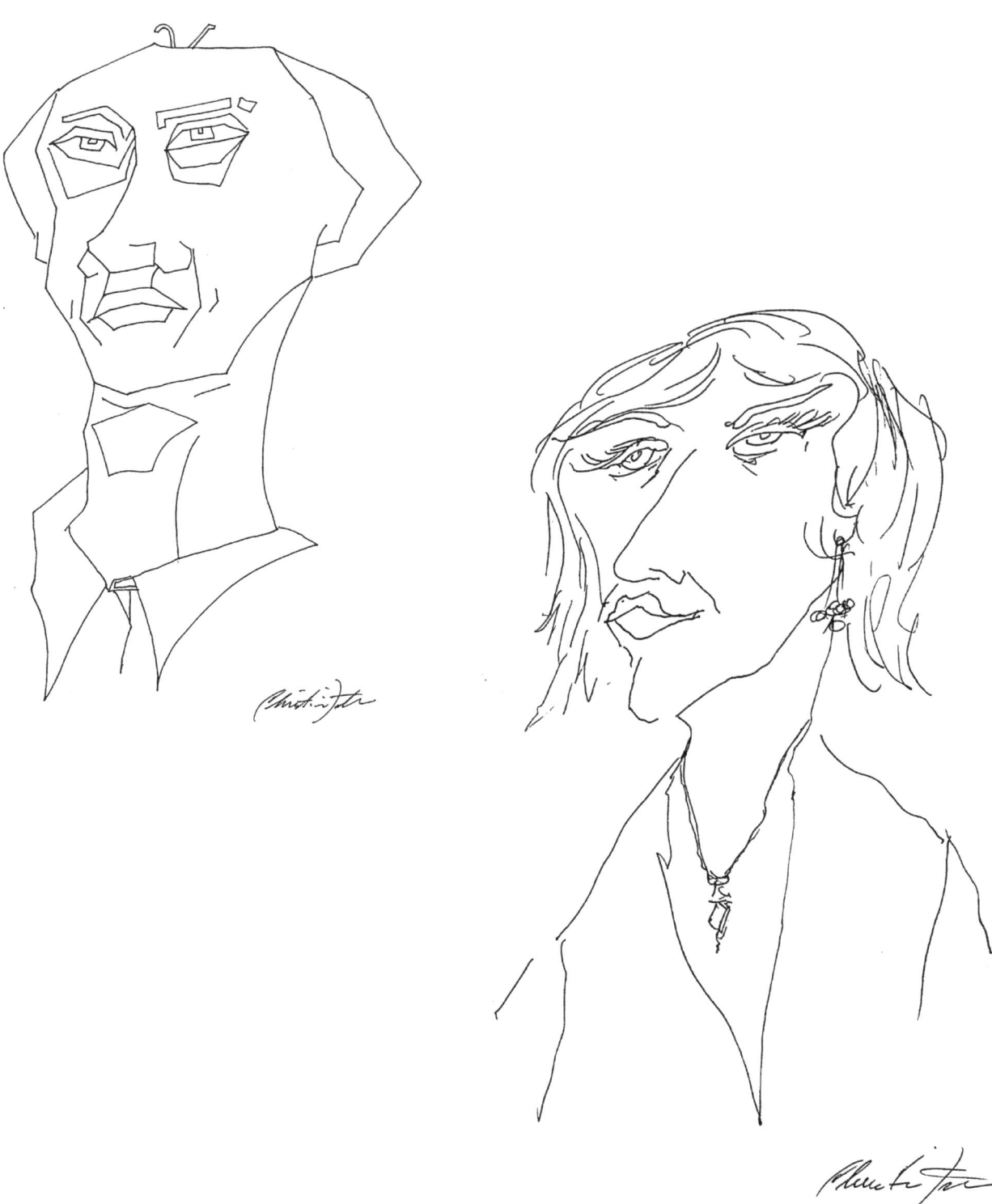

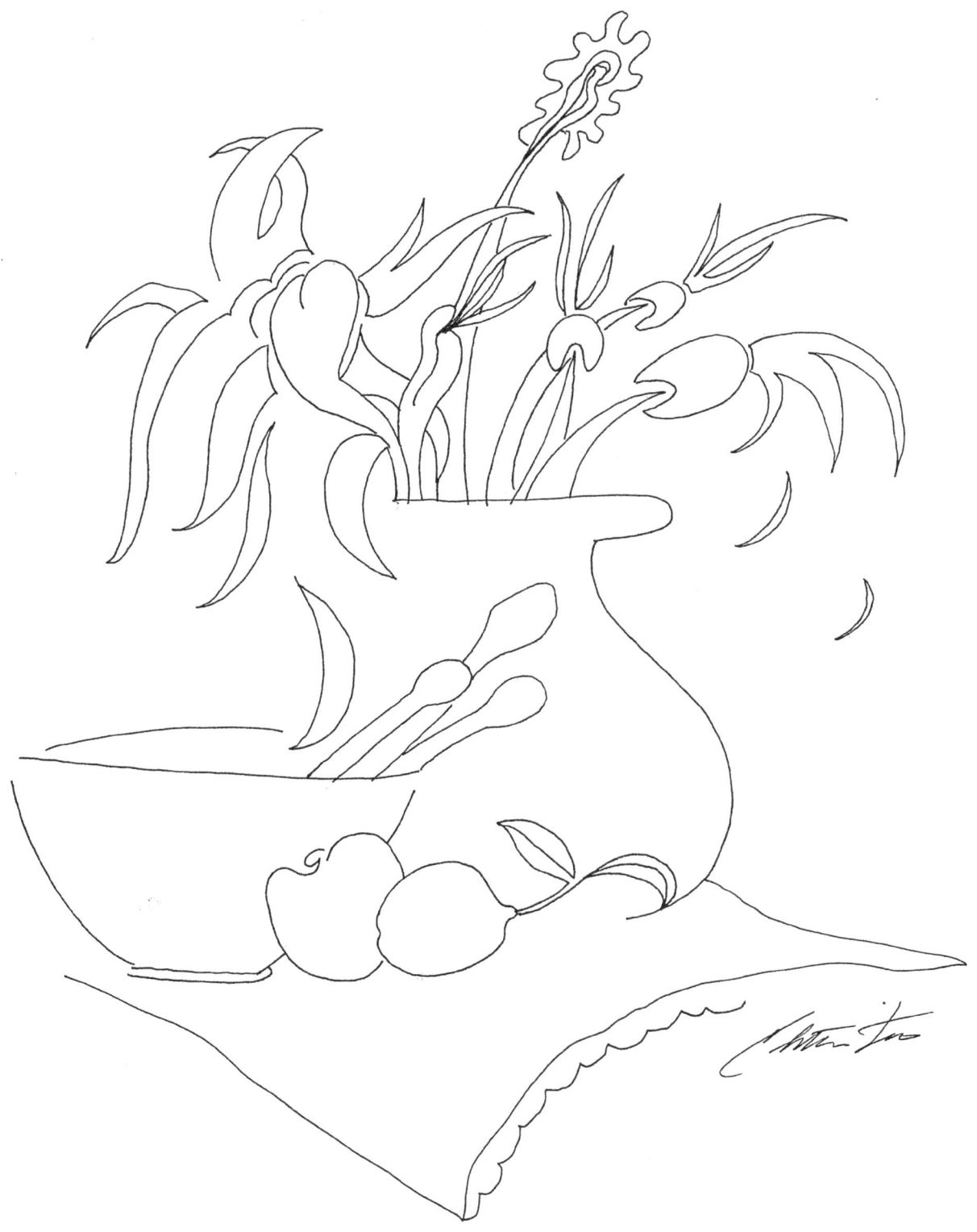

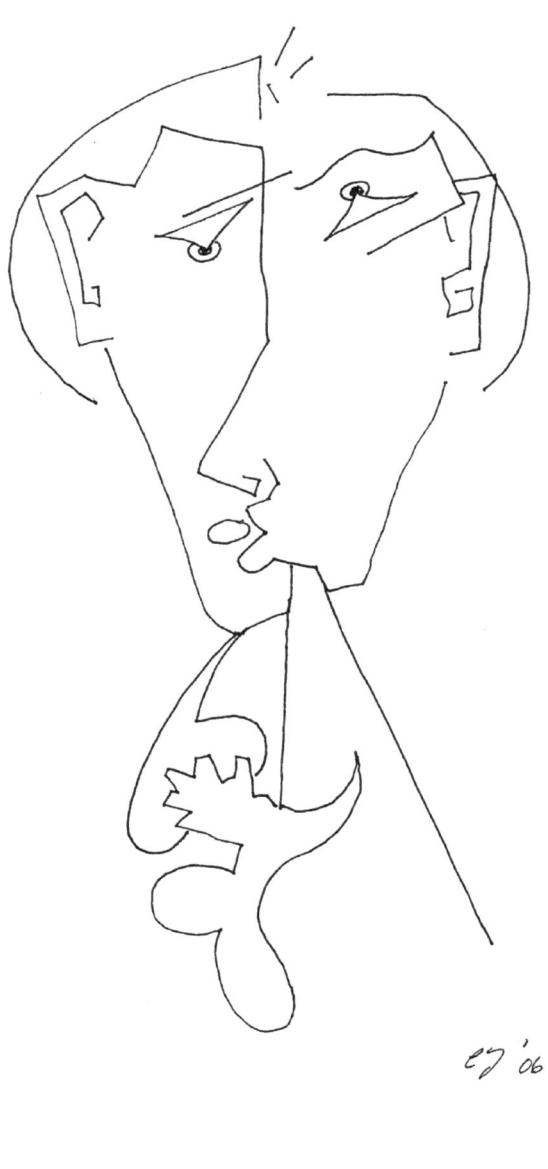

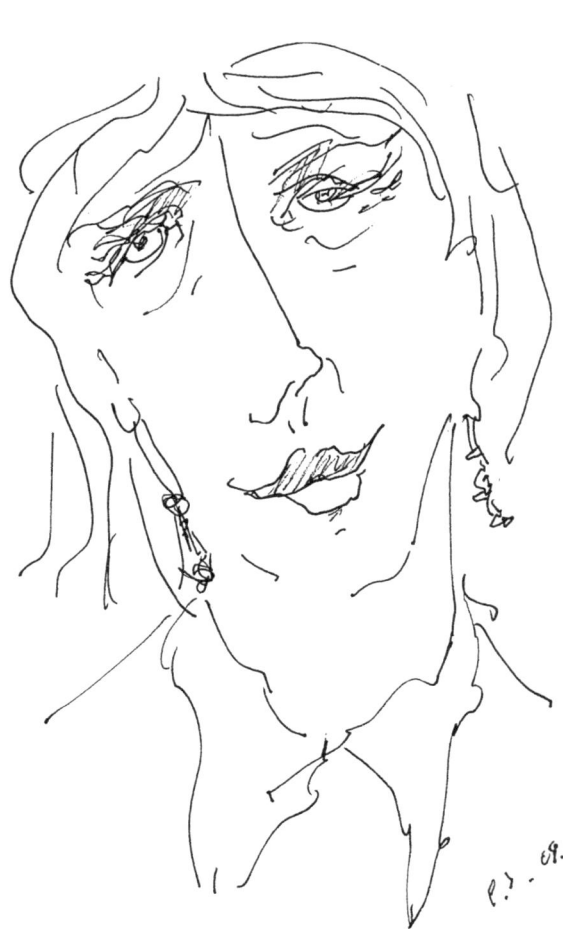

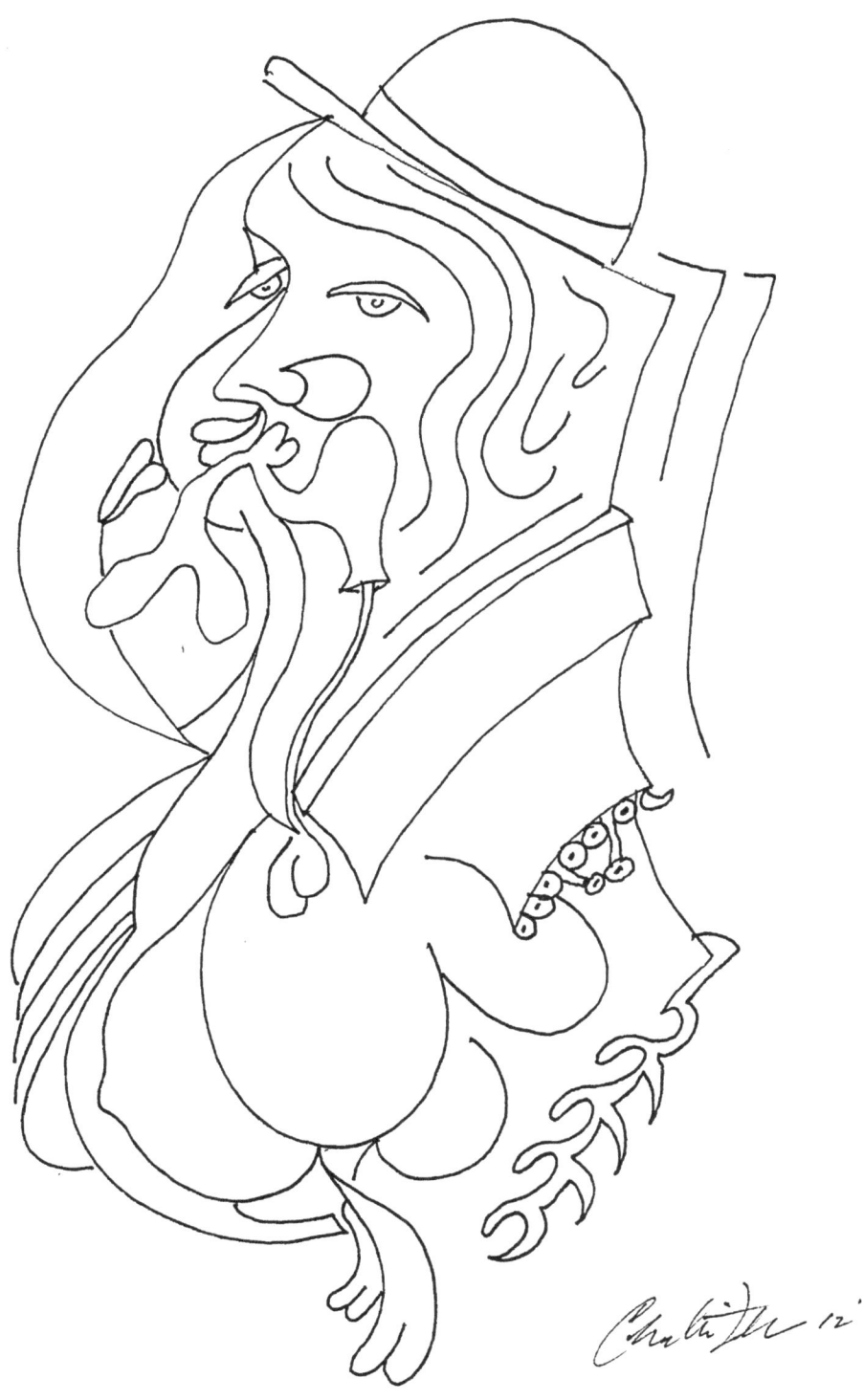

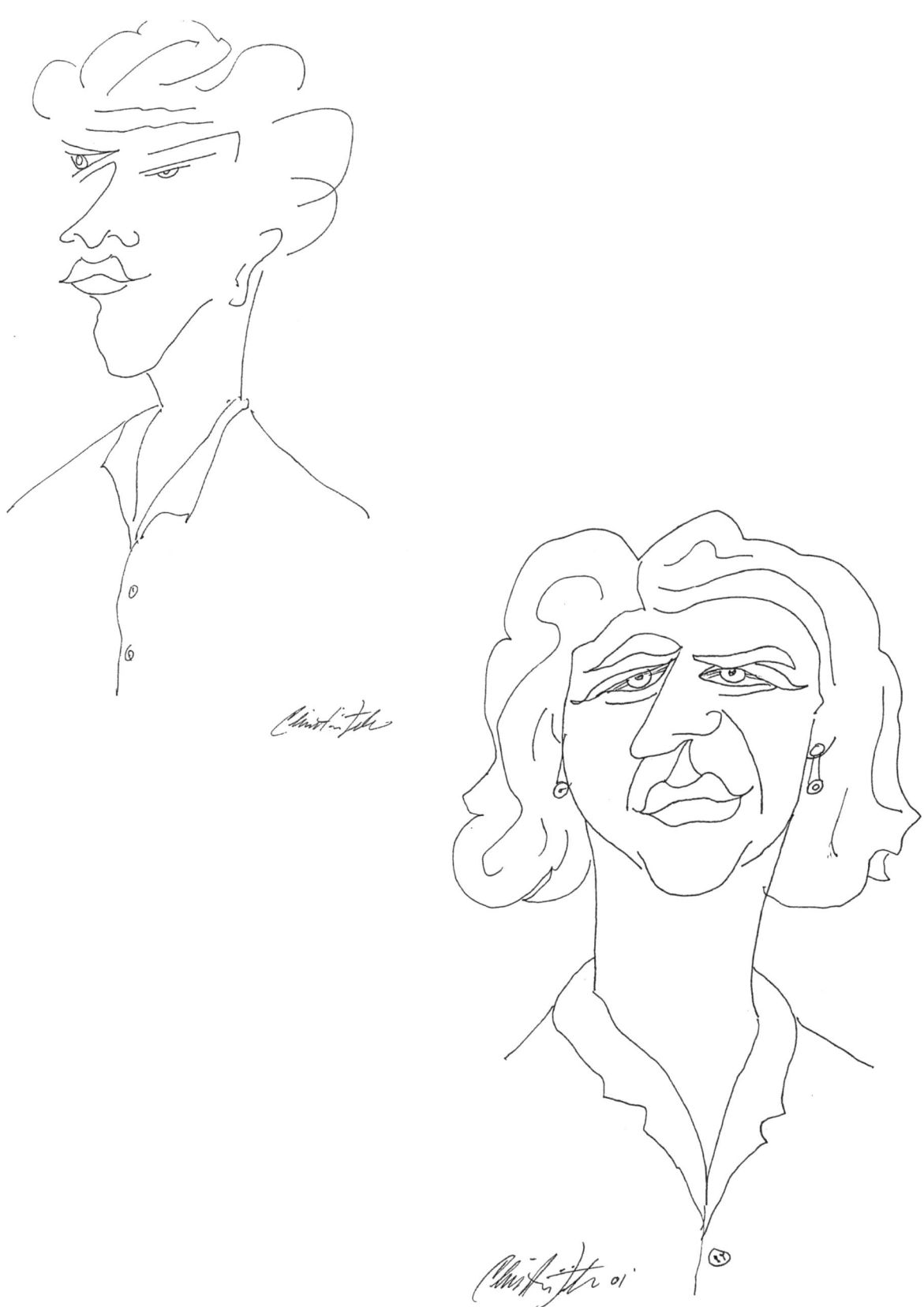

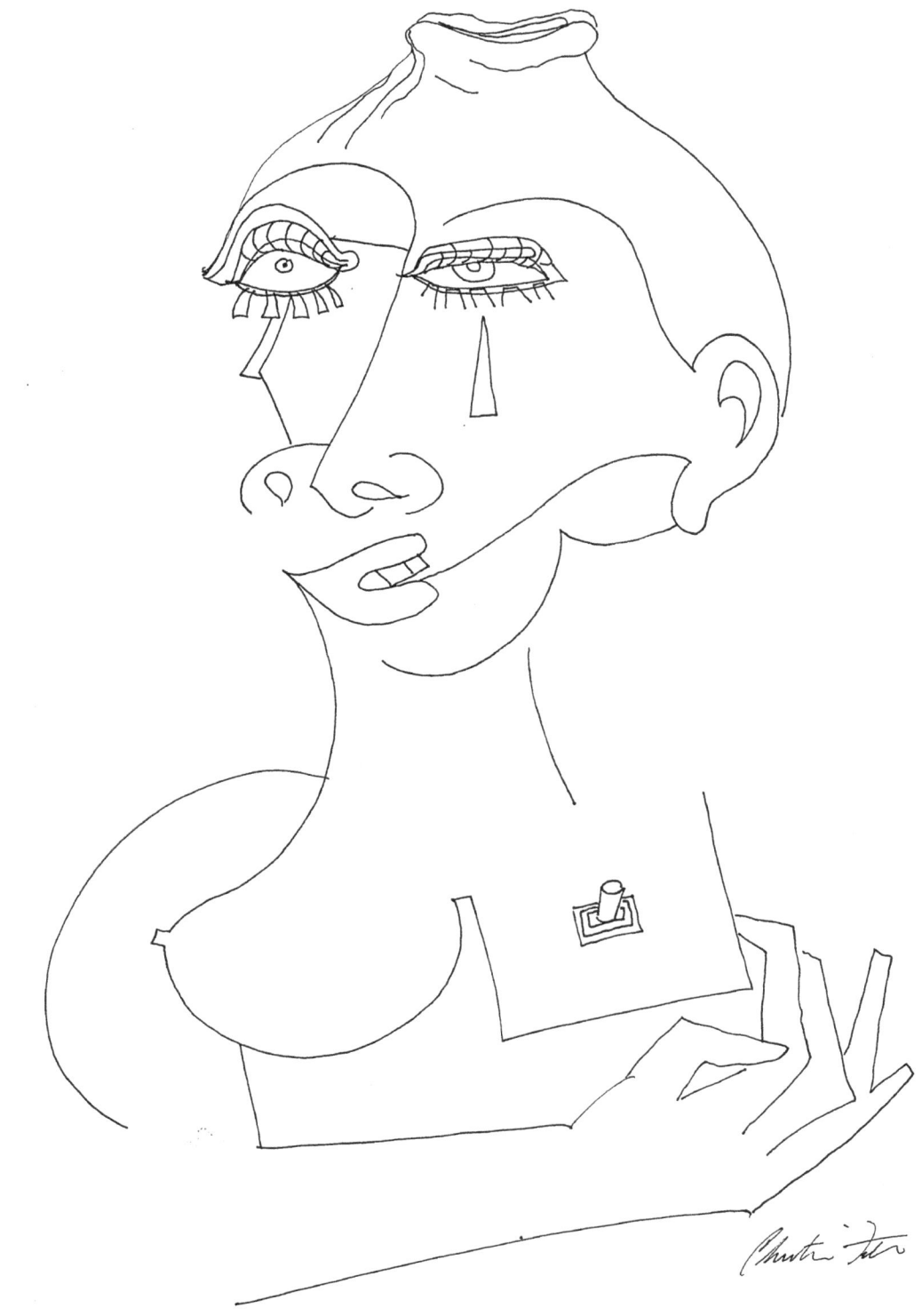

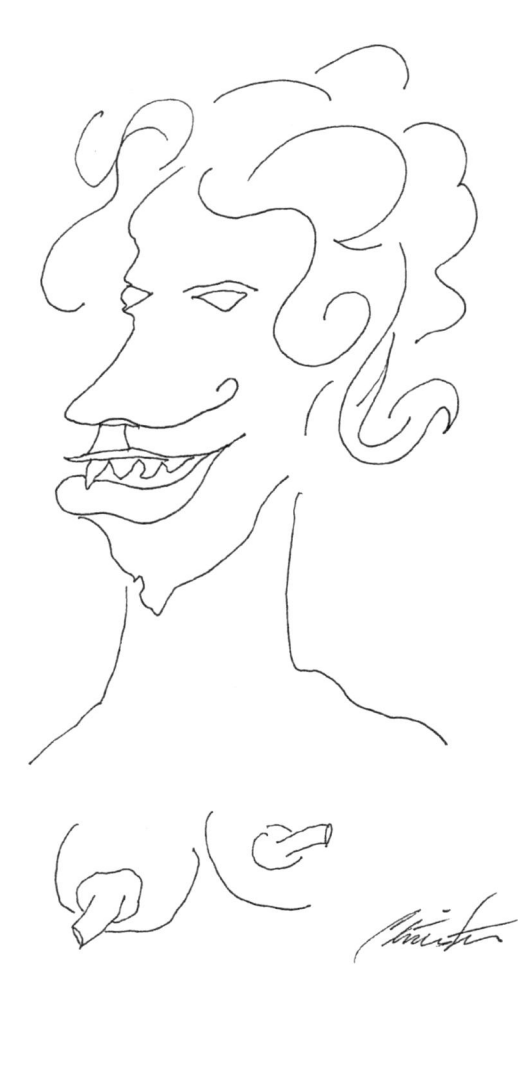

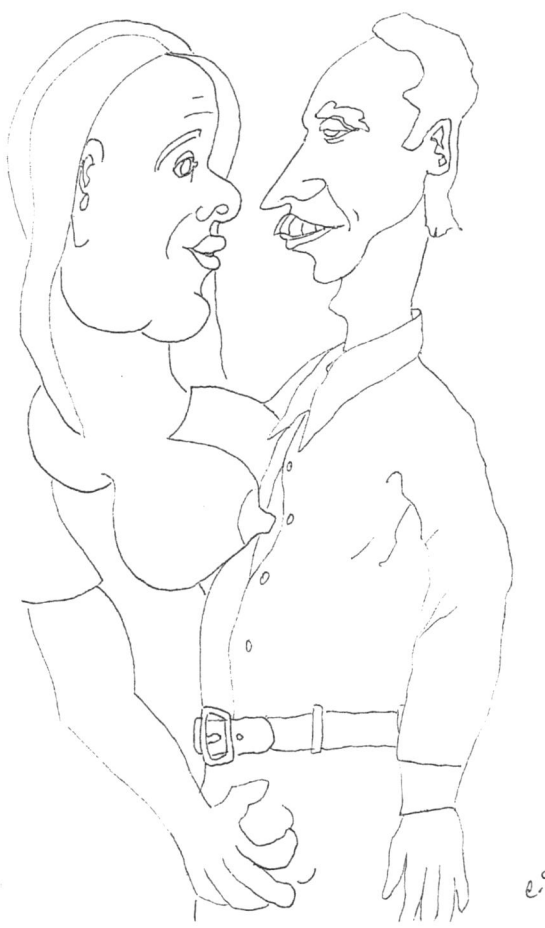

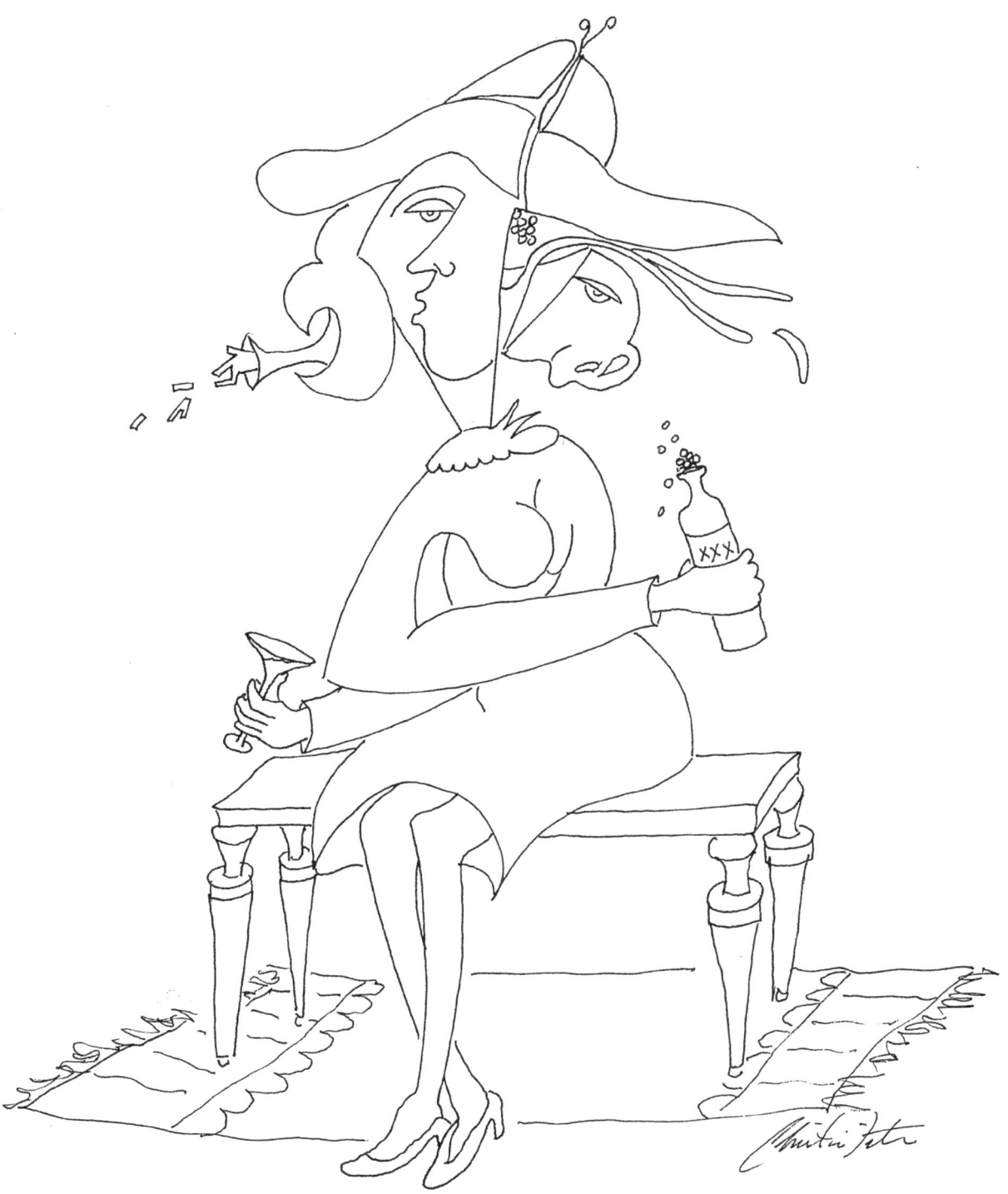

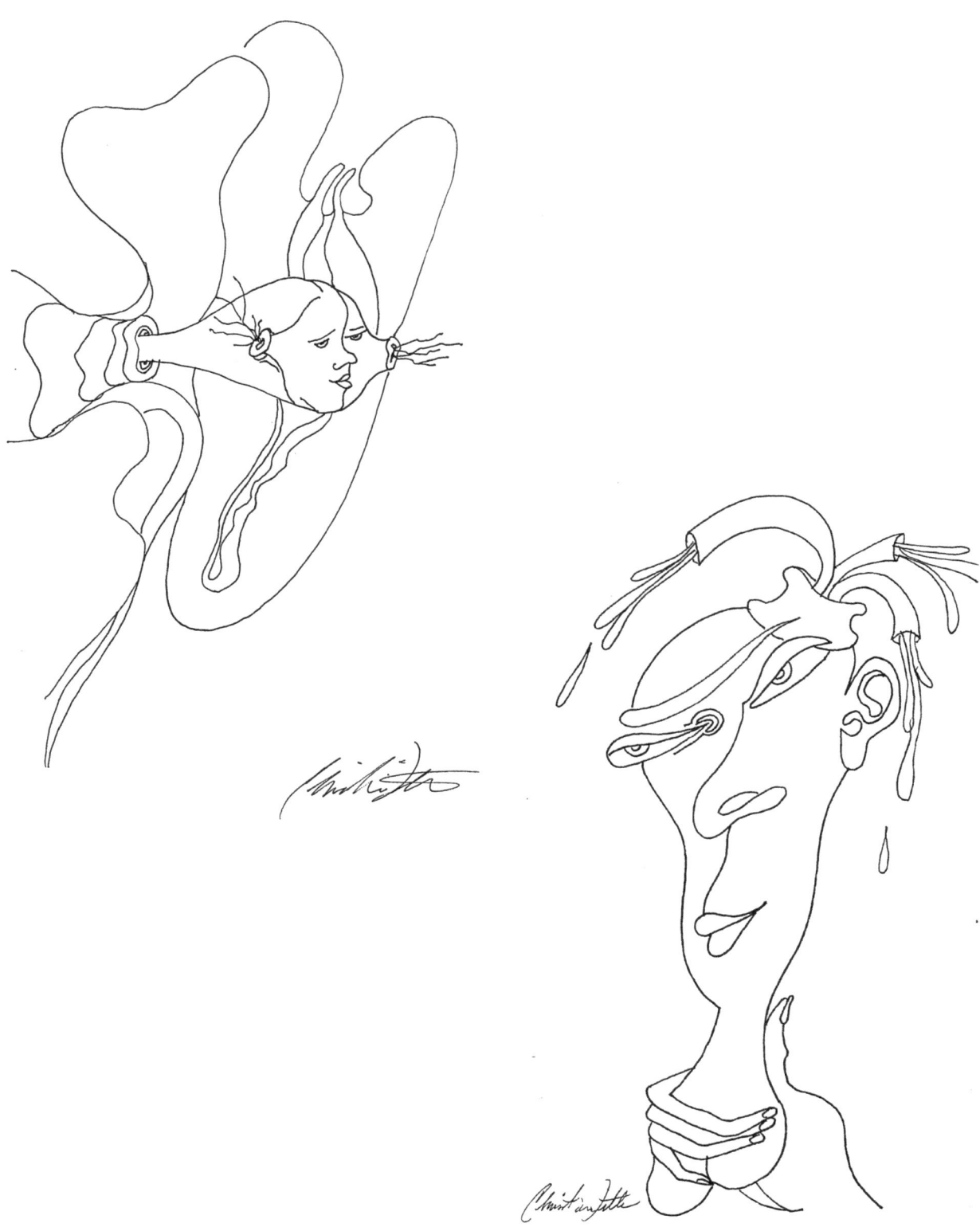

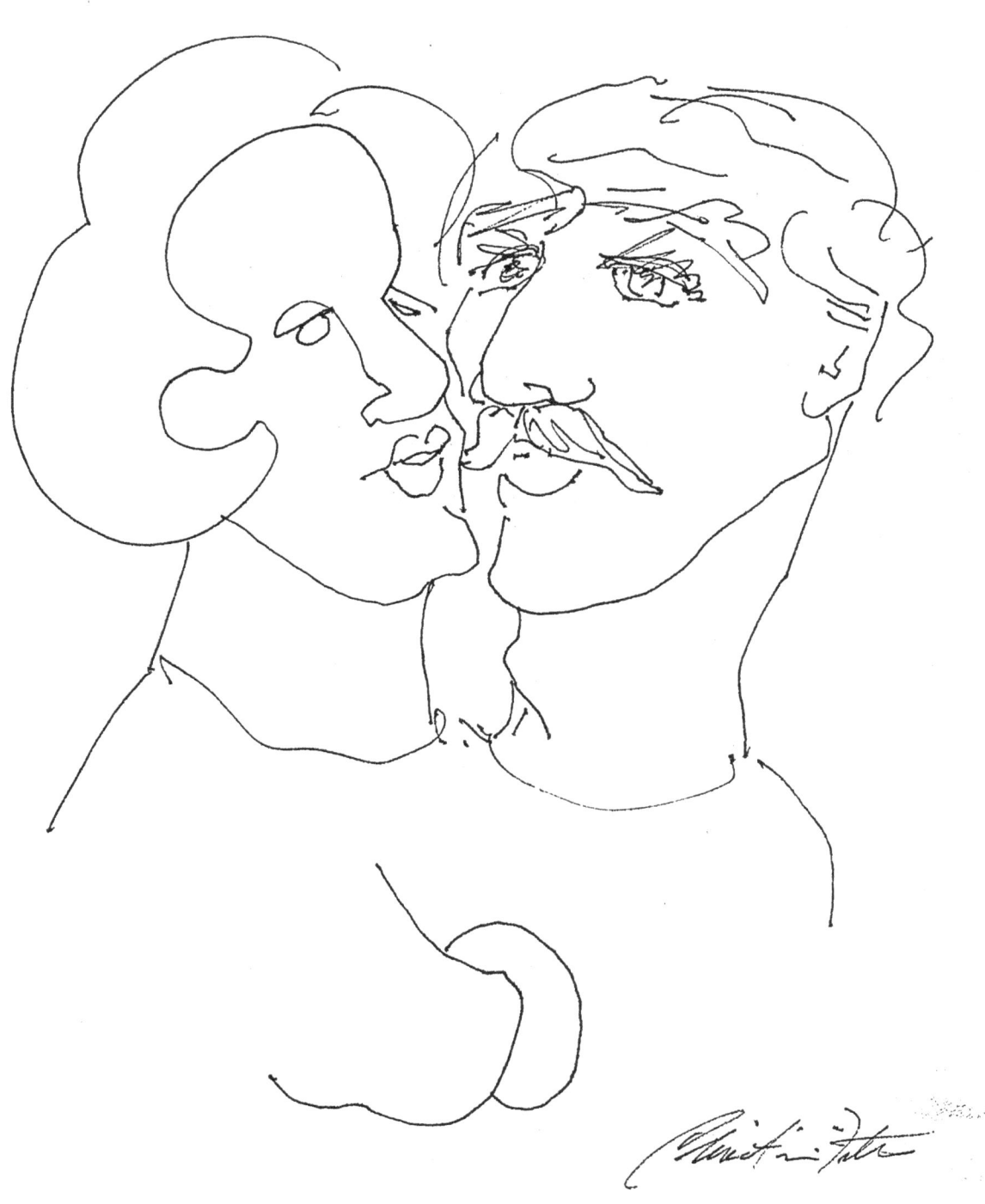

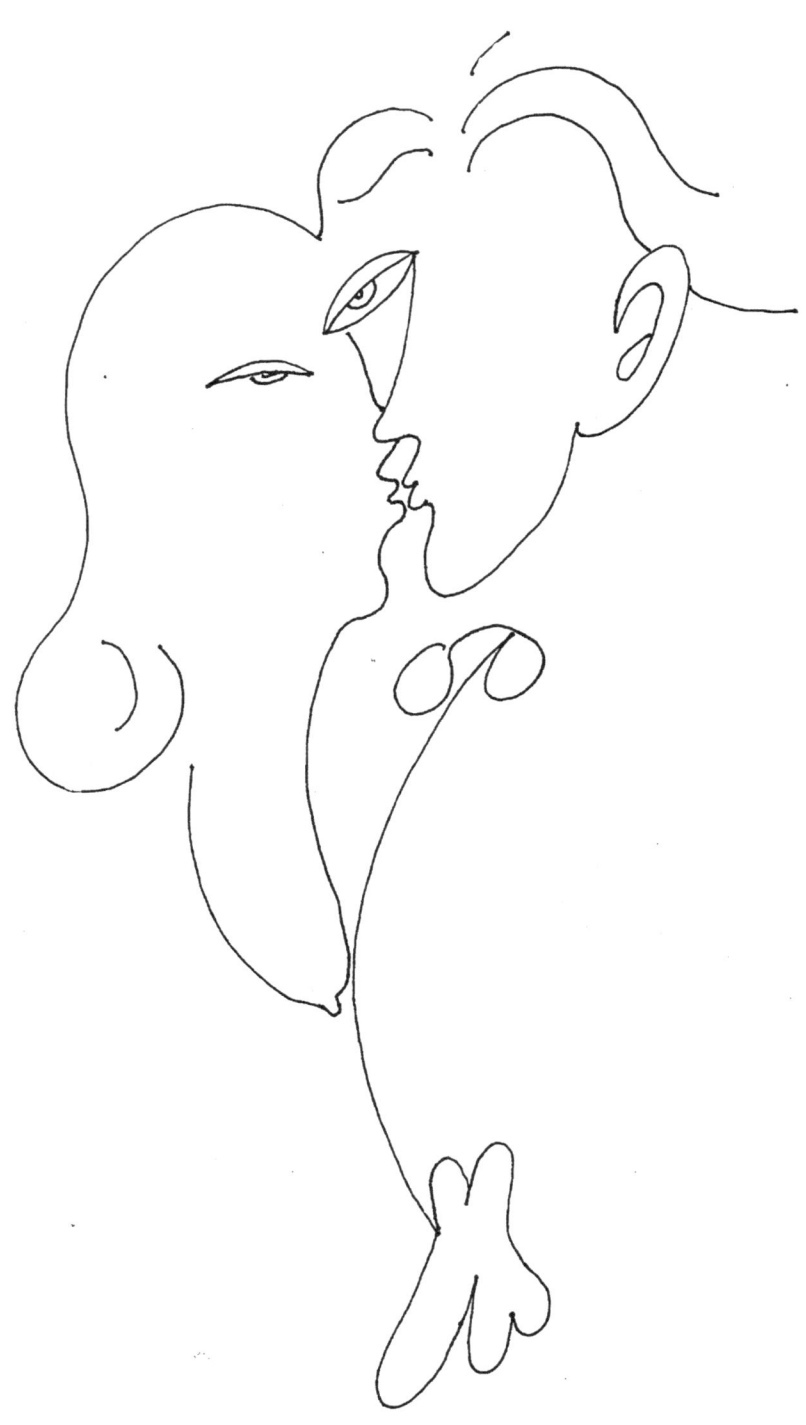

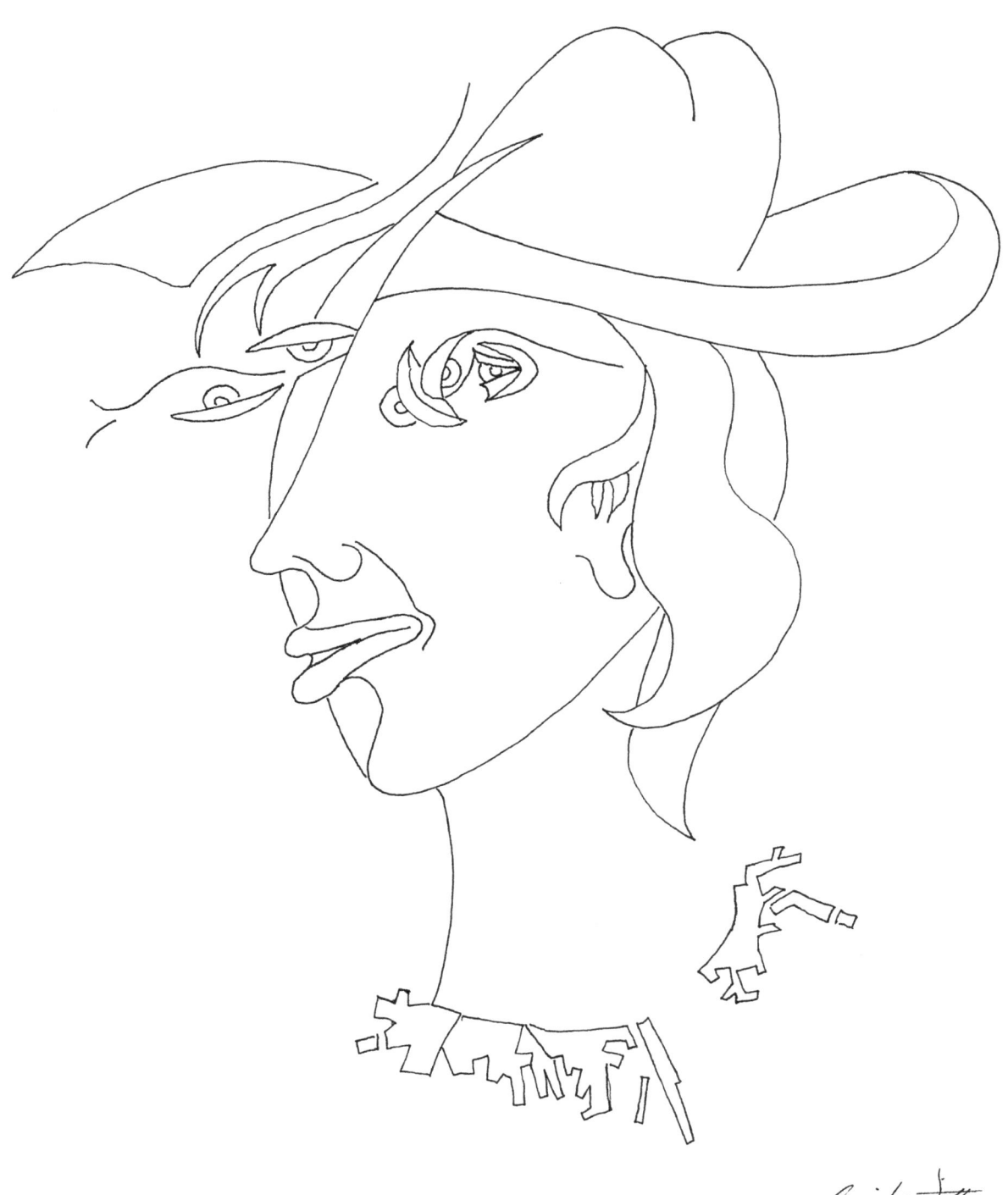

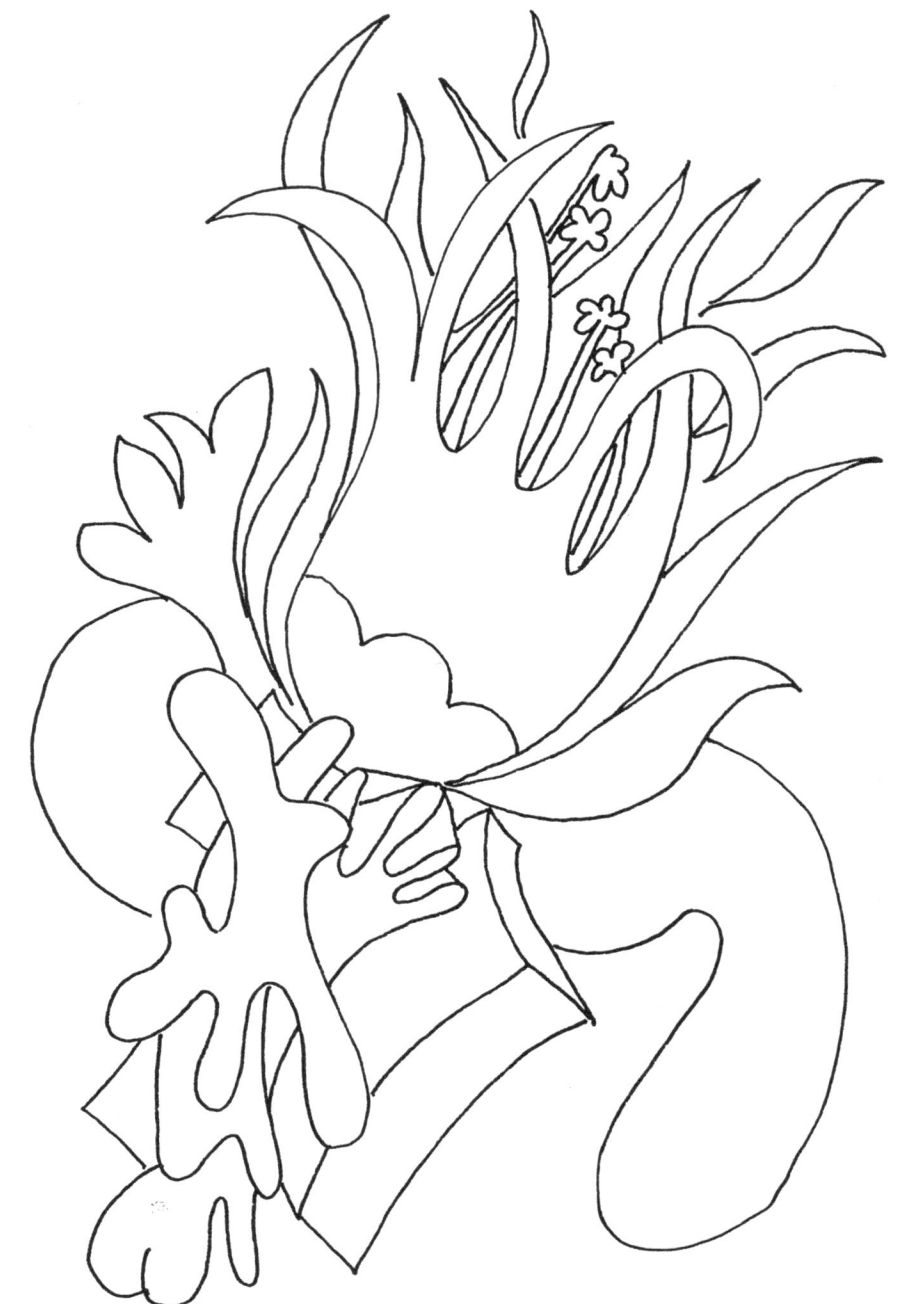

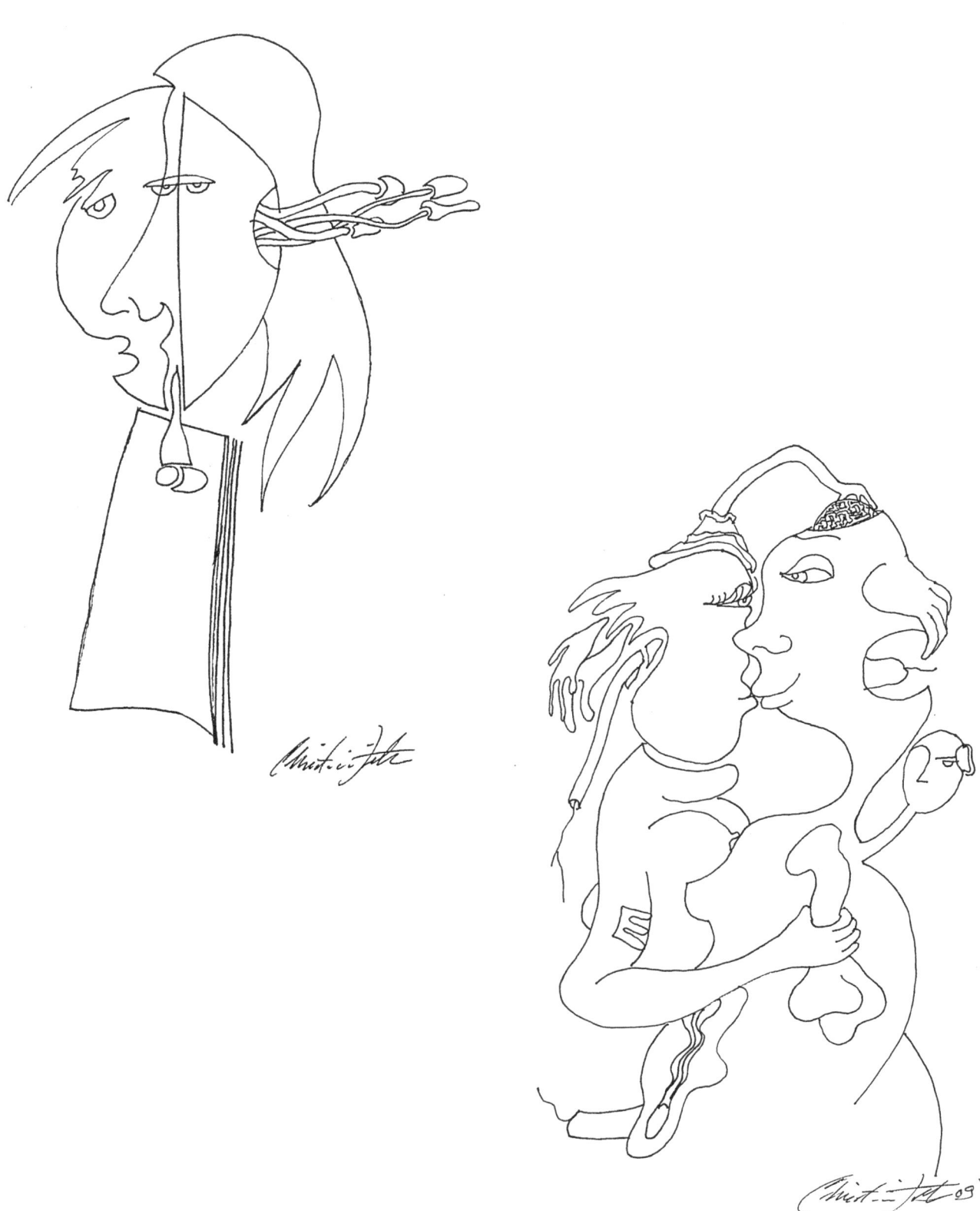

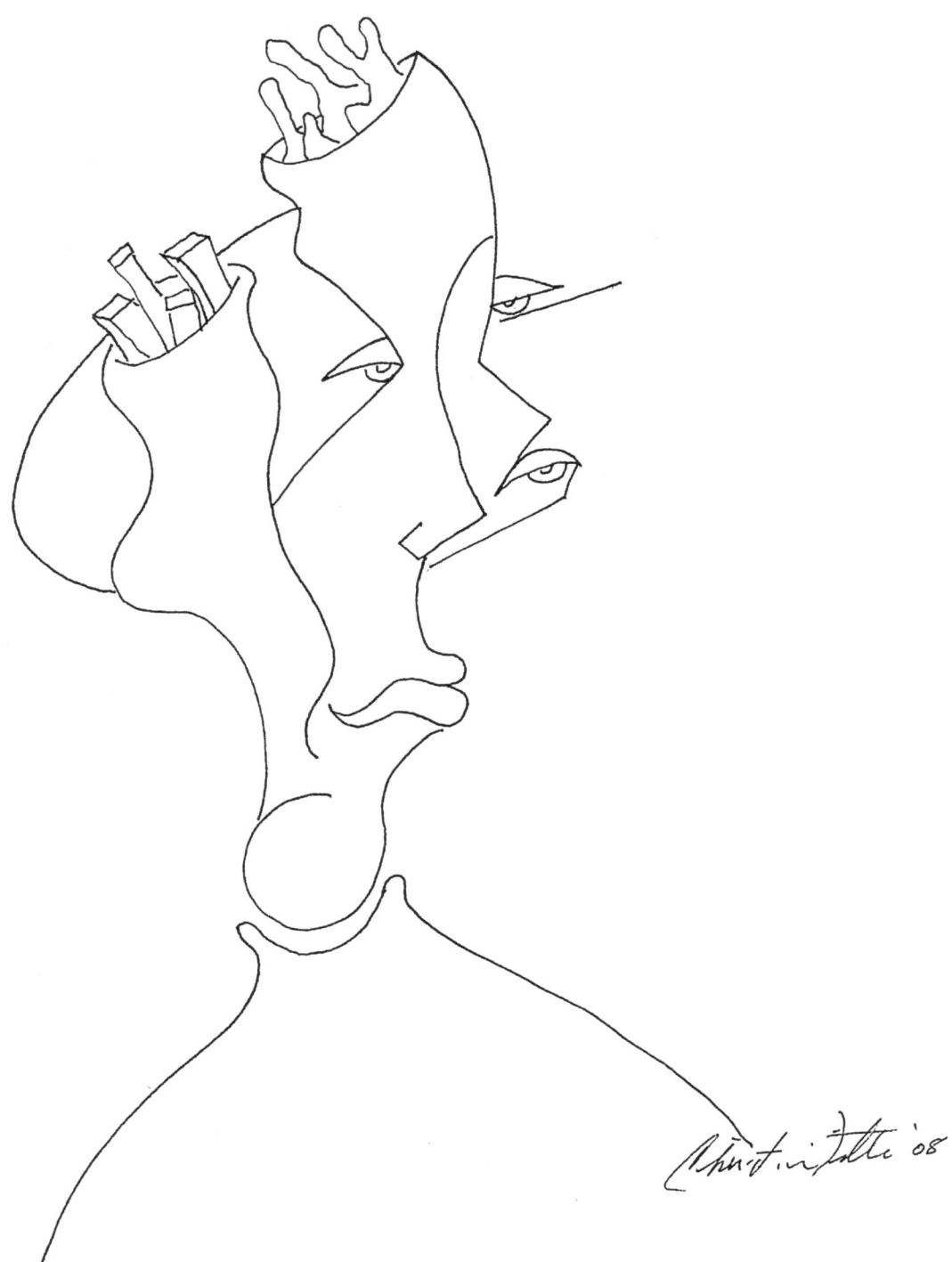

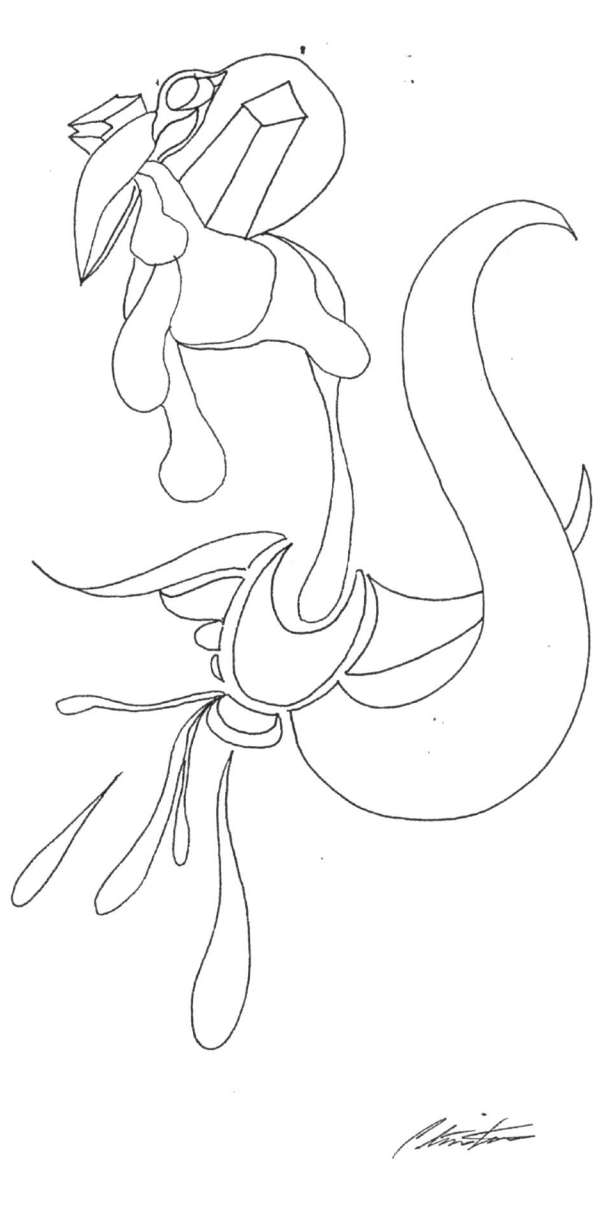

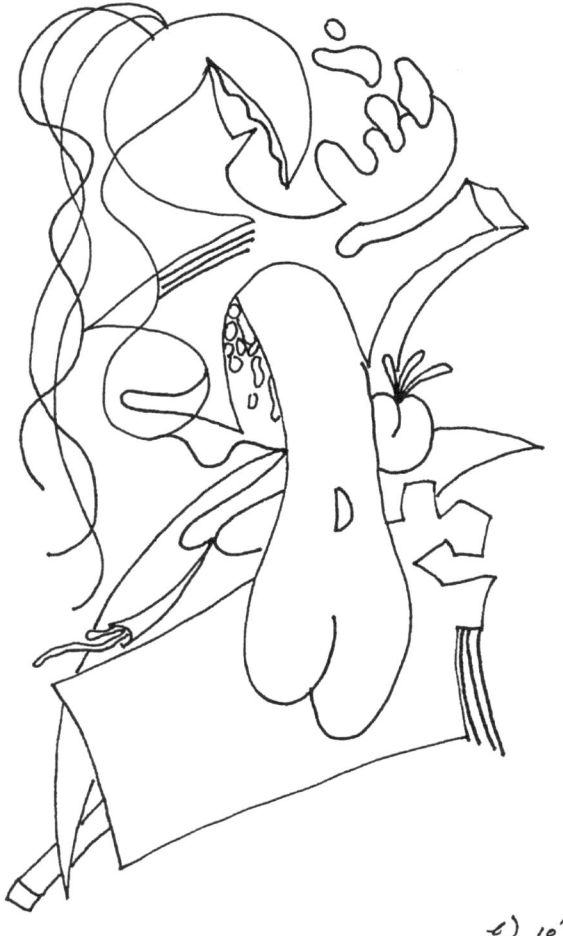

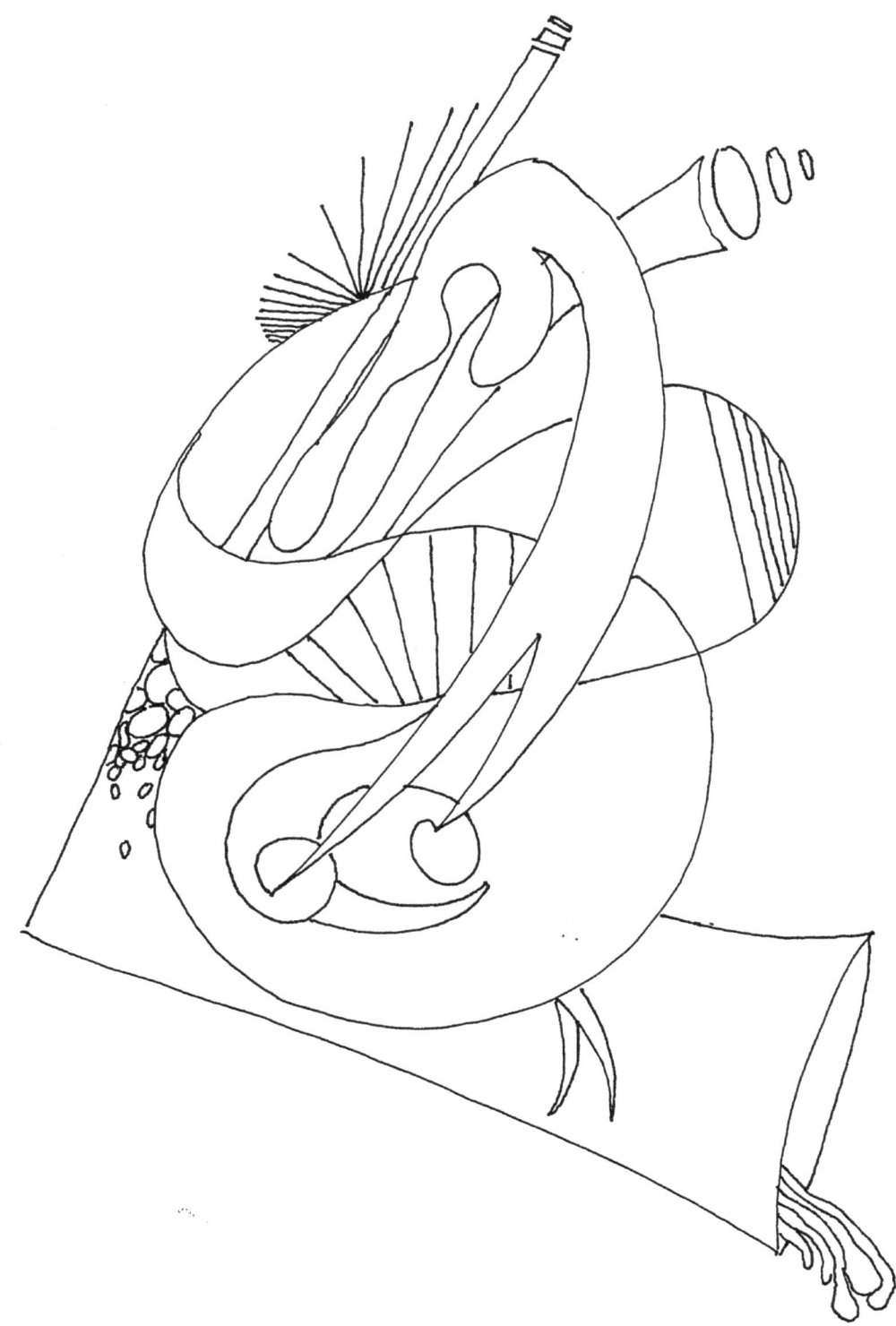

CJ. 14'

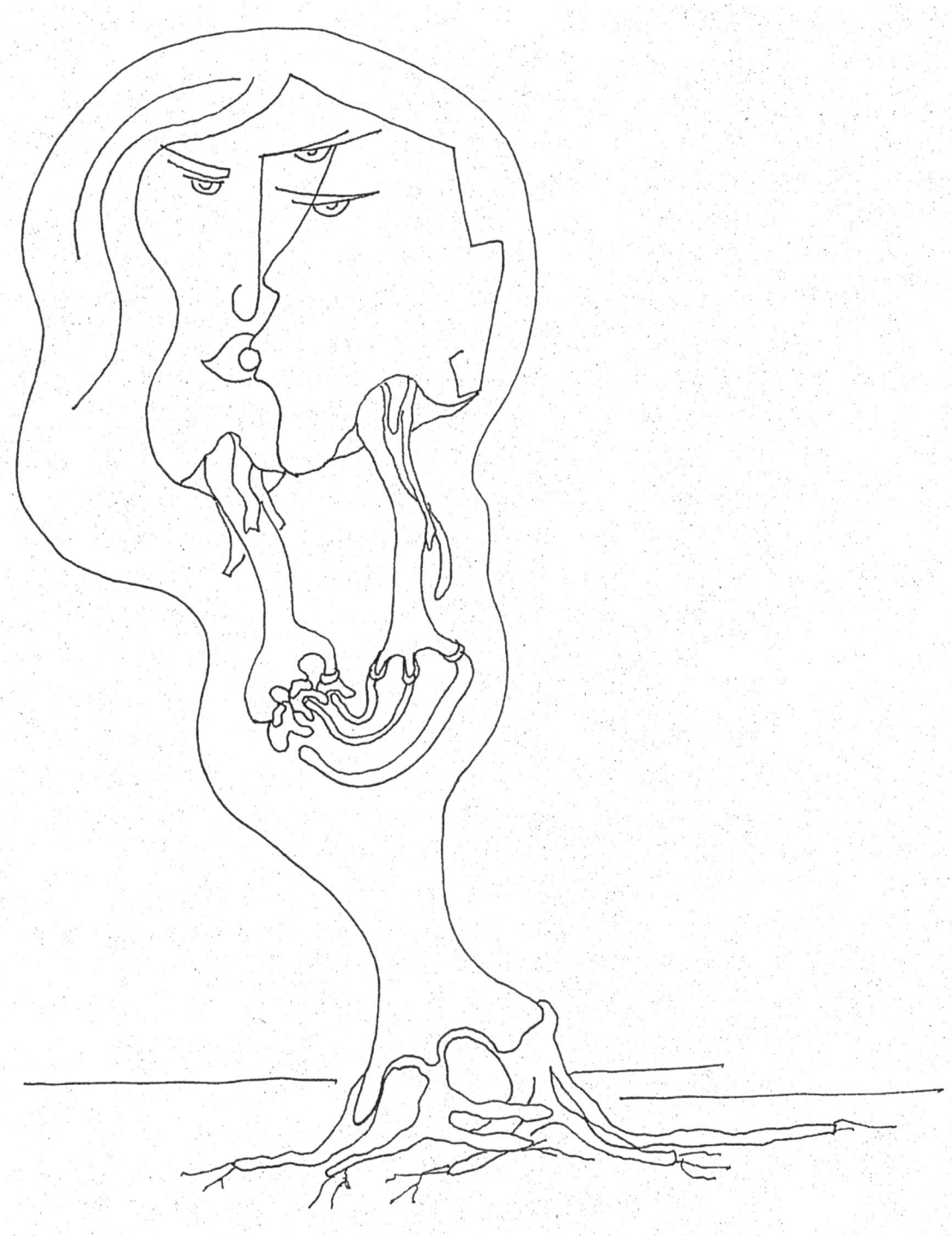

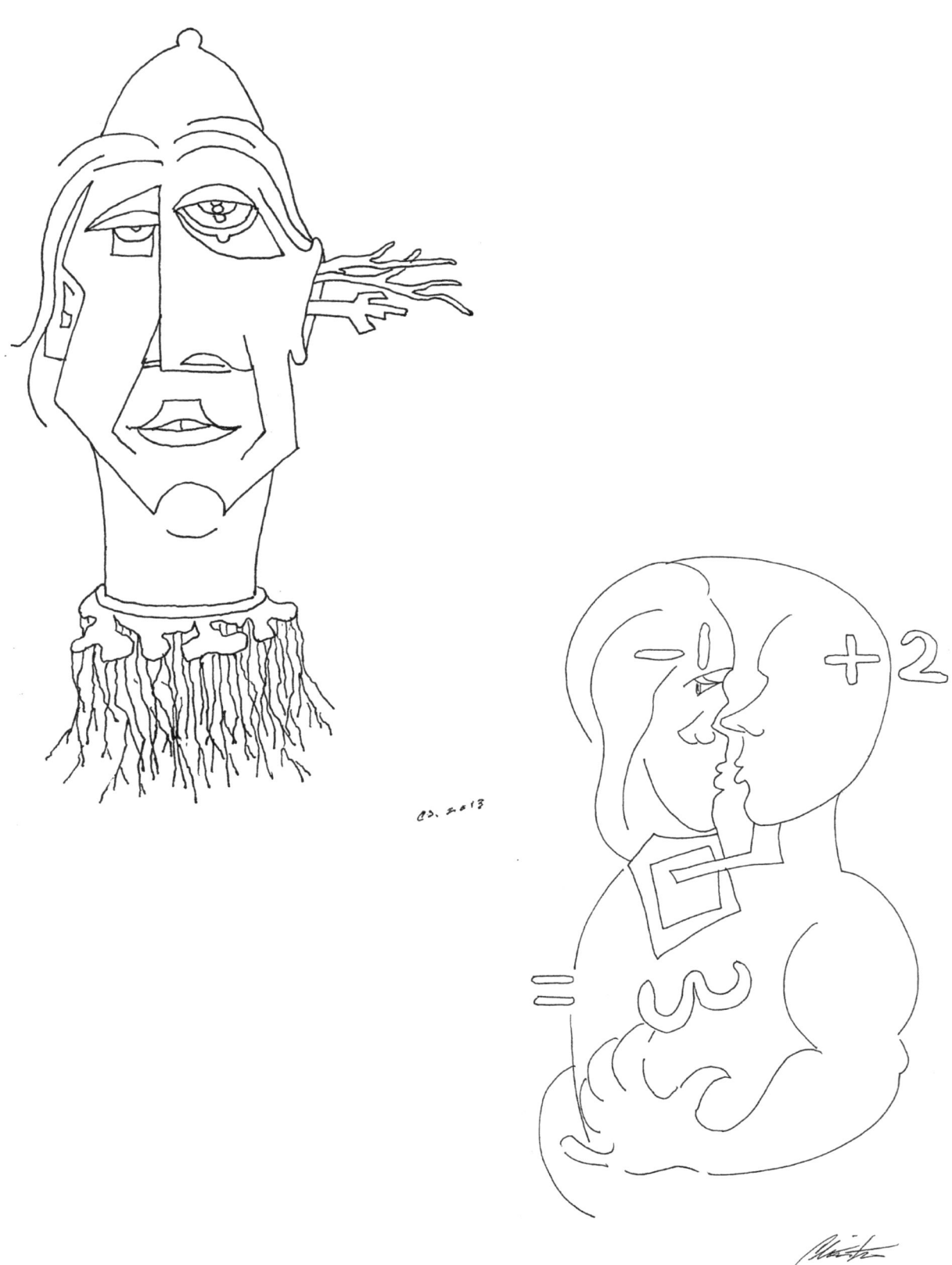

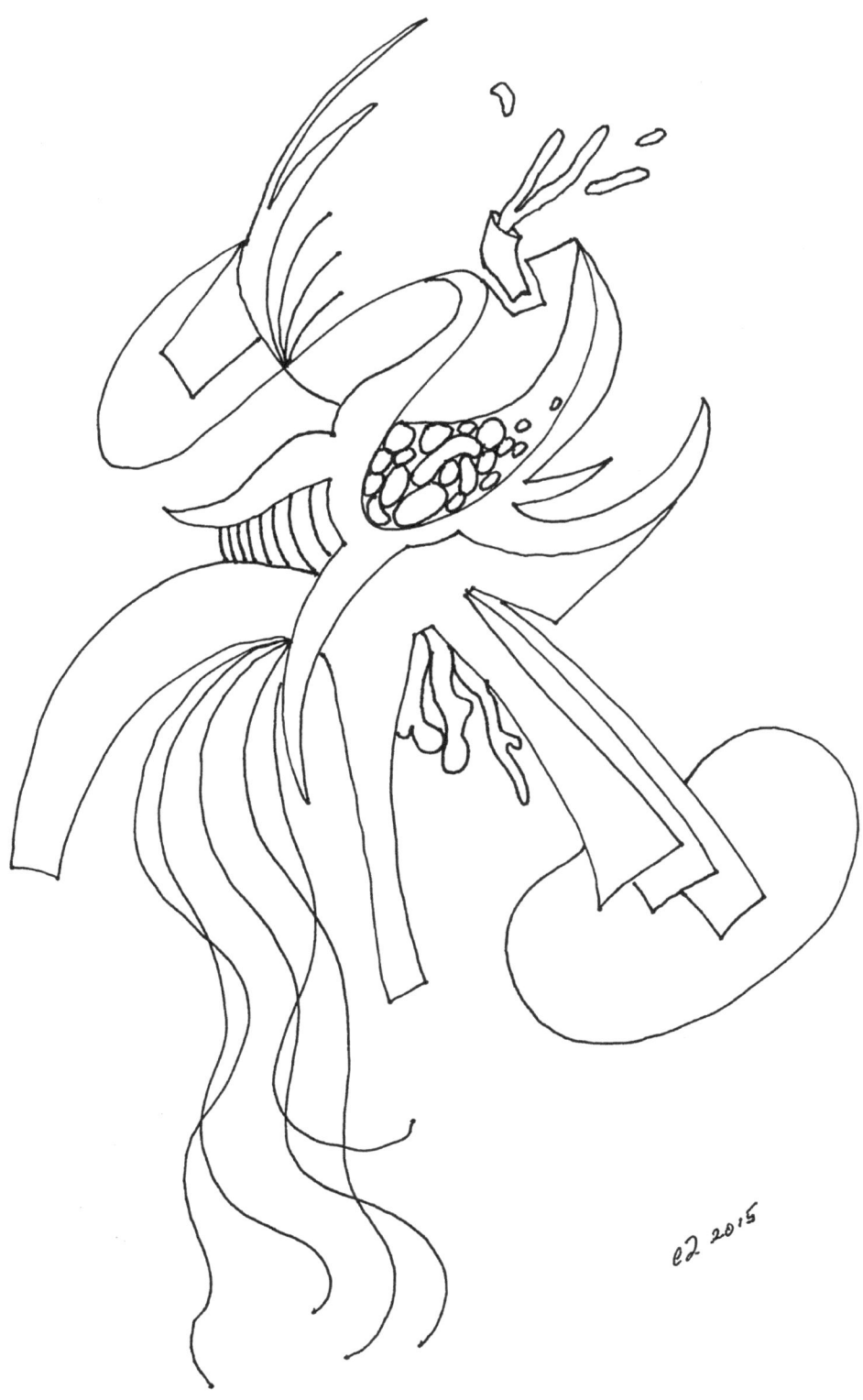

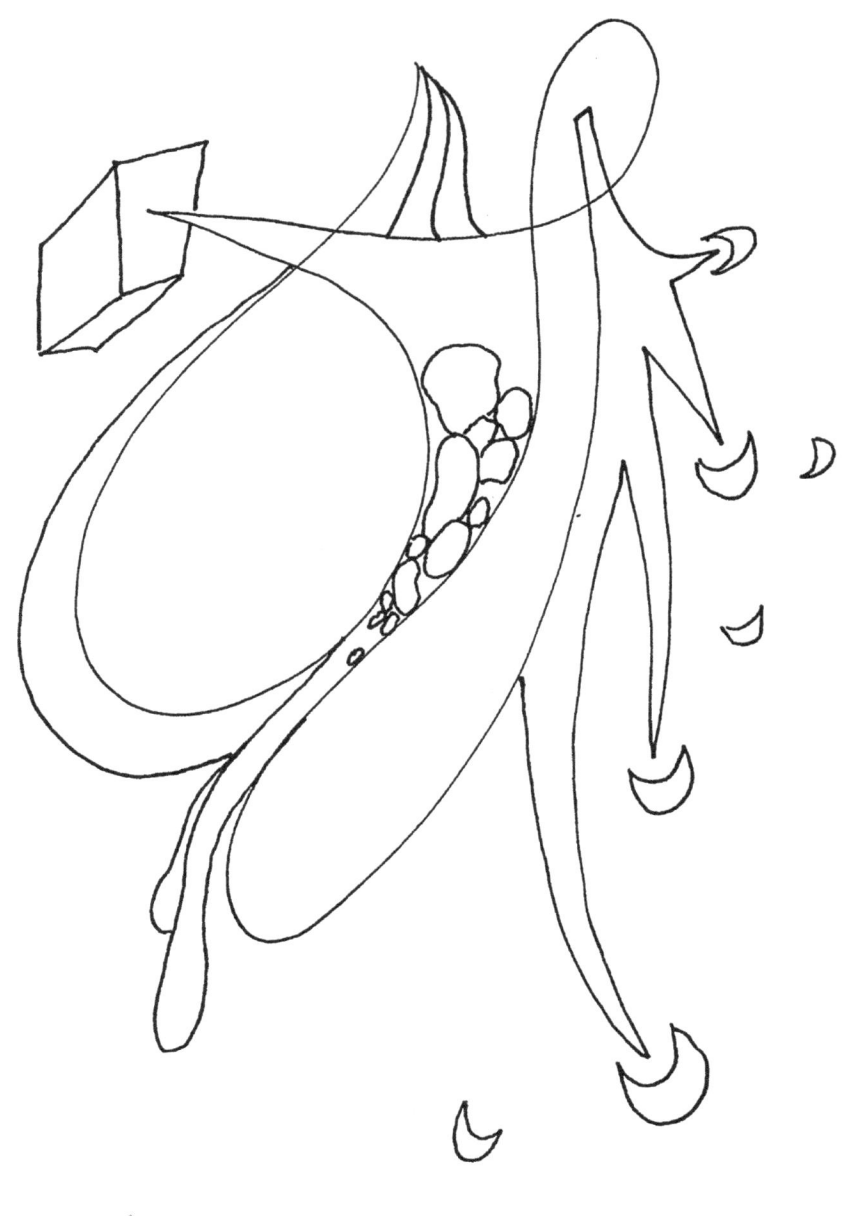

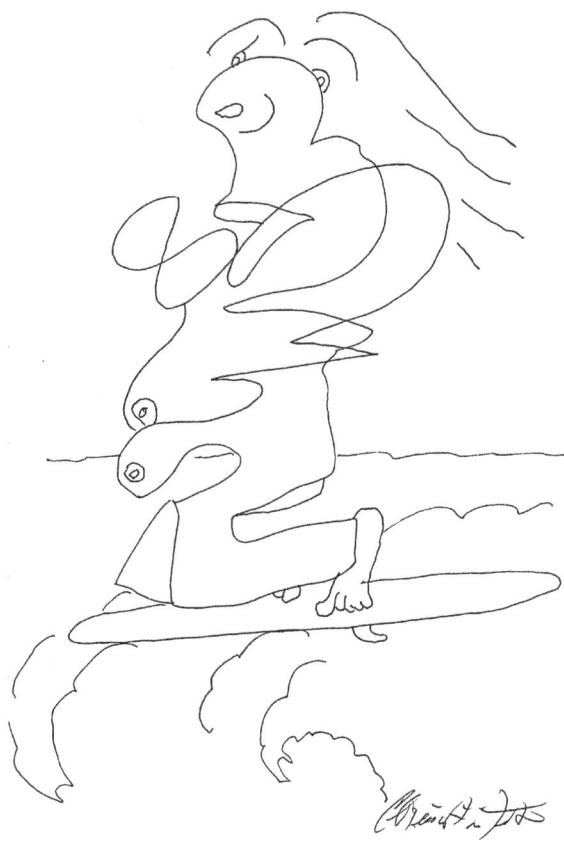

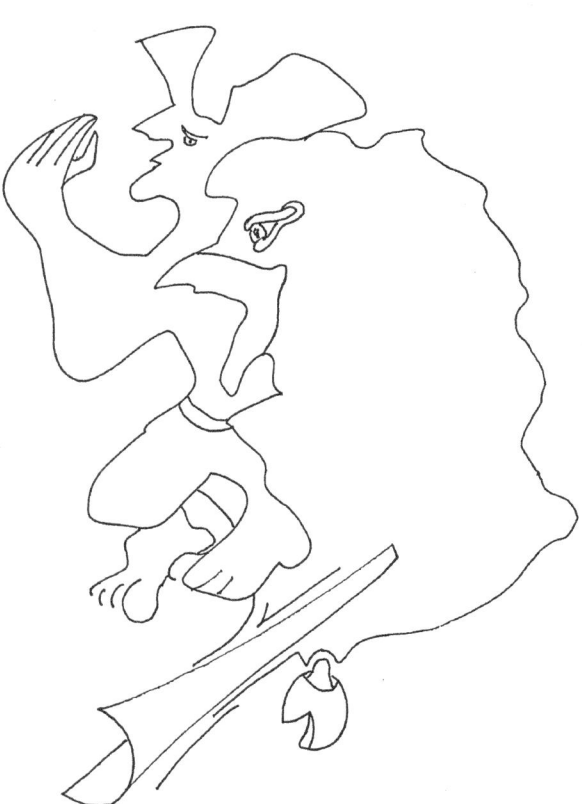

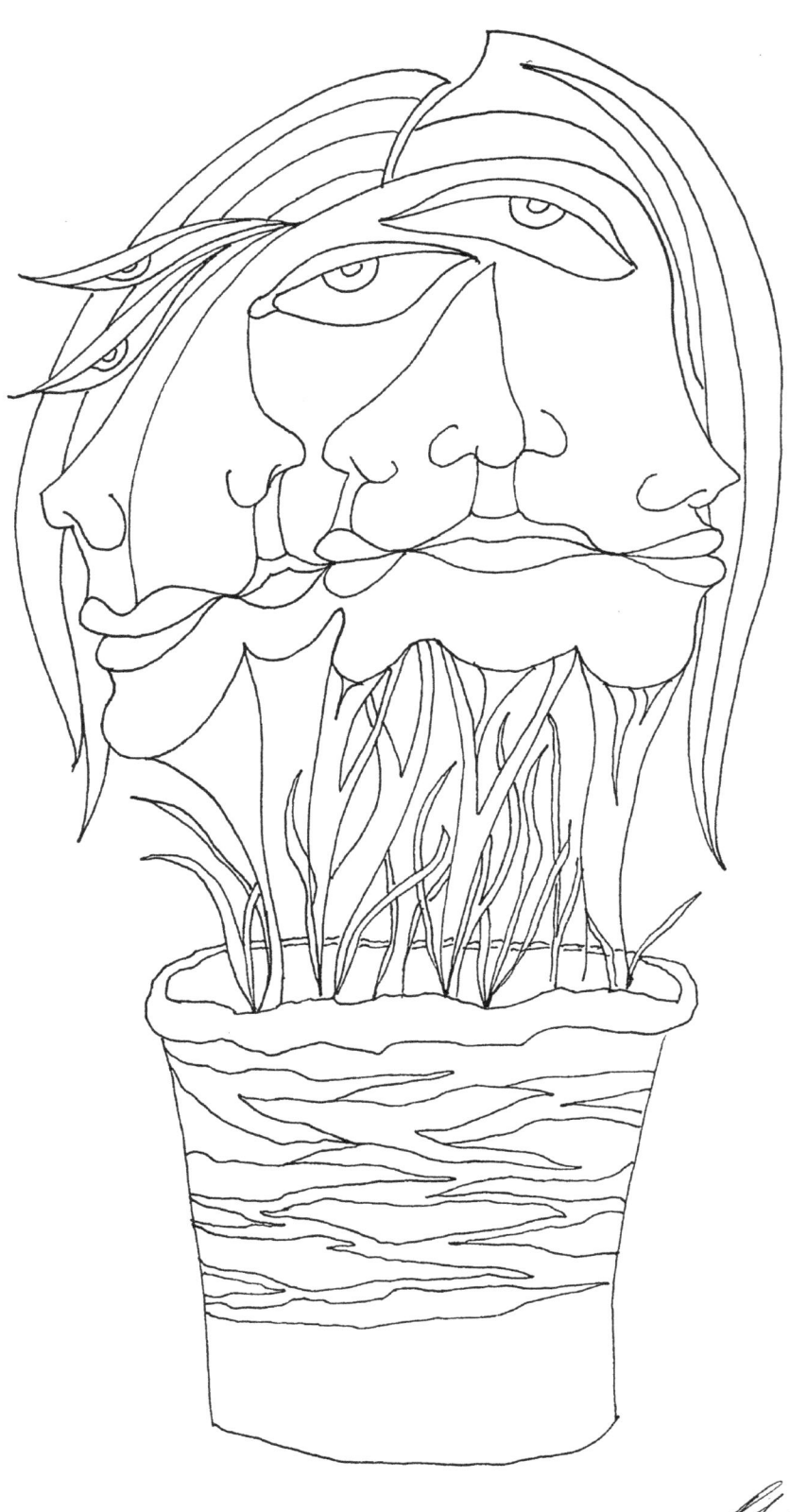

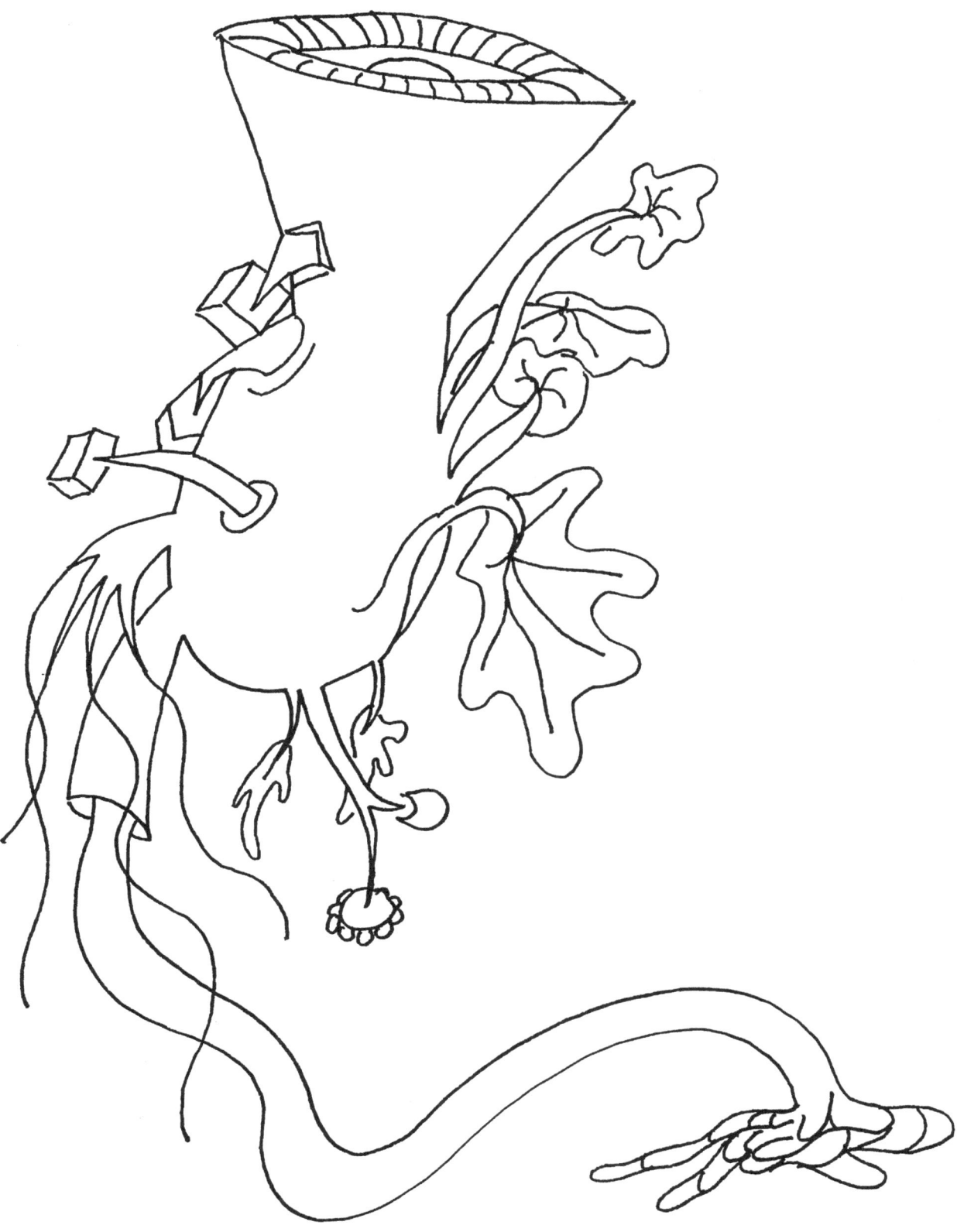

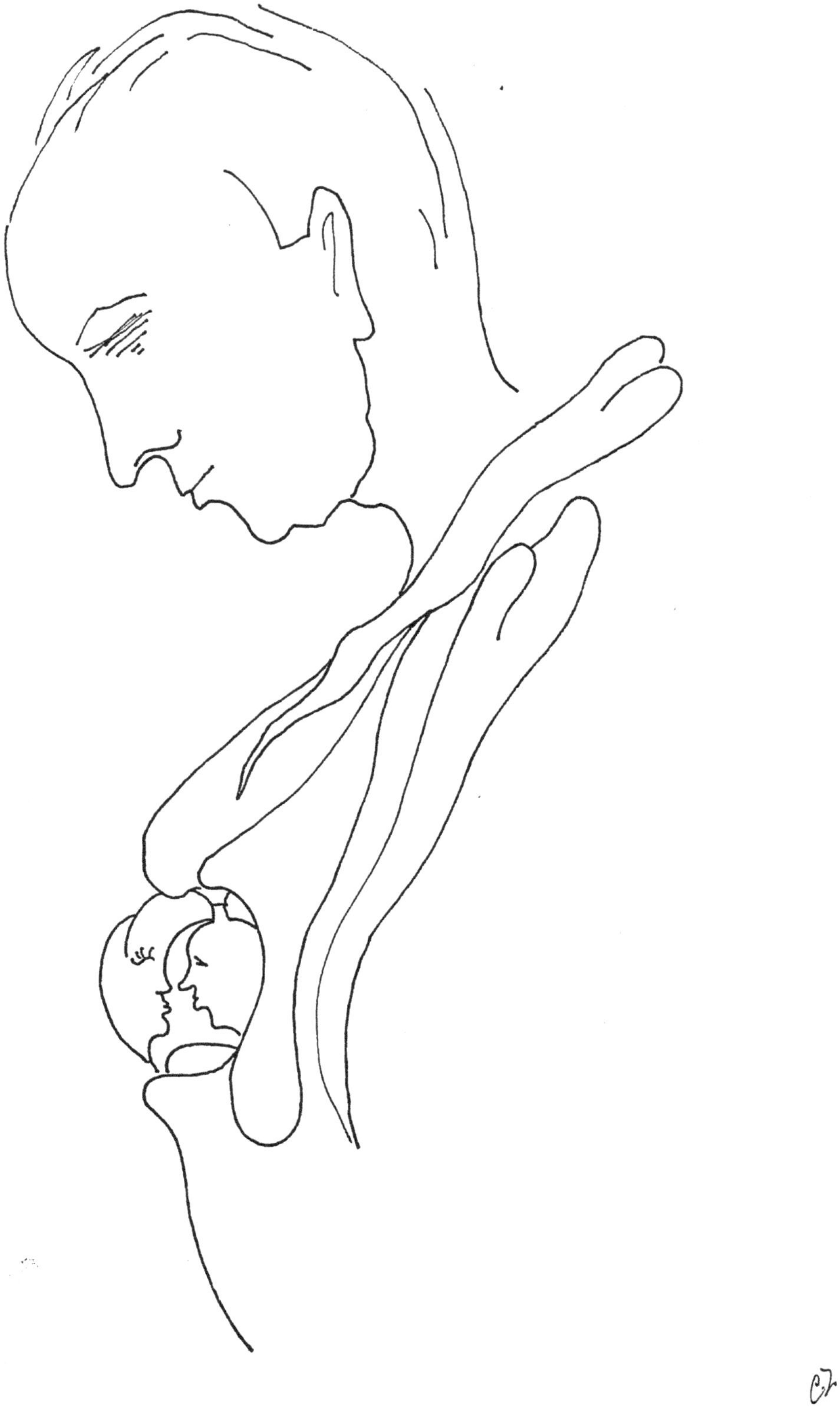

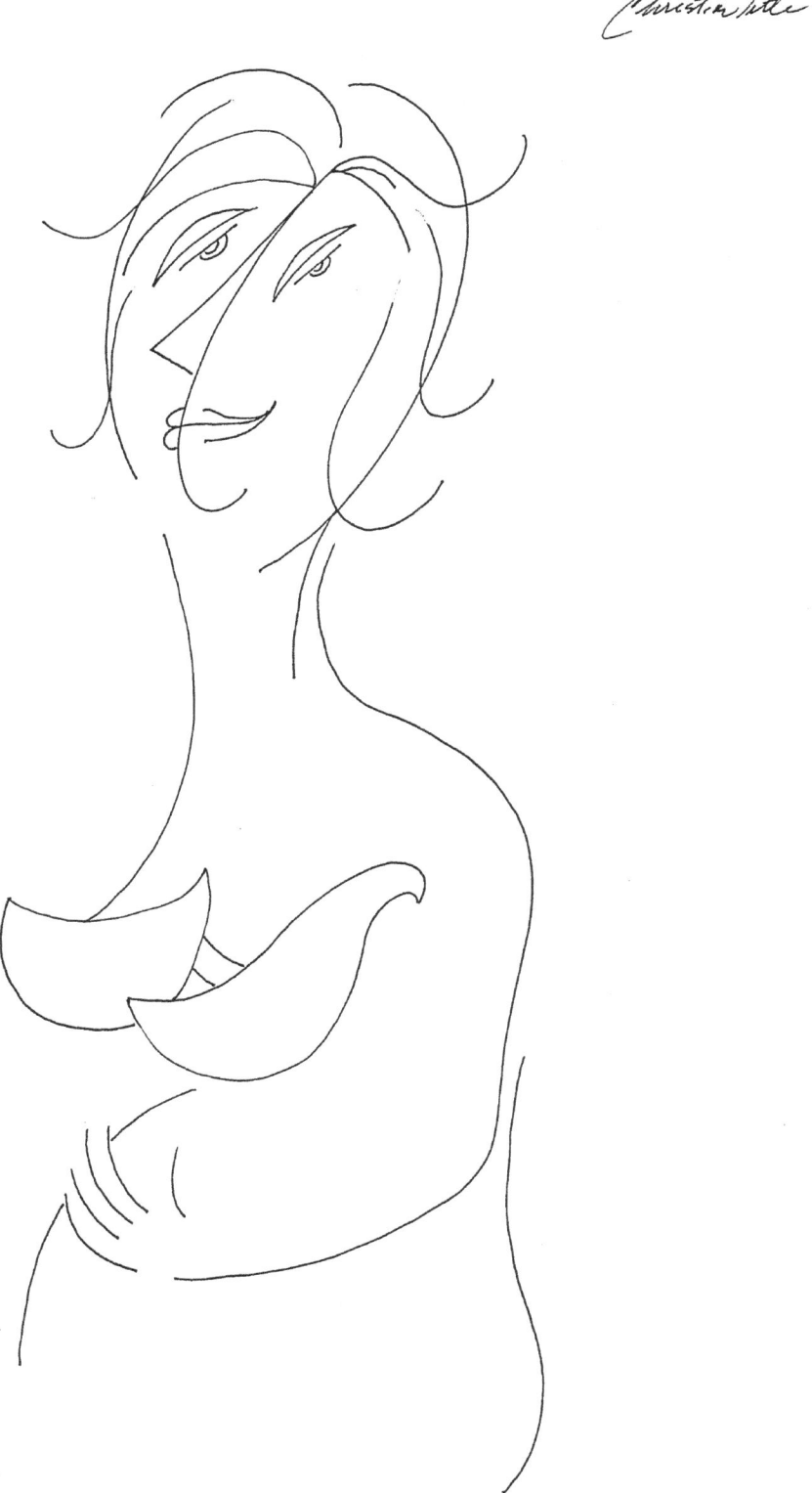

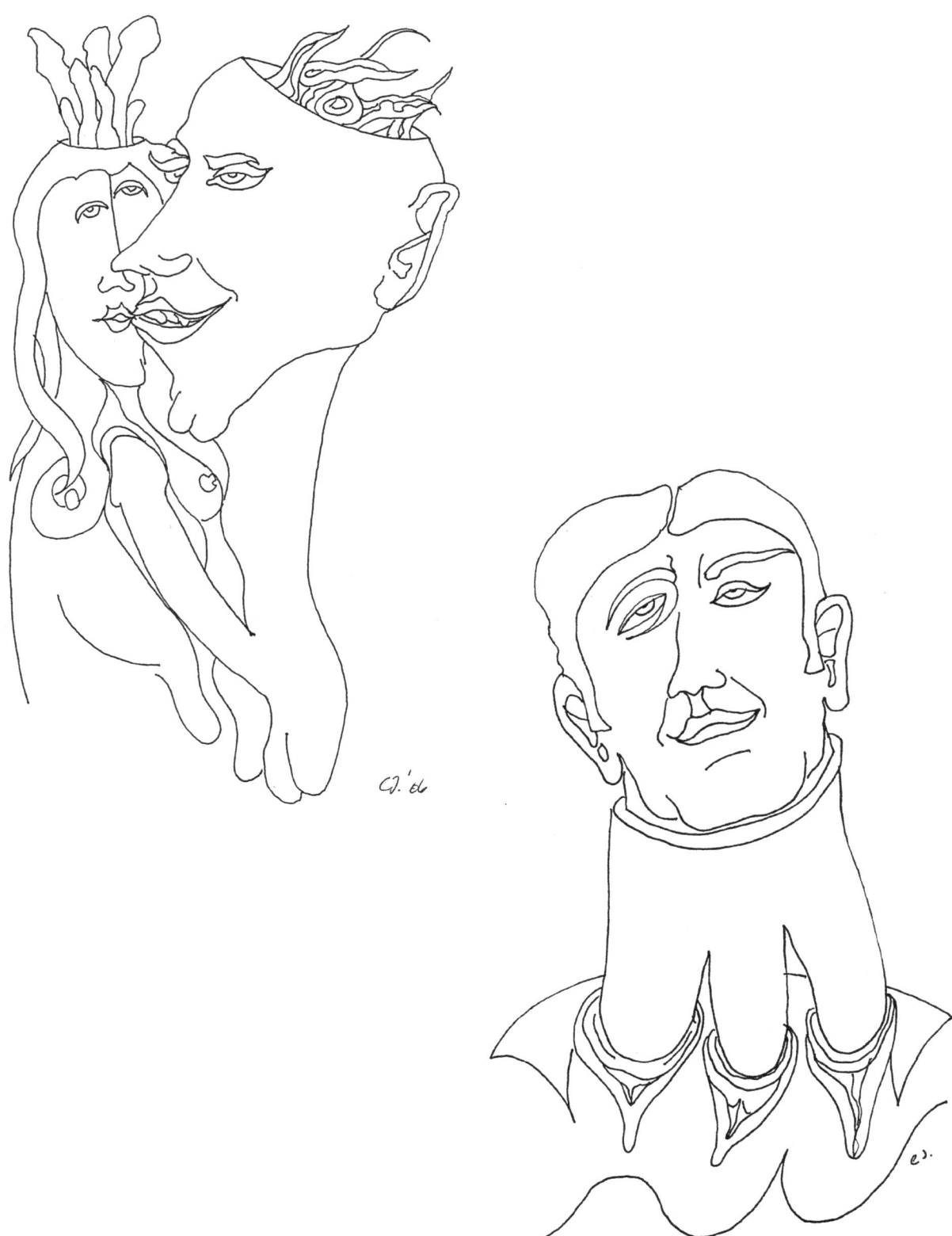

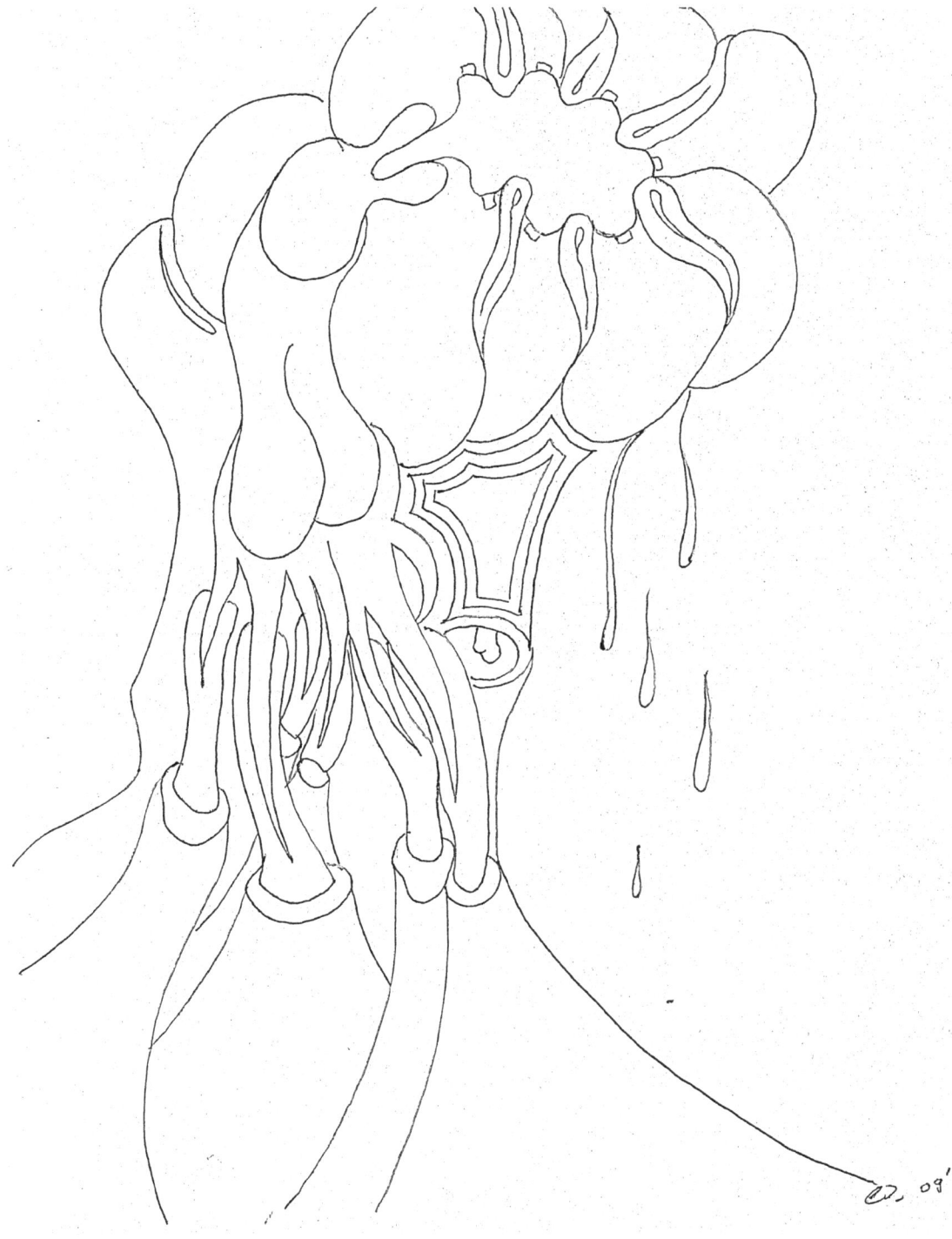

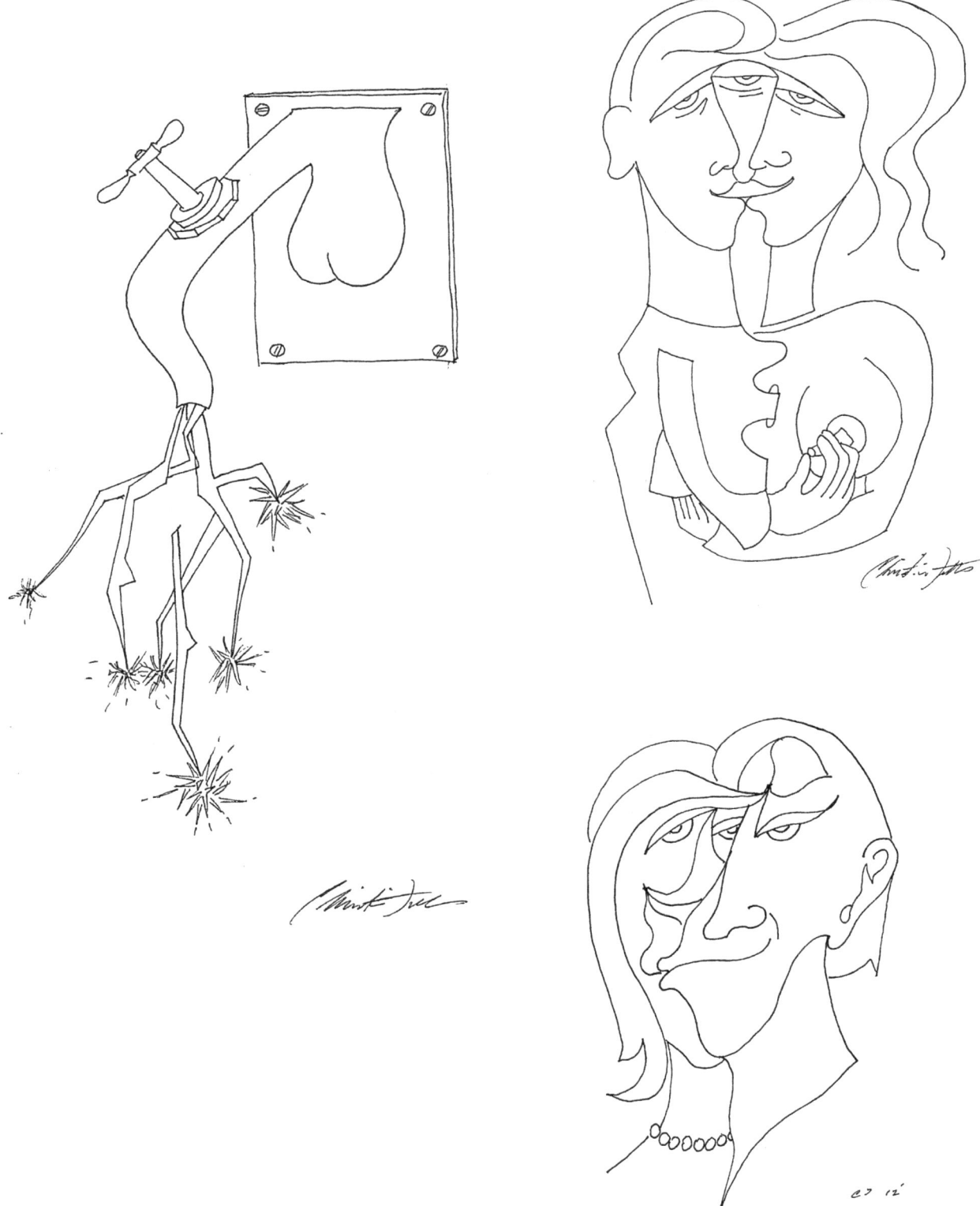

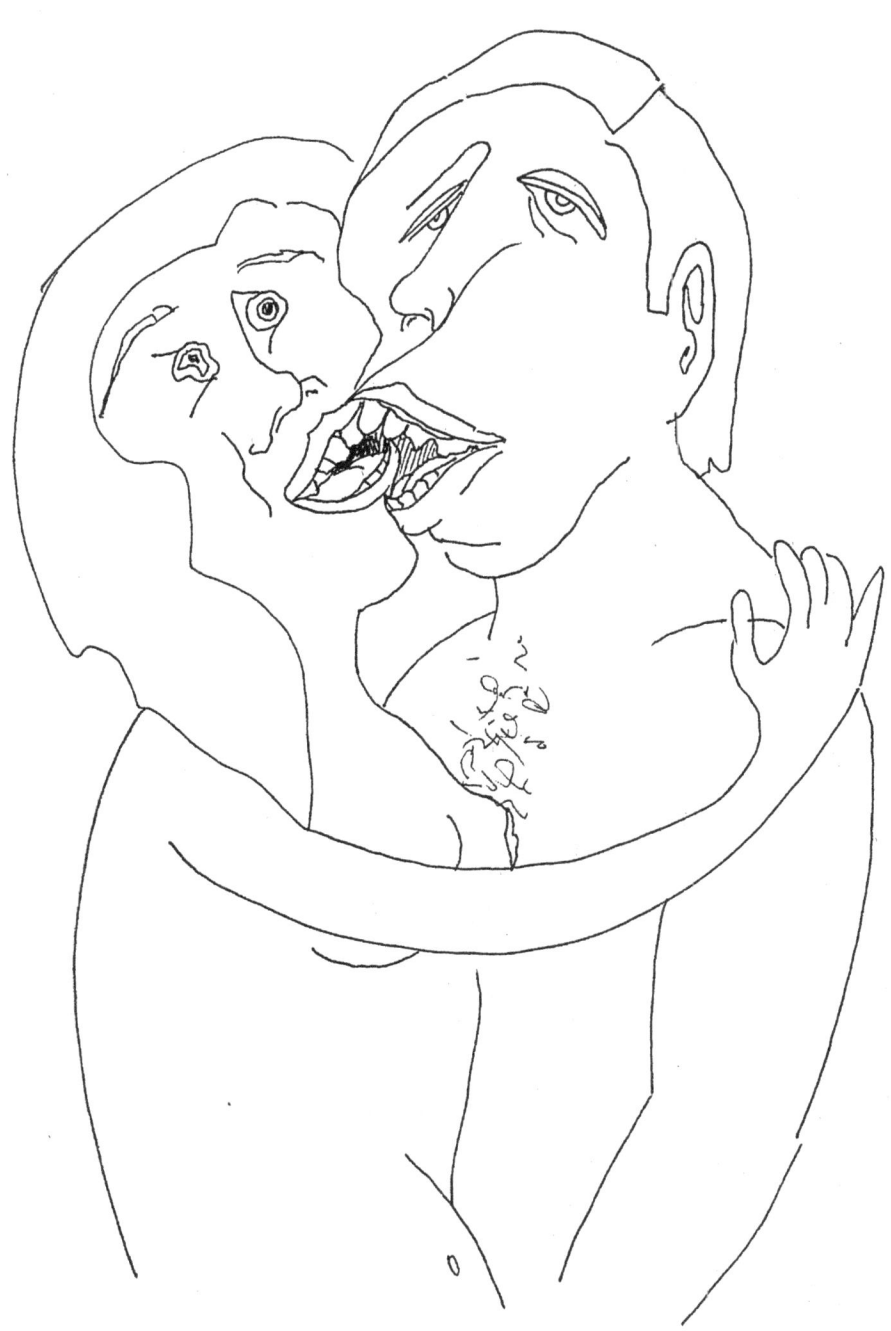

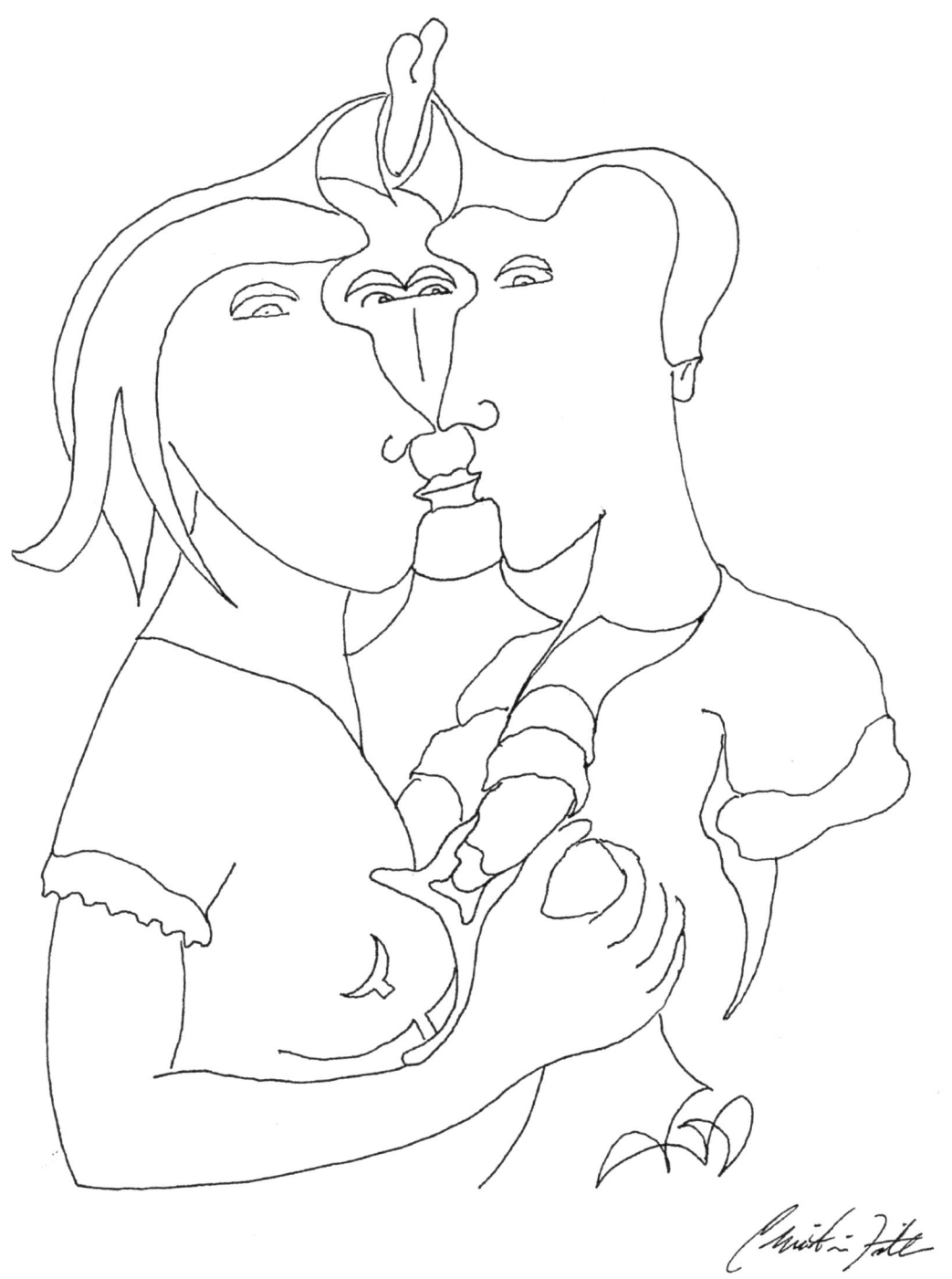

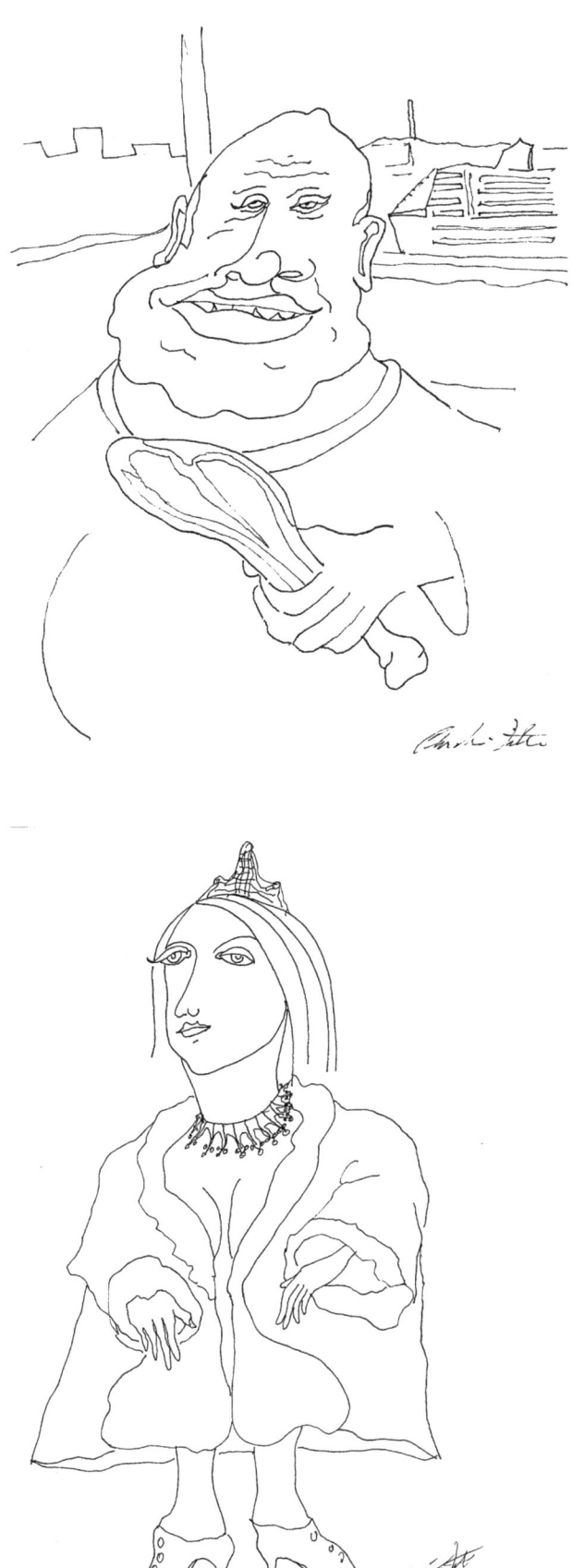

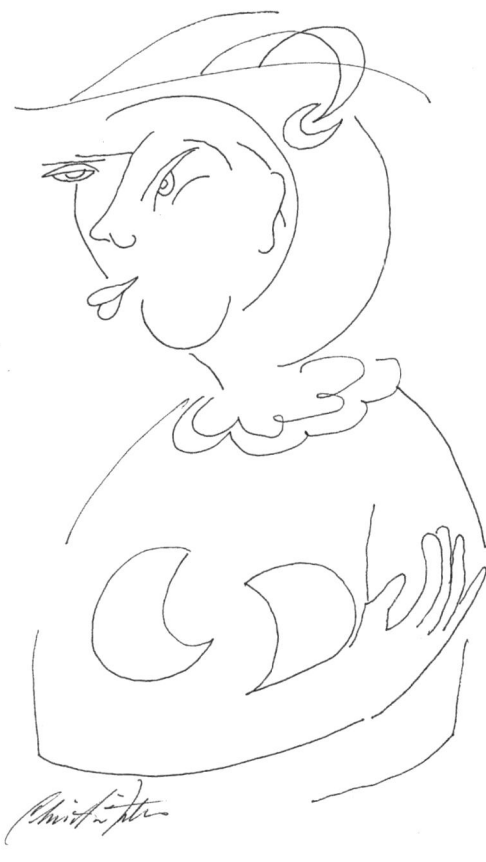

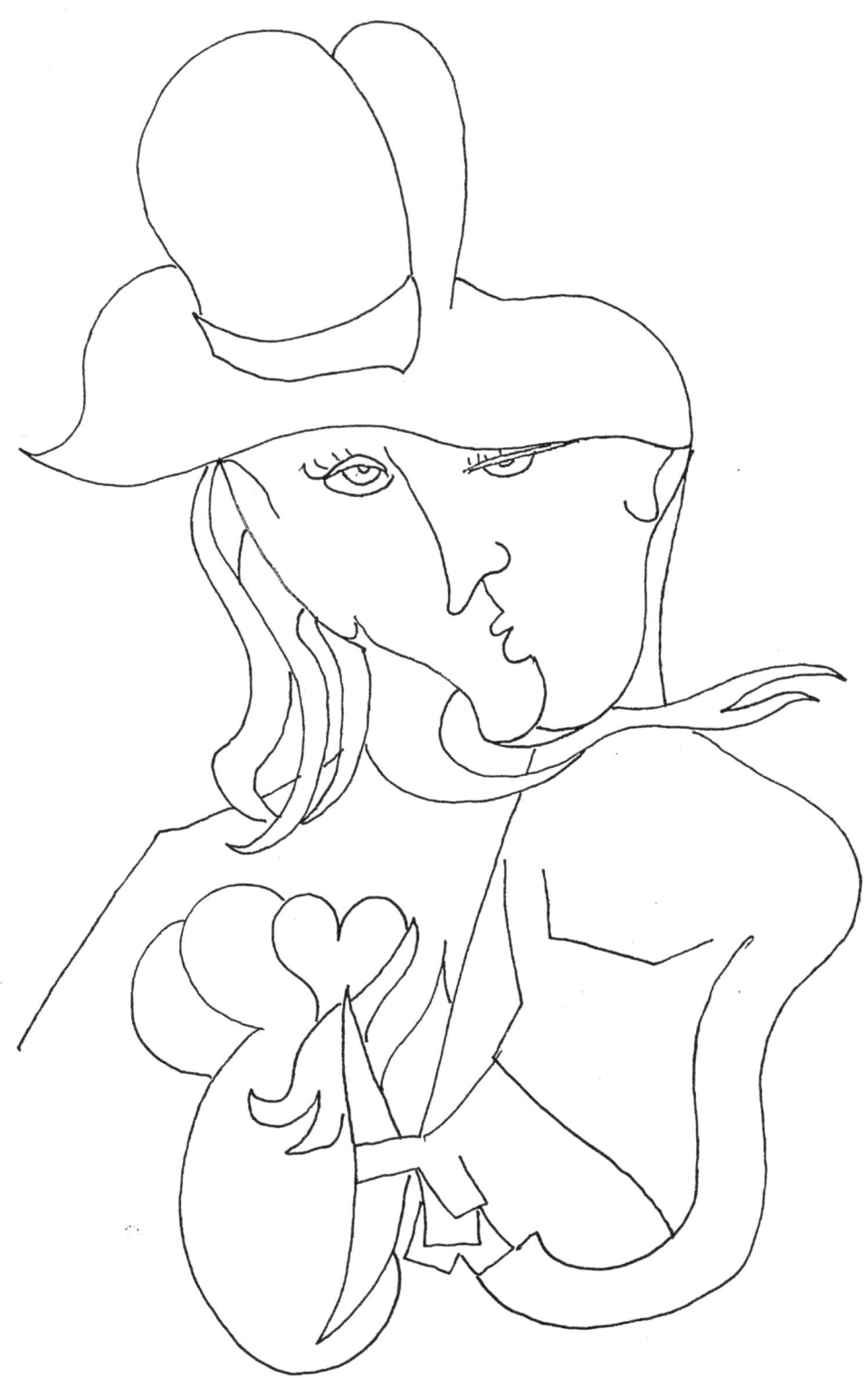

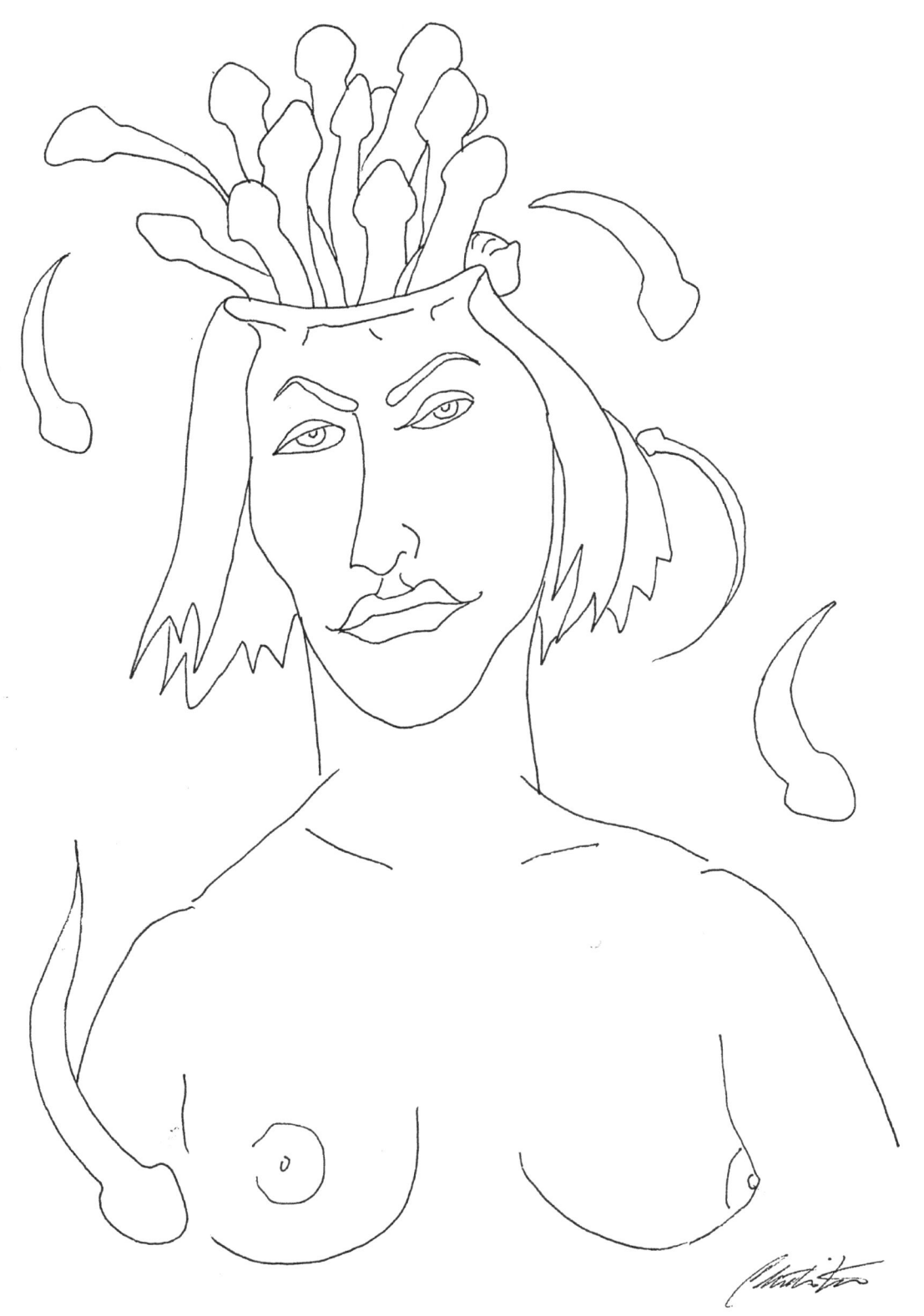

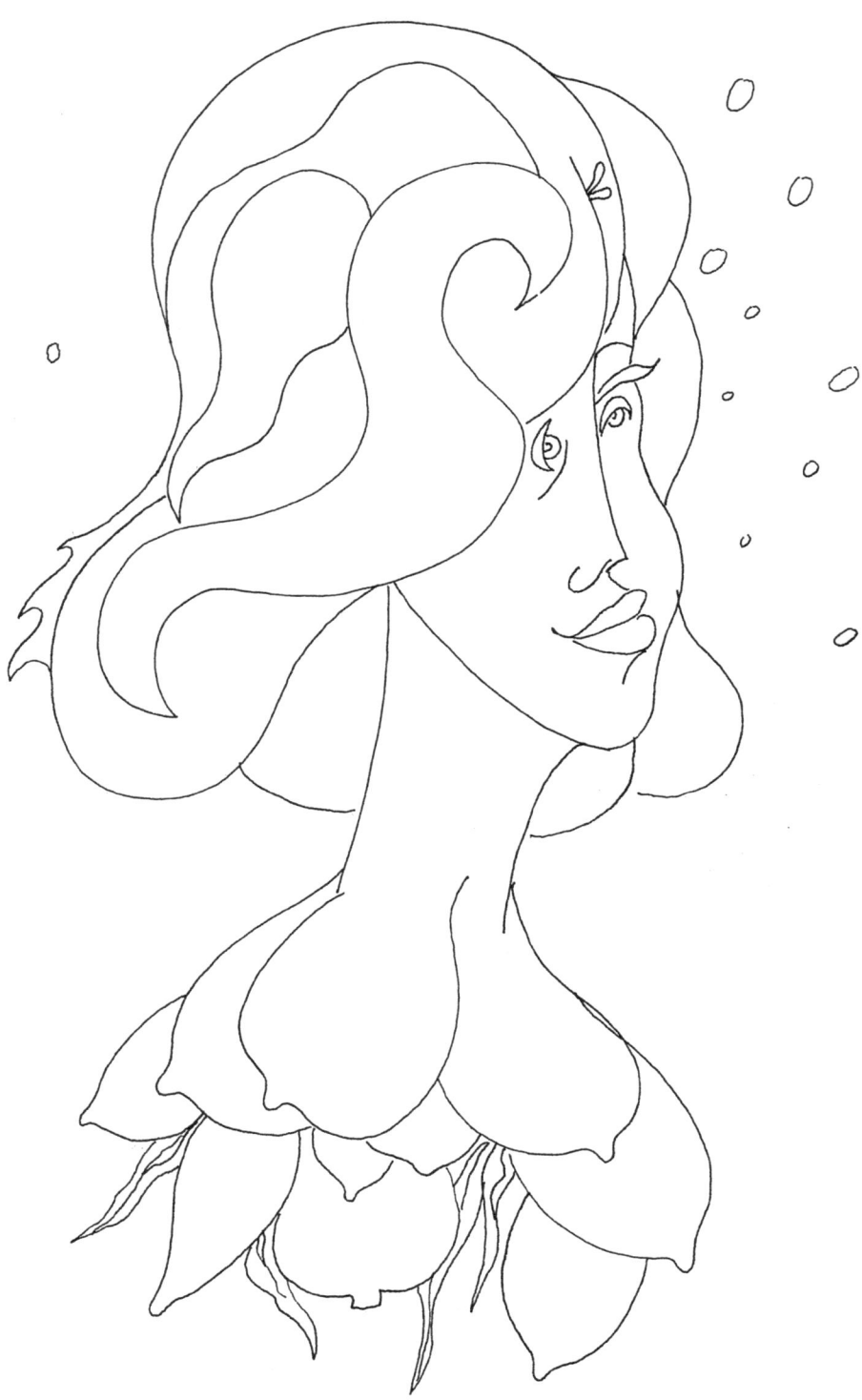

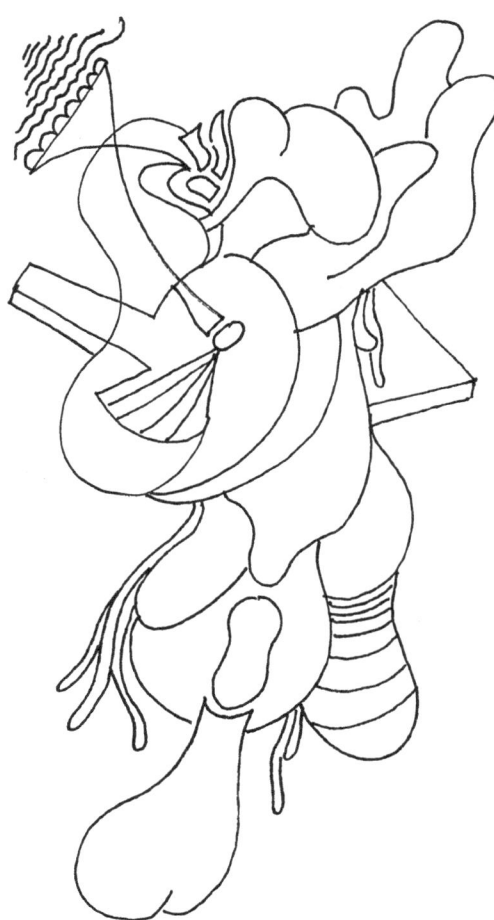

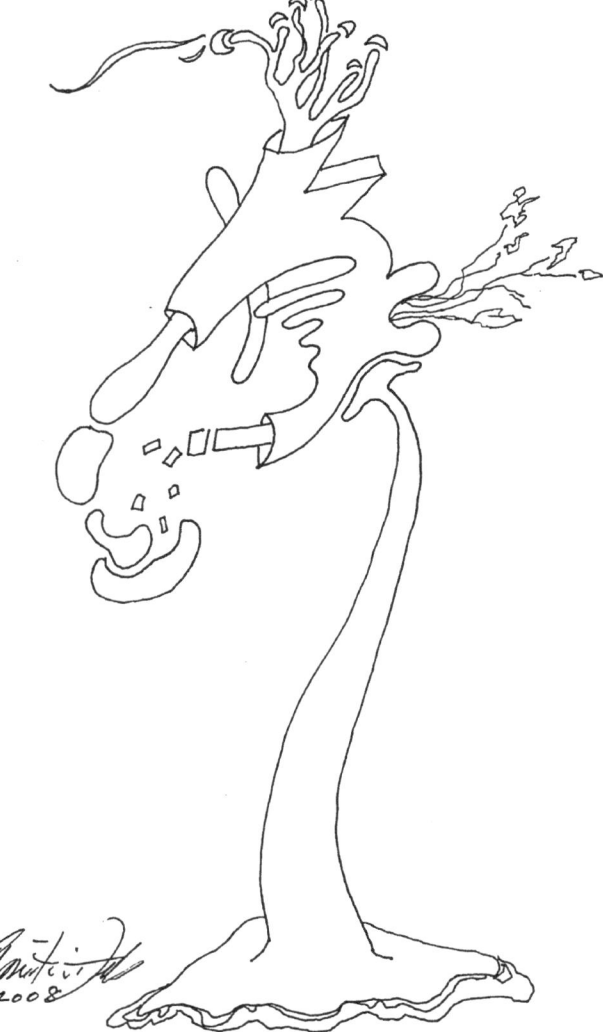

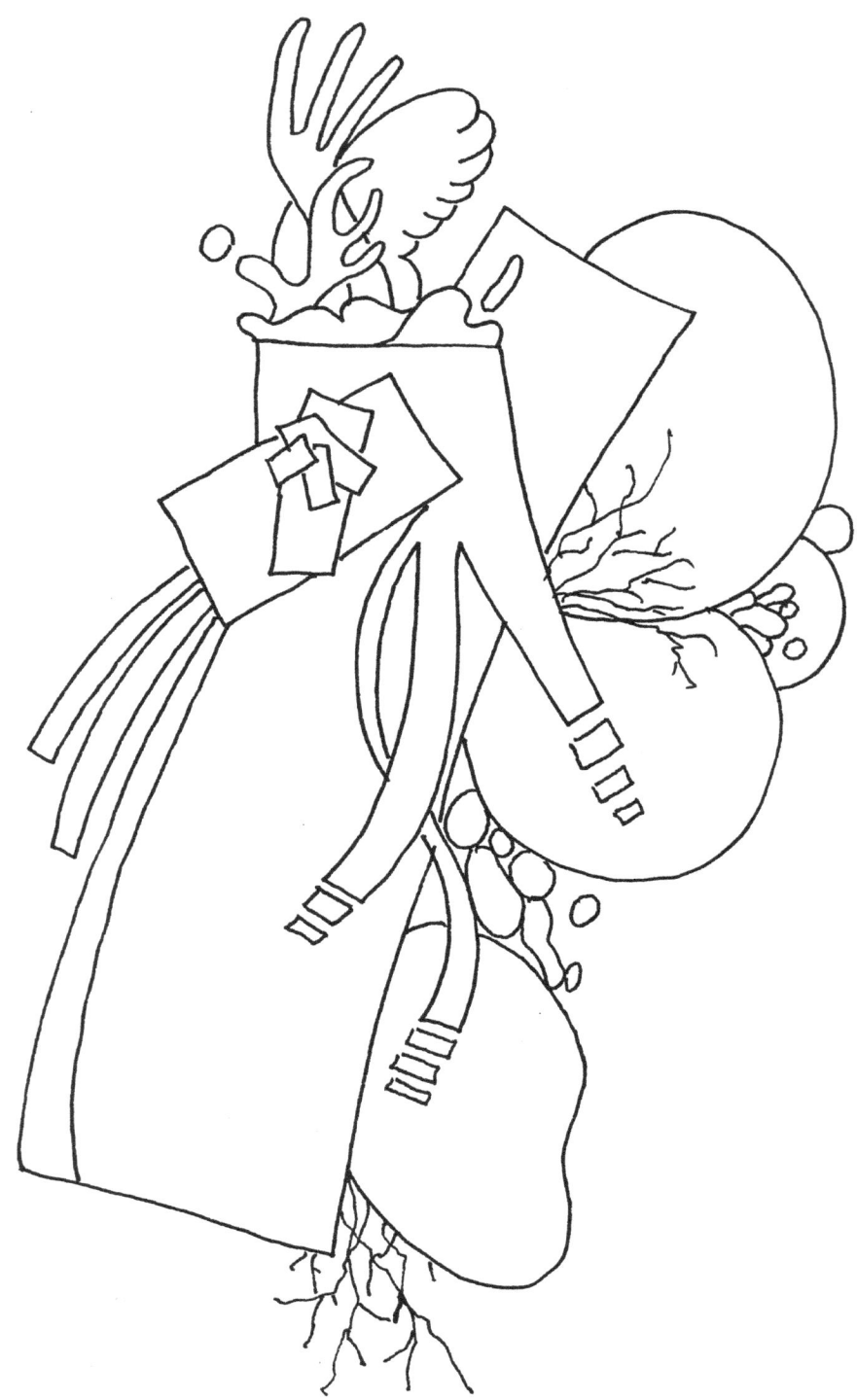

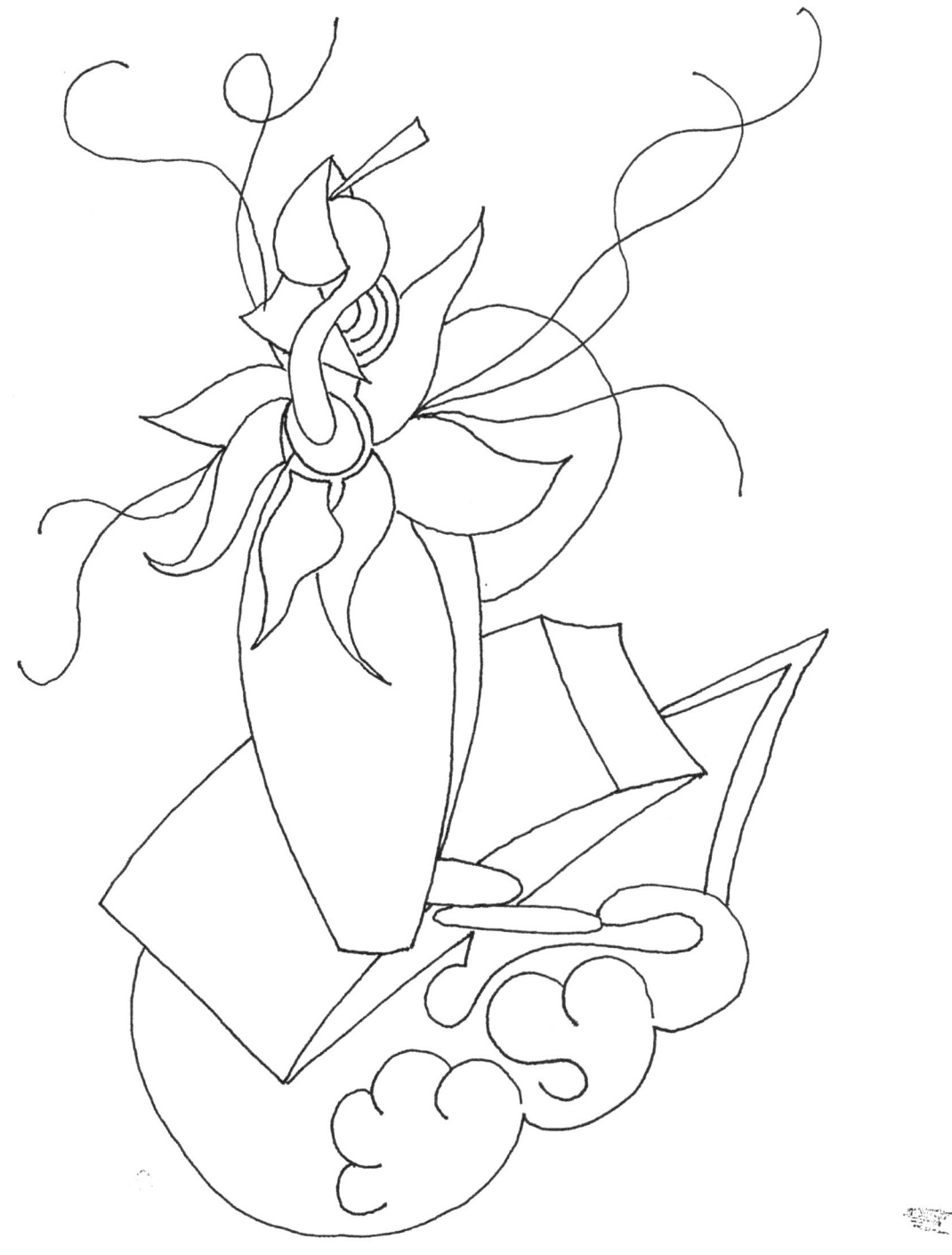

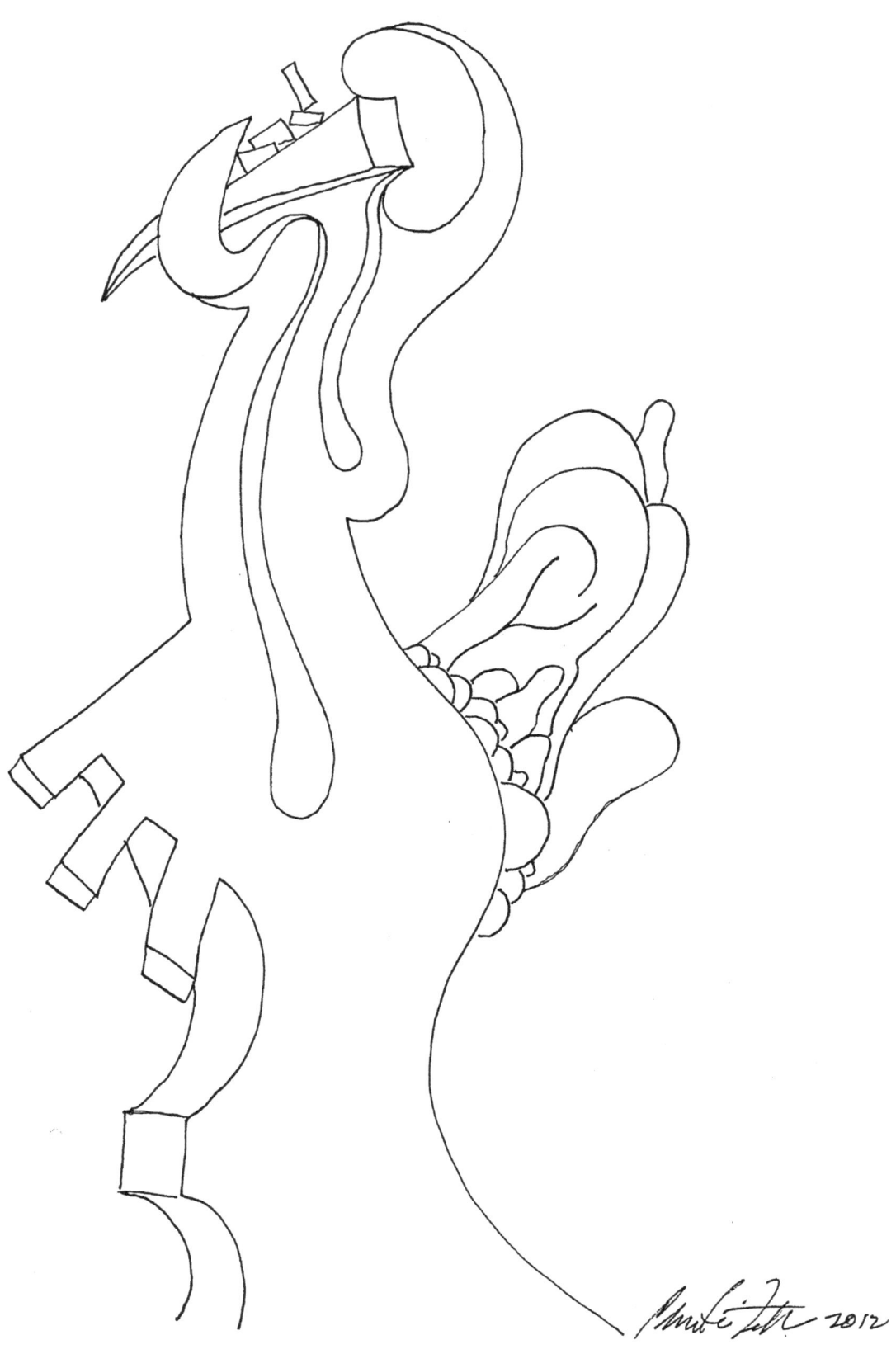

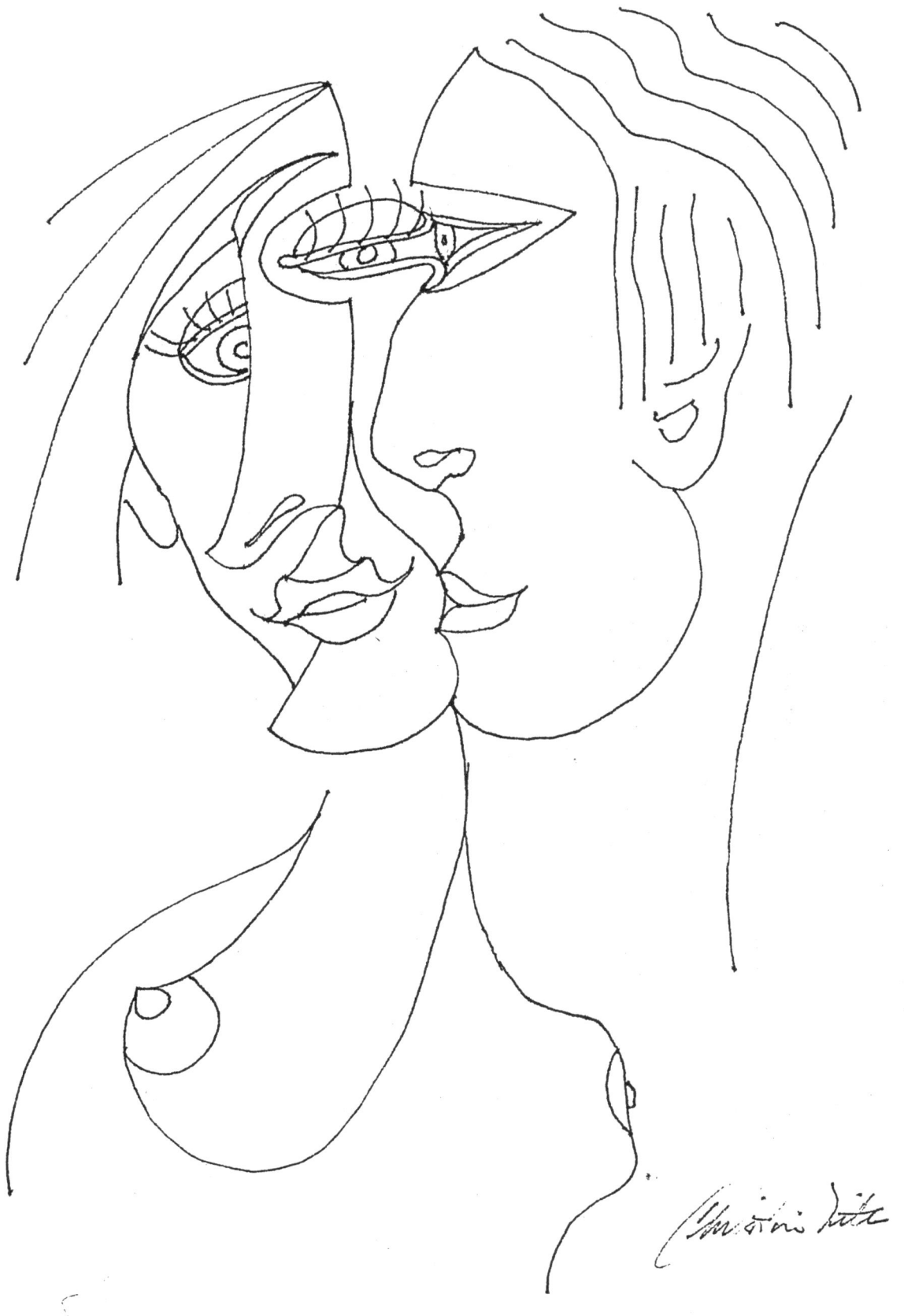

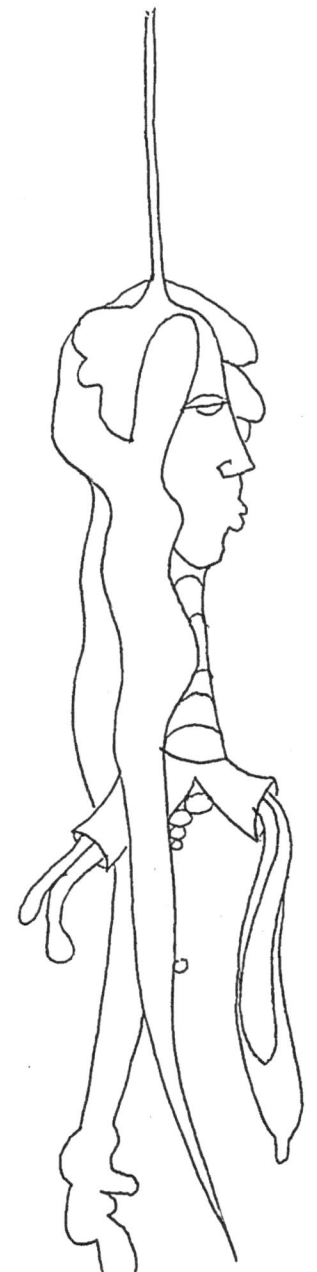

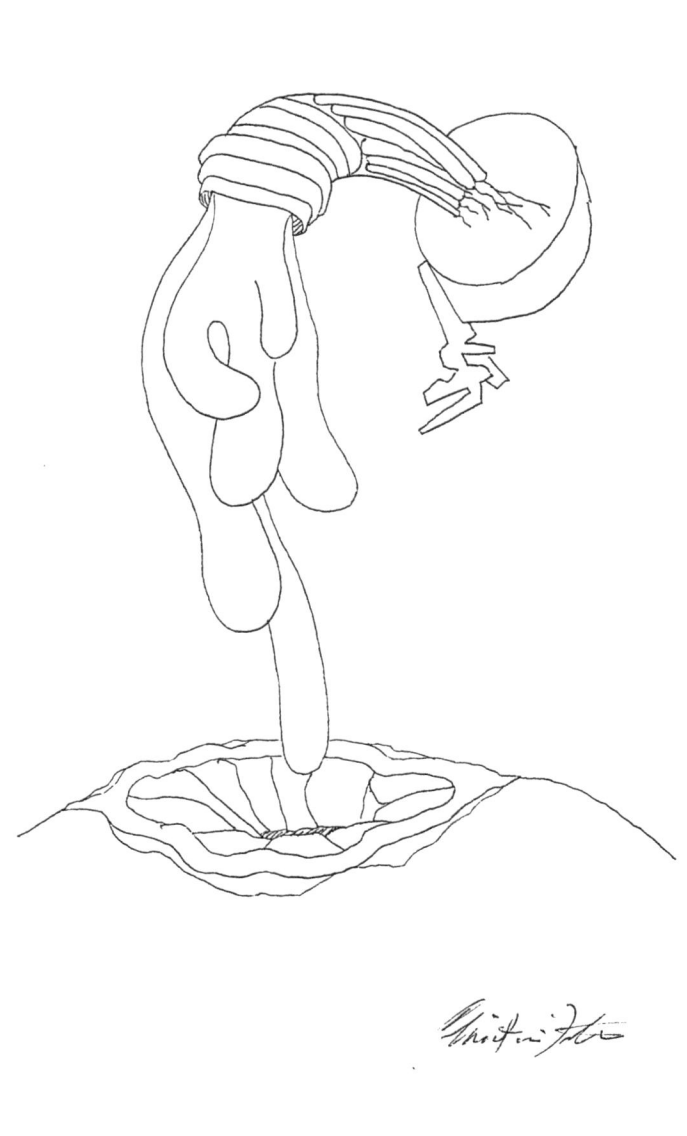

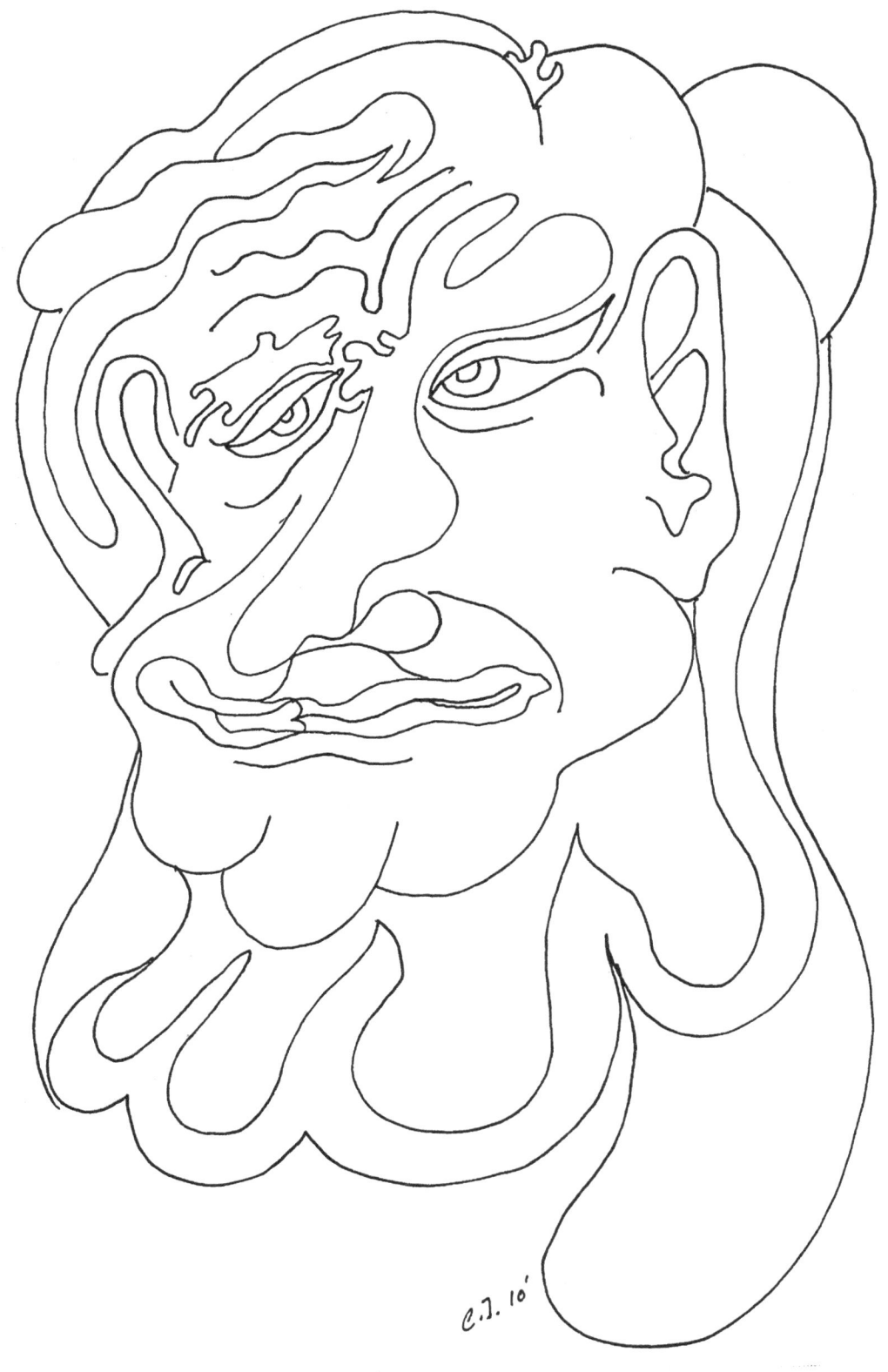

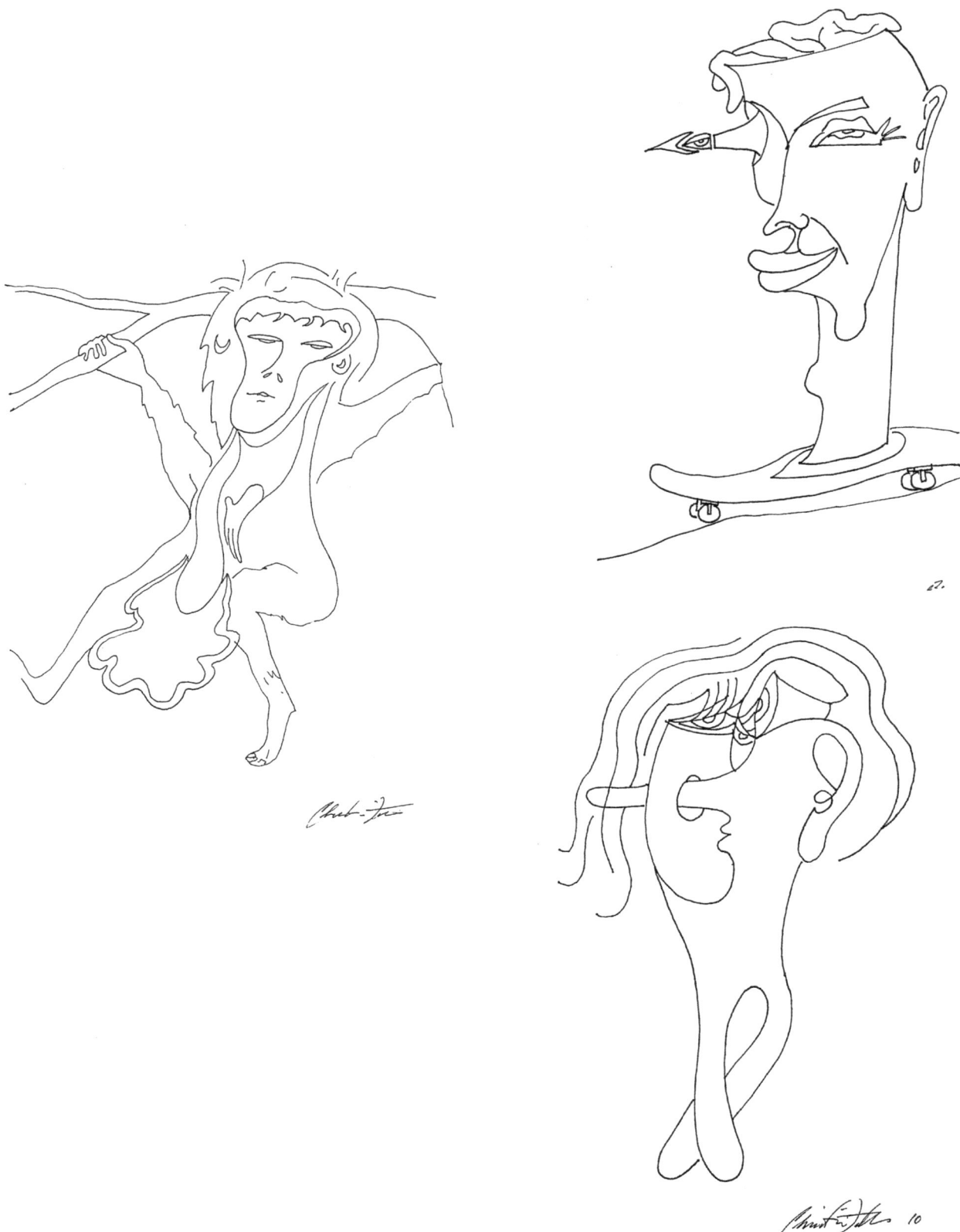

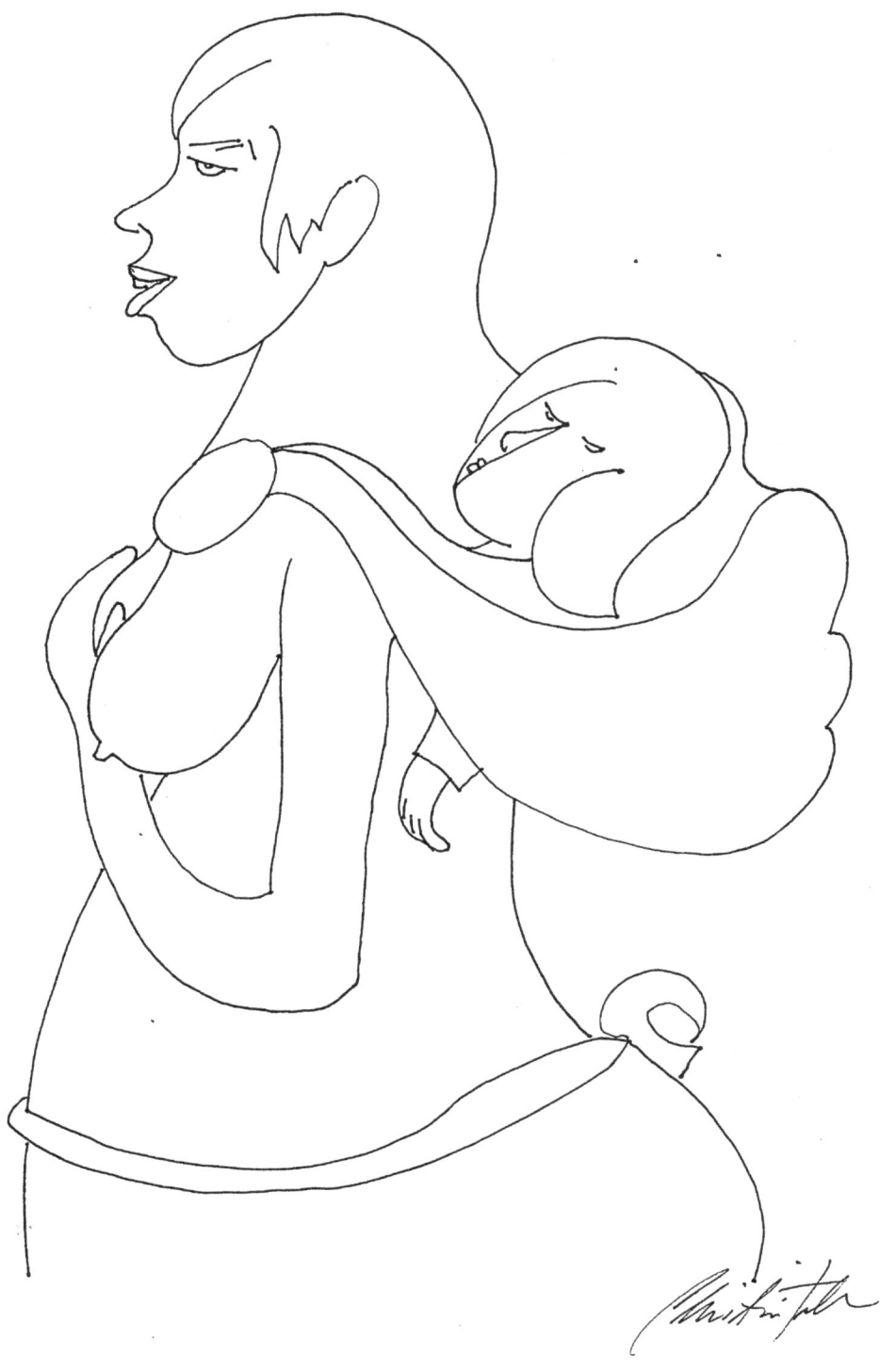

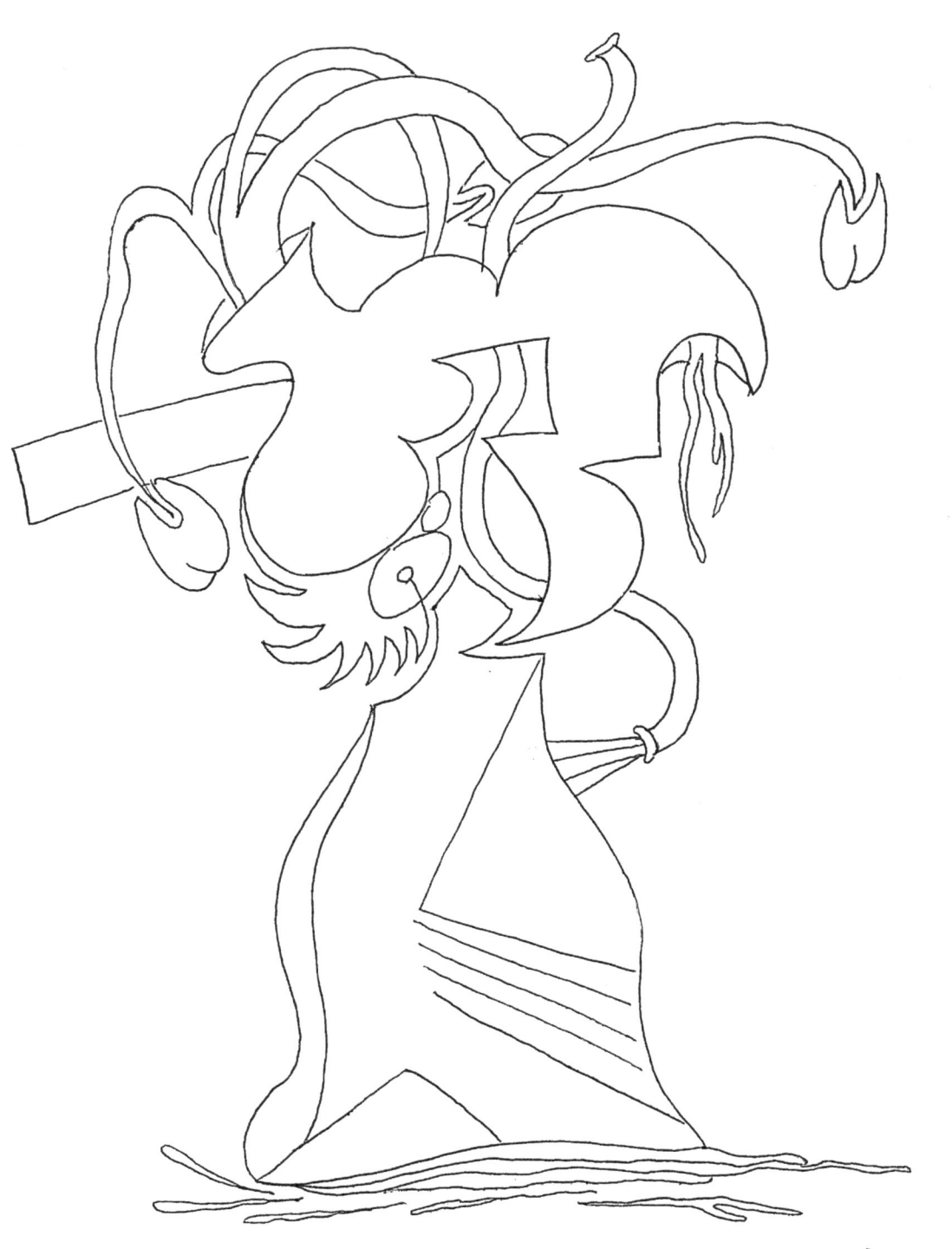

e). 2014

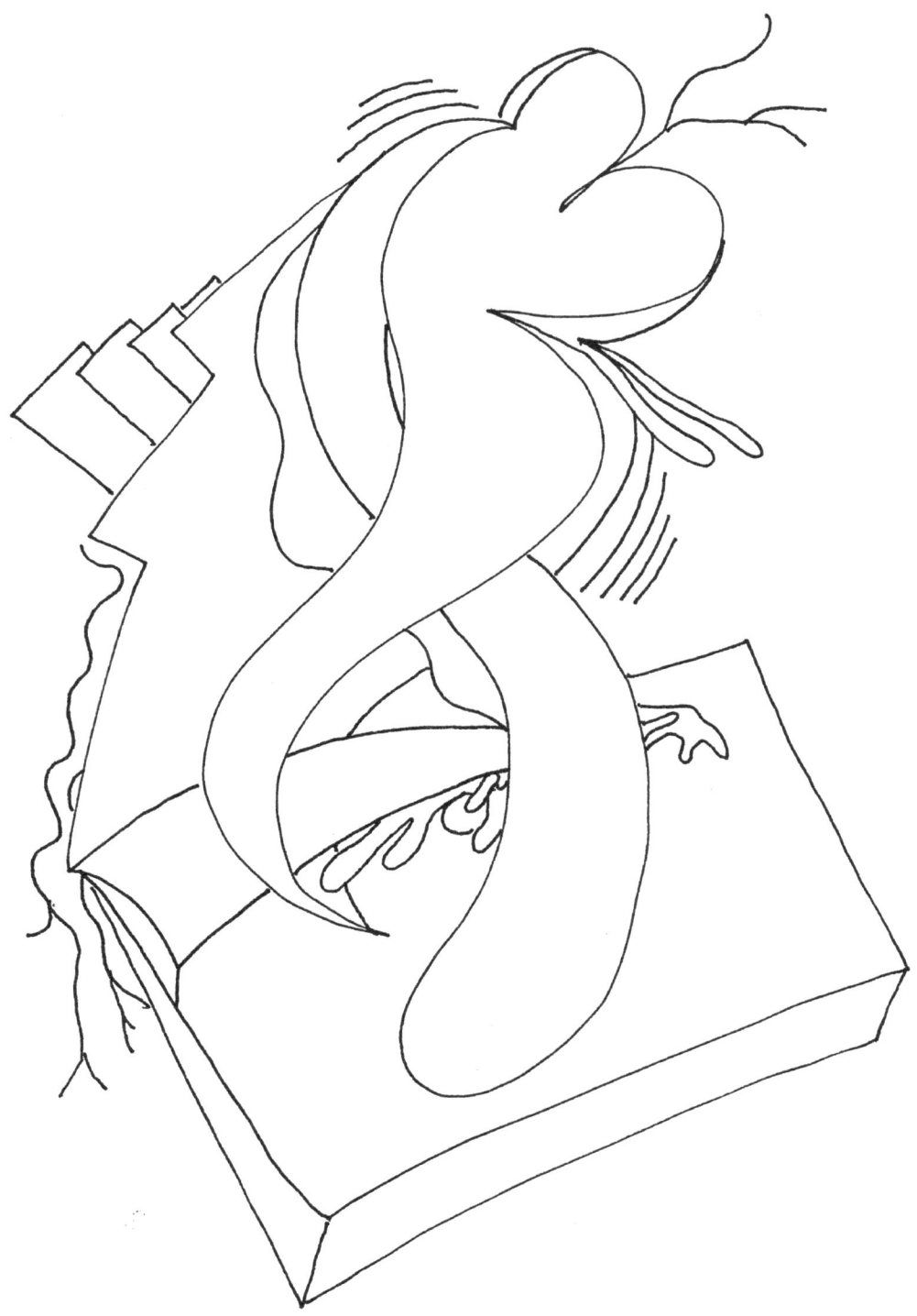

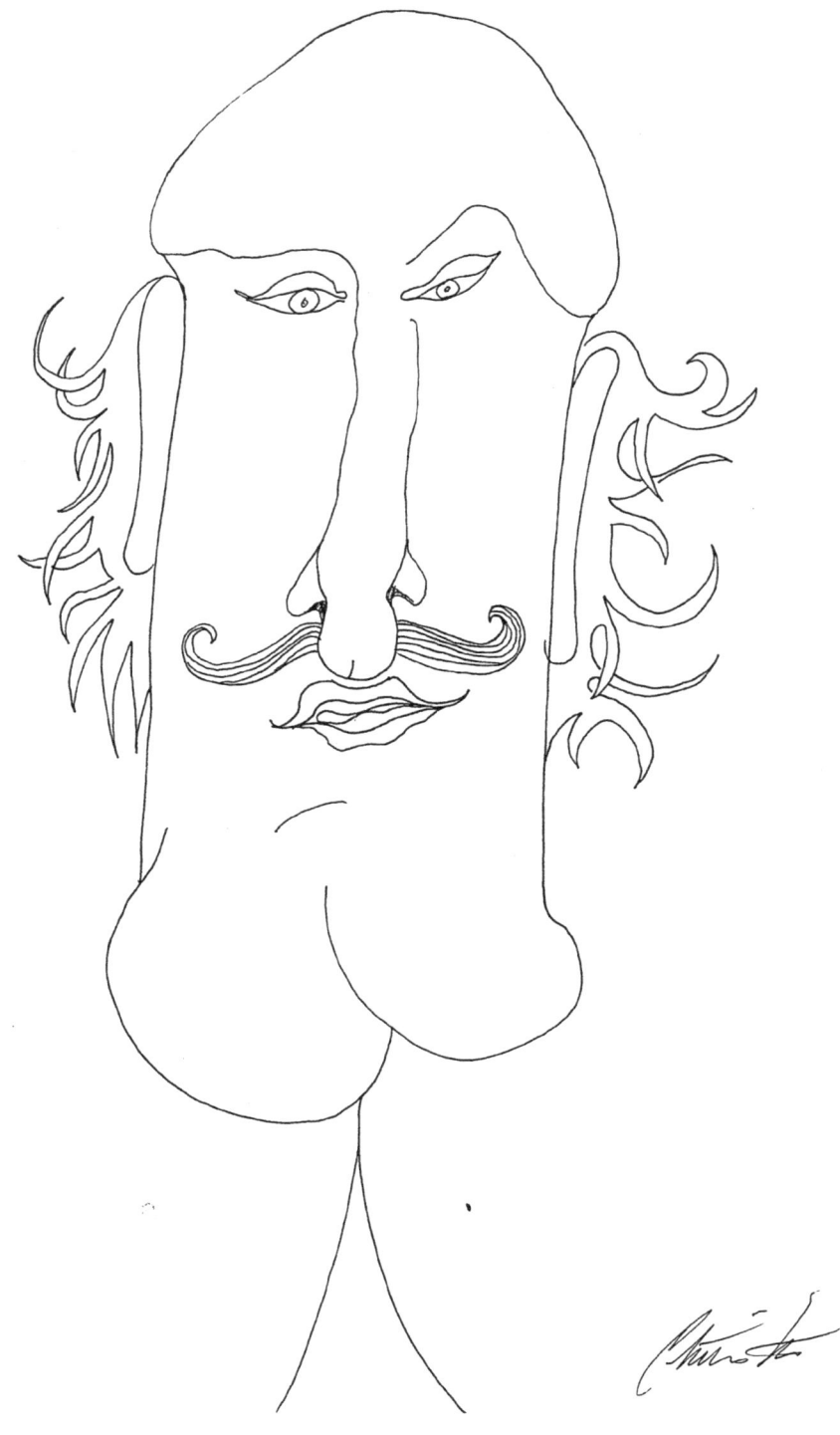

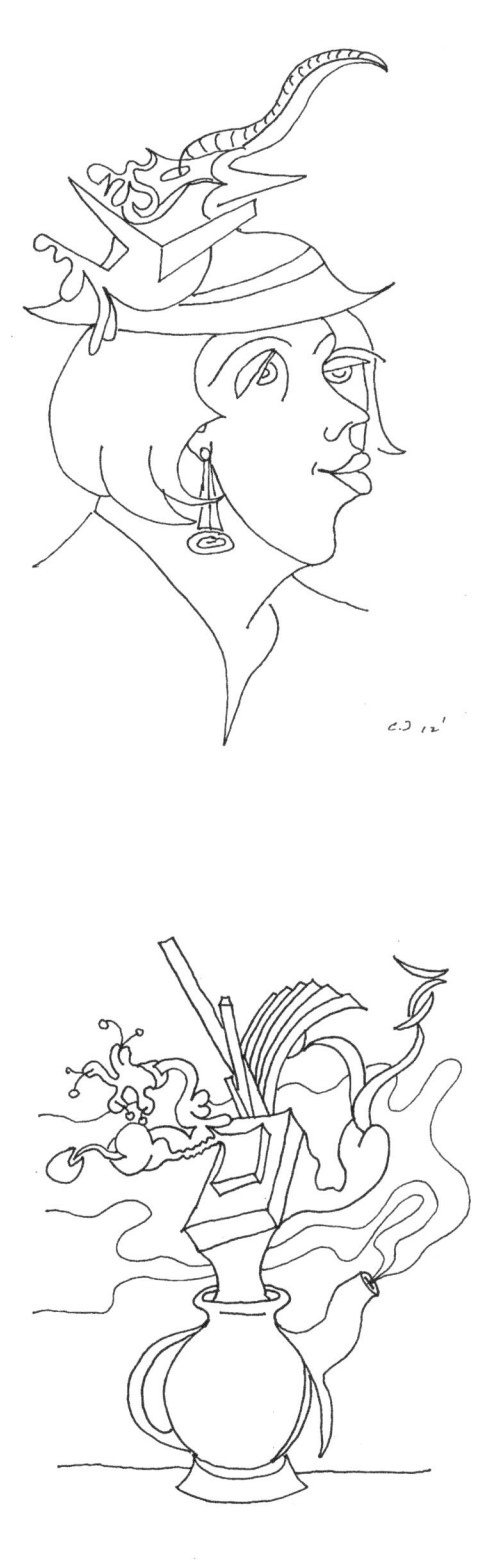

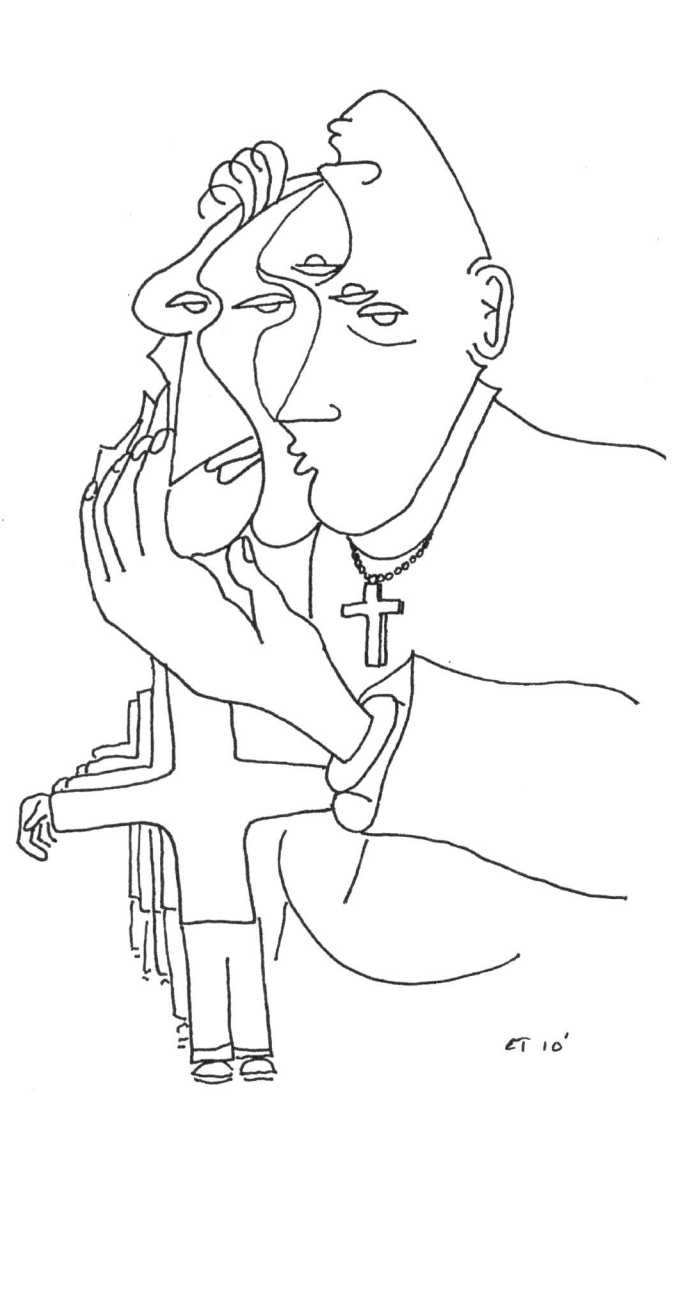

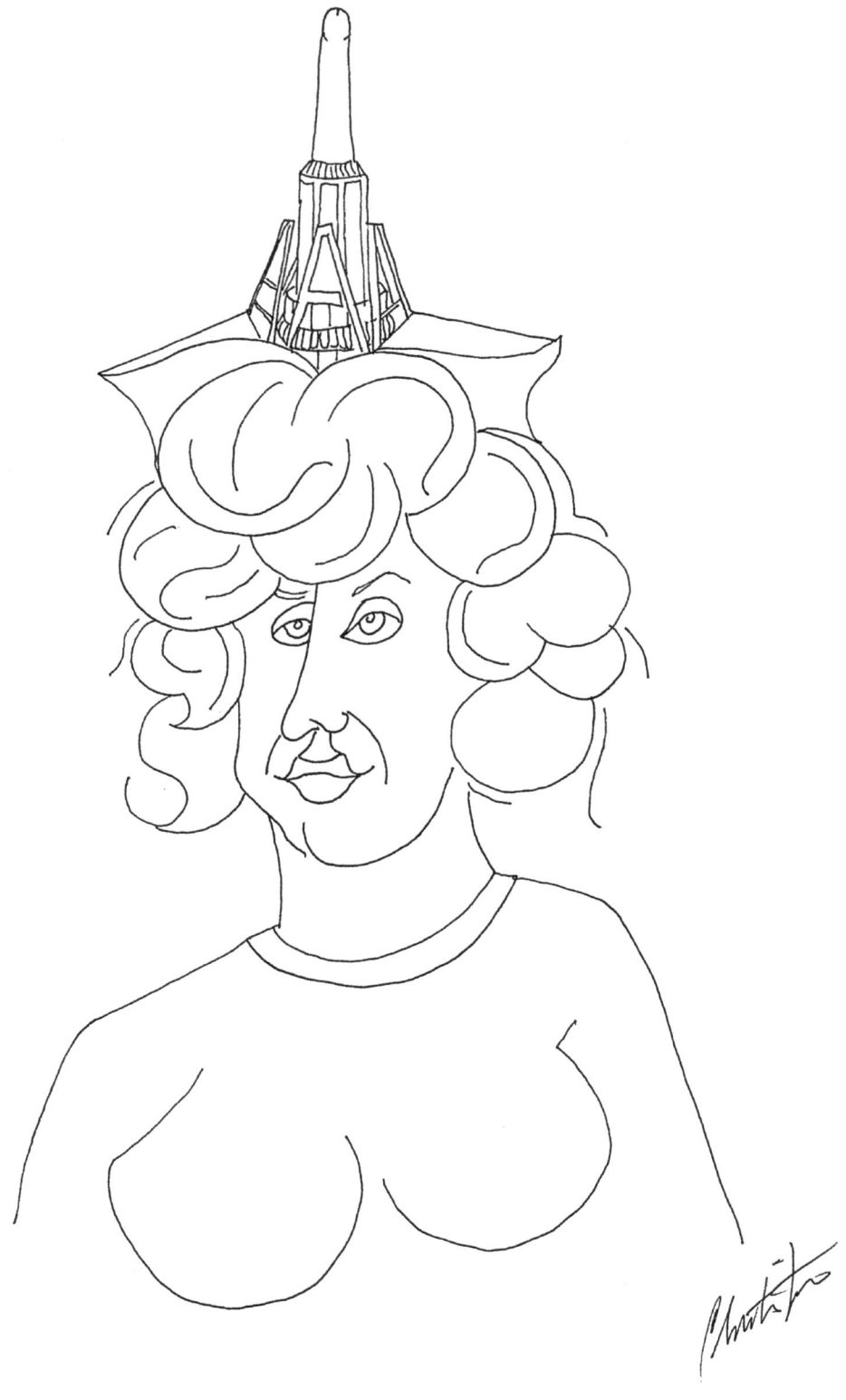

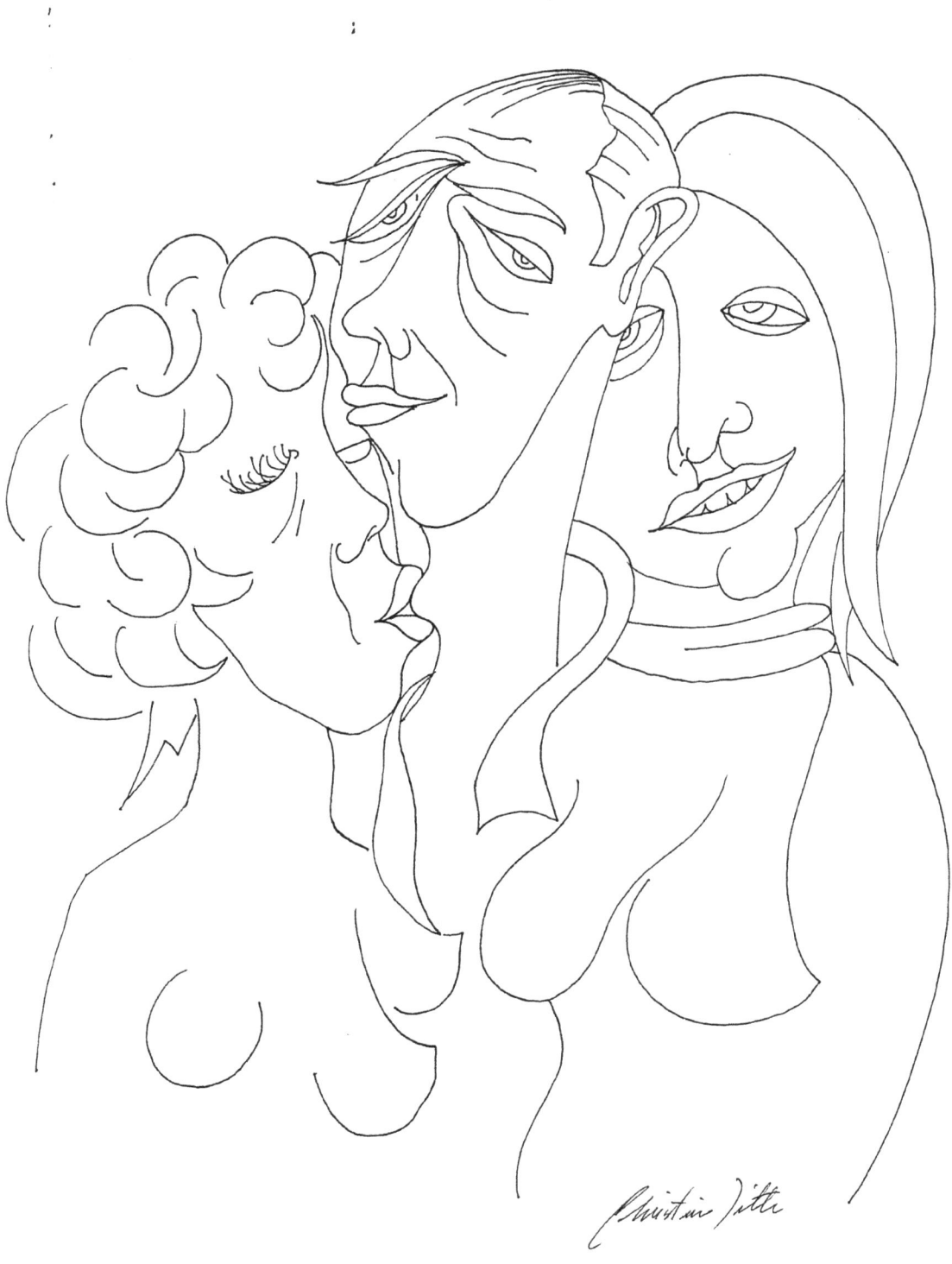

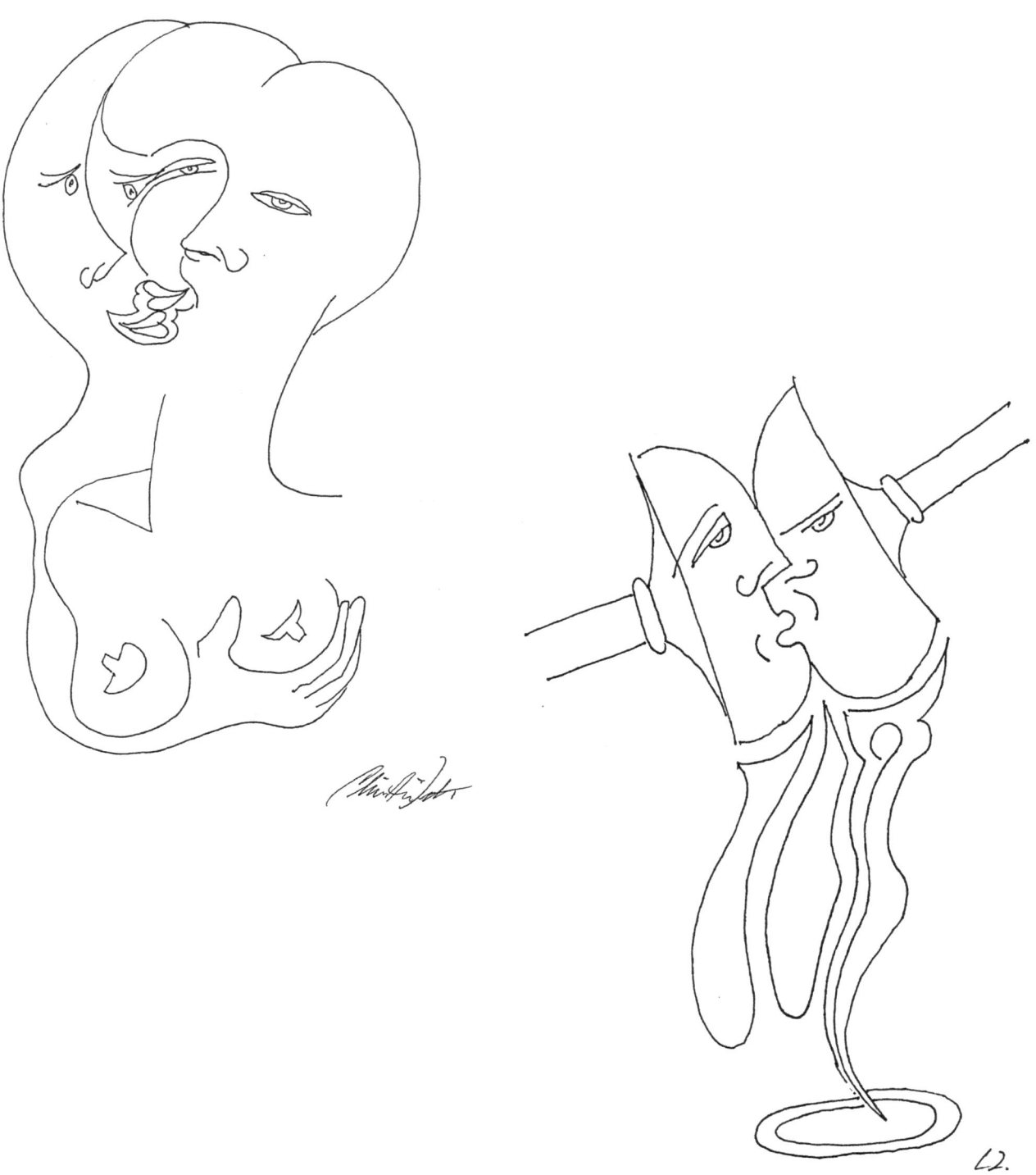

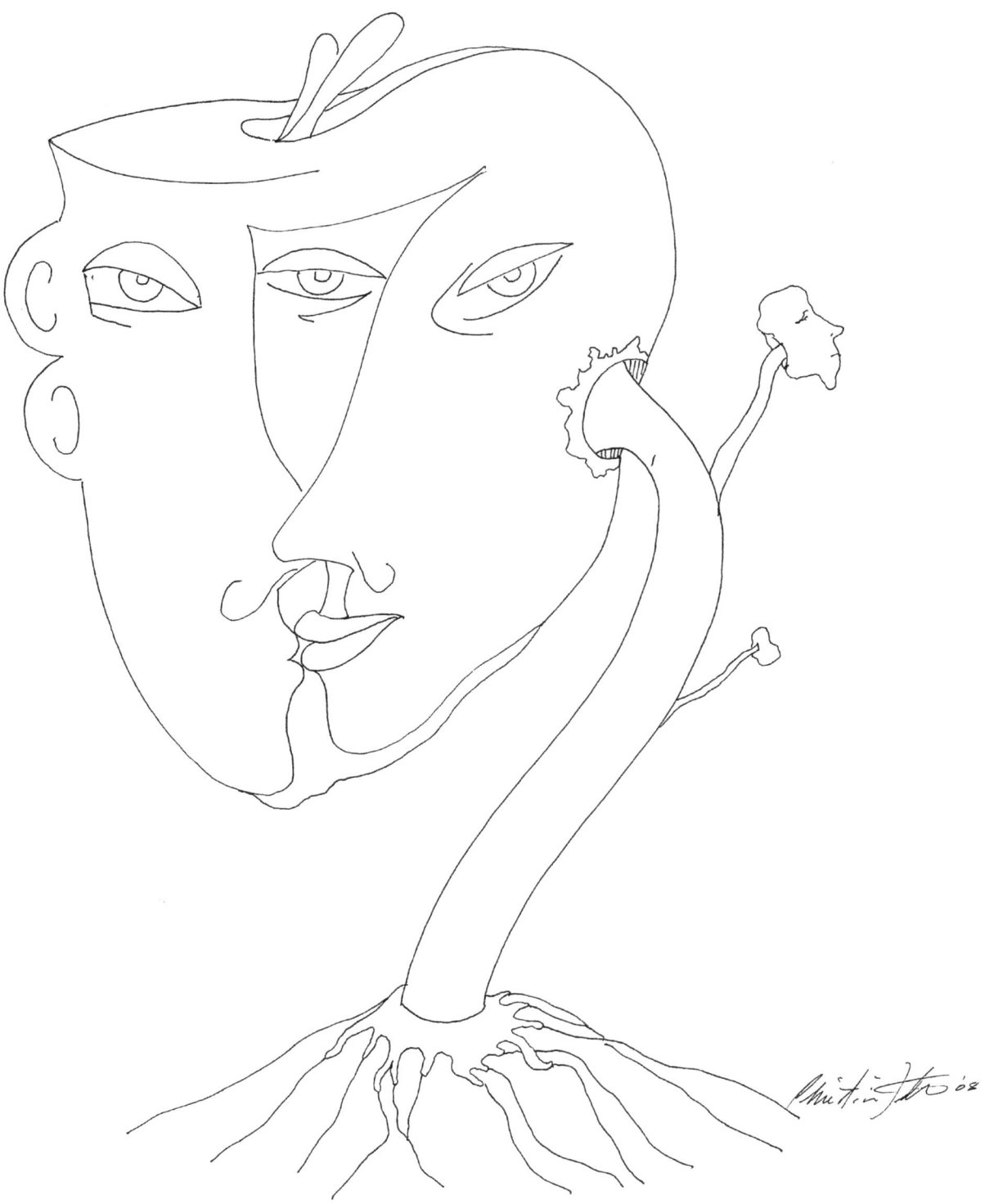

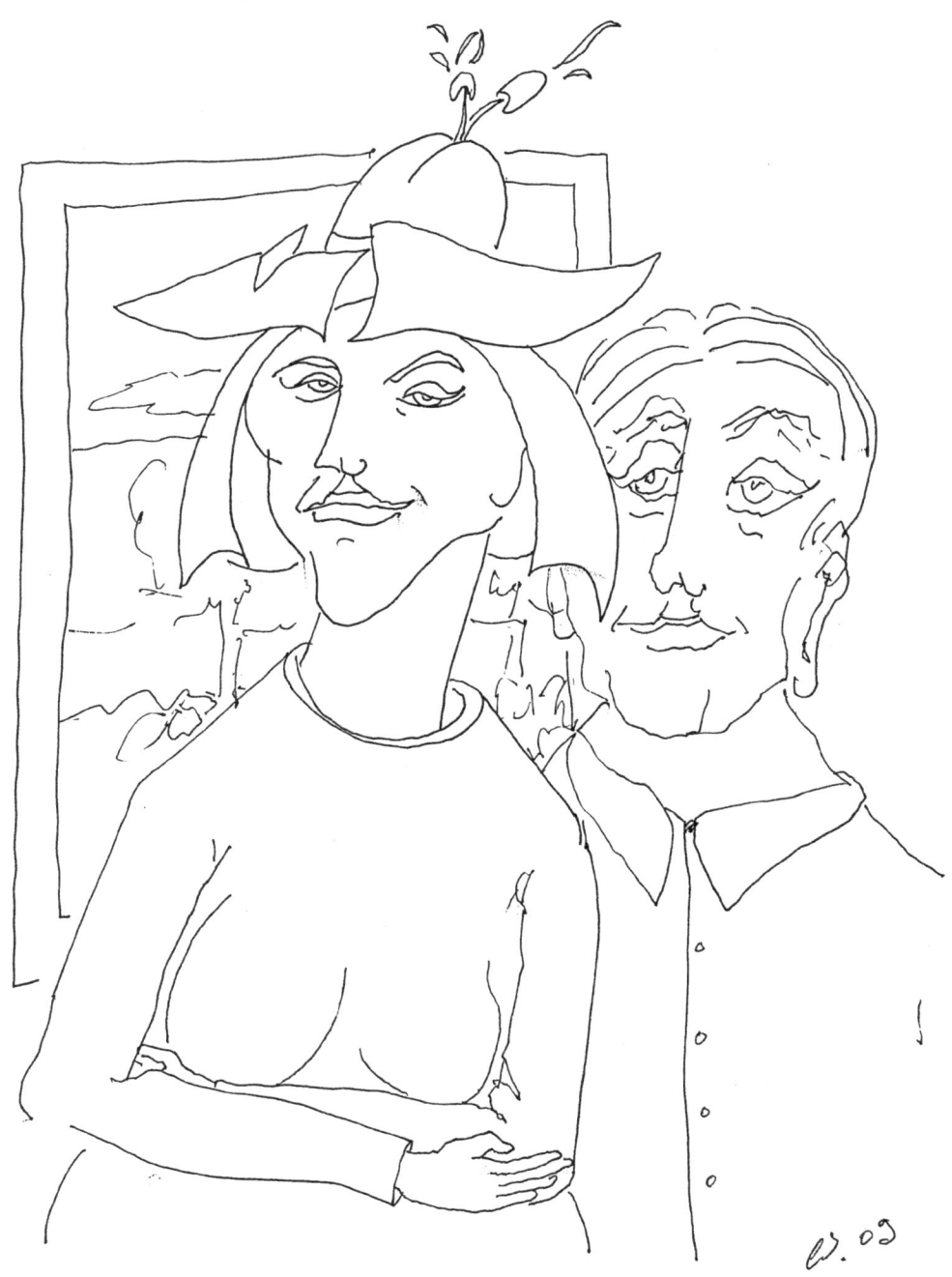

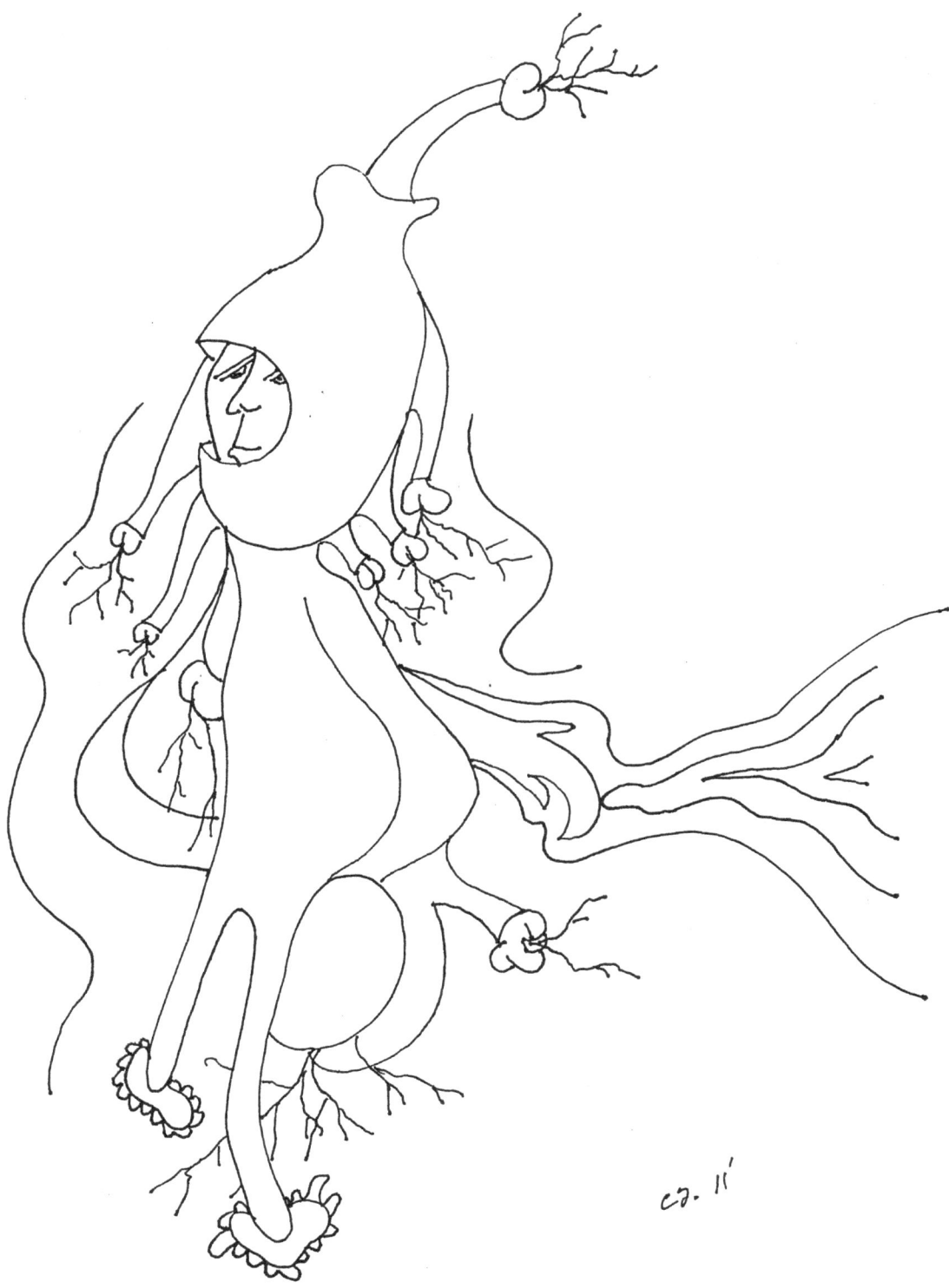

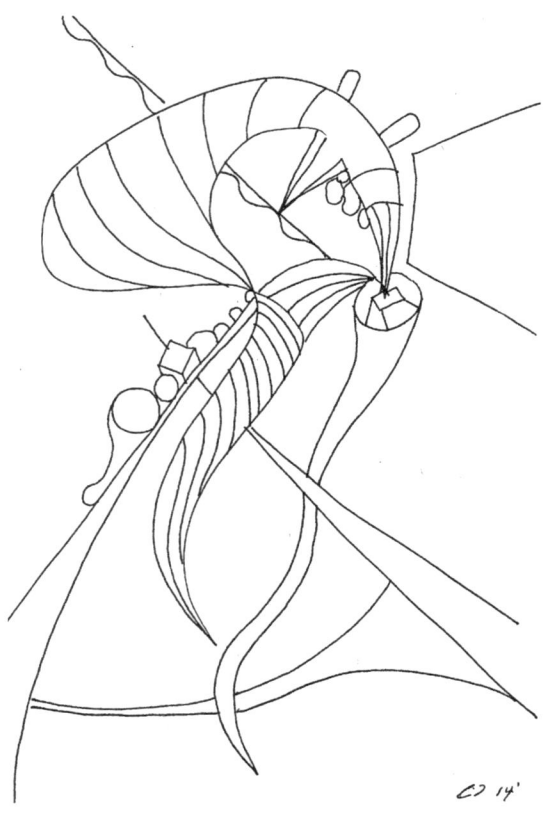

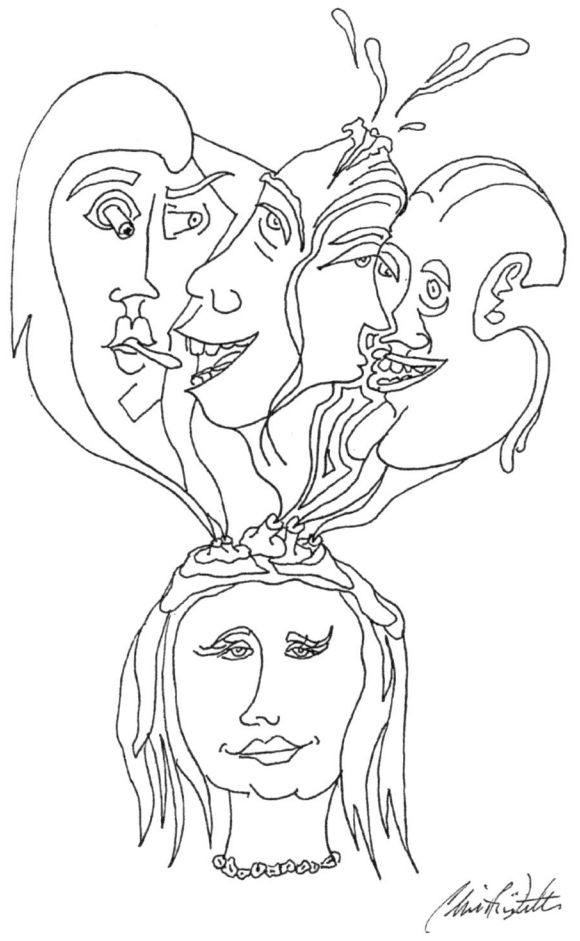

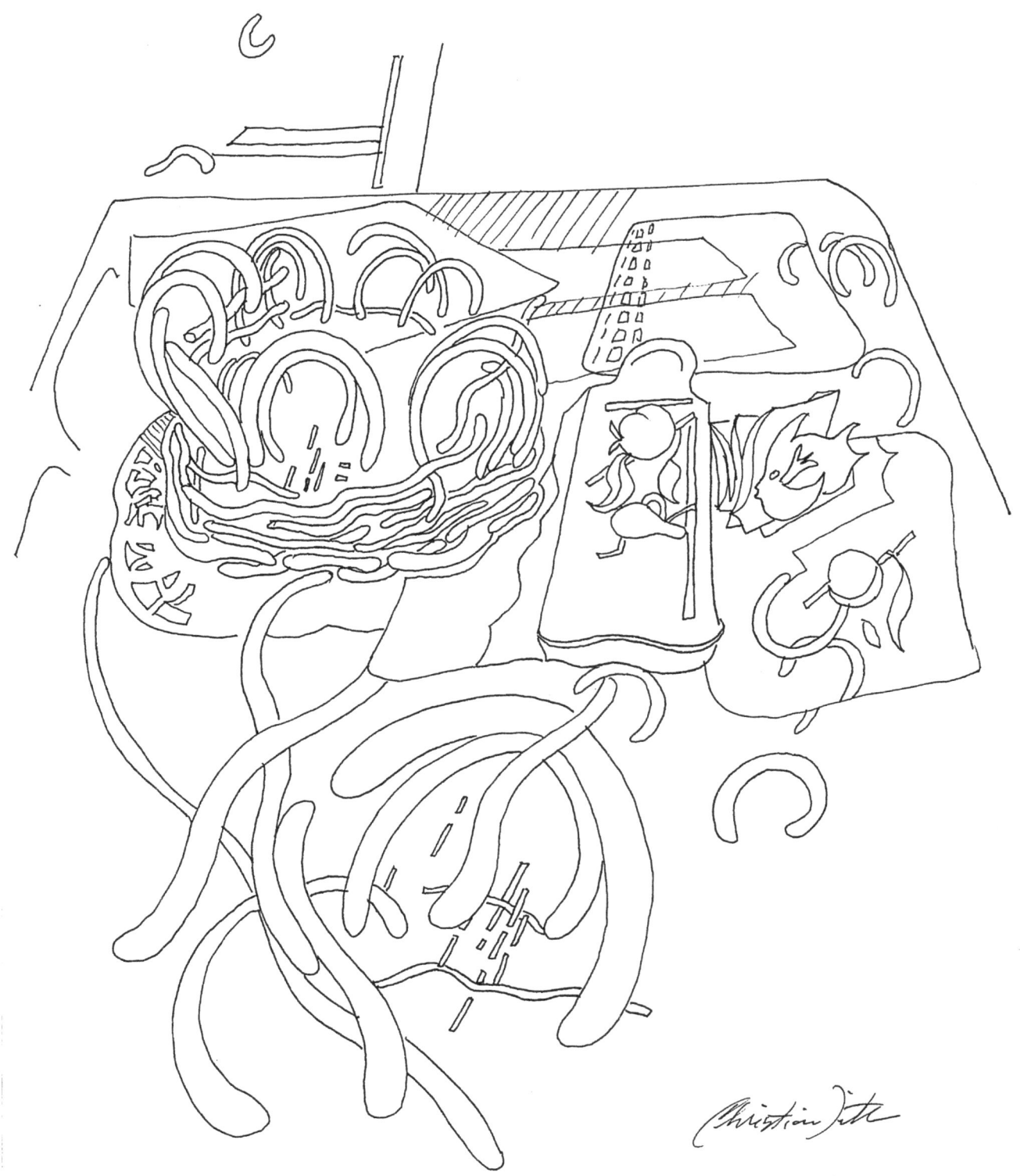

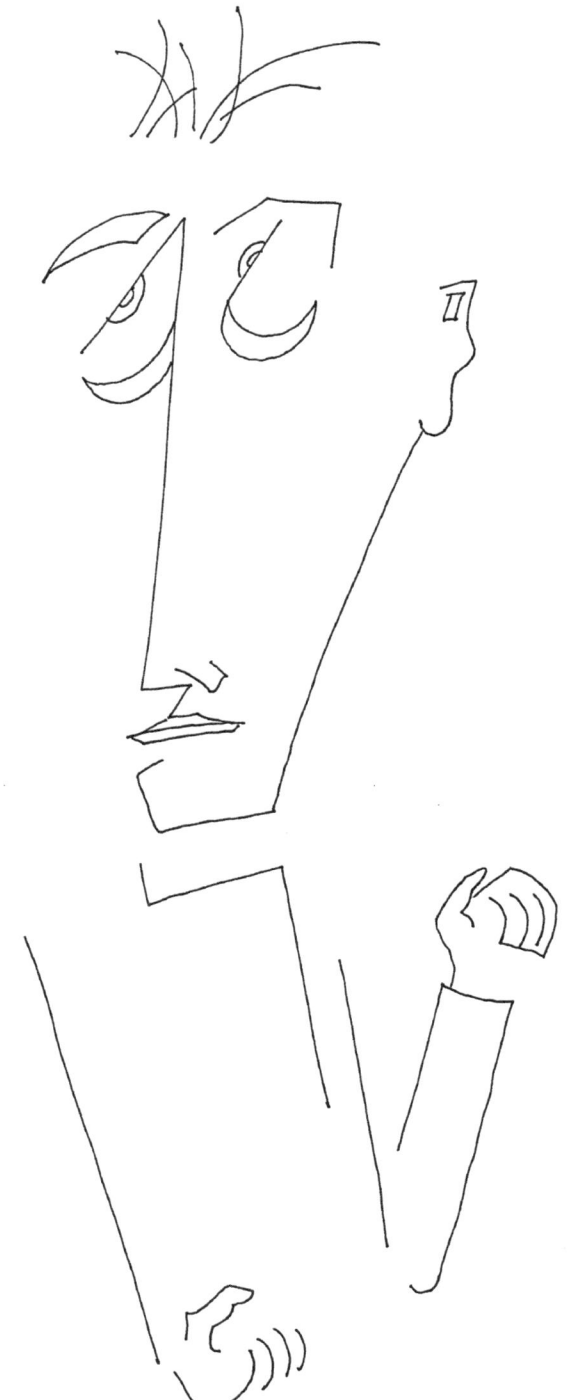

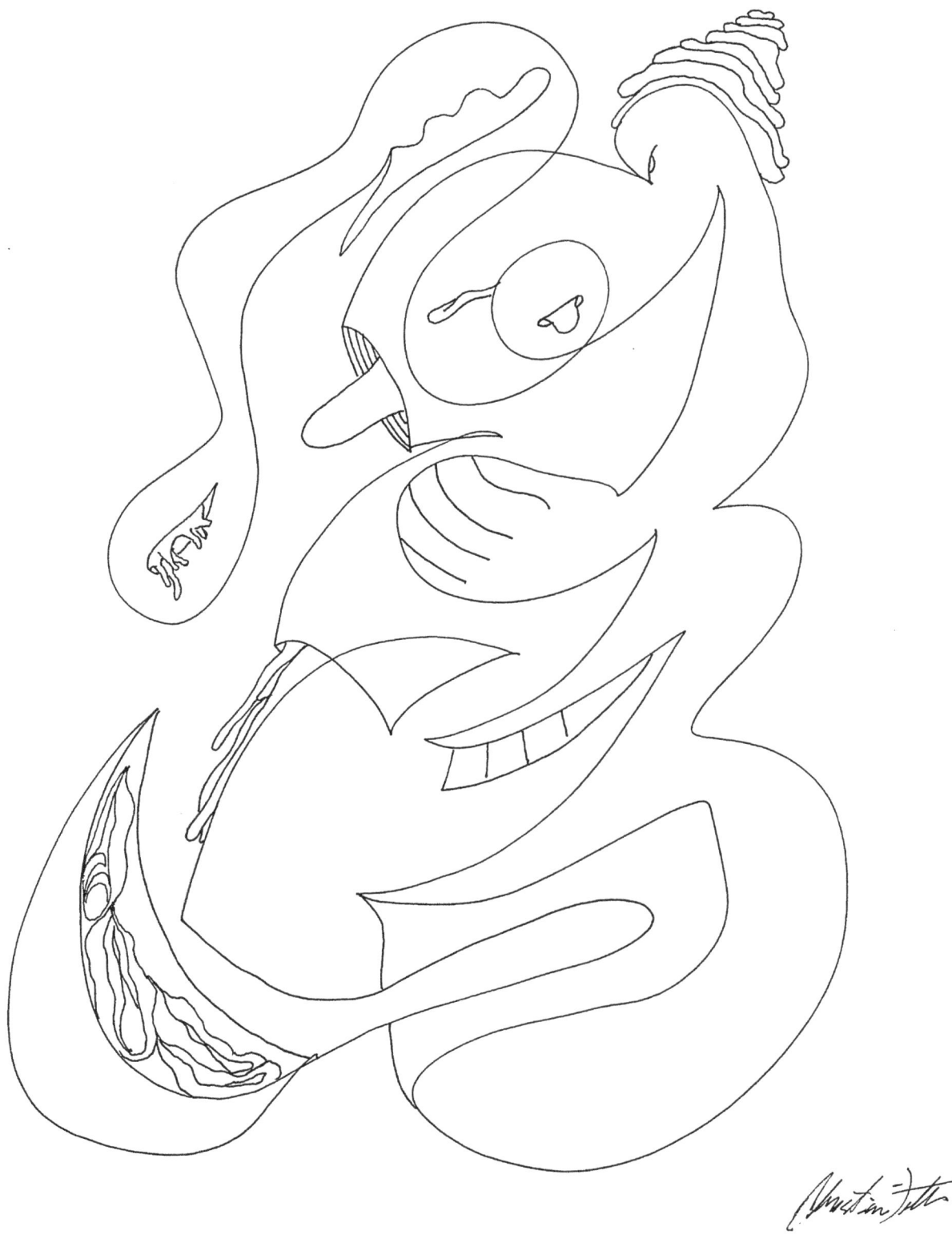

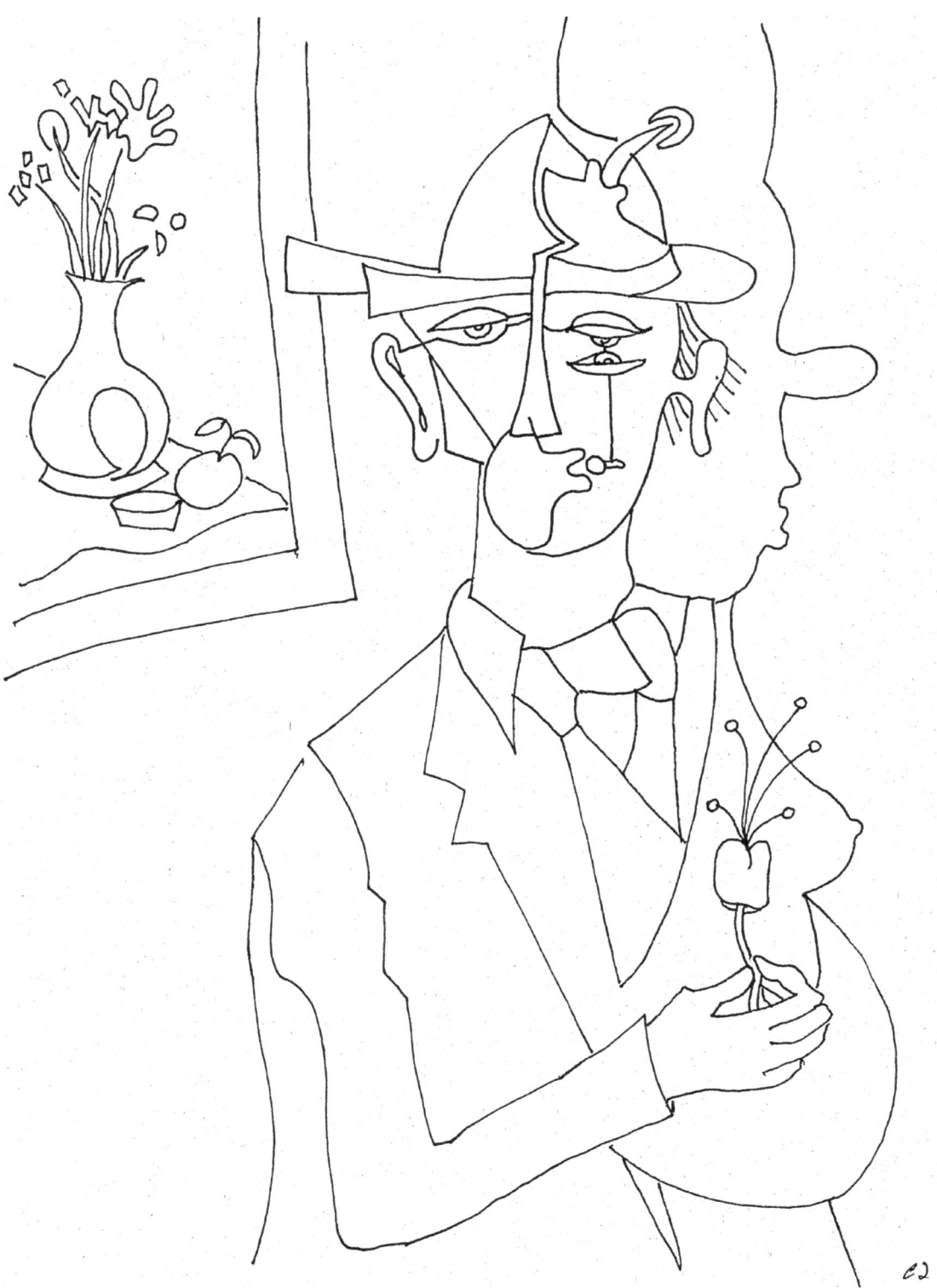

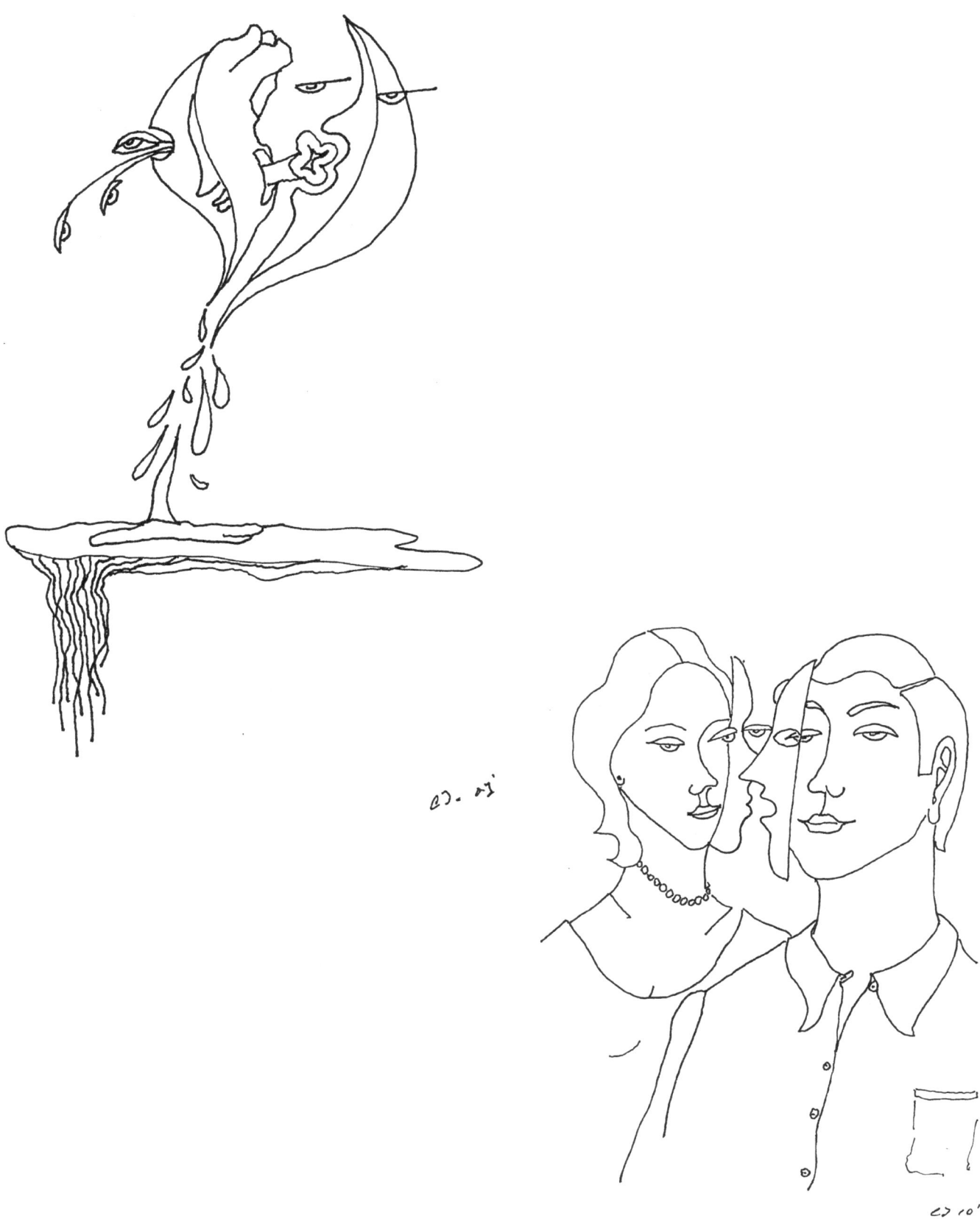

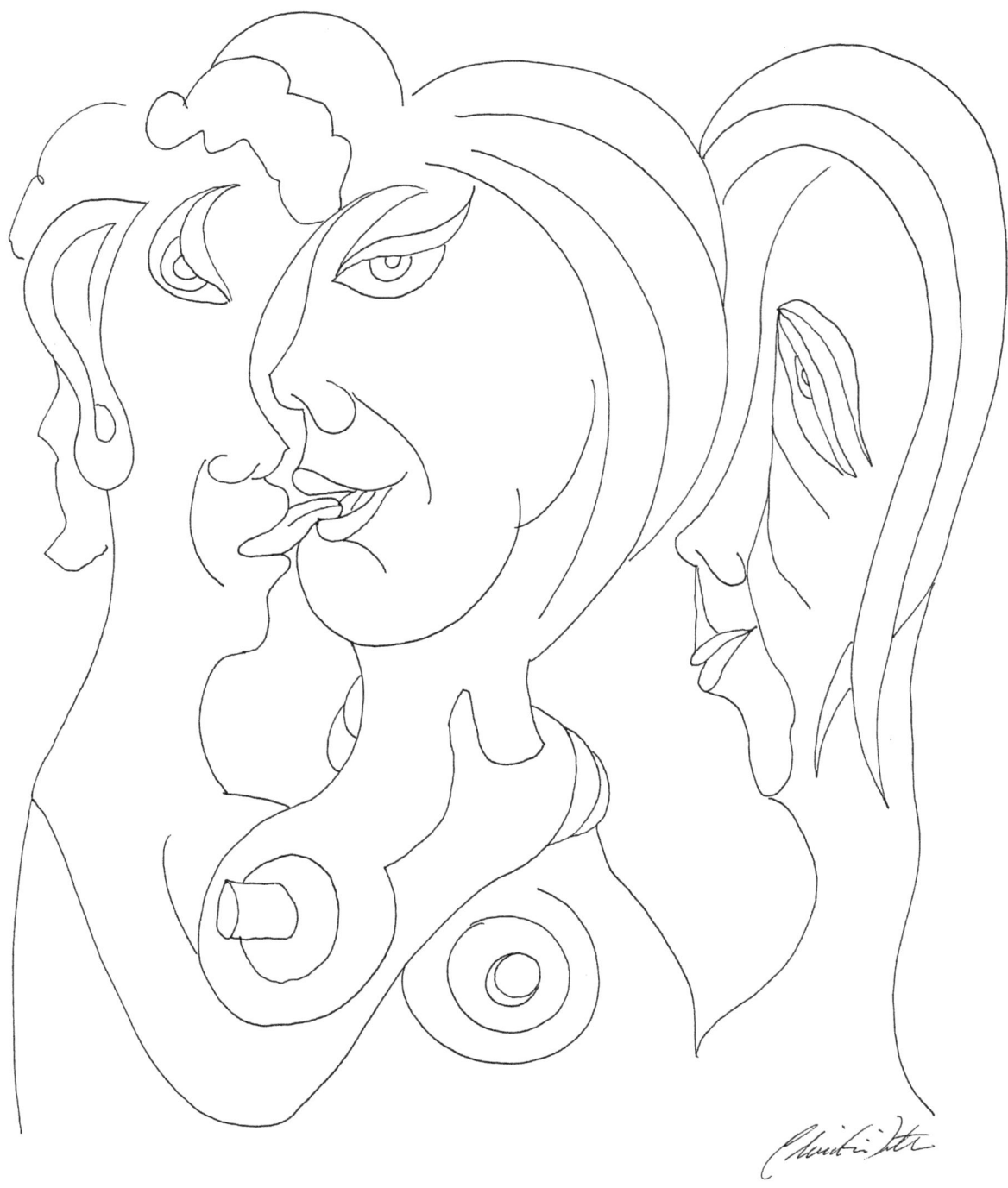

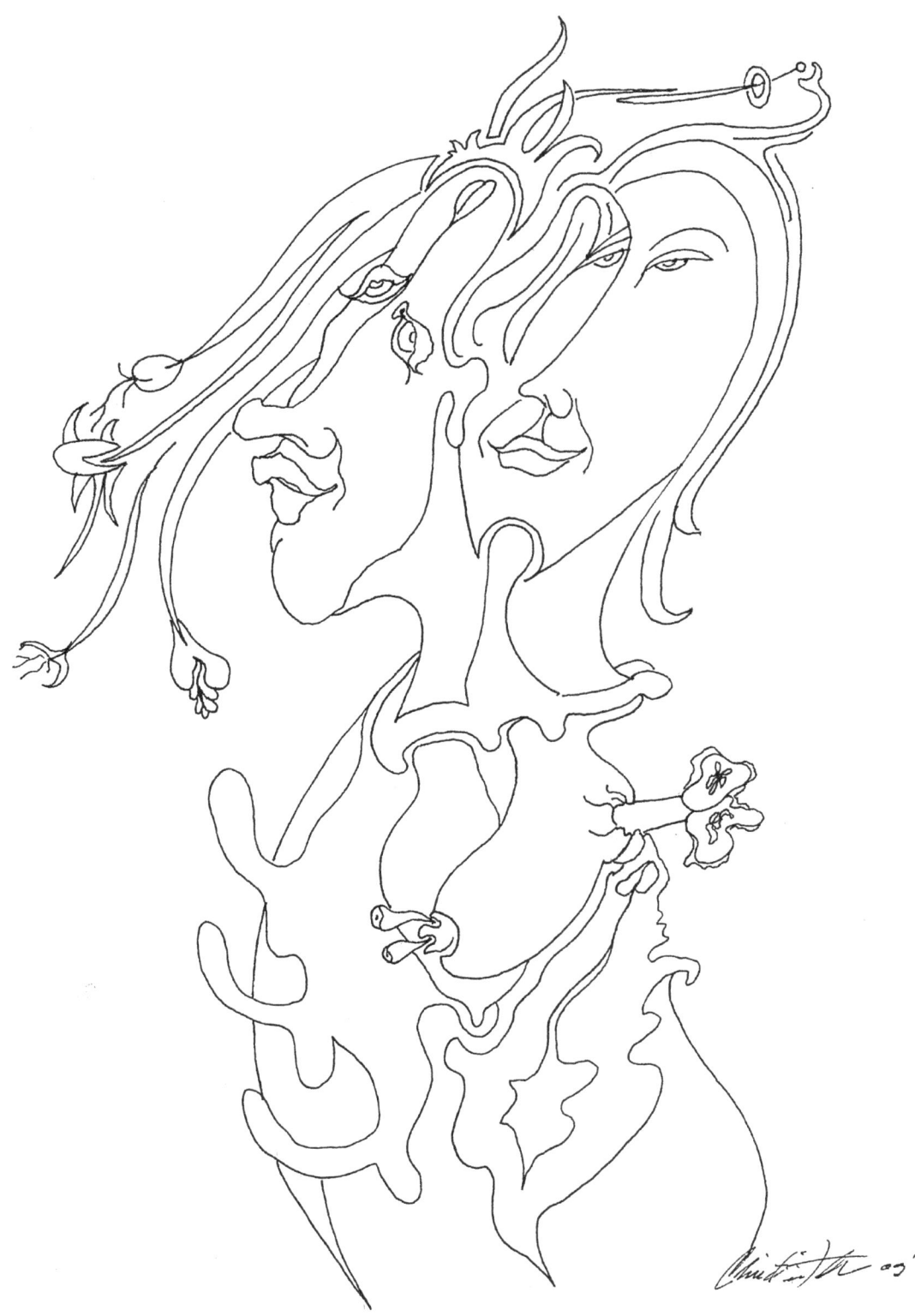

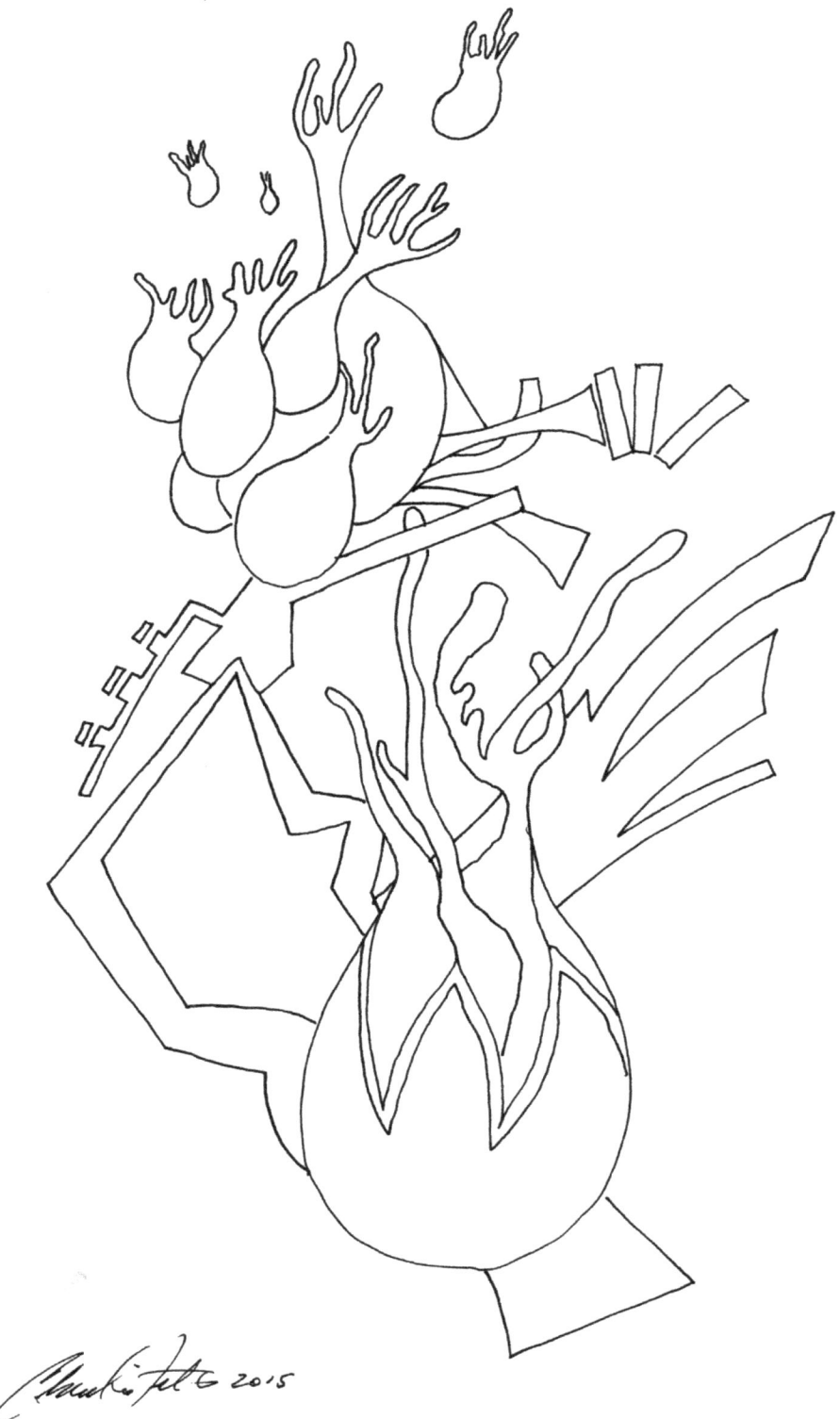

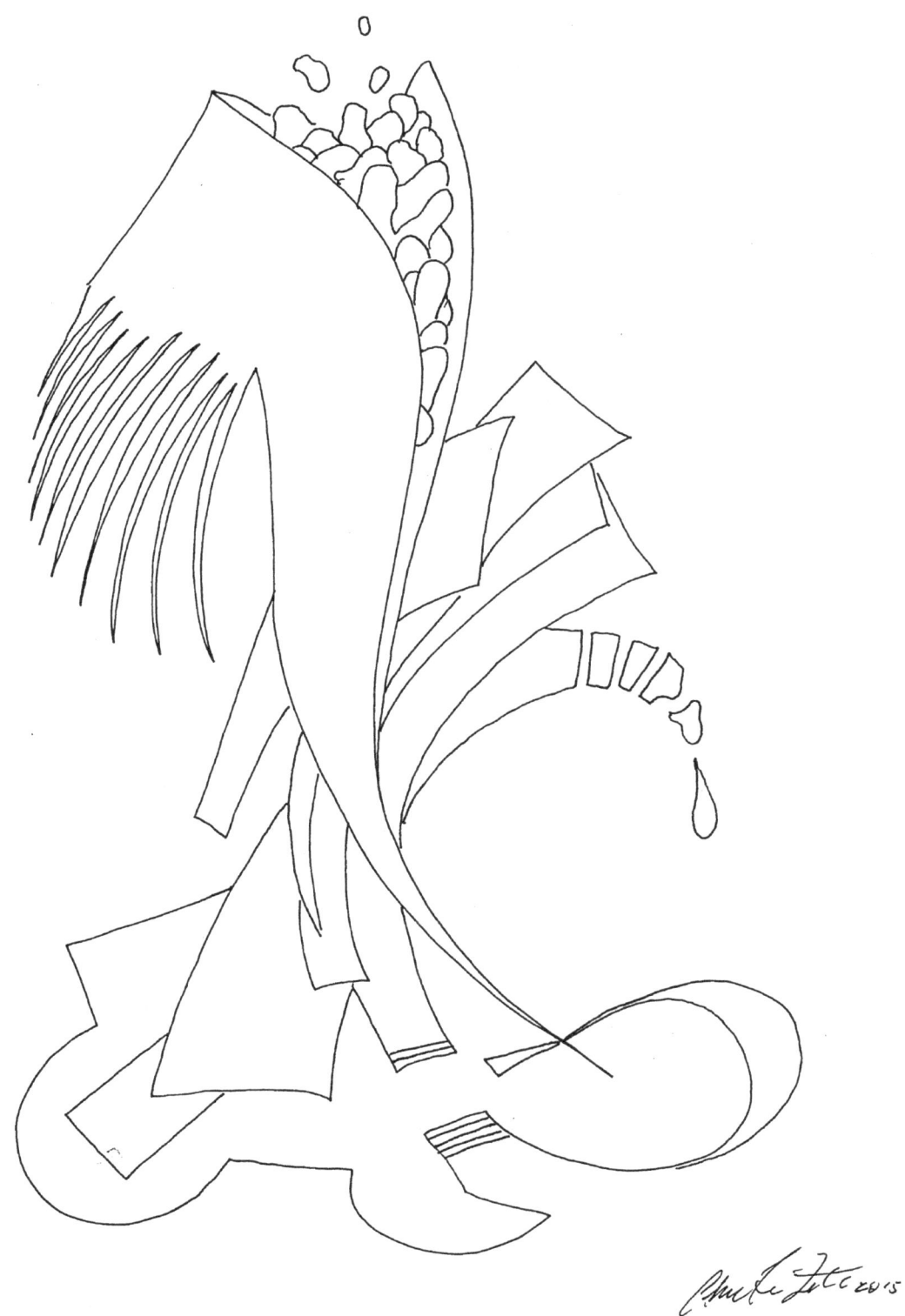

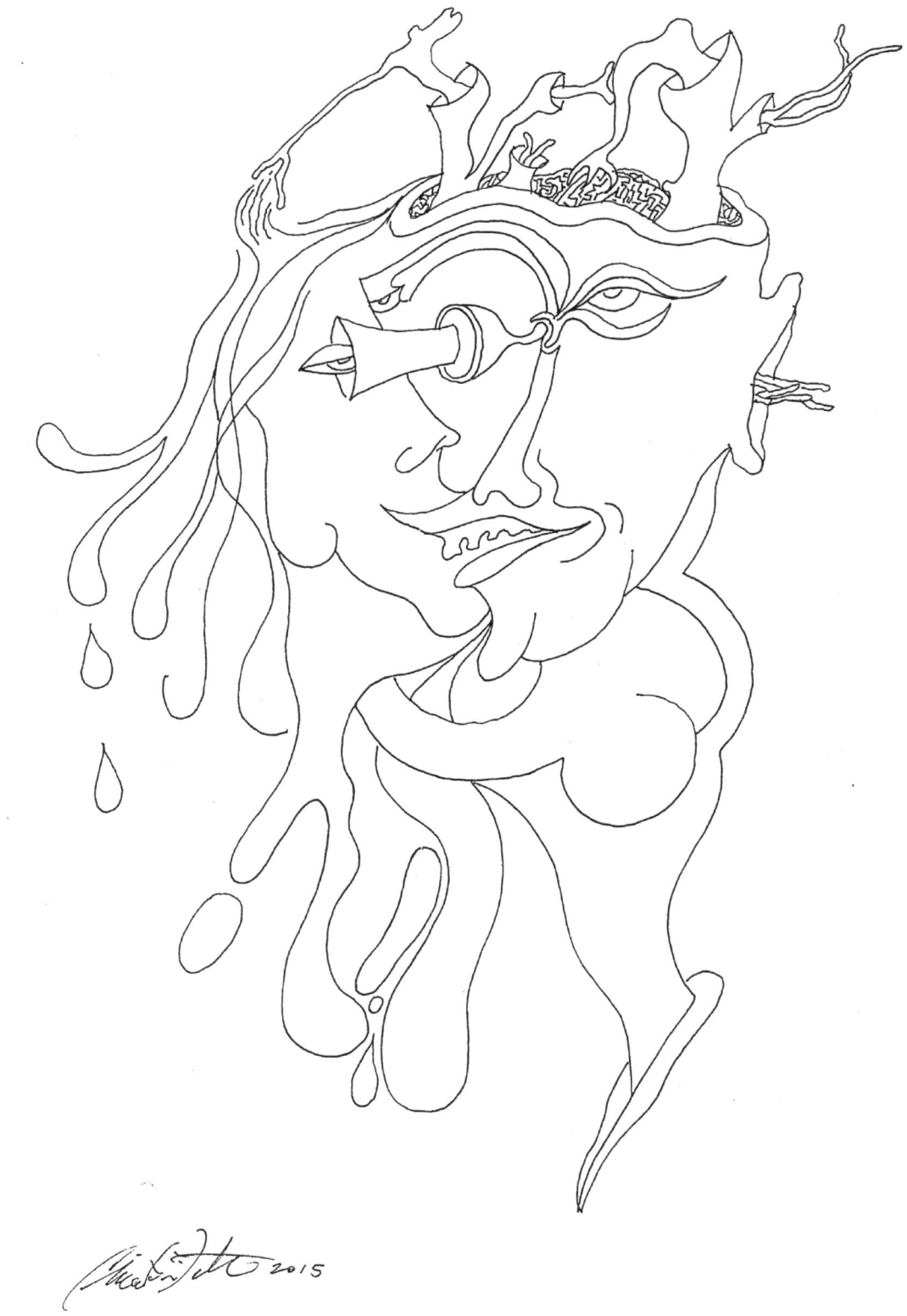

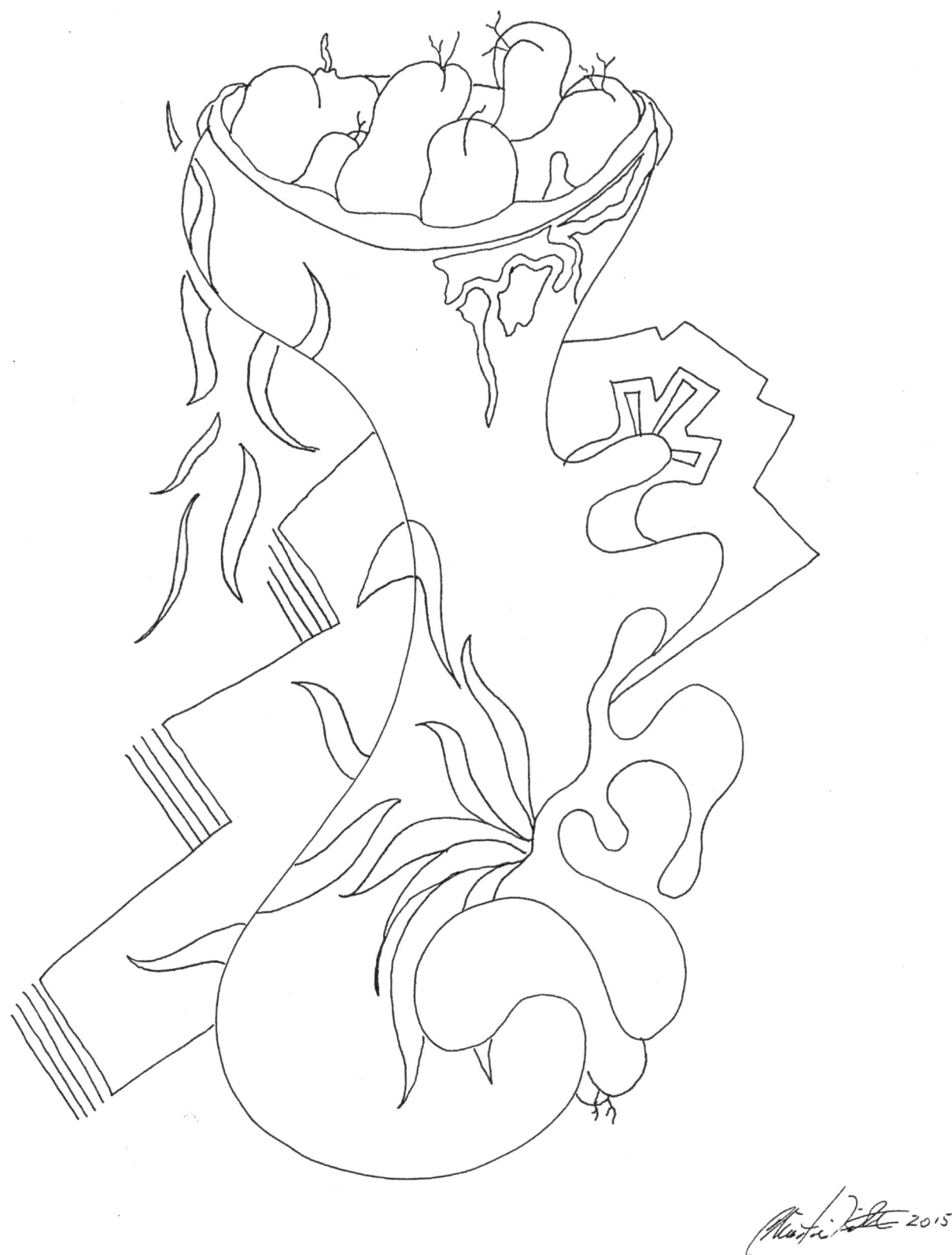